THE

TRAVELER'S

GUIDE TO

AMERICAN

GARDENS

THE TRAVELER'S

GUIDE TO

American
Gardens

Edited by Mary Helen Ray

and Robert P. Nicholls

The University of North Carolina Press

Chapel Hill & London

Library of Congress Cataloging-in-Publication Data
The Traveler's guide to American gardens.
   1. Gardens—United States—Guide-books.
2. United States—Description and travel—1981–   —
Guide-books. I. Ray, Mary Helen. II. Nicholls, Robert P.
SB466.U6T7   1988   712'.5'0973   87-40539
ISBN 0-8078-1787-2
ISBN 0-8078-4214-1 (pbk.)

The paper in this book meets the guidelines
for permanence and durability of the Committee
on Production Guidelines for Book Longevity of
the Council on Library Resources.

92 91 90 89 88   5 4 3 2 1

Illustrations by Robert P. Nicholls

For Hubert B. Owens

A garden is a lovesome thing, God wot!
    Rose plot
    Fringed pool
Fern'd grot
    The veriest school
    Of peace; and yet the fool
Contends that God is not
Not God! in gardens! when the eve is cool?

    Nay, but I have a sign;
    'Tis very sure God walks in mine.

Thomas Edward Brown, *My Garden*

Contents

Introduction

The success of the first edition of *A Guide to Historic & Significant Gardens of America* (1982) has prompted the editors to prepare this revised and enlarged second edition. Our intent is to provide the reader with concise information about and directions to gardens that are open to the public and that represent the best that each of our fifty states can offer. The guide is special in two respects: first in the inclusion of gardens from every state, and second in the use of symbols to identify "must see" (☆☆) and "superior" (☆) gardens. Our rating symbols should be viewed differently from the more conventional "four-star" rating system used by many travel guides. Such ratings imply uniform standards of quality. We feel there are too many variables affecting garden design and development in the different regions of the country, making uniform ratings impractical. Our selections are based on what travelers should consider their primary choices in a given state or region; choices should not be compared with one another across regional or state boundaries. We have only identified a small number of entries apart from the remainder. These selections are in our opinion the first choice of places the traveler should plan to see in an area if time and proposed itinerary will allow.

Irrespective of size or purpose, the creation and enjoyment of gardens has long been a means of human expression and pleasure. The term "garden" is used in this publication in the broadest sense: to define spaces of various sizes that are used for a variety of purposes, including those that preserve unique flora, that mark a culturally significant spot, or that may be referred to, or thought of, as an estate, urban park, or public square.

In selecting the entries for the guide, we were influenced by four criteria: historic importance, unique or significant features, length of settlement of the area, and nonprofit status. Historic gardens are those that have been in existence for over seventy-five years and are noteworthy examples of their time; they may also be gardens associated with a significant historic event or individual. Unique or significant gardens are those that contain rare and noteworthy plant materials and features, or that represent innovative or exemplary design. Length of settlement was considered because the earlier settled "colonial states" provided a more abundant choice of gardens for inclusion in the guide than were available in the later settled western "pioneer" states. Thus our standards for selecting an entry from Virginia were different from those we applied to selections from Nebraska. Gardens that charge entry fees and are developed as commercial undertakings for profit have not been included. Because many nonprofit foundations and publicly owned gardens must charge user fees to pay for upkeep and future development, however, such gardens appear in the guide.

Making a distinction between gardens for profit and legitimate fees for maintenance is often difficult. Our research indicates that the majority of commercially oriented gardens tend to be located close to the most popular tourist travel routes and vacation centers. An adult entry fee in excess of $6.00 is also a good indicator of probable status. In fairness it should be pointed out that many commercial enterprises provide entertainment features as value for their higher entry fees. Their larger operating budgets may also allow for immaculate landscape design and maintenance. We have listed several commercially oriented facilities at the end of each state chapter under the "Other Places of Interest" category.

To give the traveler a perspective for each state, data on area, population, and statehood are presented at the outset, followed by a brief sketch of the state's topography, climate, demography, history, and significant scenic and cultural features. The population figures are estimates for 1985, taken from the U.S. Bureau of the Census, *Statistical Abstract of the United States: 1987* (Washington, D.C., 1986). The information appearing in each entry was the best available at the time of our research. It should be noted that the times indicating when gardens are open are subject to change. To be on the safe side, visitors may wish to confirm the current schedule in advance. Telephone numbers are given whenever possible. In most instances, the number given is a direct line to the facility. However, in some instances the number will be that of a local historical society, chamber of commerce, or other organization familiar with the facility.

The editors have dedicated this edition to Hubert B. Owens, Professor Emeritus of Landscape Architecture and Dean Emeritus of the School of Environmental Design, University of Georgia, in grateful thanks for his personal interest and help over many years. Professor Owens first suggested to Mrs. Ray that the guide be developed as a project of the National Council of State Garden Clubs, Inc.

Moreover, it was he who persuaded Professor Nicholls to enter the teaching profession by joining the landscape architecture program faculty at the University of Georgia.

During his long career as an educator (1926–73), Hubert B. Owens saw many changes in the American landscape. In the 1920s few examples of developed landscapes could be observed by the average citizen. Few cities had well-designed parks, and even public squares were not attractively landscaped. There were exceptions of course, such as New York's Central Park, designed in 1867 by America's first landscape architect Frederick L. Olmsted, or Longwood Gardens, in Kennett Square, Pennsylvania, opened as a horticultural showplace by Pierre S. Du Pont in 1906.

Two events influenced the drive for civic beautification during the last decade of the nineteenth century. In 1891 the Garden Club Movement began with the founding of the first garden club in Athens, Georgia. And in 1893 the international Columbian Exposition in Chicago resulted in the City Beautiful Movement, the country's first major effort to improve the urban landscape. Most evidence of the City Beautiful Movement could be seen in the Boston area, parts of the East Coast, and around Chicago. The impact of the Garden Club Movement was more apparent in the attractive appearance of the wealthier residential areas developing in and around cities. By the 1920s, the influence of both movements was diminishing as attention was diverted by the development of the automobile and the residential suburbs that it spawned. Nevertheless, demand for the services of professionally trained architects, planners, and landscape architects was on the increase. To help meet this demand, authorities at the University of Georgia were persuaded to start a degree program in landscape architecture. In 1926 Professor Owens became the first teacher and was subsequently named head of the program.

The early years of the landscape architecture program at the University of Georgia coincided with a difficult time in our country's history. The Great Depression of the 1930s imposed acute hardships, but it also provided an opportunity for unprecedented public works. Commissions in architecture, planning, and landscape architecture were awarded by the Civilian Conservation Corps (CCC) and the Works Progress Administration (WPA) of President Franklin Roosevelt's New Deal. Many municipal, county, state, and national park and roadside development projects were designed and constructed. Also in the 1930s two of the first major historic preservation efforts were undertaken—in Charleston, South Carolina, and at Williamsburg, Virginia. Both of these privately funded projects have had a significant influence on Hubert B. Owens's teaching philosophy and on preservation nationwide.

The coincidence that Athens, home of the University of Georgia, was also the founding location of the Garden Club Movement suggested to Professor Owens that part of his educational mission should be to work with garden clubs. Since the mid-1950s, the educational programs of the National Council of State Garden Clubs, Inc., which Professor Owens initiated, have done much to stimulate an awareness of the need for and an interest in preserving, restoring, and improving the American landscape.

The development of this guide has been a cooperative effort between the two editors and the interests they both serve. Mary Helen Ray has been National Council of State Garden Clubs, Inc., Historic Preservation Chairman and an active member of the Garden Club of Georgia, Inc. The publication of the first edition of the guide was cosponsored by the Garden Club of Georgia and the University of Georgia School of Environmental Design, under the direction of Robert P. Nicholls, who succeeded Professor Owens as Dean from 1973 to 1983.

We would like to acknowledge the work of the very many people who helped in the preparation of the guide. Many of the initial listings for the first edition were suggested by various members of the National Council of State Garden Clubs, Inc., throughout the United States. Graduate students Charles Brenton, Robert Jaeger, and Barbara Koenig verified the suggestions and helped with research on additional listings. Maps were prepared by James Blume, and the original manuscript was typed by Tilda Wall with the assistance of Jarrett Brandenburg, Gloria Harber, and Deanna Kent. School librarian Claris Ingersol proofread the manuscript. Mrs. Haskell Venard, a former president of the Garden Club of Georgia, Inc., gave expert help in checking the manuscript at its various stages.

In arranging this revised edition, the editors were helped by suggestions received from readers of the first edition, by the Directors of Tourism of all fifty states, and by many members of the National Council of State Garden Clubs, Inc. Ann Knapp-English, a graduate student in the University of Georgia School of Environmental Design, was responsible for cross-checking the revised information and for typing the additions and revisions to the manuscript. The pen-and-ink sketches were prepared by Robert P. Nicholls.

The editors are also grateful for the encouragement and support of David Perry, Editor, the University of North Carolina Press, and Darrel Morrison, Dean of the University of Georgia School of Environmental Design. All funds received as royalties through the sale of this publication will be shared equally by the Garden Club of Georgia, Inc., and the School of Environmental Design. These funds will be used to help in the restoration of gardens and for educational purposes.

The editors have traveled extensively throughout the United States to gather information for the guide. During these trips we have had the opportunity to meet many fine scholars of horticulture and design and to see firsthand some of the magnificent gardens that human care, enthusiasm, inspiration, and genius have bestowed upon our land.

Ultimately, we hope that this publication will not only assist travelers and gardeners, but will also contribute to the rescue and restoration of additional landscapes, gardens, and green spaces throughout America.

Mary Helen Ray, Savannah
Robert P. Nicholls, Athens

Alabama

Area: 51,609 square miles

Population: 4,021,000

Statehood: December 14, 1819
(22nd state)

Alabama is known as the "Heart of
Dixie." It was originally part of New
France, with Mobile serving as the
capital from 1702 to 1722. This city
still retains its French and Spanish
influences. In 1814, after the defeat
of the Creek Indians, the interior of
the state was opened for settlement.
People came from the worn-out
farms of the Piedmont and the coastal
southeast. Large cotton plantations
were established in the fertile soils
of the "Black Belt," an area of rich
limestone soils stretching across the
center of the state into Mississippi.
The climate is mild in winter and hot
in summer. The planters from the
Tidewater areas brought with them
the Greek Revival architectural style
of the plantation culture and their
familiar ornamental plants.

The original forests were rich
in hardwood as well as coniferous
species. Many of the hardwoods were
removed when fields were cleared for
cultivation, and they are much slower
than the pines in growing back. A
surviving southern climax forest can
be observed at the Dismals in Phil
Campbell, near Russellville.

The U.S. Forest Service maintains
four national forests totaling 635,000

acres. An additional 14,000 acres are
held as state forests. The National
Park Service manages another 46,000
acres of public land, including Russell
Cave National Monument and Horseshoe Bend National Military Park.
Twenty-one state parks provide further recreational opportunities. Part
of the Tennessee Valley Authority
system of dams and power plants is
located in the northern part of the
state. Visitors are welcome at most
sites.

1. Auburn

Auburn Arboretum and Gardens
Auburn University Campus

The 14-acre arboretum, completed in
1977, includes three older gardens:
the Garden of Memory, a gift (1953)
from the Garden Club of Alabama to
honor the state's residents who served
in the armed forces; the Centennial
Garden; and the Collection Garden.
Open: Daily. (205) 826–4830.

2. Birmingham

Arlington Antebellum
Home and Gardens
331 Cotton Avenue, Southwest

A Greek Revival plantation house
constructed about 1850. Charles
Clemons designed the current grounds
restoration in 1969, carefully preserving ancient oaks and magnolias. Each
year, Christmas is celebrated with

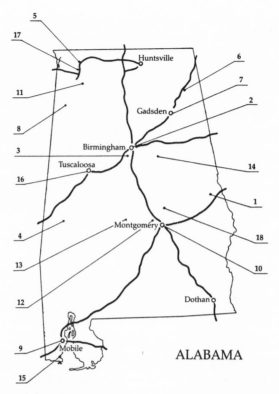

ALABAMA

1. *Auburn* 2. *Birmingham* 3. *Bucksville* 4. *Demopolis* 5. *Florence* 6. *Fort Payne* 7. *Gadsden* 8. *Hodges* 9. *Mobile* 10. *Montgomery* 11. *Phil Campbell* 12. *Prattville* 13. *Selma* 14. *Talladega* 15. *Theodore* 16. *Tuscaloosa* 17. *Tuscumbia* 18. *Wetumpka*

decorations of the type used in the nineteenth century.
Open: Tuesday–Saturday 9:00 a.m.– 4:30 p.m., Sunday 1:00–4:30 p.m. Closed: Holidays. (205) 780–5656.

Birmingham Botanical Gardens
2612 Lane Park Road

This garden has one of the largest conservatories in the Southeast, featuring orchids and other exotic plants. The iris and daylily gardens are of special interest in June and July. Other attractions include a wildflower garden and a fragrance garden for the blind. In the 7.5-acre Japanese Garden, an outstanding example of Japanese landscape art, is a teahouse where the tea ceremony is conducted occasionally on Sunday afternoon.
Open: Year-round, daily, sunrise– sunset. (205) 879–1576.

Gardens of the Episcopal Church of the Advent
2019 6th Avenue, North

Three small cloistered gardens and a miniature roof garden add color and tranquility to Birmingham's oldest church (1872). Located in the heart of downtown, the gardens demonstrate how even the smallest green space can relieve the harshness of the urban environment.
Open: Daily, sunrise–sunset. (205) 251–2324.

Ruffner Mountain Nature Center
1214 South 81st Street

This last remaining undeveloped remnant of the Red Mountain Ridge includes a wildflower garden and a nature trail.
Open: Monday–Friday 9:00 a.m.– 5:00 p.m., Saturday 10:00 a.m.– 5:00 p.m., Sunday 1:00–5:00 p.m. (205) 833–8112.

Vulcan Park and Museum
Top of Red Mountain, near Birmingham

Despite the panoramic view, formal gardens, and museum, the main attraction is Vulcan, the world's largest iron man. This colossal statue by Italian sculptor Giuseppe Moretti overlooking the city symbolizes the importance of industry in Birmingham.
Open: Year-round, daily 8 a.m.– 10:30 p.m. Fee. (205) 254–2628.

3. Bucksville

Tannehill Historical State Park
5 miles east of I-59 at Bucksville exit

Hikers, campers, naturalists, and historians come from around the nation to view the Tannehill forge remains. Begun in 1829, the #1 furnace was put into operation with Confederate bonds. More than a dozen pioneer houses have been moved from other locations in Alabama. A nature trail and wildflower area are also featured in the 1,500-acre park.
Open: Daily 7:00 a.m.–9:00 p.m. Parking fee. (205) 477–5711.

4. Demopolis

Bluff Hall
407 North Commissioner's Avenue

Originally built in 1832, the house was redesigned in the 1850s to suit the Greek Revival fashion. Small formal garden and herb garden.
Open: Tuesday–Saturday 10:00 a.m.– 5:00 p.m., Sunday 2:00–5:00 p.m. Fee. (205) 289–1666.

Gaineswood
805 Whitfield Street, East

What began as a two-room log cabin in 1821 grew between 1843 and 1861 into one of the most magnificent examples of a Greek Revival plantation mansion in the country. A National Historic Landmark, restored by the Alabama Historical Commis-

sion, the mansion has original furnishings provided by the descendants of builder General Nathan Bryan Whitfield. The north and south parterres have been well landscaped.
Open: Daily 9:00 a.m.–5:00 p.m., Sunday 1:00–5:00 p.m.
Closed: State holidays. Fee. (205) 289-4846.

5. Florence

Courtview
Court Street

This interesting Greek Revival home has magnificent boxwood gardens in the English manner. The town of Florence—one of the few in Alabama that has been preplanned—was designed by Ferdinand Sorrona, who named it after his native Florence, Italy. Courtview was built in the middle of Court Street, which required a replanning of that part of town. Alabama planter George Foster, the original owner of the house, had to obtain approval of the Alabama legislature to make the changes in Court Street. The site is now owned by the University of North Alabama.
Open: Daily 8:00 a.m.–3:30 p.m., Saturday 10:00 a.m.–3:30 p.m.
Closed: Sundays and holidays. (205) 766-4100, ext. 318.

Pope's Tavern Museum
203 Hermitage Drive

This was an old stage-stop tavern built by slave labor in 1811. It was used as a hospital during the Civil War. Restoration was completed in 1971, with the landscape design in keeping with the style of the house, including an herb garden.
Open: Tuesday–Saturday 9:00 a.m.–noon, 1:00–4:00 p.m.; Sunday 2:00–5:00 p.m.
Closed: All major holidays, 2 weeks at Christmas. Fee. (205) 766-2662.

6. Fort Payne

De Soto State Park
Little River Canyon, Highway 176 near Fort Payne

This park is noted for its impressive waterfall and a variety of native spring and fall blooming plants. Interpretative hiking trails.
Open: Daily 8:00 a.m.– sunset. (205) 845-5380.

7. Gadsden

Noccalula Falls Botanical Gardens and Park
Noccalula Road (Exit 188 off I-59 at Gadsden)

The grounds contain 246 acres of naturalized woodlands with nature trails, picnic areas, and a 100-foot-high waterfall. Ten acres have been developed into more formal gardens, including the botanical gardens and a pioneer homestead museum.

*Open: Park, 24 hours; gardens,
8:00 a.m.–sunset. Fee. (205) 534–7412.*

8. Hodges

Rock Bridge Canyon
Route 1, 2.5 miles from Hodges

This natural canyon is filled with subtropical plants among waterfalls and springs. Indigenous flowering shrubs are featured. An Annual Wildflower Festival is held in May. *Open: Daily, sunrise–sunset. Fee. (205) 935–3750.*

9. Mobile

Azalea Trail Headquarters
751 Government Street

This is the start of the 37-mile Azalea Trail tour. The tour is divided into two trails: a historic route which passes through elegant antebellum sections of Mobile, and the Spring Hill route which includes both historic and newer sections of the city. March is the best month to see azaleas and dogwoods in full bloom. Maps available for self-guided tour. *Open: Daily, sunrise–sunset. (205) 433–6951.*

Bienville Square
Dauphin and Concepcion Streets

A historic focal point of downtown Mobile, this park dates from 1849.

Some of the live oaks were planted in 1857.
Open: Daily. (205) 433–6951.

Oakleigh
350 Oakleigh Place

Designed by James W. Roper and built in 1833, Oakleigh is a former plantation house in the southern raised cottage style with Greek Revival details. It is now the headquarters of the Historic Mobile Preservation Society. Azaleas and ancient live oaks dominate the grounds. A nineteenth-century reproduction herb garden is featured.
Open: Monday–Saturday 10:00 a.m.–4:00 p.m., Sunday 2:00–4:00 p.m. Fee. (205) 432–1281.

Spanish Plaza
Government and Church Streets

This plaza commemorates Mobile's Spanish heritage. Its statues, arches, and fountains were gifts from the Spanish city of Malaga. The plaza is at the center of the nine-block De Tonti Square historic district.
Open: Daily. (205) 433–6951.

10. Montgomery

Governor's Mansion
1142 South Perry Street

Camellias are featured in this beautiful, informal setting.
Open: Weekdays 9:00 a.m.–noon, 1:00–3:00 p.m. Fee. (205) 834–3022.

Ordeman–Shaw House and Garden
310 North Hull Street

This restoration exemplifies southern town life in the 1850s. The house was originally built in 1850 by Charles Christian Ordeman and restored in 1969 by Laurence Brigham. The grounds include characteristic out-buildings and kitchen, herb, and flower gardens.
Open: Monday–Saturday 9:30 a.m.–3:30 p.m., Sunday 1:30–3:30 p.m. Fee. (205) 263–4355.

State Capitol Grounds
Bounded by Decatur, Washington, Ripley, and Monroe Streets

A formal planting was designed by the firm of Frederick Law Olmsted. The Avenue of Flags displays the flags of all 50 states.
Building open: Daily 8:00 a.m.–5:00 p.m.
Closed: Holidays. (205) 265–7886.

11. Phil Campbell

The Dismals
U.S. 43; 5 miles north of Hackleburg, 12 miles south of Russellville

Eighty acres of undisturbed southern climax forest are displayed in this natural park and arboretum. Tree, shrub, moss, fern, and wildflower varieties abound in the protected canyon. Trees are labeled. The forest is well known for its rocky bluffs, vegetation, and water features.

Open: Daily 8:00 a.m.–sunset. Fee. (205) 993–5537.

12. Prattville

Wilderness Park
Upper Kingston Road

This 26-acre bamboo forest, dedicated in 1982, was the country's first wilderness park developed inside a city's limits. Bamboo species grow to 60 feet in height.
Open: Daily 9:00 a.m.–5:00 p.m. (205) 365–9997.

13. Selma

Sturdivant Hall
713 Mabry Street

Designed by a cousin of Robert E. Lee, this Greek Revival mansion was built in 1853. Today it is owned and operated as a house museum by the city of Selma. The mansion and appropriately landscaped gardens are focal points of the social and cultural life of Selma.
Open: Tuesday–Saturday 9:00 a.m.–4:00 p.m., Sunday 2:00–4:00 p.m. Fee. (205) 872–5626.

Bellingrath Gardens, Theodore, Ala.

14. Talladega

Helen Keller Fragrance Garden for the Blind
Alabama School for the Blind

Handrails on the brick walls and Braille markers enable blind students to identify and tend the fragrant plants. A fountain adds a pleasant sound to the garden. Awarded the National Council of Garden Clubs Bronze Seal.
Open: Daily, dawn–dusk. (205) 362–1500.

Memorial Park for the Deaf
Alabama School for the Deaf

Also a winner of the National Council of Garden Clubs Bronze Seal, this garden for the deaf features seasonal colors. It is maintained by the students.
Open: Daily, dawn–dusk. (205) 362–1500.

15. Theodore

☆☆
Bellingrath Gardens
Bellingrath Road, 20 miles south
of Mobile (exit from I-10)

Described as the "Charm Spot of
the Deep South," Bellingrath comprises 905 acres, including 65 acres
of formal gardens with labeled collections of native shrubs, trees, and
flowers. The gardens are very colorful
in all seasons.
Open: Daily 7:00 a.m.–sunset. Fee.
(205) 973–2217.

16. Tuscaloosa

**Hazel Sevalley Teaching Garden
at Parklow**
Parklow School and Hospital,
University Boulevard East

A winner of the National Council
of Garden Clubs Bronze Seal, this
garden was constructed with the aid
of retarded students. A teaching area
surrounds a large fountain with constantly changing water patterns and
colors. The fountain is illuminated at
night.
Open: Daily, dawn–dusk.
(205) 553–4550.

**Japanese Garden at Gulf States
Paper Corporation**
1400 River Road

Built in 1970, this garden surrounds
the Oriental-style buildings of the
corporation's national headquarters. The work of landscape architect
David H. Engel, who was an appren-
tice to master landscape architect
Tansai Lano of Japan, it is a fine
example of functional and imagina-
tive corporate landscape design.
Open: Monday–Saturday 10:00 a.m.–
7:00 p.m., Sunday 1:30–7:30 p.m.
(205) 553–6200.

University of Alabama Arboretum
University Boulevard, 3 miles east of
campus on 15th Street

The 60-acre arboretum has nature
trails and native trees, shrubs, and
wildflowers. The campus historic
district is also of interest.
Open: Daily 10:00 a.m.–noon, 2:00–
5:00 p.m.; Sunday 2:00–4:00 p.m.
(205) 348–5960.

17. Tuscumbia

Ivy Green
300 W. North Common Street

The birthplace of Helen Keller, Ivy
Green encompasses 29 acres. Its
memorial garden of native plants
was awarded the National Council
of Garden Clubs Bronze Seal. The
original house and grounds have been
restored.
Open: Monday–Saturday 8:30 a.m.–
4:30 p.m., Sunday 1:00–4:30 p.m.
Fee. (205) 383–4066.

18. Wetumpka

Jasmine Hill
Jasmine Hill Road, off U.S. 231
south of Wetumpka

Created in the 1930s on 17 acres, the
gardens feature reproductions of ancient Greek works of art. Flowering
trees and a reproduction of the Temple of Hera create the setting for the
statuary.
*Open: Tuesday–Sunday 9:00 a.m.–
5:00 p.m. Fee. (205) 567–6463.*

William Bartram Arboretum
at Fort Toulouse
U.S. 231, 3 miles south of Wetumpka

The 30-acre arboretum is named for
the great American artist-naturalist
who visited the area in 1775–76. De
Soto crossed the site in 1540. Trails

take viewers from the ridge overlook
to a bog area and river overlook.
Plant materials are labeled.
*Open: Daily 8:00 a.m.–5:00 p.m.
Closed: Holidays. (205) 567–3002.*

Other Places of Interest

Ave Maria Grotto, Cullman
Bama Science Rock Gardens, Vance
Bankhead National Forest, Double
 Springs
Cathedral Caverns, Grant
Horseshoe Bend National Military
 Park, Dadeville
Hurricane Creek Park, Vinemont
Mound State Monument, Moundville
Natural Bridge, Haleyville
Richwood Caverns, Warrior
Russell Cave National Monument,
 Bridgeport
Sequoyah Caves, Valley Head

Alaska

Area: 586,400 square miles

Population: 521,000

Statehood: January 3, 1959
(49th state)

Alaska is the largest of the fifty states and one of the least populous. This huge land stretches across a variety of landforms and climates.

The majority of Alaska's population lives along the rugged Pacific coastline. Temperatures here are moderated by warm ocean currents. Perhaps the most striking quality of this land to the visitors from "the lower forty-eight" is the length of the days. Due to Alaska's extreme northern latitude, days are very long in summer and short in winter. The growing season is extremely brief, with less than one hundred frost-free days.

Alaska's coastal range contains some of North America's highest mountains. The native vegetation ranges from pine and spruce rain forests at the lower elevations on the coastal range to dwarfed vegetation in the extreme north. During Alaska's short alpine spring, numerous varieties of wildflowers bloom profusely in meadows and bogs. There are thousands of glaciers on the mountains. The Malaspina Glacier is as large as the state of Rhode Island.

The federal government has huge landholdings in Alaska. The U.S. Forest Service operates recreation areas in the Chugach and Tongass national forests. Near Juneau the tourist can visit the Mendenhall Glacier. Denali National Park features Mount McKinley, the continent's highest peak. In the Katmai National Park are active volcanoes. Other points of interest include the monument of Will Rogers and Wiley Post near Barrow, artifacts of Indian cultures, and historic sites from the days of Alaska's gold rush.

Alaska is North America's last great frontier. It offers the visitor a view of the wonders of unspoiled nature on a vast scale. Against this spectacular backdrop of nature Alaska's gardeners work their plots.

1. Anchorage

Alpine Strutz Garden
916 P Street

This garden was extensively damaged by the earthquake of 1964, and tons of rocks had to be brought in to contain the soil. Many interesting varieties of native wildflowers and foliage plants are featured. Privately owned but visitors are welcome. *Open: No regular hours.*

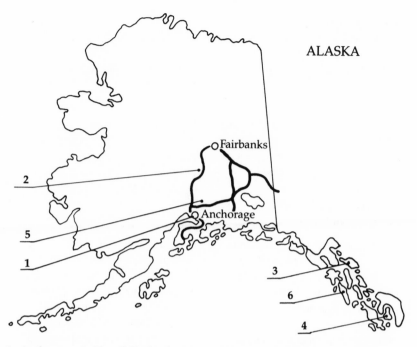

ALASKA

1. *Anchorage* 2. *Denali National Park* 3. *Juneau* 4. *Ketchikan* 5. *Palmer*
6. *Sitka*

Centennial Rose Garden
Park Strip

Displayed are rose varieties that can be grown as hardy perennials in the area.
Open: Daily. (907) 272–2401.

2. Denali National Park

Three thousand square miles of arctic-alpine wilderness surround Mount McKinley, the highest peak in North America (20,320 ft.). The area supports an outstanding variety of wildlife, mountain slope, and tundra vegetation—there are over 500 varieties of flowering plants and shrubs.
Open: Daily, June 1–mid-September.
(907) 683–2291.

3. Juneau

Governor's Mansion
9th Street and Calhoun Avenue

The grounds of the mansion have been well planted and maintained over the years.
Open: Daily. (907) 586–2201.

4. Ketchikan

Creek Street Restoration

This restoration project covers a large part of the former red-light district of old Ketchikan. Many of the buildings and grounds in the area have been revitalized. A walking tour is offered. *Open: Daily. (907) 225–6166.*

Totem Heritage House
601 Deermont Street

The restoration of the Totem House and grounds was the bicentennial project for this city. The house displays very old totem poles, no longer in tribal use, that would otherwise deteriorate. *Open: Monday–Friday 9:00 a.m.– 5:00 p.m. (907) 225–6166.*

5. Palmer

Agricultural Experiment Station
University of Alaska

An arboretum was established here in 1952 by Dr. M. F. Babb, a research horticulturist for the U.S. Department of Agriculture. The arboretum is primarily a test planting of both exotic and indigenous woody plants. There are also flower and vegetable gardens. *Open: Daily 8:00 a.m.–5:00 p.m. (907) 745–3257.*

6. Sitka

Sitka Pioneer Home
Lincoln Street

The home was built by three frontiersmen. Some original plant materials remain from early landscaping attempts. *Open: Daily 8:00 a.m.–5:00 p.m. (907) 747–8604.*

U.S. Geological Survey Station

Established in 1898 as the Alaska Agricultural Experiment Station, the facility is now the site of a Geological Survey Station. Many of the trees and woody materials from the original experimental planting are still alive and of horticultural interest. *Open: Daily 8:00 a.m.–5:00 p.m. (907) 747–3332.*

Other Places of Interest

Fort Yukon
Glacier Bay National Park
Katmai National Park
Sitka National Historical Park (for Tlingit Indian totem poles)
St. Lawrence Island
Swanson River–Swan Lake Canoe Trails

Arizona

Area: 113,909 square miles

Population: 3,187,000

Statehood: February 14, 1912
(48th state)

Arizona is a land of striking contrasts: warm deserts, lush oases, high
mesas, cool forests, and prehistoric
dwellings. The Grand Canyon of the
Colorado River is one of the seven
wonders of the world. Other natural sites include the Petrified Forest,
the Painted Desert, and Monument
Valley. The Organ Pipe and Saguaro
national monuments offer spectacular
displays of desert plants. Oak Creek
Canyon, near Flagstaff, is renowned
for its natural beauty. Indian culture,
living and past, is also of interest
as are historic landmarks of frontier
days.

The first Europeans to visit Arizona were the Spaniards. Mexico
had established missions and some
ranches when the land was taken over
by the United States. Today, Arizona's population is growing rapidly
due to the sunshine and pleasant winter climate. The Spanish and Mexican
influence on architecture and gardening can still be seen.

Summer days are hot—July temperatures in Phoenix average near
110° F. However, the desert cools
quickly at night. Most newcomers
to Arizona consider air conditioning
a necessity of life; nevertheless, the
ancient pueblos of the Indians and
certain modern structures demonstrate how human dwellings can be
well adapted to hot climates without air conditioning. The prehistoric
Indians irrigated parts of the desert.

There are nineteen national parks
and monuments in Arizona, as well
as fifteen state parks and numerous
campgrounds.

1. Carefree

Carefree Inn Japanese Garden
Mule Train Road, 0.25 miles north
of Cave Creek Road

This large motel has an interesting
Japanese garden. Principles of Japanese garden design have been adapted
using hardy desert plants.
Open: Daily. (602) 488–3551.

2. Mesa

Mormon Temple Gardens
525 East Main Street

Twenty acres of well-landscaped
grounds include sunken gardens and
water features. Citrus trees, palms,
and cedar are arranged in a desert
setting.
*Open: Daily 8:00 a.m.–9:00 p.m.
(602) 964–7164.*

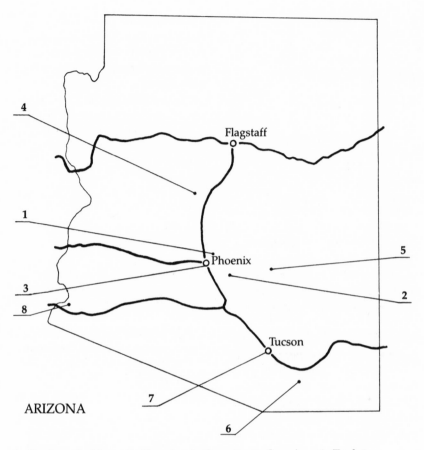

1. *Carefree* 2. *Mesa* 3. *Phoenix* 4. *Prescott* 5. *Superior* 6. *Tombstone*
7. *Tucson* 8. *Yuma*

3. Phoenix

☆☆
Desert Botanical Garden
5800 East Van Buren and
6400 East McDowell Roads,
8 miles from downtown

The garden, begun in 1935, is located
on 150 acres of natural desert in

Papago Park. At this site has been
collected over half the different kinds
of cacti in the world—some 1,400
species from miniature cacti, the
size of half-dollars, to the massive
Mexican cardon which can weigh as
much as 10 tons. Along the paths,
cacti from the southwestern United
States, Mexico, and Central and
South America display the different

Saguaro National Monument, Tucson, Ariz.

ways that plants have adapted to life in the hot and nearly waterless desert.
Open: Daily 9:00 a.m.–sunset; summer 7:00 a.m.–sunset. Fee– donation. (602) 941–1217.

**Valley Garden Center
Demonstration Gardens**
1809 North 15th Avenue

There are four interesting gardens to be seen—a Japanese garden, a semi-tropical garden, a low maintenance garden of indigenous desert plants, and a rose test garden with over 3,000 plants.
Open: Daily 9:00 a.m.–5:00 p.m. Closed: Sunday. (602) 252–2120.

4. Prescott

**Sharlot Hall Memorial
Rose Garden**
415 West Gurley Street

This circular garden was begun by citizens of Prescott to honor pioneer women; it now contains a wide variety of roses. The rose garden lies adjacent to the Old Governor's Mansion, home of the first territorial governor of Arizona. There is also an herb garden displaying 75 different plants.
Open: Tuesday–Saturday 9:00 a.m.– 5:00 p.m., Sunday 1:00–5:00 p.m. (602) 445–3122.

5. Superior

☆
**Boyce Thompson Southwestern
Arboretum**
U.S. 60, 3 miles west of Superior

Designed by Franklin Jacob Crider in 1925, this 1,075-acre site serves as a research center for desert plants and as a living museum. It was the first research center of its kind in the Rocky Mountain states and a forerunner of the U.S. Soil Conservation Service. Picnic facilities.
Open: Daily 8:00 a.m.–5:00 p.m. Fee. (602) 689–2811.

6. Tombstone

Rose Tree Inn Museum
4th and Toughnut Streets

In the courtyard of this inn is a white rose tree, planted in 1885, that is claimed to be the "world's largest." *Open: Daily 9:00 a.m.–5:00 p.m. Fee. (602) 294–2628.*

7. Tucson

Arizona–Sonora Desert Museum
2120 North Kinney Road, 14 miles west of Tucson

Located in rugged terrain, this museum features informative exhibits of desert flora and fauna in a 2.5-acre landscape setting. The nature trails and live animal collections are outstanding. *Open: Daily 8:00 a.m.–sunset; summer, from 7:00 a.m. Fee. (602) 883–1380.*

Randolph Park Rose Garden
East 22nd Street and
Country Club Road

This circular garden was started in 1960. Slightly more than one acre in size, it contains several hundred varieties of award-winning roses. Displays are best between April and July. *Open: Daily 9:00 a.m.–5:00 p.m. (602) 791–4873.*

San Xavier del Bac Mission
Mission Road, 9 miles
southwest of Tucson

Known as the "White Dove of the Desert," this is one of America's most beautiful missions. The garden displays native mesquite and cholla, as well as figs, pomegranates, and almonds. The courtyards are profusely planted with fragrant herbs. *Open: 9:00 a.m.–6:00 p.m. Masses held daily. Donation. (602) 294–2628.*

Taliesin West
East Shea Boulevard, Scotsdale

The western campus of the Frank Lloyd Wright School provides an interesting example of Wright's style of building that is integrated with the desert landscape. *Open: Daily 10:00 a.m.–4:00 p.m., Sunday noon–4:00 p.m. Fee. (602) 948–6670.*

8. Yuma

Century House Museum and Gardens
240 Madison Avenue

Situated in Yuma's old downtown, the gardens include adobe buildings, aviaries with exotic and talking birds, and a unique collection of trees, shrubs, and flowers. Over 1,300 kinds of plants and flowers can be found in these gardens, established in 1890 by E. F. Sanguinetti. Most of the

Grand Canyon National Park in Arizona.

plantings are labeled with common and botanical names.
Open: Tuesday–Sunday 10:00 a.m.–4:00 p.m.
Closed: Holidays. Tours can be arranged by calling the Arizona Historical Society. (602) 783–8020.

Other Places of Interest

Arcosanti, Cordes Junction, 38 miles north of Phoenix
Canyon de Chelly, northeastern Arizona

Casa Grande National Monument, Phoenix
Chiricahua National Monument, near Douglas, southeastern Arizona
Encanto Park, Phoenix
Grand Canyon, northern Arizona
Hoover Dam, Lake Mead, northwestern Arizona
Hopi Indian Reservation, near Flagstaff
Meteor Crater, Winslow
Montezuma Castle National Monument, near Flagstaff
Navajo Indian Reservation, eastern Arizona
Navajo National Monument, northern Arizona (off U.S. 160)
Oak Creek Canyon, between Sedona and Flagstaff
Organ Pipe Cactus National Monument, Tucson
Painted Desert, eastern Arizona
Painted Rock Park, near Gila Bend, southwestern Arizona
Petrified Forest National Park, eastern Arizona
Saguaro National Monument, Tucson
Tonto National Bridge, Phoenix
Tropical Gardens Zoo, Phoenix
Tubac Presidio Park, near Nogales, southern Arizona
Tuzigoot National Monument, Flagstaff
Walnut Canyon, near Flagstaff

Arkansas

Area: 53,104 square miles

Population: 2,359,000

Statehood: June 15, 1836 (25th state)

Arkansas borders the west bank of the Mississippi River. The southern and eastern parts of the state are low-lying alluvial plains deposited by the river and the receding Gulf of Mexico. The swampiness of these lowlands impeded early settlement. The Ouachita Mountains and Ozark Plateau occupy the northwestern part of the state. Magazine Mountain, the highest peak in Arkansas, has an elevation of 2,753 feet.

The climate is mild with ample rainfall. The growing season ranges from 176 days in the mountains to 241 days in the lowlands. There is a wide variety of vegetation. Cypress, tupelo, water oak, ash, and holly occur in the lowlands. The upland forests are dominated by oak, pine, and hickory.

There was little settlement by the French in this part of their Louisiana Territory. After its purchase by the United States, Arkansas was settled by cotton planters who had moved west when their native soils were depleted. The cotton culture reached its zenith just before the Civil War. Agriculture and lumbering remain important industries.

Arkansas has three national for-ests. Hot Springs National Park is a widely known spa. Buffalo National River is a magnificent free-flowing stream, one of the last remaining in mid-America. Crowley's Ridge State Park features a loess deposit where many types of vegetation can be found closely juxtaposed. Petit Jean, Mount Nebo, and Queen Wilhelmina state parks offer exciting panoramic views of the highlands.

1. Hot Springs

Hot Springs National Park
Central Avenue and Reserve Street (Visitor Center)

These famous thermal springs in a lush valley-park setting were visited by Hernando de Soto in 1541. Tree-lined streets surround the parks; a bathhouse and promenade overlook are of particular interest. Native plant species can be found throughout the park. There are self-guided hiking trails and bridle trails.
Open: Daily. Fee. (501) 321–1700.

2. Little Rock

Arkansas Territorial Restoration
Territorial Square,
214 East Third Street

The restoration preserves two blocks of dwellings, outbuildings, and gardens in the historic Quapaw Quarter of downtown Little Rock, including a small medicinal herb garden.

2

Jonesboro

1

Ft. Smith

3

Little Rock

Pine Bluff

Texarkana

El Dorado

ARKANSAS

1. *Hot Springs* **2.** *Little Rock* **3.** *Mena*

Adjacent to the historic buildings is a new reception center–museum where artists and craftsmen display their work.
Open: Monday–Saturday 9:00 a.m.– 5:00 p.m., Sunday 1:00–5:00 p.m. Fee, but free first Sunday of the month. (501) 371–2348.

3. Mena

Queen Wilhelmina State Park, Rich Mountain

Ark. 88, 13 miles northwest of Mena

This park began as a mountain retreat for the wealthy. The third version of a historic inn can be seen today. The park supports a great variety of mountain vegetation including some subtropical plants. It also features nature trails, deer forests, and a spectacular display of Dutch-donated

Medicinal Herb Garden in Arkansas Territorial Restoration, Little Rock.

tulips on the mountain slopes in spring.
Open: Daily. (501) 394–2863.

Other Places of Interest

Alum Cove Natural Bridge
Arkansas Post National Monument
Buffalo National River
Crater of Diamonds State Park, Murfreesboro
Devil's Den State Park, Westfork
Eureka Springs
Fort Smith National Historic Site
Mount Nebo State Park, Dardanelle
Ozark and Ouachita National Forests
Pea Ridge National Military Park
Petit Jean State Park, Morrilton

California

Area: 158,693 square miles

Population: 26,365,000

Statehood: September 9, 1850 (31st state)

The "Golden State" owes its name to the fabled gold rush of 1848. Glamour and glitter came to California again in the twentieth century when the American movie industry chose Hollywood as its home. The San Andreas Fault runs along the California coast; in 1906, fault movement caused the famous San Francisco earthquake. California's pleasant climate and great natural beauty have induced Americans from all over the nation to move here.

Mount Whitney, located in the Sierra Nevada Mountains, has an elevation of 14,494 feet. Death Valley is 282 feet below sea level. The Pacific Coast is occupied by the rugged coastal ranges. Between these ranges and the towering Sierra Nevada Mountains is the Central Valley, an extremely productive agricultural land. Along the coast and in the Central Valley, the climate is mild with little seasonal variation. Because summers are very dry, irrigation is crucial to the state's agriculture.

California has a varied and unusual vegetation. The tallest redwood on record, at 370 feet, is located in Red-wood National Forest. A sequoia tree in Sequoia National Park has a trunk diameter of 36.5 feet. California's gardeners work with a unique palette of plant materials. Many species have been imported from Australia, Asia, and Africa.

Spain and Mexico first brought European civilization to the state. In the Franciscan missions, many European plants were introduced and cultivated. Settlers from the United States moved to California in great numbers during the gold rush; many Oriental people came to work on the railroads. This variety of people, along with exceptional growing conditions, has made the state's gardens unique. Many leaders of the Modern Movement in landscape design now practice in California. The idea of the garden as an outdoor living room springs naturally from the pleasant climate.

California is an exciting place to visit. The Yosemite, Kings Canyon, and Sequoia national parks display the dramatic scenery of the Sierra Nevada Mountains. Lassen National Park features a recently active volcano. A stop at one of the many preserved missions gives the visitor an idea about California life two hundred years ago. Reyes National Seashore, Marineland Oceanarium, and San Diego's Mission Bay demonstrate the varied Pacific Coast landscape. Other points of interest include the many national monuments and state parks.

CALIFORNIA

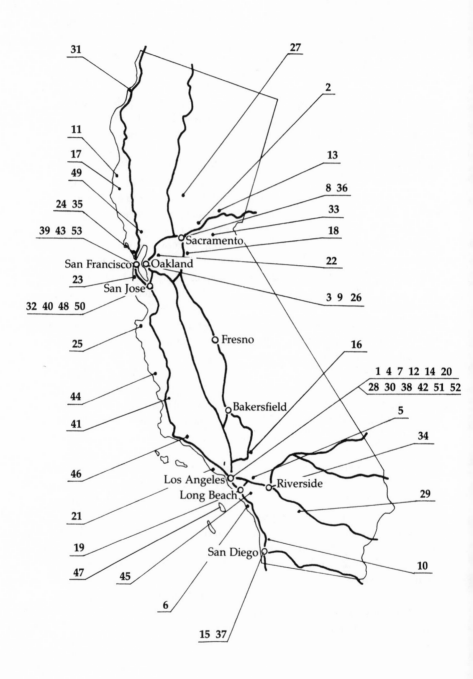

31

27

2

11

17

49

13

24 35

8 36

39 43 53

33

18

Sacramento

22

San Francisco Oakland

23

San Jose

3 9 26

32 40 48 50

25

Fresno

16

1 4 7 12 14 20

28 30 38 42 51 52

44

Bakersfield

5

41

34

46

Los Angeles

Riverside

Long Beach

29

21

19

San Diego

10

47

45

6

15 37

1. *Arcadia (Los Angeles)* 2. *Auburn* 3. *Berkeley* 4. *Canoga Park (Los Angeles)*
5. *Claremont* 6. *Corona Del Mar* 7. *Culver City (Los Angeles)* 8. *Davis
(Sacramento)* 9. *El Cerrito (Oakland)* 10. *Encinitas* 11. *Fort Bragg*
12. *Glendale (Los Angeles)* 13. *Grass Valley* 14. *La Canada (Los Angeles)*
15. *La Jolla* 16. *Lancaster* 17. *Little River* 18. *Lodi* 19. *Long Beach* 20. *Los
Angeles* 21. *Malibu* 22. *Martinez* 23. *Menlo Park* 24. *Mill Valley*
25. *Monterey* 26. *Oakland* 27. *Oroville* 28. *Pacific Palisades (Los Angeles)*
29. *Palm Desert* 30. *Palos Verdes Peninsula* 31. *Patrick's Point* 32. *Piedmont
(San Jose)* 33. *Placerville* 34. *Riverside* 35. *Ross* 36. *Sacramento* 37. *San
Diego* 38. *San Fernando (Los Angeles)* 39. *San Francisco* 40. *San Jose*
41. *San Luis Obispo* 42. *San Marino (Los Angeles)* 43. *San Mateo (San
Francisco)* 44. *San Simeon* 45. *Santa Ana* 46. *Santa Barbara* 47. *Santa
Catalina Island* 48. *Santa Clara* 49. *Santa Rosa* 50. *Saratoga (San Jose)*
51. *Sun Valley* 52. *Whittier (Los Angeles)* 53. *Woodside (San Francisco)*

1. Arcadia (Los Angeles)

☆
Los Angeles State and County Arboretum
301 North Baldwin Avenue

The 127-acre arboretum, established in 1947, displays a fine collection of indigenous and exotic plants well adapted to the southern California climate. Areas are devoted to plants of different continents, special collections, theme gardens, and *Sunset Magazine* demonstration gardens and experimental plots. The greenhouse features orchids and begonias. Two restored buildings have been listed as a State Historical Landmark.
*Open: Daily 8:30 a.m.–5:00 p.m.; greenhouses, 10:00 a.m.–4:00 p.m.
(213) 446–8251.*

2. Auburn

Esther Baker Memorial Garden
Placer County Library, 350 Nevada Street

This is a Japanese garden designed by Ray Yamasaki in 1973.
Open: Library hours only. (916) 823–4391.

3. Berkeley

Berkeley Municipal Rose Garden
Codornices Park, Euclid Avenue and Bay View Place

On a hillside above San Francisco Bay, the rose garden has a view westward across the water to the Golden Gate Bridge. Originally the rocky hillside was covered by weed and brush. From 1933 to 1937, the Civilian Conservation Corps and the Works Progress Administration

cleared the land and constructed the present garden. Designed as a rock-terraced amphitheater, the 4 acres in Codornices Park were planted and developed under the supervision of the Berkeley Parks Society. Today, the site is a demonstration garden of the American Rose Society.
Open: Daily, sunrise–sunset. (415) 644–6530.

Blake Garden
70 Rincon Road

This 10-acre Kensington showplace of fine planting design includes rare plants and a children's adventure garden. The garden is under the direction of the University of California Department of Landscape Architecture.
Open to interested individuals and groups by appointment with the superintendent. (415) 524–2449.

Botanic Gardens of Charles Lee Tilden Regional Park
6500 Broadway, Lake Temescal (2 miles east at University of California campus)

Featured on this 20-acre site are many native California species and special displays of dune, meadow, and mountain vegetation all arranged in natural geographic associations. April and May are the best months to visit.
Open: Daily 10:00 a.m.–5:00 p.m. Closed: Holidays. (415) 841–8732.

☆
University of California Botanical Garden
Strawberry Canyon and Centennial Drive

This 32-acre garden, established in 1892, enjoys a spectacular setting in Berkeley Hills. It has an outstanding collection of native California plants, cacti, and succulents from South Africa and South America, an herb garden, and an amphitheater.
Open: Daily 9:00 a.m.–5:00 p.m. Closed: Holidays. (415) 642–3343.

4. Canoga Park (Los Angeles)

Orcutt Ranch Park
23555 Justice Street

This historical monument and horticultural facility exhibits ancient native oaks, exotic specimen trees, a rose garden, children's gardens, and acres of citrus groves.
Open: Daily 8:30 a.m.–7:00 p.m. (818) 883–6641.

5. Claremont

Rancho Santa Ana Botanic Garden
1500 North College Avenue

Established in 1927, 85 acres of the 100-acre site are devoted exclusively to indigenous plants; the 19 different plant communities of the state are

represented in a collection of over 1,500 species. Fine wildflowers and native iris are displayed. Also provided are a library and herbarium. Best seen between February and June.
Open: Monday–Saturday 8:00 a.m.–5:00 p.m.
Closed: Holidays. (714) 626–3922.

6. Corona Del Mar

Sherman Foundation Library and Gardens
2647 East Coast Highway

In a small area are featured a tea garden, a fine conservatory, and an impeccable outdoor display of flowering and ornamental plants.
Open: Daily 10:30 a.m.–4:00 p.m.
Fee, but free on Mondays.
Closed: Holidays. (714) 673–2261.

7. Culver City (Los Angeles)

Kaizuka Meditation Garden
Culver City Library,
4975 Overland Avenue

The garden was designed and built in Japan, then dismantled and reassembled in Culver City—everything from the stone bridge and huge rocks to the colored gravel was shipped from Japan. A Shinto priest performed the authentic dedication ceremony in 1974. The garden is a gift of appreciation from the people of Kaizuka, Japan, to its sister city, Culver City.
Open: Daily, library hours. (213) 559–1676.

8. Davis (Sacramento)

University of California at Davis Botanic Garden and Arboretum
13 miles west of Sacramento

Founded in 1936, this garden is both a campus park and a research station to test native and exotic plants for their suitability to growing conditions in the Central Valley. Among its features are the Weier Redwood Grove, Shield's Oak Grove, and Australian plant collections.
Open: Daily, sunrise–sunset. (916) 752–2498.

9. El Cerrito (Oakland)

Persian Rug Garden
944 Arlington Avenue,
north of Berkeley

From mid-June to August, thousands of colorful annuals bloom in patterns of Persian rugs and American quilts. This unique display is the work of Sundar Shadi of India. Mr. Shadi studied tropical horticulture at the University of California, Berkeley; now retired, he sketches the pattern designs and replants the gardens each year. During the Christmas season, blooms representing the Little Town of Bethlehem and other nativity scenes cover the steep hillside garden. *Open: Daily, sunrise–sunset. (View from road only.)*

10. Encinitas

Quail Botanical Gardens
230 Quail Garden Drive

California's native plants and subtropical flowering plants and vines are featured in this 31-acre garden. Plants from 12 geographic areas are displayed, and there is an excellent collection of bamboo. Self-guided walking tour.
Open: Daily 8:00 a.m.–5:00 p.m. (619) 436–3036.

11. Fort Bragg

Mendocino Coast Botanical Gardens
18220 North Highway 1

This 47-acre seacoast site has both natural and formal gardens. Miles of trails wind through woodland gardens and rain forests. Every season has its special feature: bulbs in early spring, rhododendrons in April and May, and thousands of dahlias from July into autumn.
Open: Daily 8:00 a.m.–sunset. Fee. (707) 964–4352.

12. Glendale (Los Angeles)

Friendship Garden
Brand Park,
6501 West Mountain Avenue

This traditional Japanese garden, designed by Eljiro Nunokaura, was the product of Glendale's sister-city relationship with Hagashiosaka, Japan.
Open: Daily by appointment only; contact Parks and Recreation Division, 613 East Broadway, Room 120, Glendale, Calif. 91201. (213) 956–2000.

13. Grass Valley

Empire Mine State Historic Park
10791 East Empire Street

The 784-acre park is the site of one of the largest gold finds in California. There is a restored "baronial" cottage with formal gardens.
Open: Sunrise–sunset. Tours available April–November, by arrangement rest of year. (916) 273–4667.

Woodbridge Metcalf Fir Tree Arboretum
Condon Park, Butler and Minnie Streets

The arboretum is located on about 4 acres of gently sloping land 2,000 feet above sea level. Throughout this park, widely spaced 60- to 100-year-old ponderosa pines provide not only

Descanso Gardens, La Canada, Calif.

welcome shade but also a rich, brown pine needle carpet.
Open: Daily 8:00 a.m.–5:00 p.m.
(916) 273–4667.

14. La Canada (Los Angeles)

☆
Descanso Gardens
1418 Descanso Drive

Descanso, meaning "Where I rest," was once part of the great Rancho San Raphael. The gardens were begun in 1930 as a private estate. They contain a famous collection of over 100,000 camellias, the "History of the Rose" garden, and 30 acres of native and shade gardens. Also on the grounds are a Japanese garden and a traditional Chinese garden—one of the very few outside of China. The gardens can be viewed on foot (via nature and hiking trails) or by tram tour.
Open: Monday–Friday 8:00 a.m.–5:00 p.m., Saturday–Sunday 8:00 a.m.–6:30 p.m.
Closed: Holidays. Fee. (213) 790–5571.

15. La Jolla

Torrey Pines Mesa State Reserve
Off U.S. 101 North

The only natural groves of Torrey Pines in the world grow along the ocean in this area and on Santa Rosa Island, 195 miles away. Relics of the Ice Age, these trees were clinging to the sandstone cliffs when Cabrilho's ships first sighted California in 1542.
Open: Summer, daily 8:00 a.m.–

10:00 p.m.; winter, until 5:00 p.m.
(619) 454–1444.

16. Lancaster

Antelope Valley California Poppy Reserve
Avenue I, 15 miles west of Lancaster

This beautiful natural site, purchased as a state park, occupies 2,000 acres of "prime poppy land." The golden poppies of this area were admired by Father Junipero Serra and John Muir. Spring is an especially good time to enjoy the wildflowers.
Open: Sunrise–sunset. (805) 948–4518.

17. Little River

Pygmy Forest, Discovery Trail
Van Damme State Park
County Airport Road,
3.5 miles inland from Calif. 1

The pygmy forest presents a striking contrast to the nearby redwood forests—home of some of the tallest trees in the world; here grow some of the smallest trees. Crowded on extremely impoverished soil, thousands of trees struggle to survive. The soil has been called the "most acid in the world," with a pH of 2.8–3.9 (almost that of vinegar). Few trees in the pygmy forest are taller than 8 feet; some trees, over 100 years old, are only 3 feet tall. The dominant

tree is the pygmy cypress (*Cypressus pygmaea*).
Open: Daily, sunrise–sunset. (707) 964–3153.

18. Lodi

Japanese Rock Garden
Micke Grove Park and Zoo,
Micke Grove Road near Stockton

This 3-acre rock garden was designed by landscape architect Nagao Sakuri, who was head caretaker of the emperor's palace gardens in Tokyo. The 100-year-old Kasuga lantern was a gift from Shimizu City, Japan. Other notable features include 2 bridges, a carp pond, and 60 flowering cherry trees.
Open: Daily 8:00 a.m.–7:00 p.m.
(209) 944–2444.

19. Long Beach

El Dorado Nature Center
El Dorado Park East,
7550 East Spring Street

Awareness of the interdependence of man and nature is fostered in this 80-acre natural area.
Open: Daily 8:00 a.m.–4:00 p.m.
Closed: Christmas. Fee. Groups should make arrangements at least 2 weeks in advance. (213) 425–8569.

Rancho Los Alamitos
6400 Bixby Hill Road

The fountain, cactus garden, and courtyard of succulents reflect the style of Spanish Colonial times, when the house and garden were established. More recent additions include the Friendship Garden, a formal terrace, and an informal collection of native ornamental plants.
Open: Wednesday–Sunday 1:00–5:00 p.m. (213) 431–2511.

Rancho Los Cerritos

Restored Victorian gardens surround this Spanish colonial adobe villa built in 1850. The gardens are reputed to be the first formal design gardens in California.
Open: Wednesday–Sunday 1:00–5:00 p.m. (213) 424–9423.

20. Los Angeles

Exposition Park Rose Garden
Exposition Boulevard
at Figueroa Street

Located on the site of the 1932 Olympic Games, this 7-acre sunken garden displays 160 varieties of roses. Within easy walking distance are the Museum of Science and Industry, the Museum of Natural History, and the Aeronautical Museum.
Open: Daily, sunrise–sunset. (213) 239–0200.

University of California at Los Angeles Botanical Garden
Hilgard and LeConte Avenues

This 8-acre teaching garden, established in 1929, features collections of acacia, eucalyptus, desert plants, and other California natives.
Open: Monday–Friday 8:00 a.m.–5:00 p.m., Saturday–Sunday until 4:00 p.m. (213) 825–4321.

University of California at Los Angeles Japanese Garden
10619 Bellagio Road, Bel Air

This fine example of the traditional Japanese hill-and-pond garden was originally designed by Nagao Sakuri for the Guiberson estate; some later reconstruction was done by Koichi Kawana. The garden contains lanterns and a teahouse which were Japanese gifts.
Open: Daily 10:00 a.m.–4:00 p.m. (213) 206–8147.

21. Malibu

☆
J. Paul Getty Museum and Gardens
17985 Pacific Coast Highway

The building and grounds are a copy of the ancient Roman Villa dei Papiri, with appropriate plantings as determined from archaeological research. The gardens feature statuary, mosaics, a large reflecting pool, pomegranate trees, and many varieties

J. Paul Getty Museum and Gardens, Malibu, Calif.

of ground cover. Advance parking reservations are required; call (213) 459–8402.
Open: Tuesday–Saturday 10:00 a.m.– 5:00 p.m.

22. Martinez

John Muir National Historic Site
4202 Alhambra Avenue

Original gardens and orchards surround the 1882 home of conservationist-writer John Muir. The house museum and adjacent adobe house commemorate Muir's achievements.
Open: Daily 8:30 a.m.–4:30 p.m.
Closed: Holidays. (415) 228–8860.

23. Menlo Park

Lane Publishing Company Headquarters
Willow and Middlefield Roads

Designed by contemporary California landscape architect Thomas Church, the garden features native trees and plants of the Pacific Coast.
Open: Monday–Friday 9:00 a.m.– 4:30 p.m.
Closed: Holidays. (415) 321–3600.

24. Mill Valley

Muir Woods National Monument
Cal. 1

This famous redwood grove has both natural and historic significance. The

500-acre preserve of magnificent redwoods and their natural understory is located in a steep, humid valley only 17 miles from urban San Francisco. The land was donated by Congressman and Mrs. William Kent, proclaimed a national monument by Theodore Roosevelt in 1908, and named in honor of the great conservationist John Muir.
Open: Daily 8:00 a.m.–sunset. Donation. (415) 388–2595.

25. Monterey

Casa Amesti
516 Polk Street

This was the home of a Spanish Basque who settled in Monterey in the 1830s. The Italian-style formal gardens, within adobe walls surrounding the plot, were designed by Frances Elkins, noted interior designer who bought the house in 1918, and her brother, Chicago architect David Adler. Built in 1834, Casa Amesti is made of adobe and redwood logs, and combines architectural influences from the East Coast and California.
Open: Saturday–Sunday 2:00– 4:00 p.m. Fee. (408) 372–2608.

26. Oakland

Dunsmuir–Helleman Estate
2960 Peralta Oaks Court

This turn-of-the-century Victorian mansion is surrounded by a large, old-fashioned garden.
Open: Daily. (415) 562–7588.

Joseph McInnes Memorial Botanical Gardens
Mills College, Seminary Drive and MacArthur Boulevard

There is a 4-acre garden of native California plants on the 132-acre campus. Although the garden is primarily for instruction and research, it is open to the public.
Open: Monday–Friday 8:00 a.m.– 5:00 p.m.; daily during school term. (415) 430–2158.

Kaiser Center Roof Garden
300 Lakeside Drive

Placing the garden on the roof is a good way to maximize the development of a valuable building site while providing outdoor space for human enjoyment. Interesting plantings and excellent views of San Francisco Bay are available in this 3-acre garden.
Open: Monday–Saturday 9:00 a.m.– 9:00 p.m. (415) 271–6146.

Lakeside Park Garden Center and Japanese Garden
666 Bellevue Avenue

This contemporary garden center and park is the result of 8 years of work by over 40 garden clubs and

specialty groups. The trial gardens are intended to display flowering plants that thrive in the Bay area, particularly fuchsias (June–October), dahlias (August–September), chrysanthemums (October–November), and camellias and rhododendrons (February–April). The Japanese Garden is a fine example of spacious design within a small area.
Open: Daily 10:00 a.m.–4:30 p.m.; winter until 3:00 p.m. (415) 273–3208.

Morcom Amphitheater of Roses
400 Jean Street

This garden contains 8,000 rose bushes of 400 varieties, many of which are All-American selections. It has been referred to as the most beautiful municipal rose garden in the United States, and has nearly continuous blooms from April to December.
Open: Daily. (415) 658–0731.

Oakland Museum
1000 Oak Street

The beautiful multi-level urban plaza is planted with a great variety of trees, shrubs, vines, and ground covers.
Open: Wednesday–Saturday 10:00 a.m.–5:00 p.m., Sunday noon–7:00 p.m. (415) 273–3514.

27. Oroville

Boynton–Stapleton House and Garden
1681 Bird Street

This Queen Anne-style residence now houses law offices. The grounds feature camellias and azaleas.
Open: Tours are offered weekdays, 10:00 a.m.–4:00 p.m. (916) 533–2542.

Chinese Temple Garden
1500 Broderick Street

The temple, over 100 years old, is now a State Historical Landmark. The courtyard garden was added in 1968, according to the plans of architect Philip Choy and the planting design of Margaret Brown. All of the plants used are found in China and have symbolic significance in the Chinese garden tradition.
Open: Wednesday–Thursday noon–4:30 p.m., all other days 10:00 a.m.–4:30 p.m.
Closed: December 1–January 15. (916) 533–1646.

Judge C. F. Lott House
1067 Montgomery Street

There is an old-fashioned garden on the grounds.
Open: Daily 8:00 a.m.–5:00 p.m.
Closed: December 1–January 15. (916) 533–7699.

28. Pacific Palisades (Los Angeles)

Self-Realization Fellowship Lake Shrine
17190 Sunset Boulevard

This is a serene meditation garden with an Oriental flavor. The shrine was founded by Paramahansa Yogananda and honors Mahatma Gandhi.
Open: Tuesday–Sunday 10:00 a.m.–5:00 p.m. (213) 454–4114.

29. Palm Desert

Living Desert Reserve
47900 Portola Avenue

Here, 940 acres of desert have been set aside in a natural state for three purposes: preservation, interpretation, and education. Included is the James Irvine Garden, "An Exhibit of North American Deserts." There are also live desert animal exhibits.
Open: Daily 9:00 a.m.–5:00 p.m. (714) 346–5694.

30. Palos Verdes Peninsula

South Coast Botanic Garden
26300 Crenshaw Boulevard

Developed on a former landfill site of 87 acres, the garden features California native flora.

Open: Daily 9:00 a.m.–5:00 p.m. (213) 772–5813.

31. Patrick's Point

Stagecoach Hill
Kane Road (right turn off
U.S. 101 northbound), 2 miles
north of Patrick's Point

The 100-acre site is a 2-mile-long strip of land on a hillside overlooking the Pacific. Among many interesting species of ferns and thousands of wildflowers grow magnificent specimens of *Rhododendron occidentale.*
Open: Daily, dawn–dusk.

32. Piedmont (San Jose)

Cherry Tree Walk, Piedmont Park
Highland Avenue

This is a diverse 1-acre garden with a redwood grove, Japanese features, and a magnificent walkway lined with flowering cherries.
Open: Sunrise–sunset. (916) 626–2344.

33. Placerville

Eddy Arboretum and Institute of Forest Genetics
Carson Road

The 45-acre forest reserve, founded in 1925, is said to have the most

complete collection of pines in the world, with 70 species represented.
Open: Monday–Friday 8:00 a.m.–5:00 p.m. (916) 622–1225.

34. Riverside

Mission Inn Courtyard
3649 7th Street at Orange Street

There is an attractive Spanish-style courtyard in this still operating hotel and restaurant, which is sometimes used as a setting for movies.
Open: Daily 8:00 a.m.–9:00 p.m. (714) 784–0300.

University Botanic Gardens
University of California, Riverside

This relatively new collection (begun in 1962) of Australian and dry-climate plants is being developed by the School of Biology and Agricultural Sciences.
Open: Monday–Friday 9:00 a.m.–4:00 p.m.
Closed: Holidays. (714) 787–4650.

Victoria Avenue

Riverside is reputed to have undertaken the first municipal street tree planting in the nation, in 1890. Many original specimens remain along Victoria Avenue. (714) 787–7950.

35. Ross

Marin Art and Garden Center
Sir Francis Drake Boulevard and Laurel Grove Avenue

The center contains an art gallery, an 8-acre garden featuring specimen trees (including a 100-year-old magnolia), a Memory Garden, and a wisteria walk.
Open: Daily 9:00 a.m.–5:00 p.m. (415) 454–5597.

36. Sacramento

Goethe Arboretum
6000 J Street

Located on the grounds of California State University, the 3-acre arboretum features mainly native California conifers.
Open: Daily, sunrise–sunset. (916) 454–6494.

State Capitol Grounds
10th Street at Capitol Mall

The restored 1874 state capitol building is located in a 40-acre park setting featuring many varieties of plants, especially camellias. (Sacramento is called the "Camellia Capital of the World.")
Open: Sunrise–sunset. (916) 324–0333.

37. San Diego

☆☆
Balboa Park
Laurel Street and Sixth Avenue

In this park are very large and de-
servedly famous gardens dating
from 1868. Formal gardens include
a Spanish garden, English garden,
and Alcazar garden, patterned after
the Moorish palace in Seville. Also
featured are a Desert Garden, a Rose
Garden, and camellias; permanent
conservatory collections of shade and
tropical plants in the Botanical Building; and Garden Club exhibits and
demonstrations.
Open: Park, daily, sunrise–sunset;
Botanical Building, daily except Friday,
10:00 a.m.–4:30 p.m. (619) 239–0512.

☆
San Diego Zoological Gardens
Balboa Park, Laurel Street
and Sixth Avenue

One of the world's outstanding
zoological parks is recognized for
its plant displays as well as its animal collections. The planting design carries out the natural habitat
themes, sometimes providing the animals' food. The tropical rain forest is
especially noteworthy.
Open: Daily, winter 9:00 a.m.–
4:00 p.m.; spring until 5:00 p.m.;
summer until 6:00 p.m. Fee. (619)
231–1515.

38. San Fernando (Los Angeles)

Mission San Fernando Rey de Espana
15174 Mission Boulevard

Founded in 1797, this mission was
the seventeenth in a chain of 21 missions established by the Franciscans.
Because of its proximity to the little
pueblo of Los Angeles, the mission
was a favorite stopping place for
travelers along El Camino Real and
became one of the largest of all the
missions. The inner courtyard, with
a stream flowing through it, reflects
the Islamic influence on gardening
brought to California by way of Spain
and Mexico.
Open: 9:00 a.m.–5:00 p.m.
Closed: Holidays. (818) 361–0186.

39. San Francisco

Crown Zellerbach Plaza
1 Bush Street

The 20-story Crown Zellerbach
Building, built in 1959, is one of San
Francisco's first glass-walled office
towers. On its sloping triangular site
is a beautifully designed urban plaza,
with free-flowing paved areas, irregular steps and seating, and curving
banks of wild strawberry. The plaza
is a fine early example of the urban
office tower open space now seen in
every city.
Open: All times. (415) 951–5209.

Ghiradelli Square
North Point Beach and Larkin Streets

The restoration of this historic complex by landscape architect Lawrence Halprin is an excellent illustration of contemporary urban landscape design. *Open: All times. (415) 974–6900.*

☆☆
Golden Gate Park
and Strybing Arboretum
9th Avenue and Lincoln Way

Golden Gate Park was built in 1870 on 1,000 acres of reclaimed sand barrens. Designer William H. Hall used New York's Central Park as a model. The 40-acre arboretum utilizes the park's unusual range of microclimates to grow trees and shrubs from all over the world. There are a number of special gardens, including a Shakespeare Garden, Garden of Fragrance, and Japanese Moon-Viewing Pavilion Garden; demonstration gardens; and nature trails. Also in Golden Gate Park is the historic Japanese Tea Garden founded in 1894 by George Turner Marsh, who was assisted in the design and planting by Scotsman John McLaren and Makoto Hagiwara. Among the additions made over the years is the Classical Garden designed by Nagao Sakuri in 1953.
Open: Park, daily, sunrise–sunset; Strybing Arboretum, weekdays 8:00 a.m.–4:30 p.m., weekends 10:00 a.m.–5:00 p.m.; Japanese Tea Garden, daily 8:00 a.m.–dusk. Fee for tea garden, but free 1st Wednesday of month. (415) 661–1316.

Japanese Center Peace Plaza
Post and Geary Streets

The center features a Japanese garden and reflecting pool. There are many flowering cherry trees.
Open: Daily 9:00 a.m.–5:00 p.m. (415) 922–6776.

Lombard Street

This street is famous for its crookedness and for its hydrangeas, flowering trees, and landmark hand-carved wood arch.
Open: All times. (415) 974–6900.

Mission Dolores Cemetery
320 Dolores Street at Sixteenth Street

The cemetery adjoins the Mission Dolores, called the "Cradle of San Francisco," instituted by Father Junipero Serra in 1776. Nearly all the flowers of the western United States bloom here. The mission is now a National Historic Landmark.
Open: Summer 9:00 a.m.–5:00 p.m.; winter 10:00 a.m.–4:00 p.m. Fee. (415) 621–8203.

Octagon House
2645 Gough Street

The headquarters of the Colonial Dames, this is a fine example of the octagon plan popular in the mid-nineteenth century. The former residence is now a house museum with a period garden.
Open: Thursday 2:00–4:00 p.m., 1st Sunday of month 1:00–4:00 p.m. (415) 441–7512.

Stone Lake in Golden Gate Park, San Francisco, Calif.

40. San Jose

Japanese Friendship Garden
1300 Senter Road

At this site, a sister-city project with Okayama, Japan, is a large "stroll garden" patterned after Okayama's Kor-a-kuen Garden.
Open: Daily 10:00 a.m.–sunset. (408) 286–3626.

Japanese Garden at the Buddhist Temple
640 North 5th Street

The Japanese garden to one side of the temple features an irregularly shaped pool and fine evergreens. The garden was designed by Ernest Uenaka; the authentic temple and grounds were planned by Shinzabura Nishiura.
Open: Daily. (408) 293–9292.

41. San Luis Obispo

Dalidet Adobe
1185 Pacific Street,
off Santa Rosa Street

This 1852 home was built by a French vintner. The gardens were restored by the San Luis Obispo County Historical Society.
Open: Memorial Day–Labor Day, Sunday 1:00–4:30 p.m. (805) 543–0638.

42. San Marino (Los Angeles)

☆☆
Huntington Botanical Gardens
1151 Oxford Road

Huntington is a 200-acre estate complex including the renowned Huntington Library and Art Gallery. The gardens were begun in 1905 when Henry E. Huntington, wealthy businessman and philanthropist, purchased the San Marino Ranch. William Hestrick was the original designer and curator. Today the gardens contain the largest outdoor collection of mature desert plants in the world, an extensive camellia collection, an Australian Garden, a Palm Garden, and several fine cycad specimens. Near the Art Gallery are the formal gardens: an Italianate lawn vista, Shakespeare Garden, Rose Garden and pergola, and herb garden. The Japanese Garden, in a 5-acre canyon setting, contains a Moon Bridge, Zig Zag Bridge, Zen Garden of sand and rock, Bonsai Court, and full-sized Japanese house.
Open: Tuesday–Sunday 1:00–4:30 p.m.
Closed: Major holidays. Note: Sunday admission requires advance reservation by mail. (818) 449–3901.

The Old Mill
1120 Old Mill Road

This historic building with garden is now the headquarters of the California Historical Society.
Open: Tuesday–Sunday 1:00–4:00 p.m. (818) 449–5450.

43. San Mateo (San Francisco)

Japanese Garden in Central Park
El Camino Road and 5th Avenue

This garden designed by Nagao Saburaiana was formally opened with a Shinto ceremony in 1965. The large stone pagoda was donated by Toyanaka, San Mateo's sister city in Japan. There is a "viewing house" or *azumaza* on a high point, from which the entire garden can be seen.
Open: Teahouse (attended by a Japanese hostess), summer, 11:00 a.m.–4:00 p.m.; garden, Monday–Friday 8:00 a.m.–4:00 p.m., Saturday–Sunday 11:00 a.m.–5:00 p.m. (415) 342–1692.

44. San Simeon

☆☆
Hearst San Simeon State Historical Monument

Rarely since the day of the Medici has an estate existed as grand as La Cuesta Encantada at San Simeon. For three decades it was developed by William Randolph Hearst as a Moorish-style castle and formal gardens. The gardens include a rose garden, specimen trees, and flowering plants, enriched by one of the greatest collections of objets d'art in the world. After Hearst's death, the estate was presented to the people of California by the Hearst Corporation. It was opened to the public in 1958.

*Open: Daily guided tours only,
8:00 a.m.–3:00 p.m. Advance
reservations highly recommended. Fee.
(805) 927–4621.*

45. Santa Ana

Sarah May Downie
Memorial Herb Garden
North Flower Street and
North Park Boulevard

This small herb garden was begun
in 1954 on a boulevard strip created
in the 1920s. It received the 1975
Burlington House Award. Its main
emphasis is to demonstrate herbs
that are useful and require little
maintenance.
Open: Daily, sunrise–sunset.

46. Santa Barbara

El Cuartel Adobe
El Presidio de Santa Barbara
State Historical Park
122 East Canyon Perdito

This is the oldest remaining building
in Santa Barbara dating from the
1780s. The adjacent small gardens
were restored using plant materials of
the period.
*Open: Monday–Friday 9:00 a.m.–
4:00 p.m. (805) 965–3021.*

☆
Lotusland
695 Ashley Road (Montecito)

Dating from 1882, the 37-acre estate
was purchased in 1941 by the oper-
atic singer Madam Ganna Walska.
During her lifetime, Madam Walska transformed the European-style
gardens into an exotic botanical collection of great originality.
*Open: By reservation. Fee. (805)
969–3767.*

Santa Barbara Botanic Garden
1212 Mission Canyon Road

This garden features California native
flora in appropriate settings. The
60-acre site, established in 1926, is
located in Mission Canyon in the
foothills of the Santa Inez Mountains. Especially noteworthy are the
desert plants, wildflower meadow,
and Channel Island collection.
*Open: Daily 8:00 a.m.–sunset.
Closed when raining. (805) 682–4726.*

Santa Barbara Mission
East Los Olives and Upper Laguna
Streets

Founded in 1786, the "Queen of the
Missions" contains a small cloister
garden and a walled cemetery.
*Open: Daily 10:00 a.m.–6:00 p.m.
Closed: Holidays. Donation. (805)
682–4713.*

47. Santa Catalina Island

Wrigley Memorial Garden
1400 Avalon Canyon Road

This 37-acre botanical garden is a showcase for plants endemic to the California islands. Founded in 1934 by William Wrigley, Jr., the gardens were considerably expanded and revitalized in 1969.
Open: Daily 8:00 a.m.–5:00 p.m. Closed: Holidays. (213) 510–2288.

48. Santa Clara

Mission Gardens of Santa Clara
U.S. 101, El Camino Real

This former mission garden was begun in 1777, and many of the plant materials reflect this age. The gnarled olive trees date from 1822 and originally came from Mexico, and the wisteria arbor was planted in 1893.
Open: Daily 7:00 a.m.–7:00 p.m. (408) 296–7111.

49. Santa Rosa

**Luther Burbank
Memorial Gardens**
Santa Rosa Avenue
and Sonoma Avenue

This delightful garden of about 4 acres was designed with great care around some of the original Burbank plantings. Meticulously maintained with color at all seasons, it emphasizes the plants that Mr. Burbank introduced.
Open: House and greenhouse, April–October 12, 10:00 a.m.–3:30 p.m.; gardens, daily 8:00 a.m.–7:00 p.m. (707) 576–5115.

50. Saratoga (San Jose)

Hakone Gardens
21000 Big Basin Way

Hakone Gardens were designed in 1918 by N. Aihara. The traditional moon-viewing house, constructed without nails, was moved to its hill site from the Japanese exhibit at the San Francisco Pan Pacific Exposition of 1915. The redwood and bamboo Kamakura-style main gate was designed by Shinzabura Nishiura in 1941.
Open: Daily 10:00 a.m.–5:00 p.m. (408) 253–2506.

Villa Montalvo Arboretum
15400 Montalvo Road

This 175-acre tract exhibits ornamental plants of merit, both native and exotic, for horticultural study. The grounds are beautifully landscaped with formal gardens, fountains, and trails that lead to lookout points on the mountainside. There is a fall color festival in November. The villa itself is a public Center for the Fine Arts.
Open: Tuesday–Sunday 1:30–4:30 p.m. (408) 867–3421.

51. Sun Valley

Theodore Payne Foundation for Wildflowers and Native Plants
10459 Tuxford Street

The foundation maintains a 22-acre wildflower and native plant garden, and offers free lectures and seed distribution to perpetuate California's wildflowers. Spring is the best time to see the garden.
Open: Tuesday–Saturday 8:30 a.m.–4:30 p.m. (818) 768–1802.

52. Whittier (Los Angeles)

Rose Hills Memorial Park
3900 South Workman Mill Road

This cemetery garden is known for its 400 varieties of roses. In the Cherry Blossom Gardens section is a fine Japanese garden.
Open: Daily 8:00 a.m.–sunset. (213) 699–0921.

53. Woodside (San Francisco)

☆☆
Filoli
Canada Road

Filoli, an acronym for fidelity, love, and life, is a 654-acre estate built in 1916–17 as the residence of William B. Bourn. The gardens were designed by Bruce Porter and planted under the supervision of Isabella Bourn. Within this area are many superb specimens and plantings including a 16-acre formal garden with roses, boxwood, holly hedges, and a yew-lined allée. The gardens also contain collections of citrus and deciduous fruit trees, many espaliered on walls and trellises, and groves of indigenous trees, including redwood, live oak, madrone, and California bay. Filoli provides one of the finest horticultural displays in the San Francisco Bay area. The estate is now the property of the National Trust for Historic Preservation.
Open: Tuesday–Saturday.
Closed: Mid-November–mid-February. Tours only, call for times. Fee. No children under 12. (415) 364–2880.

Other Places of Interest

Big Basin Redwoods State Park, near Pescadero
Big Sur
Cabrillo National Monument
Carmel
Channel Islands National Monument
Cleveland National Forest, Pine Valley
Death Valley National Monument
Desert State Park, Anza-Borrego
Devil's Postpile National Monument, Yosemite Village
Humboldt Redwoods State Park, Burlington
Inyo National Forest, Mammoth Lakes
Joshua Tree National Monument, Twenty-Nine Palms
King's Canyon National Park, Three Rivers
Kruse Rhododendron State Park

Lassen Volcanic National Park,
  Mineral
Lava Beds National Park, Tule
Lompoc (commercial seed and plant
  growers area)
Mohave Desert, Barstow
Mount Whitney, Bishop
Muir Woods National Monument,
  Mill Valley
Napa Valley Wineries, Napa Valley
Pinnacles National Monument,
  Paicines
Point Reyes National Seashore
Redwood State Park, Big Basin
Sea World, San Diego
Sequoia National Park, Three Rivers
Whiskeytown-Shasta-Trinity
  National Recreation Area,
  Whiskeytown

Yosemite National Park, Yosemite
  Village

Also of special interest is the Mission Trail, where 21 missions were founded by the Franciscan Fathers from 1769 to 1784. It begins in San Diego with San Diego de Alcala and ends in the heart of the wine country, at San Francisco Solano. All of the missions had simple gardens tended by monks. Many of the gardens have been restored and can be seen today. Notable examples are San Gabriel Mission, San Juan Capistrano, La Purisma Concepcion, and San Juan Bautista.

Colorado

Area: 104,247 square miles

Population: 3,231,000

Statehood: August 1, 1876
(38th state)

The "Rocky Mountain State" is the loftiest of the fifty states. Its average elevation is 6,800 feet above sea level. There are fifty-five peaks in Colorado with elevations over 14,000 feet. The melting snow of its mountains is an important source of water for irrigating dry western lands.

The Rockies occupy the western part of the state; east of Denver stretch the Great Plains. The average rainfall on these plains is less than 20 inches per year. They are flat and treeless, sloping very gradually to the east. The Colorado Big Thompson Irrigation Project brings water from the western slopes of the Rockies across the Great Divide and through a 13.1-mile tunnel to the farms of the Great Plains.

The Rocky Mountains have long been the source of Colorado's prosperity. With the discovery of gold in 1859, settlers flocked to the state. Mining remains a major industry. The mountains are also important to the state's recreation industry, both for their wonderful scenery and for the excellent skiing they provide.

Rocky Mountain National Park in the north-central part of the state celebrates the mountains' beauty. Mesa Verde National Park in southwestern Colorado features dramatic desert scenery and the well-preserved ruins of ancient Indian pueblos. There are six national monuments in the state. In Great Sand Dunes National Monument are found spectacular sand deposits that constantly shift with the play of wind and light. Black Canyon of the Gunnison National Monument is another breathtaking work of nature. Colorado has many other features of great scenic beauty or historic interest.

1. Aspen

**Marble Garden
and Grass Mound**
Aspen Meadows Hotel,
845 Meadows Road

Two works of environmental sculpture by Herbert Bayer utilize form, plant materials, and the scenic mountain backdrop to achieve a bold character.
Open: All times. (303) 925-3426.

2. Boulder

Longs Iris Gardens
North Broadway

Longs Gardens, a commercial establishment, grows several acres of iris near downtown Boulder. The iris are

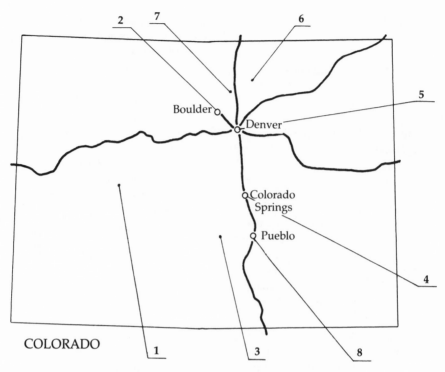

COLORADO

1. *Aspen*   2. *Boulder*   3. *Cañon City*   4. *Colorado Springs*   5. *Denver*
6. *Greeley*   7. *Longmont*   8. *Pueblo*

at their best in late May and early June.
Open: Daily, daylight hours. (303) 442–2353.

3. Cañon City

Walt's Memorial Garden
622 River Road

There are 2,000 rose bushes here, of many varieties.
Open: Daylight hours. (303) 275–2331.

4. Colorado Springs

Air Garden
U.S. Air Force Academy,
10 miles north on I-25

This is a huge water garden of precise axial, rectilinear design by contemporary landscape architect Dan Kiley; it was built in 1959.
Open: Tours by appointment only. (303) 472–2555.

Mesa Verde National Park, Cortez, Colo.

Horticultural Arts Society Garden
Glen Avenue and Mesa Road

Flowers and vegetables are displayed.
There is a garden for the blind.
Open: Daily, dawn–dusk. (303)
475–0250.

5. Denver

☆
Denver Botanic Gardens
909 York Street

The principal gardens consist of a
50-acre area in Denver and 150 acres
on Mount Goliath, 50 miles away.

(Two other areas, at Chatfield and
Evergreen, are under development.)
The Denver gardens contain an herb
collection, a Children's Garden, water
gardens, and native plants and annuals. The Boettcher Conservatory
houses cacti and tropical plants. The
Walter Pesman Trail on Mount Goliath displays native alpine plants at
an elevation of 12,000 feet.
Open: Denver gardens and
conservatory, Monday–Friday
9:00 a.m.–5:00 p.m., Saturday–
Sunday 10:00 a.m.–5:00 p.m.;
conservatory also open Friday 7:00–
9:00 p.m.; Mount Goliath, June–
August, daily 10:00 a.m.–4:00 p.m.
(303) 575–2547.

Elitch Garden
4620 West 38th Avenue

Formal gardens take up to 30 acres in this amusement park-recreation area. *Open: May–Labor Day, daily noon–midnight. Fee. (303) 455–4771.*

Harper Humanities Garden
University of Denver,
University Park Campus
South University Boulevard
and East Evans Avenue

Plant materials and water features create areas to unify the campus plan. *Open: Daily. (303) 871–2000.*

Skyline Parks
Arapahoe Street between 15th
and 18th Avenues

Three downtown parks designed by contemporary landscape architect Lawrence Halprin provide variations on a single theme. *Open: Daily. (303) 892–1112.*

Washington Park
South Downing Street and
East Louisiana Avenue

Here is a replica of the Colonial Gardens at George Washington's estate, Mount Vernon. *Open: Daily, daylight hours. (303) 575–2168.*

6. Greeley

University of Northern Colorado
11th Avenue

This 243-acre campus has a well-designed display of nearly all the indigenous plants of Colorado. *Open: Daily during school term. (303) 351–1890.*

7. Longmont

Longmont Memorial Rose Garden
Roosevelt Park, 7th Avenue

The garden contains 1,500 rose bushes of many varieties. *Open: Sunrise–sunset. (303) 776–5295.*

8. Pueblo

Mineral Palace Park
Main Street, 15th–19th Streets

The park has a rose garden with 4,000 plants representing many varieties that bloom from June to September. *Open: Daily, sunrise–sunset. (303) 542–1704.*

Other Places of Interest

Black Canyon of the Gunnison
National Monument, Montrose

Denver Red Rocks Amphitheater, Denver

Dinosaur National Monument, Dinosaur

Florissant Fossil Beds National Monument, Colorado Springs

Garden of the Gods, Colorado Springs

Great Sand Dunes National Monument, Alamosa

Loveland Pass, I-70

Mesa Verde National Park, Cortez

Pikes Peak, Colorado Springs

Rocky Mountain National Park, Estes Park

Royal Gorge, Canyon City

Connecticut

Area: 5,009 square miles

Population: 3,174,000

Statehood: January 9, 1788
(5th state)

Connecticut rises from the low sandy
coast of Long Island Sound to an
elevation of 2,380 feet at Mount Fris-
sell in its northwestern corner. The
topography is gently hilly with many
rock outcrops and loose stones. The
Connecticut River cuts the state in
two from north to south. Glaciers
have stripped much of the topsoil
away and deposited innumerable large
boulders. Colonial farmers carefully
piled these up to make stone walls to
enclose their fields, and to build their
massive fireplaces and the foundations of their homes. Connecticut was
well settled in colonial times. Numerous historic homes and thousands
of stone walls recall early agricultural days. The state's thin soils were
rapidly depleted by farming, and by
the time of the Civil War manufacturing was becoming the dominant
economic base. Today much former
agricultural land has returned to forest, which covers 60 percent of the
state.

Many Connecticut towns still
preserve their colonial character. Old
town greens where Revolutionary
War militiamen once drilled remain
the center of social life. Around them
can be found simple but stately white
clapboard colonial homes and high-
steepled wooden churches. The state
park system features many beautiful
natural areas. In June, mountain
laurel, the state flower, blooms beside
streams that flow swiftly between
massive boulders. Fall is the time of
brilliant foliage.

Connecticut's Merritt Parkway is
one of the nation's first parkways
and, with its mature landscaping, one
of the most attractive. No two bridges
over the road are detailed in the same
way.

1. Bloomfield

**Connecticut General Life
Insurance Company**
900 Cottage Grove Road

This corporate complex, designed by
Skidmore, Owings, and Merrill in
1957, is surrounded by a 280-acre
naturalized setting with scenic vistas
recalling the eighteenth-century
English landscape style. Terraces and
interior courts of the office buildings
use shrubs and flowering plants in
formal patterns.
*Open: Daily, business hours. (203)
726–6000.*

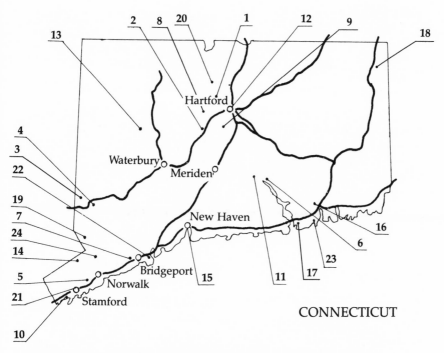

CONNECTICUT

1. *Bloomfield*   2. *Bristol*   3. *Brookfield*   4. *Danbury*   5. *Darien*   6. *East Haddam*   7. *Fairfield*   8. *Farmington*   9. *Glastonbury*   10. *Greenwich* 11. *Haddam*   12. *Hartford*   13. *Litchfield*   14. *New Canaan*   15. *New Haven* 16. *New London*   17. *Old Saybrook*   18. *Putnam*   19. *Ridgefield* 20. *Simsbury*   21. *Stamford*   22. *Stratford*   23. *Waterford*   24. *Wilton*

2. Bristol

American Clock and Watch Museum Garden
100 Maple Street

This small garden is made particularly interesting by its location next to the American Clock and Watch Museum. Designed in 1973 by Rudy J. Favretti and David Dickson, it is an authentically restored colonial flower and herb garden, appropriate to a small townhouse built in 1801. *Open: April–October, daily 1:00–5:00 p.m. Fee. (203) 583–6070.*

3. Brookfield

Brookfield Center and Historical Museum
Brookfield Center,
Junction of Routes 133 and 25

At this site is an attractive colonial herb and flower garden, designed by Rudy J. Favretti. All of the plantings have been carefully researched and are true to the period.
Open: Daily. For museum hours call the Town Hall, (203) 775–2515.

4. Danbury

Scott–Fanton Museum Garden
43 Main Street

The eighteenth- and early nineteenth-century flower garden adjacent to the historic Rider House (1785) contains old-fashioned roses, peonies, tree peonies, and foxglove. A separate herb garden with labels was established for public education.
Open: Wednesday–Sunday 2:00–5:00 p.m. (203) 743–5200.

5. Darien

Bates–Scofield House
45 Old King's Highway, North

This restored eighteenth-century house is now the headquarters of the Darien Historical Society. The garden (designed in 1968) features collections of plants used in colonial times, especially shrub roses and herbs and native plants used for medicinal purposes.
Open: Wednesday–Thursday 9:30 a.m.–12:30 p.m., 2:00–4:00 p.m.; Sunday 2:00–4:00 p.m. Open by appointment at other times. (203) 655–9233.

6. East Haddam

Gillette Castle State Park
South of Conn. 82

The castle was built by actor William Gillette on 190 acres overlooking the Connecticut River. There are formal gardens in the conservatory, and informal lawns, native trees and shrubs outdoors.
Open: June–mid-October, daily 11:00 a.m.–5:00 p.m.; grounds, 8:00 a.m.–sunset. (203) 526–2336.

7. Fairfield

Greenfield Hill
Congress Street and Hillside Road

Designated a National Historic Site, this village is landscaped with spring-flowering trees, especially white and pink dogwood. It is best seen in mid-May.
Open: All times. (203) 255–1011.

8. Farmington

Stanley–Whitman House
37 High Street

Regarded as "one of the finest" restored seventeenth-century houses in New England. The gardens feature herbs and flowers representative of the period.
Open: May–October, Tuesday–Sunday 1:00–4:00 p.m.; rest of year, Sunday. Closed: January. Fee. (203) 677–9222.

9. Glastonbury

Wells–Shipman–Ward House and Gardens
972 Main Street

The historic house has an excellent collection of early needlework and fine antiques. The garden is both herb-medicinal and culinary as well as ornamental. Researched and designed by Rudy J. Favretti, this modern garden is an authentic representation—in content and form—of the period of the house.
Open: Sunday 2:00–4:00 p.m. Fee. (203) 633–6652.

10. Greenwich

Audubon Center
613 Riversville Road

This is a National Audubon Wildlife Sanctuary containing 485 acres of natural habitats for many species of flora and fauna. There are exhibits in the Wildlife Garden and Trailside Museum.
Open: Year-round, Tuesday–Sunday 9:00 a.m.–5:00 p.m. Closed: Holidays. (203) 869–5172.

Mianus River Gorge Wildlife Refuge and Botanical Preserve
Millers Mill Road and Route 104

The 325 acres of rugged, scenic terrain contains over 800 species of trees, shrubs, vines, and wildflowers as well as native fauna. The area has been designated as a Natural History Landmark.
Open: April–November, daily 9:30 a.m.–5:30 p.m. (203) 322–9148.

Putnam Cottage
243 East Putnam Avenue

Built in 1690, the restored cottage is now maintained as a museum. On the grounds is an authentic eighteenth-century kitchen garden, including fruits, with plants and herbs that were available before this period.
Open: House, Monday, Wednesday, Friday, and by appointment; garden, daily year-round. Fee. (203) 869–9697.

11. Haddam

Wilhelmina Ann Arnold Barnhart Memorial Gardens
Hayden Hill Road at Walkley Hill Road

The historic house was built in 1794. Its extensive, authentic gardens of 1800 were planted with culinary and medicinal herbs, flowers, vegetables, and fruits. This site, which in 1975 received the Award of Merit from the Connecticut League of Historical Societies, provides insights into the tastes as well as the industry of a typical small New England family. *Open: June–September, Saturday–Sunday 2:30-5:00 p.m. (203) 345–2400.*

12. Hartford

Constitution Plaza
Hartford Downtown Redevelopment Area

This was one of the first successful urban renewal projects to employ contemporary urban landscape design, by landscape architects Sasaki, Walker, Dawson and Demay of Boston. It provides examples of roof garden design, water gardens, paving textures, and sitting areas. *Open: All times. (203) 782–6789.*

Elizabeth Park Municipal Rose Garden
Prospect Street and Asylum Avenue

Established in 1903, this is reputed to be the oldest municipal rose garden in the country, with over 1,000 species. Peak bloom is in mid-June. *Open: Daily, sunrise–sunset. (203) 722–6541.*

Harriet Beecher Stowe House
77 Forest Street

Well-planted Victorian gardens surround the restored home of the author of *Uncle Tom's Cabin*, now a registered National Historic Landmark. *Open: Year-round, Sunday 1:00–4:00 p.m.; September–May, Tuesday–Saturday 9:30 a.m.–4:00 p.m.; June–August, Tuesday–Saturday 10:00 a.m.–4:30 p.m. (203) 525–9317.*

Mark Twain House and Nook Farm
351 Farmington Avenue

The nineteenth-century Victorian house and grounds have been restored. *Open: Year-round, Sunday 1:00–4:00 p.m.; September–May, Tuesday–Saturday 9:30 a.m.–4:00 p.m.; June–August, Tuesday–Saturday 10:00 a.m.–4:30 p.m. Fee. (203) 525–9317.*

Noah Webster Foundation
227 South Main Street (West Hartford)

The restored eighteenth-century birthplace of Noah Webster, who

Constitution Plaza, Hartford, Conn.

wrote the first American dictionary, has a small herb and flower garden. *Open: June 15–September 30, Thursday–Tuesday 10:00 a.m.–4:00 p.m.; rest of year and Sundays, 1:00–4:00 p.m. (203) 521–5362.*

13. Litchfield

Tapping–Reeve House and Garden
1173 South Street

The building dates from 1774. There is a small restored period garden. *Open: May–October, Thursday–Monday. Fee. (203) 567–5862.*

14. New Canaan

Oliver W. Lee Memorial Gardens
89 Chichester Road

This woodland setting contains over 1,000 species of plants including many native and endangered plants as well as imported ornamentals. *Open: Daily 9:00 a.m.–5:00 p.m. (203) 742–7244.*

15. New Haven

Edgerton Park
Whitney Park

This large, former private estate features old specimen trees and shrubs and a perennial border.
Open: 10:00 a.m.–dusk. (203) 787–8367.

Pardee–Morris House
325 Lighthouse Road,
4 miles southeast of New Haven
(Exit 50 Conn. Tpk.)

This is a restored eighteenth-century colonial residence with formal and herb gardens.
Open: June–August, Tuesday–Sunday 1:00–4:00 p.m.
Closed: Holidays. (203) 562–4183.

Pardee Rose Gardens
East Rock Park, Amhryn and Park Roads

A fine collection of roses, annuals, flowering trees, and shrubs can be seen in the 647-acre public park. Conservatories provide seasonal displays.
Open: June–October, daily. (203) 787–8021.

16. New London

Connecticut Arboretum, Connecticut College
William Street

This woodland arboretum covers 415 acres of the 680-acre campus and includes native plant communities for research. A woody plant collection, wildflowers of the Northeast, and flowering trees are featured.
Open: Daily, daylight hours. (203) 447–1911.

Shaw Mansion Gardens
11 Blinman Street

The gardens of this eighteenth-century house were designed in 1924 by twentieth-century pioneer landscape architect Christopher Tunnard. They are currently maintained by the New London Historical Society.
Open: Tuesday–Saturday, 1:00–4:00 p.m. Fee. (203) 443–1209.

17. Old Saybrook

General William Hart House
350 Main Street

This Georgian-style house (ca. 1767) has some interesting and unusual architectural features. On the grounds are a re-created colonial garden and an award-winning herb garden.
Open: Mid-June–mid-September, Friday–Sunday 11:00 a.m.–3:00 p.m. Donation. (203) 388–2622.

18. Putnam

Bowen Cottage
7 miles northwest of Putnam
via Conn. 171 and 169

The structure is an important example of Gothic Revival architecture and has one of the oldest parterre gardens in New England.
Open: June–September 15,
Wednesday–Sunday noon–5:00 p.m.;
Friday–Sunday to October 21. (203)
928–4074.

19. Ridgefield

Ballard Garden
Ballard Park

This garden was designed by Frederick Law Olmsted, pioneer American landscape architect (1822–1903), and donated to the town by Mrs. Edward L. Ballard.
Open: Daily 9:00 a.m.–5:00 p.m.
(203) 438–7301.

20. Simsbury

Simsbury Historic Center
800 Hopmeadow Street

Several of the buildings in this eighteenth-century restoration have gardens appropriate to the period. All have been carefully researched to include plant material in use at that time. Of particular interest are the Phelps House Parlour Garden—a charming small space in the ell of the house—and the Hendricks Cottage Herb Garden.
Open: May–October for daily tours;
gardens, daily.
Closed: Holidays. (203) 658–2500.

21. Stamford

Bartlett Arboretum
151 Brookdale Road

The 62-acre garden, operated by the University of Connecticut, contains a large collection of evergreens.
Open: Daily, sunrise–sunset. (203)
322–6971.

Stamford Old Fort Period Garden
Westover Road

The fort was built in 1781 and is a designated National Historic Site. In 1930, a formal, walled garden was designed to represent a typical eighteenth-century garden. The garden, which has been renovated, includes roses, shrubs, and perennials.
Open: By arrangement. (203) 322–
0545.

22. Stratford

Judson House, Grounds, and Gardens
967 Academy Hill

The eighteenth-century homestead is surrounded by perennial, annual, and herb gardens of the period.
Open: April–November, Wednesday, Saturday–Sunday.
Closed: Holidays. (203) 378–0630.

23. Waterford

Harkness Memorial State Park and Gardens
275 Great Neck Road

Formal and informal gardens, begun in 1902, surround the Italianate mansion of the late philanthropist Edward S. Harkness. A continuous flower display, ancient boxwoods, and specimen trees are featured. The 235-acre site presently serves as a recreation area for the handicapped.
Open: June–October, daily 10:00 a.m.–sunset. Fee. (203) 443–5725.

24. Wilton

Old Town Hall Community and Garden Center
Ridgefield Road

The Town Hall was constructed in 1832. Renovation was begun in 1934, and today the structure forms the nucleus of the town's designated historic district. The Wilton Garden Club maintains a Garden Center with demonstration garden and greenhouse.
Open: By appointment.
Mrs. Bigelow (203) 762–8708 or Mrs. Demarest (203) 762–0100.

Other Places of Interest

Audubon Center, Greenwich
Betsy Barnum House, Stamford
Bruce Park and Museum, Greenwich
Campbell Falls State Park, Canaan
Children's Museum and Roaring Brook Nature Center, Sharon
Flanders Nature Center, Woodbury
Fort Nathan Hall Restoration, New Haven Harbor
Haddam Meadows State Park, Connecticut River
Harkney Memorial State Park, Housatonic River
Housatonic Meadows State Park, Housatonic River
Litchfield Nature Center and Museum, Litchfield
Mohawk Mountain State Park, Cornwall
Montgomery Pinetum, Cos Cob
New Canaan Nature Center, New Canaan
Ogden House, Fairfield
Pardee–Morris House, New Haven
Roy and Margot Larsen Audubon Sanctuary and Wildlife Refuge, Fairfield
Seaside Park, Bridgeport
Sleeping Giant State Park, Mount Carmel

Stamford Museum and Nature
 Center, Stamford
West Rock Park, New Haven

Towns of special interest include
Essex, Farmington, Greenwich, Guil-
ford, Lebanon, Litchfield, Madison,
Mystic, Old Saybrook, Stonington,
Wethersfield, Windsor, and Wood-
bury.

Delaware

Area: 2,057 square miles

Population: 622,000

Statehood: December 7, 1787
(1st state)

The small state of Delaware occupies a stretch of low coastal plain lying between the Delaware and Chesapeake bays. This low sandy region, 96 miles long and ranging in width from 9 to 35 miles, forms the northern section of the Delmarva Peninsula. The surrounding waters give the state a mild climate. Only at its extreme northwestern corner does Delaware rise to the Piedmont region; its maximum elevation is 442 feet. Wilmington, the state's major city, is 26 miles from Philadelphia.

The first Europeans to settle Delaware were the Swedes, who established a colony in 1638 in present-day Wilmington. The colony was later ruled by the Dutch and then by the English. Plantations grew up on the flat alluvial land, which was easily accessible to the numerous creeks and rivers in the area. As a state, Delaware became part of the great urban industrial complex that stretches from Washington, D.C., to Boston. The Chesapeake Bay long separated lower Delaware from the Washington area and helped preserve the rural character of that part of the state. But, in 1952, a 3.5-mile bridge was constructed across the Chesapeake Bay near Annapolis, Maryland. Since then, the Delmarva Peninsula has become more closely linked to the lifestyle of the Baltimore-Washington area, and industry has filtered into the lower counties of the state.

Delaware, one of the original thirteen colonies, offers an interesting capsule survey of the history of American gardening. Its treasures include restored gardens from the colonial period; an 1804 residence that was landscaped in 1847 by Andrew Jackson Downing, leader of the Picturesque School of gardening; an urban park of the late nineteenth century designed by Frederick Law Olmsted, who recognized the importance of open space to urban areas; and a great garden of the early twentieth century.

1. Dover

John Dickinson Mansion
Kitts Hummock Road

A restored colonial home with a formal English garden displays thousands of nineteenth-century bulbs. *Open: Tuesday–Saturday 10:00 a.m.–5:00 p.m., Sunday 1:00–5:00 p.m. (302) 734–9439.*

DELAWARE

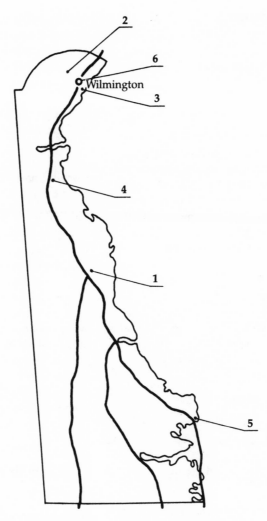

1. *Dover* 2. *Greenville* 3. *New Castle* 4. *Odessa* 5. *Rehoboth Beach*
6. *Wilmington*

2. Greenville

Eleutherian Mills
and Hagley Museum
Barley Mill Road
and Brandywine Creek

Eleutherian Mills is the former residence of E. I. Du Pont and the site of some of the original Du Pont Company powder mills and workers' cottages. The estate was used for experimental planting by Mr. Du Pont, whose hobby was botany. North American flora is featured.
Open: Grounds, mid-April–mid-June and month of October, Tuesday–Saturday 9:30 a.m.–4:30 p.m., Sunday 1:00–5:00 p.m.; estate by appointment only, contact Information Office, Hagley Museum, Greenville, Wilmington, Del. 19807. (302) 658–2400.

3. New Castle

Read House and Garden
42, The Strand

The Read House garden surrounds the stately Federal mansion built by George Read II, son of one of Delaware's signers of the Declaration of Independence. The garden was installed in 1847 by William Couper, the second owner of the house, and has changed little since then. Its design, which is traditionally attributed to Andrew Jackson Downing, was definitely influenced by his writings. In fact, this is one of the few gardens in the country in which Downing's principles can be seen unaltered.
Open: Tuesday–Saturday 10:00 a.m.–4:00 p.m., Sunday noon–4:00 p.m. (302) 322–8411.

4. Odessa

Corbit–Sharp House
Main Street

This house was built between 1772 and 1774. Its architecture resembles that of elegant pre-Revolutionary Philadelphia houses, and the furnishings include many locally crafted antiques as well as those owned by the Corbit family. A spacious lawn sweeps down to the banks of Appoquinimink Creek. Next to the house is an herb garden laid out in formal geometric patterns.
Open: Tuesday–Saturday 10:00 a.m.–5:00 p.m., Sunday 2:00–5:00 p.m. Fee. (302) 378–4069.

5. Rehoboth Beach

Homestead Boxwood Gardens
10 Dodd's Lane, Henlopen Acres

A colonial-style boxwood garden was established here in 1930 and has been restored by the Sussex Gardeners.
Open: Daily, daylight hours. (302) 227–8408.

6. Wilmington

Brandywine Park
North Park Drive
and Van Buren Street

This urban park was designed by
Frederick Law Olmsted, the father
of American landscape architecture. Along the promenade through
Josephine Gardens are Oriental cherries, a Florentine fountain, and a rose
garden.
*Open: Daily, daylight hours. (302)
571–7788.*

Buena Vista
Route 13, 8 miles
south of Wilmington

Buena Vista is known for its gardens,
tree-lined lane, landscaped drives,
outbuildings, and meadows.
*Open: Tuesday, Thursday, Saturday,
11:00 a.m.–4:00 p.m. (302) 323–4430.*

☆☆
Nemours Foundation
Rockland Road, off Route 141

The Louis XIV-style mansion was
built on this 300-acre estate in the
early 1900s. The beautiful French
Renaissance gardens patterned after
the work of Le Notre were completed
in 1932.
*Open: By tour reservation only,
May 1–November 30, Tuesday–
Sunday; 2-hour tours leave every 2
hours Tuesday–Saturday 9:00 a.m.–
3:00 p.m., Sunday 11:00 a.m.–
3:00 p.m. Under 16 not admitted. Fee.
(303) 573–3333.*

Rockwood Museum
610 Shipley Road

In 1851, architect George Williams
designed the stone house, Delaware's
only surviving example of Rural
Gothic architecture. The grounds and
gardens were laid out by the original owner, Joseph Shipley, and his
gardener, Robert Salisbury. Shipley,
who made his fortune in England,
had taken an interest in the prevalent theories of English landscape
architecture of the 1840s; his library
contained all the prominent texts on
the Gardenesque School of Landscape
Design. The grounds and gardens of
his former home still reflect those influences. The 6.5-acre estate contains
unusual species of trees, including
unique monkey puzzle trees, and
shrubs.
*Open: Tuesday–Saturday 11:00 a.m.–
4:30 p.m. Fee. (302) 571–7776.*

☆
Winterthur Gardens
Route 52, 6 miles north
of Wilmington

This great 960-acre estate was land-
scaped under the personal supervision
of its owner, Henry Francis Du Pont.
The carefully planned vistas of lawns
and naturalized plantings are illus-
trated by the Azalea Woods, the
Quarry Garden, and the formal Sun
Dial Garden—among others. The
Henry Francis Du Pont Winterthur
Museum of Decorative Arts houses
one of the best private collections of
American furnishings.
*Open: Garden, mid-April–October,
Tuesday–Saturday 10:00 a.m.–*

4:00 p.m.; other times by appointment, (301) 655–8591. Museum, south wing, Tuesday–Saturday 10:00 a.m.–4:00 p.m., Sunday noon–4:00 p.m.; main museum tours by reservation. Fee. (302) 654–1548.

Other Places of Interest

Bombay Hook National Wildlife Refuge
Brandywine River Trail
Cape Henlopen State Park
Christina Trail
Delaware Dunes, Delaware Seashore State Park
New Castle Colonial Town, Wilmington
The Rocks, Wilmington
Tucssion Pond (4,500-acre Hadley Press Swamp)
University of Delaware Campus, Newark
Valley Gardens State Park, Greenville

Towns of special interest include Dover, Lewes, Odessa, and Seaford.

District of Columbia

Area: 67 square miles

Population: 626,000

In 1791, when the Potomac site was chosen for the nation's capital, the Constitutional government was only three years old. An important consideration in selecting the area at the western limit to navigation on the Potomac River was the promise that the city could be tied to the "West" (the Ohio River Valley) by a canal, making it an important commercial port. At that time, Georgetown was a thriving little tobacco port. The canal was used until 1830, when the Baltimore and Ohio Railroad made it obsolete. Development of the Chesapeake and Ohio National Historic Parks has transformed the old canalway into a modern recreational area.

Pierre Charles L'Enfant, a French soldier, engineer, and artist, who had served under George Washington in the Revolutionary War, was thrilled at the opportunity to design a capital city for the new nation. With great sensitivity to the character of the area selected, with its knolls and views of the Potomac River, he laid out a scheme for the city according to the baroque canons of design then fashionable in Europe. Many similarities of style can be perceived between L'Enfant's plan for Washington and the plan of Versailles. The architectural style thought appropriate for the young republic was that of ancient Rome, a city lauded by Enlightenment thinkers as a model republic. The White House and parts of the capitol building are architectural monuments of this time. European visitors to Washington in the early nineteenth century found humor in the contrast between the monumental skeleton of the city and the huts and barns that lined its broad, unpaved avenues. Charles Dickens labeled it "the city of great intentions." One hundred and ninety-five years later, however, the wisdom of L'Enfant's vision in laying out a city for half a million people is confirmed.

Modern Washington is a cosmopolitan city. The embassies of foreign nations in the Northwest District offer an interesting variety of architectural styles. The Oriental cherry trees given by the Japanese government provide a brilliant spectacle in early spring. The Washington Tourist Information Center (1400 Pennsylvania Avenue, NW; Telephone [202] 789–7000) in the "Great Hall" of the U.S. Department of Commerce is open to provide up-to-date local information: Year-round, Monday–Saturday 9:00 a.m.–5:00 p.m.; also Sunday 9:00 a.m.–5:00 p.m. from April to October.

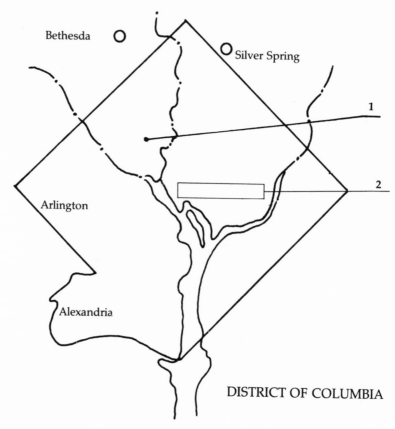

Bethesda

Silver Spring

1

2

Arlington

Alexandria

DISTRICT OF COLUMBIA

1. *Washington, D.C.* 2. *The Mall Area*

1. Washington, D.C.

Bishop's Garden at the Washington National Cathedral
Massachusetts and Wisconsin Avenues, Northwest

The architecture and planting relate well to this natural setting; basically a formal boxwood garden in medieval style, it is skillfully adapted to the sloping, irregular terrain consisting of 54 acres. Interesting features include the twelfth-century Wayside Cross and sun dial, herb garden, and yew walks.

Open: Sunrise–sunset. Tours available Monday–Saturday 10:00 a.m.–3:15 p.m. (202) 537–6200.

Decatur House and Garden
748 Jackson Place, Northwest

Decatur House—an elegant Federal townhouse designed by Benjamin

Latrobe in 1818—is owned by the National Trust for Historic Preservation. The walled garden, enclosed by buildings on all sides, has brick paved areas that are used for entertaining. The plantings include camellias, azaleas, and ground covers that thrive in shade and city conditions.
Open: Tuesday–Friday 10:00 a.m.– 2:00 p.m., Saturday-Sunday, noon–4:00 p.m.
Closed: Thanksgiving, Christmas. Fee. (202) 637–4030.

☆☆
Dumbarton Oaks and Gardens
1703 32nd Street, Northwest

The outstanding Georgetown estate garden was designed in 1922 by Beatrix Farrand, pioneer American landscape architect (1872–1959). Plant materials were chosen especially for spring and autumn enjoyment. The design uses brick, stone, pebbles, and decorative materials and ornaments. Established in the 1920s, the 10-acre garden has been carefully maintained; it is now owned by Harvard University.
Open: Daily 2:00–5:00 p.m. April– October. Fee. (202) 342–3290.

Franciscan Monastery
14th and Quincy Streets

Styled after the Franciscan missions of California, the courtyard garden of Saint Francis features many tropical plants.
Open: Daily 8:00 a.m.–5:00 p.m. Tours hourly, except during Mass.
Closed: Holidays. (202) 526–6800.

Dumbarton Oaks and Gardens, Washington, D.C.

Hillwood
4155 Linnean Avenue, Northwest

The grounds of this 25-acre estate include a rose garden, a fine Japanese garden, and a French formal garden. Plantings feature azaleas and other flowering shrubs, bulbs, and chrysanthemums for fall color.
Open: Daily 11:00 a.m.–4:00 p.m. Closed: Tuesday and Sunday. Fee. Reservations to tour house but not garden. (202) 324–3447.

Ippakutei—Ceremonial Teahouse and Garden at the Embassy of Japan
2520 Massachusetts Avenue, Northwest

The ceremonial teahouse was designed by architect Nahiko Emori

and built in Japan, then dismantled and reconstructed in the United
States. The garden, also designed
by Mr. Emori, represents three traditional styles: the first style is the
sand and rock Zen meditation garden, and the second that of an early
nineteenth-century formal garden;
the third style uses stones deliber-
ately placed to slow the visitor's pace
in approaching the teahouse.
Open: By appointment only, April–
November. (202) 234–2266.

Islamic Center
2551 Massachusetts Avenue,
Northwest

This is the leading Muslim religious
facility in the United States. The
architectural style of the building is
Islamic. The lovely interior courtyard
is an example of the Middle Eastern
style of courtyard gardens.
Open: Daily 10:00 a.m.–5:00 p.m.
(202) 332–8343.

Kenilworth Aquatic Gardens
Kenilworth Avenue and Douglas
Street, Northeast

Fourteen acres of ponds, streams,
and environments display water lilies
and lotus, native and topical aquatic
vegetation.
Open: Daily 7:00 a.m.–sunset. (202)
426–6905.

Lafayette Square
Pennsylvania Avenue, Northwest

Located across from the White
House, the park was designated as the
"President's Park" on the L'Enfant

plan for the capital. A taped tour is
available from the National Trust for
Historic Preservation.
Open: All times. (202) 485–9666.

Organization of American States Building
Constitution Avenue and 17th Street

The courtyard garden of the Pan
American Union features tropical and
semitropical plants native to Central
and South America.
Open: Monday–Friday 9:30 a.m.–
4:30 p.m.
Closed: Holidays. (202) 789–3751.

Rock Creek Park and Nature Center
Beech Drive, north of
National Zoological Park
(Entrance to Nature Center
on Glover Road)

The 1,754 acres of recreational facilities and scenic trails make this one of
the largest urban parks in the world.
Open: Park, sunrise–sunset; Nature
Center, Tuesday–Sunday 9:00 a.m.–
5:00 p.m. (202) 426–6829.

☆☆
U.S. National Arboretum
3501 New York Avenue, Northeast

The arboretum's dual purpose is to
educate the public and to conduct research on woody plants. Established
in 1927, the 415 acres display several
fine collections in a predominantly
naturalized setting. Highlights include the Morrison Azalea Garden,
the Camellia Collection, and other
collections of Oriental plants, particu-

larly the National Bonsai Collection. Additional features are the flowering tree collections, a trail for the visually handicapped, the Fern Valley, the Gotelli dwarf conifer collection, the National Herb Garden, and many species of spring-flowering bulbs and shrubs.
Open: Weekdays 8:00 a.m.–5:00 p.m., weekends 10:00 a.m.–5:00 p.m.; National Bonsai Collection, daily 10:00 a.m.–2:30 p.m. Buildings open on weekends for scheduled events only.
Closed: Christmas. (202) 475–4815.

White House Gardens
1600 Pennsylvania Avenue, Northwest

The East Garden and Rose Garden of the White House have been the pride of every president and first lady. Over the years, many changes have been made according to whim or by design.
Open: Tours only, Tuesday–Saturday 10:00 a.m.–noon.
Closed: Christmas, New Year's Day, and during presidential functions. Free tickets from Ellipse booth, 8:00 a.m.–noon. Note: Views of gardens from White House interior only; gardens open briefly in spring and fall. (202) 456–7041.

Woodrow Wilson House Gardens
2340 S Street, Northwest

The Woodrow Wilson House, built in 1915, was the home of President and Mrs. Wilson from 1921 until Wilson's death in 1924. The garden is a fine example of early twentieth-century neoclassic gardens and one of the few formal gardens left on Embassy Row. Property of the National Trust.
Open: March 1–December 31, Tuesday–Friday 10:00 a.m.–2:00 p.m.; Saturday–Sunday and holidays noon–4:00 p.m.; February 1–28, Saturday–Sunday only, noon–4:00 p.m.
Closed Thanksgiving, Christmas. Fee. (202) 387–4062.

2. The Mall Area

Between Constitution and Independence Avenues

The Mall is the core of the national government, and the location of many monuments, museums, and other public buildings. According to L'Enfant's plan of 1791, this area would be a grand public open space. Throughout the nineteenth century, however, buildings and transportation encroached haphazardly into L'Enfant's formal vistas. In 1851, Andrew Jackson Downing (1815–52) proposed a comprehensive landscape design for the areas from the White House south to the Washington Monument and then east to the Capitol. Downing's plan was in the picturesque Romantic tradition, with curvilinear paths and roads and naturalistic plantings. Little of this plan was accomplished; all that remains today is the White House Ellipse area.

In the 1870s, Frederick Law Olmsted, Sr., designed the plantings, terraces, and serpentine paths of the West Front of the Capitol. The Senate Park Commission, created in 1901 by Senator McMillan, called on architects Daniel Burnham, Frederick Law Olmsted, Jr., and Charles Follen McKim to re-create the grand formal mall envisioned by L'Enfant. The straight rows of elms, long reflecting pools, and formal vistas seen today date from the 1901 plan. The East and West Potomac parks and the Tidal Basin were created by draining and filling swamp areas near the river. Since 1910, a seven-member National Commission of Fine Arts —usually including one landscape architect—has served as an advisory body for major capital planning decisions.

Significant garden features of the Mall area are described below.

Constitution Gardens
Constitution Avenue west
of 17th Street, Northwest

The irregularly shaped pond and curvilinear planting on this 50-acre site, completed in 1976 as a memorial to the signers of the Declaration of Independence, provide a striking contrast to the formal monumental character that dominates the Mall.

☆

Enid A. Haupt Garden
Independence Avenue, south
of Smithsonian Institution

Completed in 1987, this garden incorporates and replaces the former "Victorian Garden," which occupied part of the site. Instead of building new museum structures on the site, the 4.2 acres were excavated and the museums were built underground, leaving the surface available for this colorful garden. In front of the entrance pavilion to the Arthur M. Sackler Gallery there is an Oriental garden with a 9-foot moongate. In front of the entrance pavilion to the national Museum of African Art there is an African garden.
Open: All times. (202) 357–2700.

Frederic Auguste Bartholdi Park
Independence Avenue, south of
U.S. Botanic Garden

The centerpiece of the park is the historic Bartholdi Fountain, designed in 1876 by Frederic Auguste Bartholdi for the Philadelphia Centennial Exposition and purchased in 1877 by Congress. The park is an outdoor floral display area for the U.S. Botanic Garden.

☆

Hirshhorn Museum and Sculpture Garden of the Smithsonian Institution
8th Street and Jefferson Drive,
Southwest

Formal terraces and plantings create an outdoor setting for a portion of the Hirshhorn sculpture collection. The garden and circular museum building were completed in 1974.
Open: Sunrise–sunset. (202) 357–3235.

National Museum of American Art and National Portrait Gallery Gardens

8th Street and Constitution Avenue, Northwest

These gardens contain formal, architectonic exterior plantings. Interior courtyard gardens are tiny gems, rich in plant variety and detail.
Open: Monday–Saturday 10:00 a.m.–5:00 p.m., Sunday noon–9:00 p.m.; summer, daily until 9:00 p.m. (202) 357–3111 or 357–2920.

U.S. Botanic Garden

Maryland Avenue and First Street, Southwest

The Botanic Garden was founded in 1856 for the purpose of collecting and cultivating exotic plant materials for exhibit. A 38,000-square-foot conservatory allows for indoor collections of tropical and temperate zone plants; annuals and perennials are displayed outdoors.
Open: Daily 9:00 a.m.–5:00 p.m.; June–August, until 9:00 p.m.
Closed: Saturday. (202) 225–8333.

Other Places of Interest

Arlington National Cemetery, Virginia
Chesapeake and Ohio Canal, Georgetown
Columbus Plaza, at Union Station
Congregational Cemetery, 1801 E Street, Southeast
Embassy Row, Massachusetts Avenue between Sheridan and Observatory Circles, Northwest
Georgetown, Wisconsin Avenue and M Street, Northwest
Glen Echo Park Garden, MacArthur Boulevard, Northwest
Jefferson Memorial, Tidal Basin, Southwest
Lincoln Memorial, west end of the Mall
Lincoln Park, 11th and E Streets, Southeast
Meridian Hills Park, 16th Street and Euclid, Northwest
National Zoological Park, 3000 Connecticut Avenue
Oak Hill Cemetery, 30th and R Streets, Northwest
Pershing Park, between 14th & 15th Streets, Northwest, on Pennsylvania Avenue
Rawlins Park, 18th and E Streets, Northwest
Theodore Roosevelt Island, Potomac River
Tidal Basin, 25th Street, Southwest
Washington Monument, The Mall at 15th Street

Florida

Area: 58,560 square miles

Population: 11,366,000

Statehood: March 3, 1845
(27th state)

Florida is known as "the Sunshine State." Each year millions of Americans flock to its sandy golden beaches to escape winter's cold. Florida's first tourist was Ponce de Leon, who explored the area in 1513. Today, tourism is vital to the state's economy; recreational opportunities are many and varied. On the low, flat peninsula has developed a vacationland of natural beauty, fantasy, and fun. The grand style of great estates and gardens, the fantasy lands of Walt Disney World and Busch Gardens, the subtropical plant communities unique to Florida among all of the states, invite the visitor.

Florida has a mild, temperate-to-subtropical climate. Rainfall is ample in summer and fall; sunshine predominates in winter and spring. Winter temperatures are warm; the average January temperature is 55° F in Jacksonville and 67° F in Miami. Frosts do occur occasionally and pose a threat to the state's important citrus-growing industry. The entire state lies on a low coastal plain only 345 feet above sea level at its highest point. In northern and central Florida are thousands of crystal-clear lakes

and springs—a result of the limestone bedrock underlying this area. Because of this flat topography, much of the state is poorly drained, and there are many swamps and glades. In Everglades National Park, at Florida's southern tip, 2,300 square miles of the unique River of Grass, which flows from Lake Okeechobee south to Florida Bay, are protected as a wilderness area and wildlife refuge. Florida created the nation's first underwater park, at John Pennekamp Coral Reef off Key Largo.

The first permanent European settlement on the North American mainland was established by the Spanish at St. Augustine in 1565. In 1821, the United States acquired Florida from Spain. Cotton plantations flourished in northern Florida before the Civil War, but lower Florida was long considered too remote, swampy, mosquito-infested, and hot for settlement. By 1890 railroads began to make southern Florida more accessible, and in the early twentieth century many wealthy industrialists established winter homes along the coast. Soon, the mild climate and unusual environment attracted tourists and vacationers. Today many retired Americans make Florida their home year-round.

The gardeners of Florida enjoy a unique range of climates and a colorful palette of plants. Their gardens reflect the exuberant patterns and colors of the Mediterranean world and the Caribbean, as well as the stately grandeur of the Old South. The state is rich in gardens of great drama, diversity, and beauty.

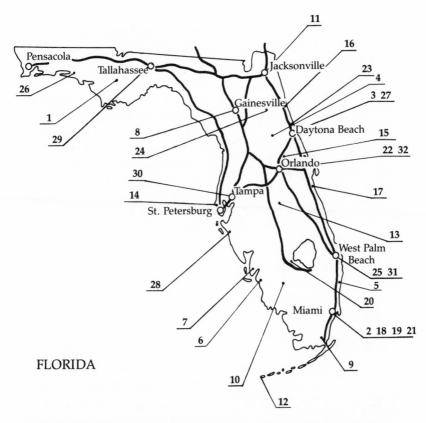

FLORIDA

1. *Bristol* 2. *Coral Gables* 3. *Daytona Beach* 4. *De Leon Springs* 5. *Delray Beach* 6. *Estero* 7. *Fort Myers* 8. *Gainesville* 9. *Homestead* 10. *Immokalee* 11. *Jacksonville* 12. *Key West* 13. *Lake Wales* 14. *Largo* 15. *Longwood* 16. *Marineland* 17. *Melbourne* 18. *Miami* 19. *Miami Beach* 20. *Moore Haven* 21. *North Miami Beach* 22. *Orlando* 23. *Ormond Beach* 24. *Palatka* 25. *Palm Beach* 26. *Point Washington* 27. *Port Orange* 28. *Sarasota* 29. *Tallahassee* 30. *Tampa* 31. *West Palm Beach* 32. *Winter Park*

1. Bristol

Gregory House at Torreya State Park
Highway 12, between
Bristol and Greensboro

This 1,063-acre park, named for the Torreya, a tree found only within a 20-mile radius of the park, has been called the "Garden of Eden" because trees described in the Bible grow here. The house, built in the 1830s, is now a museum.
Open: 8:00 a.m.–sundown; house tours, Monday–Friday 11:00 a.m.– 2:00 p.m., weekends 9:00 a.m.– 1:00 p.m. (904) 643-2674.

2. Coral Gables

☆☆
Fairchild Tropical Garden
10901 Old Cutler Road

This 83-acre tropical garden is one of America's major botanical gardens, established in 1936 with the assistance of the greatest botanists of the time. The palm collection is outstanding; cycads, bromeliads, and tropical flowering trees from around the world are also displayed.
Open: Daily 9:30 a.m.–4:30 p.m. Closed: Christmas. Fee. (305) 667-1651.

U.S. Agricultural Research Service
13601 Old Cutler Road

Miami is one of four locations where the U.S. Department of Agriculture has established stations specializing in plant evaluation and research. The Miami station conducts research on tropical and subtropical fruits and on ornamentals for use in the nation's subtropical regions, including disease-free germ plasm collections of coffee, cacao, and rubber.
Open: Monday–Friday 8:00 a.m.– 4:30 p.m. Visitor registration required. (305) 238-9321.

3. Daytona Beach

Bellevue Biblical Garden
Bellevue Memorial Park,
1425 Bellevue Avenue

The plants in this 1-acre garden are those described in the Bible, laid out in chronological order according to the New Testament life of Jesus Christ. The garden has been restored.
Open: Daily 8:00 a.m.–5:00 p.m. (904) 253-2534.

Tuscawilla Park
Volusia Avenue and Nova Road

This 88-acre park in the center of Daytona Beach includes a natural hummock with native hardwood forest, nature trails, and a 10-acre museum site. Children's nature study programs are offered.
Open: 8:00 a.m.–sunset. (904) 258-3170.

4. De Leon Springs

De Leon Springs State Recreational Area
U.S. 17, 6 miles north of De Leon

Camellias, azaleas, a 1,000-year-old bald cypress tree, and ancient oaks are featured in this 54-acre subtropical park. There are exotic birds and an Indian burial ground.
Open: Daily 8:00 a.m.–sundown. Fee. (904) 985–4212.

5. Delray Beach

Morikami Museum of Japanese History
Carter and Morikami Roads

The museum, begun in 1975, presents Japanese culture and horticulture to visitors. Exhibits are housed in an authentic Japanese residence, with a typical Japanese garden setting. In a 140-acre park surrounding the museum are lakes, waterfalls, nature trails, and a bonsai collection.
Open: Tuesday–Sunday 10:00 a.m.–5:00 p.m.
Closed: January 1, Easter, July 4, Thanksgiving, Christmas. (305) 499–0631.

6. Estero

Koreshan State Historical Site
U.S. 41

Originally a tropical fruit orchard, this 305-acre park was transformed by the Koreshan Brotherhood. It now contains hundreds of tropical, subtropical, and rare fruit trees.
Open: Daily 8:00 a.m.–sundown. Fee. (813) 992–0311.

7. Fort Myers

☆
Thomas A. Edison Winter Home and Botanical Gardens
2350 McGregor Boulevard

The botanical gardens consist of more than 1,000 varieties of tropical trees and plants from all over the world. Edison collected the trees between 1890 and 1930 in his search for useful by-products. One of his projects at the time was the extraction of rubber from goldenrod. Edison's chemical laboratory and a museum of his inventions are located on the estate. The gardens cover approximately 14 acres.
Open: Daily 9:00 a.m.–4:00 p.m., Sunday 12:30–4:00 p.m. Guided tour only.
Closed: Christmas. Fee. (813) 334–3614.

Thomas A. Edison Winter Home and Botanical Gardens, Fort Myers, Fla.

8. Gainesville

Kanapaha Botanical Gardens
4625 63rd Boulevard

With 62 acres, this is Florida's second largest botanic garden. There are nine specialized garden areas, including the state's largest bamboo garden and the South's largest herb garden.
Open: Weekdays, except Thursday, 9:00 a.m.–5:00 p.m., Saturday 9:00 a.m.–sunset, Sunday 1:00–5:00 p.m. (904) 372-4981.

Wilmot Memorial Gardens
University of Florida, Archer and Stadium Roads

The gardens are used as an outdoor laboratory for university students of horticulture. The main collections consist of azaleas, camellias, juniper, hardy palms, hollies, other specimen trees, and an orchid greenhouse. The peak flowering season is mid-January through March.
Open: Monday–Friday 8:00 a.m.–5:00 p.m. (904) 392-1830.

9. Homestead

Everglades National Park
Main entrance on State Road 27, two other entrances off U.S. 41

The park comprises more than 1 million acres of southern Florida wilderness—a unique, fragile ecosystem that supports an extraordinary variety of plant communities and wildlife. The vast sawgrass marshes,

hardwood hammocks and cypress
bays, and coastal mangrove swamps
and waterways form a landscape un-
like any other.
Open: Daily 8:00 a.m.–5:00 p.m. Fee
at main entrance. (305) 247–6211.

**Preston B. Bird and Mary
Heinlein Fruit and Spice Park**
24801 Southwest 187th Avenue

This 20-acre public park and tropical
arboretum displays fruit, nut, and
spice trees from all over the world.
Open: Monday–Saturday 10:00 a.m.–
5:00 p.m., Sunday 1:00–3:00 p.m.
Tour fee only. (305) 247–5727.

10. Immokalee

Corkscrew Swamp Sanctuary
1.5 miles from County Road 846
on County Road 849, 14 miles from
Immokalee

Corkscrew Swamp is a wildlife sanctuary maintained by the National
Audubon Society. It covers 11,000
acres of Florida swamp wilderness,
including a magnificent virgin stand
of bald cypress. A 1.5-mile, self-
guided boardwalk trail is provided.
Open: Daily 9:00 a.m.–5:00 p.m. Fee.
Groups may request naturalist-directed
tours; write Sanctuary Director, Box
1875, R.D. #2, Sanctuary Road,
Naples, Fla. 33940. (813) 657–3771.

11. Jacksonville

**Cummer Art Gallery
and Memorial Gardens**
829 Riverside Avenue

The gardens were begun in 1903 by
Mrs. Cummer. She based the design
on English and Italian prototypes she
had seen in her travels abroad. The
gardens include a formal evergreen
garden, arbors and brick walkways, a
riverfront garden, naturalized bulbs,
and flowering shrubs. There is a 400-
year-old oak tree in the gardens.
Open: Tuesday–Friday 10:00 a.m.–
4:00 p.m., Saturday noon–5:00 p.m.
Closed: Sundays and major holidays.
(904) 794–0997.

12. Key West

Audubon House and Garden
Whitehead and Greene Streets

Made famous by the visit in 1832 of
conservationist John James Audubon,
the 1830 house was the first (1958)
restoration project in Key West. The
garden features rare exotic plants.
Open: Daily 9:00 a.m.–noon,
1:00–5:00 p.m. Fee. (305) 294–2116.

**Ernest Hemingway
House and Garden**
907 Whitehead Street

Hemingway was the first of many
writers who have called Key West
their home. He purchased this house
in 1931. His wife, Pauline, designed

the 1-acre garden, using exotic plants from all over the world. The swimming pool, built in the late 1930s, was the first in Key West.
Open: Daily 9:00 a.m.–5:00 p.m.; last tour begins at 4:30 p.m. Fee. (305) 294–1575.

Key West Garden Center and West Martello Fort
Higgs Beach and White Street Pier

An old fort, constructed in 1861, is now the Key West Garden Center. Plantings are within the walls and moat of the fort structure.
Open: Wednesday–Sunday 10:00 a.m.–noon, 1:00–3:30 p.m. (305) 294–3210.

Oldest House and Gardens
322 Duval Street

The house was built in 1835; both the house and gardens have been restored.
Open: 10:00 a.m.–4:00 p.m. Closed: Wednesday. Fee. (305) 294–9502.

13. Lake Wales

Bok Tower Gardens
U.S. 27, 3 miles north of Lake Wales

The sanctuary was established by Edward W. Bok in the early 1900s as a peaceful natural retreat and wildlife refuge. The grounds contain 128 acres of naturalized planting atop Iron Mountain, the highest point in the Florida peninsula. The landscaping

was done between 1924 and 1928.
Open: Daily 8:00 a.m.–5:30 p.m. Parking fee. (813) 676–1408.

14. Largo

Suncoast Botanical Garden
102nd Avenue North, at 125th Street

This 60-acre subtropical garden was established in 1962. Special gardens and collections feature eucalyptus, citrus, hibiscus, subtropical flowering trees, and many more native and exotic species.
Open: Daily 8:00 a.m.–sunset. (813) 896–3186.

15. Longwood

Big Tree Park
General Hutchison Highway, off U.S. 17–92

"The Big Tree" is reported to be the oldest and largest bald cypress tree in the world. It is 17 feet in diameter and over 3,500 years old.
Open: Monday–Friday 7:00 a.m.–sunset, Saturday–Sunday 9:00 a.m.–sunset. (305) 831–1622.

16. Marineland

**Washington Oaks Gardens
State Park**
Fla. A1A, 2 miles south
of Marineland

The 340-acre state park, bounded
by the Intercoastal Waterway on
the west and the Atlantic Ocean
on the east, contains a plantation,
gardens, and citrus groves. First
established in 1815, the gardens and
other plantings have been expanded
since 1930 by Mr. and Mrs. Owen D.
Young. Native and exotic plants and
shrubs are featured in naturalized
gardens.
*Open: Daily 8:00 a.m.–sunset. (904)
445–3161.*

17. Melbourne

Florida Institute of Technology
150 West University Boulevard

A quarter of this 125-acre campus is
taken up by a botanical palm garden,
with 200 species represented. The
Dent Smith Trail winds through the
subtropical gardens.
*Open: Daily, sunrise–sunset. (305)
768–8000.*

18. Miami

☆
Charles Deering Estate
16701 Southwest 72nd Avenue

Purchased in 1985 from the Charles
Deering heirs, this 368-acre estate is
now owned by the state and operated
by Dade County Recreation and Parks
Department. The site is the largest
undisturbed natural area of South
Florida coastal plant communities
in an urbanized area. Rich in both
ecological and archaeological finds,
the site combines areas of pinegrove,
hammock, and mangrove swamp. The
Richmond Cottage and Inn are the
only remains of the town of Cutler,
which existed before Miami and was
purchased in its entirety by Deering
at the turn of the century. Deering's
Mediterranean-style mansion was
built in 1922.
*Open: Weekends and holidays,
9:00 a.m.–5:00 p.m. and by
appointment. Fee. (305) 235–1668 or
579–2676.*

**San-Ai-An Garden
and Japanese Teahouse**
Watson Island, MacArthur Causeway

Created in 1961 as a gift of Kiyoshi
Ishimura, the circular garden is a
small but peaceful retreat within view
of the Miami skyline. Landscape
architect Kingo Sakamuto of Japan
designed the garden.
*Open: Daily 9:00 a.m.–6:00 p.m.
(305) 285–1027.*

Vizcaya Gardens, Miami, Fla.

Simpson Park
55 Southwest 17th Road

This natural hammock of 8.5 acres is located near downtown Miami. It is a remnant of the 600-acre tract owned by the Brickell family, early Miami pioneers. Naturalist guided tours can be arranged by calling (305) 856–6807.
Open: Daily, sunrise–sunset.

☆
Vizcaya Gardens
3251 South Miami Avenue

Vizcaya, the residence of the late James Deering, is an American recreation of an Italian Renaissance villa and gardens. The house, begun in 1912, contains fine period furniture, textiles, and sculpture.

Ten acres of the estate are devoted to superb formal gardens containing Italianate fountains, sculpture, and ornate parterres. There is a walled secret garden.
Open: Daily 9:30 a.m.–4:30 p.m. Closed: Christmas. Fee. (305) 579–2708.

19. Miami Beach

Miami Beach Garden Center and Conservatory
2000 Garden Center Drive

Plants indigenous to southern Florida are housed in a glass conservatory.
Open: Daily 10:00 a.m.–3:30 p.m. (305) 673–7256.

20. Moore Haven

The Lone Cypress
Bank of the Caloosahatchee Canal

This tree has been a landmark since the early years of recorded history on Lake Okeechobee. It has been a guide to boatmen and a silent witness to settlement, destructive fire, and tragic storms. A small park to commemorate the tree has been developed.
Open: Daily, sunrise–sunset.
(813) 946–0711.

21. North Miami Beach

Gardens and Cloisters of the Monastery of St. Bernard
16711 West Dixie Highway

Twenty acres of formal tropical gardens provide the setting for this reconstructed Spanish Cistercian monastery of the twelfth century, now a museum.
Open: Monday–Saturday 10:00 a.m.–5:00 p.m., Sunday noon–5:00 p.m.
Fee. (305) 945–1461.

22. Orlando

Leu Botanical Gardens
730 Forest Avenue

The 56-acre garden contains a formal rose garden, azalea and camellia collections, and a large orchid house.

Open: Daily 9:00 a.m.–5:00 p.m.
Closed: Christmas. Fee. (305) 894–6021.

23. Ormond Beach

Ormond Beach Memorial
70 East Granada Boulevard

This densely wooded natural garden provides a welcome retreat in the middle of the city, with dunes, ponds, streams, waterfalls, and a small Japanese garden.
Open: Garden, daylight hours; gallery, October 1–August 31, Thursday–Tuesday noon–5:00 p.m.
Closed: January 1, Easter, Thanksgiving, Christmas. (904) 677–1857.

Rockefeller Gardens
25 Riverside Drive

This riverfront garden was constructed in the 1920s by John D. Rockefeller as part of his winter home. The original gardens, credited to Swedish landscape architect P. Frederick Seabloom, have been restored. The garden is designed in three sections: the north lawns are planted in citrus, the central areas have stylized plantings and seasonal flowers, and the south sections represent natural woodlands with pools and footbridges.
Open: Monday–Friday 9:00 a.m.–5:30 p.m., Saturday 10:00 a.m.–noon.
(904) 673–4701.

24. Palatka

Ravine Gardens State Park
Twigg Street, off State Road 20

In this 85-acre park, over 50 varieties of azaleas bloom on the banks of three natural fingerlike formations. The gardens are enhanced by camellias, dogwood, and flowering annuals.
Open: Daily 8:00 a.m.–sunset. Fee. (904) 328–4366.

25. Palm Beach

Cluett Memorial Gardens at Church of Bethesda-by-the-Sea
South County Road
and Barton Avenue

Given by Nellie B. Cluett in memory of her parents, this garden provides a quiet retreat from city noise. In the formal garden are a raised terrace, walled garden, and canal fish pond flanked by flower beds; an ancient gumbo-limbo tree overhangs two corner gazebos.
Open: Daily 9:00 a.m.–5:00 p.m. (305) 655–4554.

Harbor Island
Waterway side of Juniper Island

This island garden, approached by a Japanese bridge, features typical southern Florida native flora. Plants are labeled.
Open: Daily, sunrise–sunset. (305) 964–4420.

Henry Morrison Flagler Museum and Gardens
Whitehall Way

Flagler began to develop Florida's East Coast in the 1880s, establishing the first railroads and resort areas. The home, "Whitehall," and its magnificently landscaped gardens and grounds were built for his wife in 1901. The plantings are identified by markers with botanical names.
Open: Tuesday–Saturday 10:00 a.m.–5:00 p.m., Sunday noon–5:00 p.m. Fee. (305) 655–2833.

Society of the Four Arts
Royal Palm Way

A tropical garden, herb garden, and fine Chinese Courtyard Garden share this site with a library, art gallery, and auditorium. The Chinese Garden, constructed in 1938, is notable for its antique Chinese sculptures.
Open: Garden and library, November 1–April 30, Monday–Saturday 10:00 a.m.–5:00 p.m., Sunday 2:30–5:00 p.m.; rest of year, Monday–Friday 10:00 a.m.–5:00 p.m. Galleries closed at 1:30 p.m. on Tuesday, January 1–March 31. (305) 655–7226.

26. Point Washington

Eden State Gardens
Off U.S. 98 on State Road 395

A restored mansion and grounds of Eden reflect the life-style along Florida's northwestern Gulf Coast

in the 1890s. The Greek Revival
house was built by William Henry
Wesley in 1895; restoration began
in 1953. Beneath the magnolias and
evergreen oaks hung with moss are
beautiful formal gardens, including a
rose garden and azalea groupings.
*Open: Daily 8:00 a.m.–sunset. (904)
231–4214.*

27. Port Orange

Sugar Mill Gardens
On Herbert Street, west of U.S. 1

The ruins of an old English sugar mill
sit in a beautiful garden setting under
giant oaks. The 12 acres contain
native "jungle" vegetation and a
hammock trail.
*Open: Daily 9:00 a.m.–4:00 p.m.
Closed: Christmas and New Year's
Day. (904) 767–1735.*

28. Sarasota

Marie Selby Botanical Gardens
800 South Palm Avenue

These gardens were founded in 1973
for the study of epiphytic plants such
as orchids, bromeliads, gesneriads,
ferns, and cacti. They were originally
created in the 1920s by the late Marie
Selby as a private tropical garden.
*Open: Daily 10:00 a.m.–5:00 p.m.
Closed: Christmas. (813) 366–5730.*

Ringling Museums
U.S. 41, 3 miles north of Sarasota

Built during the 1920s, the museums
include the Museum of Art, Asolo
Theater, Museum of the Circus, and
"Ca'd'Zan," the former Ringling
residence. All the buildings are of
Italian Renaissance style, Ca'd'Zan
being modeled after the Doge's Palace
in Venice. The formally landscaped
68-acre estate features rare tropical
plants and Mable Ringling's rose garden. There is also a formal sculpture
garden.
*Open: Monday–Friday 9:00 a.m.–
7:00 p.m., Saturday 9:00–5:00 p.m.,
Sundays and holidays 11 a.m.–
6:00 p.m. Fee. (813) 355–5101.*

29. Tallahassee

Alfred B. Maclay State
Ornamental Gardens
3540 Thomasville Road

This 300-acre tract was developed by
Alfred Barmore Maclay, landscape
architect, who purchased the land
in 1923. The 50 acres of formal and
woodland gardens feature some of the
finest massed plantings of azaleas and
camellias in the South, together with
mountain laurel and other native
trees.
*Open: Park, daily 8:00 a.m.–sunset;
gardens, daily 9:00 a.m.–5:00 p.m.
Fee. (904) 893–4232.*

Broucaw–McDougall House
329 North Meridian Street

Originally constructed in 1856, the house and grounds were restored in 1974. Archaeological research provided the information for the authentic garden reconstruction. *Open: Daily 9:00 a.m.–5:00 p.m. (904) 488–3901.*

Lemoyne Garden
125 North Gadsden Street

Beautiful ivy-covered walls surround the English-style garden of the 1852 Ivan Monroe House. The garden was restored in 1969 by Helen Lind; it features a fountain, gazebo, and sculpture. *Open: Tuesday–Saturday 10:00 a.m.– 2:00 p.m., Sunday 2:00–5:00 p.m. Fee. (904) 222–8800.*

30. Tampa

Lowry Park
North Boulevard and Sligh Avenue

This park features tropical plants, including bamboo, banana trees, and flowering shrubs. *Open: Monday–Saturday 10:00 a.m.– 5:00 p.m., Sunday until 6:00 p.m. (813) 935–5503.*

31. West Palm Beach

Mounts Botanical Garden
531 North Military Trail

This 3.5-acre teaching garden, designed by Eugene Joyner, exhibits a large array of rare tropical fruit trees, citrus, ferns, and flowering trees. *Open: Monday–Saturday 8:30 a.m.– 5:00 p.m., Sunday 1:00–5:00 p.m. Closed: Holidays. (305) 683–1777.*

Norton Gallery of Art and Patio Garden
1451 South Olive Avenue

In formal, individual garden areas, tropical plants are abundantly and effectively used. The gardens feature sculpture, a fountain, and seasonally flowering borders. Beautiful orchids and platyclinis hang from taller trees. Most plants are labeled. *Open: Tuesday–Saturday 10:00 a.m.– 5:00 p.m., Sunday 1:00–5:00 p.m. (305) 832–5194.*

32. Winter Park

Mead Botanical Gardens
1400 South Denning Drive

This 40-acre site features azaleas and other native plants, and specializes in orchids. Adjacent to the botanical gardens is the headquarters of the Florida Federation of Garden Clubs. The gardens here include a formal raised garden and a wildflower garden.

*Open: Botanical gardens, daily
9:00 a.m.–5:00 p.m. (305) 644–5770;
Garden Club headquarters, Monday–
Friday 9:00 a.m.–5:00 p.m. (305)
647–7016.*

Other Places of Interest

Note: Places marked with an aster-
isk (*) are recommended for their
superior garden displays, which are
incidental to their main tourist attractions.

Big Cypress National Preserve,
  Naples
Biscayne National Monument,
  Homestead
*Busch Gardens, Tampa
Caladesi Island State Park, Dunedin
Canaveral National Seashore,
  Titusville
Castillo de San Marcos National
  Monument, Saint Augustine
Cedar Key
Central Florida Zoo, Sanford
Collier-Seminole State Park, Naples
*Cypress Gardens, Winter Haven
De Soto National Monument,
  Bradenton
Everglades Wonder Gardens, Bonita
  Springs

Florida Caverns State Park, Marianna
Fort Caroline National Monument,
  Jacksonville
Fort Matanzas National Monument,
  Saint Augustine
Gulf Islands National Seashore, Gulf
  Breeze
John Pennekamp Coral Reef State
  Park, Key Largo
Jungle Gardens, Sarasota
Kennedy Space Center, Titusville
Lake Okeechobee
Mar-A-Lago National Historic Site,
  Palm Beach
Marineland, Saint Augustine
Ocala National Forest, Ocala
Orchid Jungle, Homestead
Parrot Jungle, Miami
Pine Island Wildlife Refuge
Sea World Florida, Orlando
Slocum Water Gardens, Winter
  Haven
Stephen Foster State Folk Culture
  Center, White Springs
*Sunken Gardens, Saint Petersburg
U.S. Department of Agriculture Plant
  Introduction Station, Miami
*Walt Disney World and Epcot
  Center, Orlando
Weeki Wachee Spring, Weeki
  Wachee

Georgia

Area: 58,876 square miles

Population: 5,976,000

Statehood: January 2, 1788
(4th state)

Georgia is the largest state east of
the Mississippi River. The last of
the original thirteen colonies, it was
founded in 1733 by General James
Oglethorpe. The colony was first used
as a buffer between the Carolinas and
Spanish Florida. The British and the
Spaniards were not the first settlers
of Georgia, however. Cherokee and
Creek Indians had inhabited the land
for countless generations. Indian
mounds, which date back over 2,000
years, are the only remnants of these
earlier civilizations.

The landscape of Georgia varies
from coastal plains to mountains and
from semiarid to swamp. Its main
physiographic regions are the Coastal
Plain, which includes several undeveloped coastal islands, marshes, and
the famous Okefenokee Swamp; the
rolling hills of the Piedmont Plateau,
which extend northeast to southwest across the upper half of the
state; and the Blue Ridge Mountain
region along the northern border.
Many rivers and lakes occur throughout Georgia. The largest lakes are
man-made and provide excellent recreational facilities as well as irrigation
and hydroelectricity. Natural vegeta-

tion in the northern half of the state
is the oak-hickory climax forest. In
the southern half of the state are pine
forests, with cypress and live oak
along the coast. The climate is warm
to temperate; there are 185 growing
days in the mountainous northern region and over 300 days in the south.
The average rainfall is over 45 inches
per year.

Since 1945, Georgia has changed
from a largely agricultural economy
to one that is predominantly industrial. The agricultural economy based
on cotton created an open landscape.
Today, much of that open space has
been replaced with timber stands to
provide forest products, now Georgia's second largest industry, rivaling
the textile industry.

With its abundant water supply, its
temperate climate, and its diversity
of landscape and recreational opportunities, Georgia has become one of
the most attractive states for "Sunbelt
migration."

1. Athens

Founders Memorial Garden
South Lumpkin Street and Bocock
Drive, at northern end of University
of Georgia Campus

The centerpiece of this 2.5-acre garden is the 1857 Lumpkin House, a
former university faculty residence.
The house has been restored, along
with its adjacent smokehouse and
kitchen buildings, and is now the
headquarters of the Garden Club of

GEORGIA

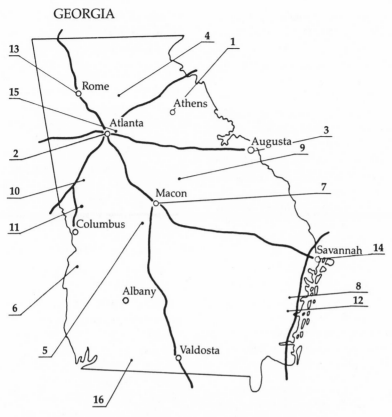

1. *Athens* 2. *Atlanta* 3. *Augusta* 4. *Canton* 5. *Fort Valley*
6. *Lumpkin* 7. *Macon* 8. *Midway* 9. *Milledgeville* 10. *Newnan*
11. *Pine Mountain* 12. *Riceboro* 13. *Rome* 14. *Savannah*
15. *Stone Mountain* 16. *Thomasville*

Georgia, Inc. The garden commemorates the founding in 1891 of the
Ladies Garden Club of Athens, the
first garden club in the world. It contains formal and informal areas, with
ornamental plant materials suitable
for use in the Upper Piedmont section
of the South.
Open: Garden, daily, sunrise–sunset;
house, Monday–Friday 9:00 a.m.–
4:00 p.m. and by appointment. (404)
542–3631.

State Botanical Garden of Georgia
2450 South Milledge Avenue,
1 mile south of Athens bypass

These 293 acres represent a broad
cross section of the Georgia Piedmont
landscape. Five miles of trails allow
the visitor to observe the characteristic plants of floodplain, upland slope,
ravine, and stream, as well as the
successional stages of revegetation
in areas farmed as recently as 1960.

The conservatory building at the site houses a collection of tropicals and is also used as a display and instructional area. The garden is committed to the preservation of rare and endangered species, and includes a collection of native flora. Special collections of roses, perennials, azaleas, camellias, dogwoods, magnolias, redbuds, laurel, viburnum, and rhododendron are being developed and improved. *Open: Daily 8:00 a.m.–sunset; Visitors' Center, Monday–Saturday 9:00 a.m.–4:30 p.m., Sunday 11:00 a.m.–4:30 p.m. (404) 542–1244.*

2. Atlanta

Atlanta Botanical Garden
Piedmont Park, Prado entrance off Piedmont Drive

Located on 60 acres in midtown Atlanta, the garden combines attractive spaces with an educational purpose. Features include herb, rose, vegetable, and Japanese gardens as well as a 15-acre mature hardwood forest with walking trails. The garden has been approved as a test site for All-American seed selections and for the Wildflower Research Center. *Open: Monday–Saturday 9:00 a.m.–8:00 p.m., Sunday noon–dusk. Fee, Tuesday–Sunday; children under 6 free. (404) 876–5858.*

Atlanta Historical Society, McElreath Hall
3101 Andrews Drive, Northwest

The Atlanta Historical Society owns and operates a 26-acre complex of historic homes and gardens, including the Quarry Garden, Swan House and Gardens, and Tullie Smith House. Tickets may be purchased at McElreath Hall to view all houses, gardens, woodlands, and exhibits (see descriptions below). *Open: Monday–Saturday 9:00 a.m.–5:30 p.m., Sunday noon–5:00 p.m. Fee, adults and senior citizens. (404) 261–1837.*

Quarry Garden. An abandoned 3-acre rock quarry on the grounds of the Atlanta Historical Society was used to create a pleasant, informal area displaying plants native to the Piedmont and Coastal Plain of Georgia.
Swan House and Gardens. The Palazzo Corsini in Rome was the inspiration for this elegant house and gardens built for the Inman family by architect Phillip Shutze in 1928. The gardens include fountains, cascades, formal vistas, and a delightful nature trail (with educational markers) known as Swan Woods.
Tulie Smith House. This restored 1835 Georgia farmhouse with outbuildings was moved to the grounds of the Atlanta Historical Society. The garden—of authentic nineteenth-century design—is planted in vegetables, field crops, flowers, and herbs. Native plants can be seen in adjacent woodland areas.

Callanwolde Fine Arts Center
980 Briarcliff Road, Northeast

A 24-room Tudor-style mansion, once occupied by Coca-Cola heir Charles Howard Candler and his family (1921–59), now houses numerous art activities. Administered by the Callanwolde Foundation, Callanwolde's landscaping and beautification projects are being conducted by the DeKalb Federation of Garden Clubs.
Open: By appointment. (404) 872–5338.

Fernbank
Heaton Park Drive, off Artwood Road (Artwood Road is off Ponce de Leon Avenue)

Fernbank consists of the DeKalb County Board of Education Science Center and the Fernbank Forest. The 60-acre forest, consisting of climax oak, hickory, and beech in primeval condition, is unique in the Piedmont area. There are nature trails and observation stations throughout the forest, allowing the visitor to study the various ecological habitats of the Piedmont.
Forest open: Sunday–Friday 2:00–5:00 p.m., Saturday 10:00 a.m.–5:00 p.m.
Exhibit Center open: Tuesday–Friday 8:30 a.m.–10:00 p.m., Monday and Saturday 8:30 a.m.–5:00 p.m., Sunday 1:30–5:00 p.m. (404) 378–4311.

Piedmont Park
Piedmont Avenue at 12th Avenue

"To understand Piedmont Park is to understand the South." Originally the site of the 1895 Cotton States Exposition which helped bring capital from the North to the South, the 180-acre park is a significant resource for Atlanta. Its general design still follows the pattern used for the exposition. Frederick Law Olmsted was consulted on the original design, but his ideas were not used. In 1909, his sons, the Olmsted brothers, prepared an improvement plan which was implemented.
Open: Sunrise–sunset. (404) 658–6116.

3. Augusta

Pendleton King Park and Sunken Blue Garden
Kissingbower Road

This 64-acre park, privately owned and leased, is located in the heart of Augusta. In the park is a formal garden that is more than 100 years old. Known as "The Sunken Blue Garden," it features only blue-blooming plants, including a rare Lilac Chaste tree. There is also a touch-and-smell herb garden. Picnic areas.
Open: Daily 8:00 a.m.–10:00 p.m. (404) 826–4722.

4. Canton

Gardens de Pajarito Montana (Gardens of Little Bird Mountain)
Ga. 140, 4 miles south of Canton

The 20-acre garden, part of the old Byrd Plantation, was developed by its owners, Margaret and Gene Cline. Certain large collections of native and exotic plants are used for study and research by individuals and institutions.
Open: By appointment; Rt. 4, Box 1181, Canton, Ga. 30114. (404) 479–4471.

5. Fort Valley

Massee Lane Camellia Gardens
Route 49, between Fort Valley and Marshallville

The 7-acre garden of camellias and other plants is the headquarters of the American Camellia Society (P.O. Box 1217, Fort Valley, Ga. 31030). Camellias are in flower from November to April.
Open: Gardens, daily; headquarters, Monday–Friday 9:00 a.m.–4:00 p.m. and on Sunday 1:00–5:00 p.m. during blooming season. (912) 967–2358.

6. Lumpkin

Bedingfield Inn Garden
Town Square

The garden of this 1835 inn displays popular designs and plants of the period.
Open: September–May, Saturday–Sunday 1:00–5:00 p.m.; June–August, daily 1:00–5:00 p.m. Fee. (912) 838–4201.

Westville Living History Museum and McDonald House
U.S. 27, 0.5 miles from Lumpkin

Westville is a living history village of relocated and restored buildings representative of Georgia's preindustrial life and culture. The McDonald House is one of several historic buildings of the 1850s. The half-acre Edwards Garden is typical of the period. It features American boxwood trimmed into hedges and is a copy of the historic Kilb-Pou-Newton House Garden in Madison, Ga.
Open: Monday–Saturday 10:00 a.m.–5:00 p.m., Sunday 1:00–5:00 p.m. Fee. (912) 838–6310.

7. Macon

Rose Hill Cemetery
1091 Riverside Drive

This 50-acre cemetery, designed by Simri Rose in 1839, is a landscape gardening landmark. Many rare and unusual trees grace the picturesque

landscape. Much of Macon's history is reflected in the finely carved nineteenth-century sculptures situated here.
Open: Daily, sunrise–sunset. (912) 744–7276.

Sydney Lanier Cottage
935 High Street

The poet was born in this Victorian cottage in 1842. An old-fashioned garden has been re-created in the backyard.
Open: Weekdays 9:00 a.m.–1:00 p.m., 2:00–4:00 p.m. Fee. (912) 743–3851.

8. Midway

Midway Church and Museum
U.S. 17, just north of
U.S. 82 and Ga. 38

The New England-style Puritan church has retained its original character. Close by is a 1,200-grave cemetery. The museum is a re-created raised plantation plain-style house. The design of the garden is contemporary with the house.
Open: Tuesday–Saturday 10:00 a.m.–4:00 p.m. (912) 884–5837.

9. Milledgeville

Lockerly Arboretum
U.S. 441, 44 Irwinton Highway

The arboretum was founded in 1966 to promote conservation and beautification. Located just north of the fall line, it is comprised of 40 acres of wooded terrain with nature trails, 2 greenhouses with 370 named varieties of cacti and succulents and several unnamed varieties, and extensive garden areas.
Open: Monday–Friday 8:00 a.m.–4:00 p.m. (912) 452–2112.

Memory Hill Cemetery
South Liberty Street

The historic (1804) cemetery is located in one of the public squares laid out in the original plan of the city.
Open: Daily 9:00 a.m.–5:00 p.m. (912) 452–4687.

Old Governor's Mansion
Georgia College,
120 South Clark Street

The mansion, with its elegant Palladian rotunda, is typical of the Greek Revival period of the 1840s. Gardens have been re-created in the appropriate style.
Open: Tuesday–Saturday 10:00 a.m.–5:00 p.m., Sunday 1:00–5:00 p.m. Fee. (912) 452–4687.

10. Newnan

Dunaway Gardens
Route 70, Roscoe Road,
6 miles north of Newnan

During the Great Depression, a 20-
acre garden was created on a 64-acre
tract of worn-out cotton land by
hundreds of black laborers under the
direction of the actress Hetty Jane
Dunaway Sewell. Six small but complete gardens are incorporated into
the overall landscape, which includes
7 natural springs. Featured are an
Outdoor Theater with 14 unique
magnolia trees, the Hanging Garden, a sunken garden, "Little Stone
Mountain," and a Japanese rock garden. Currently under restoration, the
gardens were once used as a national
center to train aspiring actors and
actresses, drama coaches, and directors. "Tara," the filmset house made
famous in *Gone with the Wind*, and a
re-creation of a southern plantation
will be incorporated on an adjoining
160 acres, scheduled to open in 1989.
Tours of gardens by appointment.
(404) 251–2109.

11. Pine Mountain

☆
Callaway Gardens
Off I-185, just south of Pine
Mountain and west of U.S. 27

One of the South's most unique
combinations of public gardens and
recreational facilities, this 2,500-acre
estate emphasizes environmental
education and family-oriented recreational activities. Visitors may use
extensive walking and bicycling trails
through natural and horticultural
display areas. There are over 700
varieties of azaleas and year-round
displays of many plant varieties, as
well as a Horticultural Center with
5 acres of greenhouses and display
gardens.
*Open: Daily, March 21–October
25, 7:00 a.m.–6:00 p.m.; October
26–November 30, 7:00 a.m.–5:00
p.m.; December 1–January 30, 8:00
a.m.–5:00 p.m.; February 1–March
20, 7:00 a.m.–5:00 p.m. Fee. (404)
663–2281.*

12. Riceboro

LeConte–Woodmanston
40 miles south of Savannah
on U.S. 17

In 1810, the botanical gardens
of Louis LeConte (father of John
LeConte, first president of the University of California, Berkeley) were
internationally famous. Now a project
of the Garden Club of Georgia is
under way to re-create LeConte's
botanical gardens and a demonstration rice-growing area on this
63.8-acre site.
*Open: Tuesday–Saturday 10:00
a.m.–4:00 p.m., Sunday 2:00–4:00
p.m. by reservation. (912) 884–5837.*

13. Rome

Marshall Forest
Horseleg Creek Road

This 200-acre preserve, called "the first natural area in the Southeast," is now owned by the Nature Conservancy. In 1966 it was named Georgia's first National Natural Landmark. More than 100 acres consist of virgin forest protected for over a century by the Marshall family. For many years botanists and ecologists have been using the area as a research facility. There are observation trails, markers, and a Braille trail.
Open: Early spring–late fall. Tours by appointment. (404) 232–3520.

Oak Hill, Martha Berry Museum and Art Gallery
Mount Berry Highway (U.S. 27)

Oak Hill, Miss Berry's home, was built in 1847. Groomed lawns, giant oak trees, and formal gardens give a sense of serenity to this classic Southern home. Visitors are welcome to see the museum and tour the scenic Berry College and Berry Academy campuses.
Open: Tuesday–Saturday 10:00 a.m.–5:00 p.m., Sunday 1:00–5:00 p.m. (404) 291–1883.

☆☆
14. Savannah

The distinctive quality of this historic city is demonstrated by the unique system of public squares incorporated in James Oglethorpe's original plan. Of the original 24 squares, 22 remain. Today they form the core of the Savannah Historic District, now recorded in the National Register of Historic Sites. A walking tour is recommended to view the green, open spaces, and gracious townhouses, many of which have been preserved or restored. For further information call the Savannah Convention and Visitors' Bureau, (912) 233–6651. Gardens of special significance are described below.

Andrew Low House
329 Abercorn Street

The front garden of this 1848 house is one of only three in the city to have retained its original design. The house is now the Georgia headquarters of the Colonial Dames of America. In the carriage house was founded the Girl Scouts of America by Juliette Gordon Low.
Open: Daily 10:30 a.m.–4:00 p.m. Closed: Thursdays and national holidays. Fee. (912) 233–6854.

Bethesda Home for Boys
9520 Ferguson Avenue

Founded in 1740 by George Whitfield, an eighteenth-century evangelist, this is the oldest orphanage in

America. The home is located on a
natural sweep of land, enhanced by
the landscape design which includes
plantings in the English manner.
*Open: Daily, by appointment. (912)
355–0905.*

Bonaventure Cemetery
350 Bonaventure Road

Originally a plantation, the property
was purchased in 1847 for use as a
cemetery. The peacefulness of the
area is enhanced by the profusion
of camellias, azaleas, jasmine, and
wisteria growing under a canopy of
live oaks and Spanish moss.
*Open: 8:00 a.m.–5:30 p.m. (912)
232–0238.*

Colonial Park Cemetery
Abercorn and Liberty Streets

Burials occurred here between 1750
and 1850. Among the graves of several notable Georgians is that of
Button Gwinnett, a signer of the
Declaration of Independence. Outstanding specimen trees are featured.
*Open: Daily, sunrise–sunset. (912)
233–6651.*

Emmet Park
East Bay Street

This handsome, tree-bordered green
space is part of the unique historic
area known as Factors' Walk.
Open: All times. (912) 233–6651.

Forsyth Park
Gaston, Whitaker, Park,
and Drayton Streets

Named for Governor Forsyth, the 32-
acre park was laid out in 1851. The
multi-use park was probably designed
in response to the sentiment of the
period for public spaces in urban
areas, even though Savannah was
already well endowed with them. A
handsome 1858 cast-iron fountain is
a focal point of the park.
*Open: Daily, sunrise–sunset. (912)
233–6651.*

Green–Meldrim House
14 West Macon Street

The Gothic Revival house (1856)
has a garden of authentic Victorian
design.
*Open: Tuesday, Thursday–Saturday
10:00 a.m.–4:00 p.m. Fee. (912)
233–3845.*

Isaiah Davenport House
324 East State Street

This is an American Federal-style
house (1821) with a restored period
garden.
*Open: Monday–Friday 9:30 a.m.–
4:30 p.m., Saturday 10:00 a.m.–4:00
p.m., Sunday 1:00–4:30 p.m. Fee.
(912) 233–3597.*

Juliette Gordon Low Birthplace
124 Bull Street

Now the National Girl Scouts Center,
this registered landmark is enhanced
by a re-created Victorian garden
designed by landscape architect Clermont Lee.

Forsyth Park, Savannah, Ga.

Open: Monday–Saturday 10:00 a.m.–4:00 p.m., Sunday 11:00 a.m.–4:30 p.m.
Closed: Wednesday; also Sunday in December, January. Fee. (912) 233–4501.

Laurel Grove North
802 West Anderson Street

A beautiful Victorian cemetery (1852) contains the graves of 616 Confederate soldiers.
Open: Daily 8:00 a.m.–5:30 p.m. (912) 233–9225.

Laurel Grove South
101 Kollock Street

This area comprises part of the original 1852 cemetery that was divided by the construction of Interstate 16. Listed in the National Register of

Historic Places, it is called "the jewel among black historic sites."
Open: Daily 8:00 a.m.–5:30 p.m. (912) 233–9225.

Owens–Thomas House
124 Abercorn Street

This house, designed by William Jay, is an outstanding example of Regency architecture. The 1820-era garden is surrounded by tabby walls.
Open: Tuesday–Saturday 10:00 a.m.–4:30 p.m., Sunday–Monday 2:00–5:00 p.m.
Closed: September, major holidays. Fee. (912) 233–9743.

Rousakis Riverfront Plaza
Savannah Riverfront

The recently revitalized riverfront area is paved with cobblestones brought over in ships from England. The statue of a waving girl and plantings in square beds along the river repeat the design of the original plan of Savannah.
Open: All times. (912) 233–9225.

The Scarbrough House
41 West Broad Street

Designed by William Jay, an English architect, for William Scarbrough, a principal investor in the SS *Savannah*, the first steamship to cross the Atlantic, this 1819 house now serves as headquarters for Historic Savannah Foundation, Inc. The garden was restored by the Trustees Garden Club. It combines historically accurate design details and plant materials with contemporary adaptations appropriate for the many functions for which the gardens are now used.
Open: Monday–Friday 9:00 a.m.–4:00 p.m., or by appointment. (912) 233–7787.

Wormsloe Plantation
Isle of Hope, 8 miles southeast of Savannah, via Skidaway Road

This estate is now owned in part by descendants of the original owner, Noble Jones, and in part by the state of Georgia. Jones received the land grant from the king of England in 1739.
Open: Renowned avenues of oaks, interpretive museum, and trails,

Tuesday–Saturday 9:00 a.m.–5:00 p.m., Sunday 2:00–5:30 p.m.; house and grounds by invitation only. Fee. (912) 352–2548.

15. Stone Mountain

**Antebellum Plantation,
Stone Mountain Park**
Stone Mountain Freeway,
U.S. 78, east of Atlanta

Buildings were collected from various locations in the state to reproduce this pre-Civil War Georgia plantation. At the site are a formal garden with gazebo, vegetable gardens, tobacco and cotton plots, and various plantation buildings.
Open: Daily 10:00 a.m.–9:00 p.m.; September–March, until 5:30 p.m. Parking fee. (404) 498–5600.

**Thornton House,
Stone Mountain Park**
Stone Mountain Freeway,
U.S. 78, east of Atlanta

This completely restored 1783 Piedmont settlement house was relocated in Stone Mountain Park. Also featured are an authentically re-created boxwood garden and a kitchen garden.
Open: Daily 10:00 a.m.–5:30 p.m.; summer, until 9:00 p.m. Fee. (404) 498–5600.

16. Thomasville

The "Big Oak"
Corner of Crawford
and Monroe Streets

A landmark since 1688, this tree is 68 feet tall with a 162-foot limb span. The trunk has a 24-foot circumference.
Open: All times. (912) 226–9600.

Paradise Park
Broad and Hansell Streets

This 26.5-acre virgin forest tract was acquired by the city in 1889.
Open: All times. (912) 226–9600.

Pebble Hill Plantation
U.S. 319, 5 miles south
of Thomasville

The plantation was established in 1820 and purchased by the Hanna family of Cleveland, Ohio, in the 1920s as a winter home. The present house, designed in 1930 by Abraham Garfield, is an elegant replacement of the original home which was destroyed by fire.
Open: Tuesday–Saturday 10:00 a.m.–5:00 p.m., Sunday 1:00–5:00 p.m.
Closed: September after Labor Day, Thanksgiving, Christmas. Fee. (912) 226–2344.

Rose Test Gardens of the American Rose Society
Thomasville Nurseries, U.S. 84 East

One of the society's 26 test gardens, this garden was founded in 1898. The roses are best viewed in March–April.
Open: Monday–Saturday 8:00 a.m.–5:00 p.m., Sunday 2:00–5:00 p.m. (912) 226–9600.

Other Places of Interest

Antebellum Trail (Many fine historic houses, some with restored gardens, can be seen on this trail which begins in Athens and ends in Macon. Towns on the route include Madison, Eatonton, Milledgeville, and Clinton. Tour itinerary from P.O. Box 948, Athens, Ga. 30603. [404] 549–6800.)
Chickamauga National Military Park, Ringgold
Cumberland Island National Seashore, Saint Mary's
Cyclorama, Grant Park, Atlanta
Etowah Indian Mounds, Cartersville
Fort Frederica, Saint Simon's Island
Fort Jackson, Savannah
Fort McAllister, Richmond Hill
Fort Pulaski National Monument, Savannah
Georgia Agrirama, Tifton
Golden Isles, Brunswick to Savannah
Jarrell Plantation, Juliette
Kennesaw Mountain National Battlefield, Kennesaw
Kolomoki Indian Mounds, Blakely
Little White House, Warm Springs
Okefenokee National Wildlife Refuge, Waycross
Panola Mountain Conservation Park, Stockbridge
Providence Canyon, Lumpkin
Scarborough House Garden, Savannah

Hawaii

Area: 6,450 square miles

Population: 1,054,000

Statehood: August 21, 1959
(50th state)

Hawaii's isolated location in the middle of the Pacific Ocean permitted the development of life on the island to follow unique paths. Today, this mid-ocean location makes Hawaii an important crossroads between East and West.

Because of Hawaii's tropical location, temperatures vary little from season to season. The trade winds striking the islands from the northeast are major determinants of local climates. The windward sides of mountains receive extreme amounts of precipitation. The island of Kauai, considered to be the rainiest spot on earth, receives in some parts an average of 480 inches of rain annually. Yet on the same island, in the wind shadows of the mountains, an arid climate occurs.

Hawaii's plant and animal life is unique in the world. No large mammals were found on the island before Polynesian adventurers first arrived 1,200 years ago. Polynesian colonists introduced familiar plant species for use as food and fiber. The Europeans, who arrived after Captain Cooke discovered the islands in 1778, had an even greater impact on the ecology. Goats, pigs, and cattle which they introduced ravaged the forests. Plantations of sugarcane and pineapple were established. The cultivation of these crops and cattle grazing are important land uses in modern Hawaii. Like so many of its plant species, Hawaii's native cultural traditions have almost disappeared. Japanese, Chinese, Filipino, and American holidays have replaced ancient ceremonies.

Public parks in Hawaii preserve many natural areas of great interest. Haleakala National Park occupies the eroded sides of an ancient volcanic crater. This park preserves the habitat of the rare silversword plant. Located at Hawaii Volcanoes National Park, the site of Mauna Kea and Moana Loa, is a volcano observatory. Kalopa State Recreation Area displays especially abundant native wildlife, trees, and ferns. Relics of the ancient Polynesian culture are also preserved in public parks. At Kieawa Heiau State Park, a garden of traditional medicinal plants is cultivated. Waipahu Cultural Garden Park interprets life on the nineteenth-century plantation, which had a formative influence on modern Hawaii's ways.

Oriental and Occidental peoples have brought their rich gardening traditions with them to the islands, and their efforts have been rewarded bountifully. Hawaii's small gardens are spectacular. A more difficult task is to make the islands' total environment like its small gardens. So it was for the ancient Polynesians.

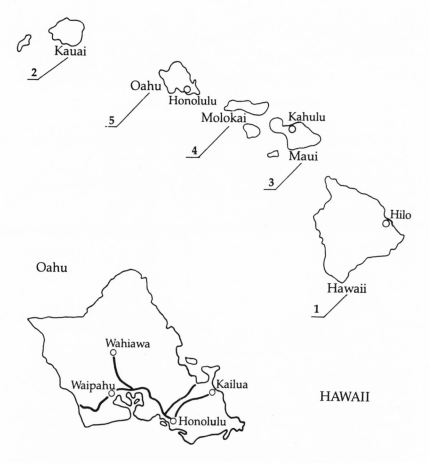

1. *Hawaii Island* 2. *Kauai Island* 3. *Maui Island* 4. *Molokai Island*
5. *Oahu Island*

Hawaii's adoption of a statewide land use plan is a hopeful first step in this direction.

Hawaii consists of a group of islands; the principal ones are, in alphabetical order, Hawaii, Kauai, Maui, Molokai, and Oahu. Honolulu, the capital, is located on Oahu. Below, features are listed by island.

1. Hawaii Island

Akaka Falls State Park
Highway 19, 10 miles north of Hilo

One of the most beautiful parks in the Hawaiian Islands, this 66-acre state park is resplendent with giant gingers, ferns, ti, orchids, and

bamboos. There is also a breathtaking view of the falls.
Open: Daily, sunrise–sunset. (808) 961–7200.

Hawaii Tropical Botanical Garden
4-mile scenic route, 5 miles north of Hilo on Route 19

This is a 17-acre tropical rain forest preserve of great natural beauty. The wide variety of naturally occurring tropical plant material is being augmented with rare species from around the world.
Open: Daily 9:00 a.m.–5:00 p.m. Closed: Holidays. Donation. (808) 964–5233.

Kalopa
5 miles southeast of Honokaa on Highway 19

This state recreation area is located in a forest rich with native wildlife, indigenous trees, and ferns. It has a native ohia forest.
Open: Daily, sunrise–sunset. (808) 961–7200.

☆
Liliuokalani Garden Park
Banyan Drive and Lihiwai Street, Hilo Bay

This authentic 30-acre Japanese garden was listed as one of the "Treasures of America" by *Reader's Digest*. Conceived in 1914, the gardens have been twice destroyed by tidal waves. They have been painstakingly restored by native Hawaiians with the support of many gifts and authentic design advice from Japan.

Open: Daily, sunrise–sunset. (808) 961–5797.

Manuka State Park
Hawaii 11, 20 miles south of Kailua-Kona

A small wayside arboretum features a collection of exotic and indigenous shrubs.
Open: Daily, sunrise–sunset. (808) 961–7200.

2. Kauai Island

The Gardens of Kiahuna Plantation
Opposite Sheraton and Kauai Hotels, Poipu Beach

Former estate of Hector Moir, the gardens are noted for their unsurpassed collection of cacti and succulents and for one of the largest plantings of African aloes in the world.
Open: Daily 9:00 a.m.–6:00 p.m.

Menehune Gardens
Highway 58, Nawiliwili

Kauai is known as the "Garden Island" because of its rich tropical vegetation. This garden represents the efforts of people sensitive to the island's ecology. It contains a replica of a primitive Hawaiian house and a stage where ancient Hawaiian chants and dances are performed.
Private, but visitors are welcome between 8:30 a.m.–4:30 p.m. Fee.

Olu Pua Botanical Garden and Plantation
Hawaii 50, Kalahoe

The 12-acre estate of a former plantation manager has been divided into 8 separate garden areas with over 3,000 varieties of plants, many unique to Kauai.
Open: 8:30 a.m.–5:00 p.m. Fee. (808) 332–8182.

☆
Pacific Tropical Botanical Garden
Lawai Valley, off Highway 50

This 186-acre garden was chartered in 1964 by Congress as a national research center for tropical botany and horticulture.
Open: Monday, Tuesday, Thursday, tours at 9:00 a.m. and 10:15 a.m.; advance registration required; tour accommodates 14 persons. Fee. (808) 332–7361.

3. Maui Island

Kahanu Gardens
4 miles north of Hana

At this 120-acre site are a well-preserved Pandanus forest and a vanilla orchid collection. Scenic coastlines, historic trails, and the legendary Piilanihale Heiau shrine add to the interest of the area.
Open: Daily 8:00 a.m.–2:30 p.m. Closed: Holidays. (808) 332–8131.

Kepaniwai Heritage Gardens
Hawaii 32, Wailuku, near entrance of Iao State Park

These gardens commemorate the ethnic groups that settled the area: American, Filipino, Portuguese, Chinese, Japanese, and Hawaiian. A typical house design and garden represent each group. The Chinese and Japanese houses have been imported from their respective countries; others are authentic copies. Plant materials are authentic for each culture.
Open: Daily 9:00 a.m.–5:00 p.m. Fee. (808) 572–7749.

Kula Botanical Gardens
0.7 miles from Kula Highway (Hawaii 37) on Kakaulike Avenue (Hawaii 377)

This modern garden is situated on land once owned by Chieftess Kakaulike at the 3,300-foot level of the dormant volcano, Haleakala. The site covers 23.5 acres and features proteas, orchids, bromeliads, and rare native Hawaiian plants.
Open: Daily 9:00 a.m.–4:00 p.m. Fee. (808) 878–1715.

4. Molokai Island

Palaau State Park
Highway 47, 3 miles north of Kualapuu

This forested mountain area of historic interest has an arboretum of native and exotic trees.
Open: Daily, sunrise–sunset. (808) 244–4354.

5. Oahu Island

Byodo-in Temple
Valley of the Temples Memorial Park
47–200 Kahekili Highway

A Japanese garden of 7 acres surrounds a temple that is almost an
exact replica of the famous Byodo-in
Temple near Kyoto, Japan.
*Open: Daily 8:30 a.m.–4:00 p.m. Fee.
(808) 239–8811.*

☆
Foster Botanic Gardens
180 North Vineyard Boulevard,
Honolulu

In 1855, Queen Kalama sold the
property to William Hillebrand, a
German who wrote the botanic trea-
tise "Flora of the Hawaiian Islands."
Captain Foster purchased the garden in 1867 and gave it to the city
of Honolulu in 1930. Its original 5.5
acres have grown to 20, and thousands of new species of trees and
shrubs have been added.
*Open: Daily 9:00 a.m.–4:00 p.m.
Closed: Christmas, New Year's Day.
Fee. (808) 533–3406.*

Harold L. Lyon Arboretum
3860 Manoa Road,
Manoa Valley, Honolulu

The arboretum is a research unit of
the University of Hawaii. Established
in 1918 by the experiment station
of the Hawaiian Sugar Planters'
Association, it was presented to the
university in 1953 to use as an arboretum and botanical garden. The 124

acres extend from an elevation of 450
to 1,300 feet and feature a variety of
plant types.
*Open: Monday–Friday 9:00 a.m.–
3:00 p.m.; general public tour, 1st
Friday and 3rd Wednesday of the
month at 1:00 p.m., and 3rd Saturday
at 10:00 a.m. Groups may arrange for
special tours. (808) 988–3177.*

Ho'omaluhia
Luluku Road in Kaneohe

This 400-acre nature forest preserve
is operated by the Honolulu Botanic
Gardens. It features plants native and
unique to Hawaii, including many
fruit-bearing trees and shrubs.
*Open: Daily 9:00 a.m.–3:00 p.m.
(808) 533–3406 or 235–6636.*

Japanese Garden
at the East-West Center
University of Hawaii,
1777 East-West Road

This garden is located behind the
Jefferson Hall Administration Building of the East-West Center. Covering about three-quarters of an acre,
it was landscaped in the traditional
Japanese style by Kenzo Ogata of
Tokyo.
*Open: Daily, daylight hours.
(808) 944–7193.*

Kyoto Gardens
Honolulu Memorial Park,
22 Craigside Place

Located here is a beautiful cemetery
for those of the Buddhist faith and
others who practice cremation. In
1966, copies of two historic Japa-

nese temples were completed: the Kinkaku-ju, the famous "Golden Pavilion" of Kyoto; and the Sanju or three-tiered, sixteenth-century pagoda of the Minami Hokko-ji Temple of Nara. The area is surrounded by the Mirror Lake Garden, fashioned after the Muromachi style.
Open: Daily, daylight hours.
(808) 523–4525.

Moanalua Gardens and Valley

Established in 1884 by Samuel M. Damon on land left to him by Princess Bernice Bishop, the gardens were a favorite recreation spot for later Hawaiian royalty. On the grounds are a Hawaiian taro patch, a carp pond, and numerous indigenous plants. The valley, also known as Kamananui Valley, is a wilderness area penetrated only by a jeep road. Archaeological sites of interest are located primarily at the upper part of the valley and may be reached by a 2–3 hours' walk.
For permission to enter and information on guided tours, write Damon Estate, Suite #1210, First Hawaiian Bank Building, Honolulu, Hawaii.

Wahiawa Botanical Garden
1396 California Avenue

This botanical garden is the rural division of the Foster Botanic Gardens in downtown Honolulu. It is full of exotic plants, including spreading fig and banyan trees, Hawaiian toro and tree fern, and spreading eucalyptus.
Open: Daily 9:00 a.m.–4:00 p.m.
(808) 533–3406.

Waimea Arboretum at Waimea Falls Park
59–864 Kalanianole Highway, Haleiwa

Rippling streams, waterfalls, lush green plant life, and thousands of labeled plants, some rare and endangered, can be observed here. Many of Hawaii's rare birds, geese, and ducks are also seen. In the area, which is the site of the first settlement on Oahu, are numerous historic remains. Guides available.
Open: Daily 10:00 a.m.–5:30 p.m.
Fee. (808) 638–8511.

Other Places of Interest

Haleakala National Park, Maui
Hawaii Volcanoes National Park, Hawaii
Na Pali Wilderness, Kauai

Idaho

Area: 83,557 square miles

Population: 1,005,000

Statehood: July 3, 1890 (43rd state)

A large part of Idaho is occupied by the northern Rocky Mountains. There are more than 50 peaks with elevations of over 10,000 feet. The mountains are a land of clear lakes and pine forests. Sheep and cattle graze the meadows.

The Snake is Idaho's most important river. It runs through the Columbia plateau, the fertile bread basket of southcentral Idaho, where most of the state's population lives. Potatoes are a major crop there. The deepest canyon on the continent, Hell's Canyon, is cut by the Snake River as it runs north through the mountains to join the Columbia River.

The first large influx of settlers followed the discovery of gold in 1860. Today, many ghost towns recall those brief-lived days of glory. Mining is still important to the economy, as are lumbering and grazing. Tourism is a fast-growing industry. The world famous Sun Valley ski resort is located in Idaho.

Almost 70 percent of the state consists of public land; Idaho has more officially designated wilderness than any other state except Alaska. There are ten national forests. The new Sawtooth National Recreation Area features spectacular mountain scenery. The Nez Percé National Historic Park offers the visitor a fascinating interpretation of one American Indian tribe's sad history.

1. Boise

Howard Platt Gardens
1701 Eastover Terrace

The gardens were planned and built to complement the Union Pacific passenger depot, marking Boise's first mainline service. The depot is now listed in the National Register of Historic Buildings. It was built on a moderately sloping hillside of Capitol Boulevard with great landscaped lawns and flowerbeds. The central section consists of rock, a grotto, waterfalls, goldfish, lily ponds, benches, and walks. The depot is flanked on both sides with mature deciduous trees and a rose arbor.
Open: Daily, sunrise–sunset. (208) 345–4140.

Idaho State Capitol Grounds
8th and Jefferson Streets

The trees on the capitol grounds date from 1885 to the present. President Howard Taft planted the first tree in 1885, an Ohio Buckeye that was brought in by stagecoach. A water oak was planted by President Harrison in 1891.
Open: Daily, sunrise–sunset. (208) 344–7777.

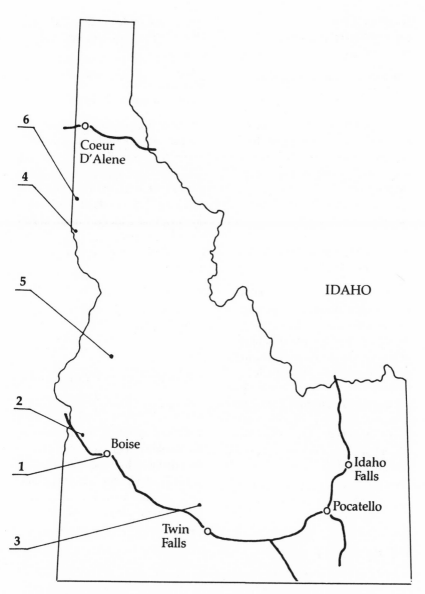

1. *Boise* **2.** *Caldwell* **3.** *Gooding* **4.** *Lewiston* **5.** *McCall* **6.** *Moscow*

Julia Davis Park
Between Capitol Boulevard
and Broadway

Established in 1902, the park is located along the Boise River with beautiful old trees, a picnic area, fireplaces, a rose garden, a zoo, and several old pioneer buildings. It now forms the first unit of the Boise Goldenbelt Plan which will connect several parks.
Open: Daily, sunrise–sunset. (208) 384–4240.

Veterans Memorial State Park
960 Veterans Way

Located at the Old Veterans Home, the Veterans Memorial is the first urban park to be established in Idaho. The grounds are landscaped with paths for the handicapped and wheelchair patients, and Braille markers for the blind. There are lakes for fishing and canoeing as well as many beautiful trees, shrubs, and flower beds planted by the Southwest District of the Idaho State Federation of Garden Clubs.
Open: Daily 9:00 a.m.–5:00 p.m. (208) 334–2812 or 334–3360.

2. Caldwell

Caldwell Rose Garden
700 North Illinois Street

This was begun as a small rose garden in 1920. Land was added by local business and civic organizations to enlarge the garden to its present size.
Open: Daily, sunrise–sunset. (208) 459–3641.

Memorial Park
South Kimball Avenue

This area was set aside to house the two cabins built by the Johnson brothers in 1864. The Johnson family was one of the first pioneer families in this part of Idaho. The cabins, which hold many relics of the past, are surrounded by the Memorial Park for public enjoyment.
Open: Daily, sunrise–sunset. (208) 454–8252.

3. Gooding

Fragrance Garden for the Blind
Gooding School for the Blind,
Main Street

The Gooding School for the Blind was established in 1908. The garden, designed by Mrs. Robson, is maintained with the help of the blind students. Braille markers identify each fragrant shrub or herb.
Open: School hours. (208) 934–4457.

4. Lewiston

Luna House
3rd and C Streets

Built in 1902 as a private residence, the house and grounds have been restored.
Open: Tuesday, Wednesday, Friday, 8:00 a.m.–5:00 p.m. (208) 743–2535.

5. McCall

Charlie's Gardens
Warren Wagon Road

Mostly the work of Mr. Charles Davidson, these gardens combine native plant materials with popular ornamentals.
Open: June 1–Labor Day. (208) 634–7631.

6. Moscow

Charles Huston Shattuck Arboretum
College of Forestry,
University of Idaho

The arboretum encompasses about 70 acres and has 200 species of trees, largely natives of the northern Rocky Mountains.
Open: Daily 8:00 a.m.–5:00 p.m. (208) 885–6280.

Plant Sciences Arboretum
University of Idaho Campus

The arboretum contains a fascinating set of gardens that show various kinds of evergreen shrubs, ground covers, flowering shrubs, annuals, perennials, and succulents. In addition, over 100 varieties of crab apple trees have been underplanted with peonies, spring bulbs, and iris.
Open: Daily 8:00 a.m.–5:00 p.m. (208) 885–6424.

Other Places of Interest

Anningham Arboretum, Boise
Bruneau Dunes State Park, south of
   Mountain Home
Coena d'Alene Indian Reservation,
   Plummer
Craters of the Moon National
   Monument, south of Arco, U.S.
   20–26
Heyburn State Park, St. Maries, U.S.
   95
Lucky Peak Nursery, U.S. Forest
   Service, Ogden
Morrison Memorial Park, Boise
Ross Park, Pocatello
Snake River, Idaho Falls
Sun Valley, Ketchum

Illinois

Area: 56,400 square miles

Population: 11,535,000

Statehood: December 3, 1818
(21st state)

The last Ice Age enveloped Illinois over a million years ago, smoothing its surface and depositing a thick layer of rich soil. The southern parts of the state were covered with hardwood forests when the French explorers Marquette and Joliet first arrived by way of the Mississippi River. Large parts of the central lowlands were covered with bluestem prairie grass, interrupted by trees along the water courses. In these great seas of grass grew multitudes of wildflowers. Along the Great Lakes were found some coniferous forests.

As part of France's Louisiana Territory, Illinois was sparsely settled. In 1787, it was included in the Northwest Territory of the United States by way of the Ohio River Valley. In 1825, the Erie Canal connected the Great Lakes with New York, bringing an influx of settlers from New England. The invention of the steel plow by John Deere in 1837 and McCormick's invention of the reaper led to a new form of agriculture in the state's fertile plains. Farm machinery production has long been an important industry.

Chicago, enjoying a favorable site at the intersection of the Great Lakes and Mississippi Valley transportation systems, grew rapidly to prominence. In 1893, the city hosted the Columbian Exposition. Photographs of the exposition's Great White Way inspired a movement throughout the country to make cities more beautiful. In the late nineteenth century, the Chicago School of Architecture led the world in the development of the skyscraper. Today, skyscrapers crowd the shore of Lake Michigan, giving the city an awesome skyline. The famous American architect, Frank Lloyd Wright, left the Chicago School to develop the architectural style of the Prairie School, which emphasized the character of the vast, flat prairie by the use of dominant horizontal lines. His first office and some of his early works were located in the Chicago suburb of Oak Park. The farseeing 1909 plan for Chicago by Daniel Burnham has guided the great city's orderly growth and has served as a model for many other communities.

Illinois has one national forest, Shawnee, at the southern end of the state. There are sixty-six state parks and twenty-four conservation areas. Mississippi Palisades State Park features wooded crags, strange rock formations, and Indian mounds. Here are found many of the wildflowers that once covered the state. New Salem State Park reconstructs the frontier town where Abraham Lincoln lived as a young man. The Mormon church has re-created the town of Nauvoo, where its people lived before their migration to Utah.

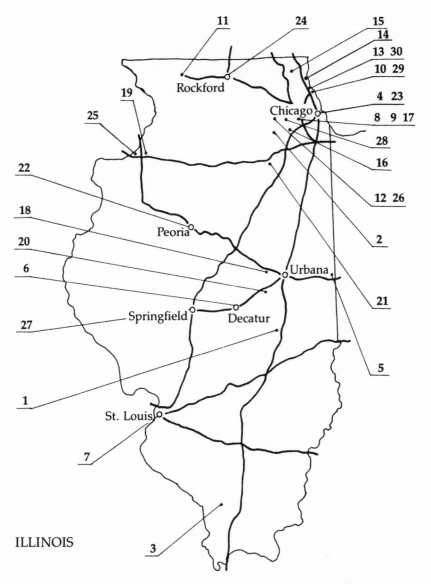

ILLINOIS

1. *Arcola* 2. *Aurora* 3. *Carbondale* 4. *Chicago* 5. *Danville* 6. *Decatur*
7. *East St. Louis* 8. *Elgin* 9. *Elmhurst* 10. *Evanston* 11. *Freeport*
12. *Geneva* 13. *Glencoe* 14. *Lake Forest* 15. *Libertyville* 16. *Lisle*
17. *Lombard* 18. *Mahomet* 19. *Moline* 20. *Monticello* 21. *Morris*
22. *Peoria* 23. *Riverside* 24. *Rockford* 25. *Rock Island* 26. *Saint Charles*
27. *Springfield* 28. *Wheaton* 29. *Wilmette* 30. *Winnetka*

An old barn in southern Illinois.

1. Arcola

Rockome Gardens
Route 2, 5 miles west of Arcola

This fantasy garden of rock sculpture and walks has formal and informal plantings, which include roses, herbs, and lily ponds.
Open: May 26–October 17, daily 10:00 a.m.–5:00 p.m.; May 1–25, Wednesday–Sunday. Fee. (217) 268–4216.

2. Aurora

Sensory Gardens in Pioneer Park
Barnes Road, off East-West Toll Road at Sugar Grove exit

These gardens were designed for people with impaired vision, although they are also enjoyed by the general public. The gardens lie in the middle of the 60-acre park, where a variety of demonstration plantings are planned.
Open: April–October, daily 9:00 a.m.–5:00 p.m. (312) 892–1550.

3. Carbondale

Southern Illinois University Outdoor Laboratory
University Campus

This university arboretum specializes in hollies.
Open: Daily, sunrise–sunset. (618) 453–3493.

4. Chicago

Chicago Park District

Chicago's network of large urban parks has a significant history. In

1871, the firm of Frederick Law Olmsted and Calvert Vaux completed a plan for the Chicago South Parks Commission from which Washington Park, Midway Plaisance, and Jackson Park were created; Jackson Park later was altered to become the site of the 1893 Columbian Exposition. In 1903, the South Parks Commission authorized Olmsted Brothers to develop plans for Grant Park and several smaller parks. By the time of Daniel Burnham's 1909 plan of Chicago, an extensive system of parks and boulevards had been established. Burnham identified the Grant Park landfill area, already the site of the Art Institute and the Field Museum of Natural History, as the "intellectual center" of the city, as well as its focal public garden. This aspect of Burnham's grand plan is evident today.

Another notable figure in the development of Chicago's parks was Danish-American landscape designer Jens Jensen (1860–1951). Hired in 1886 as a gardener in the Chicago West Parks, in 1906 he became landscape architect and superintendent for the entire Western Park system. During his 14 years in this post, he designed Garfield Park and Columbus Park, and began the natural open space belt now known as the Cook County Forest Preserves. Jensen is especially noted for his use of indigenous plant materials to achieve a Prairie School of landscape design, in which native plants symbolized rather than copied the natural prairie landscape. For additional information, write Chicago Convention and Tourism Bureau, McCormick Place, Chicago, Ill. 60616. (312) 567–8500.

Chicago River Garden
West Bank of the Chicago River, between Washington and Randolph Streets

Through the efforts of the Garden Club of Illinois, this derelict riverfront land was transformed into a lovely garden. Every day commuters can enjoy the view of this little spot of relief in the urban environment. *Open: Daily 10:00 a.m.–4:00 p.m.* *(312) 225–5000.*

Douglas Park
South of Ogden Avenue, east of Sacramento Boulevard

The formal garden at Douglas Park features the finest collection of hardy waterlilies in the Chicago area, as well as extensive beds of annuals. *Open: Daily, sunrise–sunset. (312) 521–3244.*

First National Bank Plaza
Dearborn and Monroe Streets

This plaza is a premier example of successful urban open space, both functional and exciting, located in the heart of Chicago's highest-density office sector. The multi-level plan, extending more than a full story below street level, provides shelter from Chicago's well-known winds, welcome greenery, and an informal amphitheater for lunchtime entertainment. On warm days, office workers of Chicago's Loop flock to the plaza for lunch and sunshine. The

depth of the plaza exaggerates the awesome view of surrounding shapes and opens on the soaring parabola of the First National Bank Building. The building and plaza were designed in 1969 by C. F. Murphy Associates and by the Perkins and Will partnership. Two important features of the plaza are the huge, two-sided mosaic "Four Seasons" by Marc Chagall (1974), situated on the upper level near Dearborn Street, and, on the lower level, the grand-scale granite pool and fountain of 400 jets designed by Samuel Hamel.
Open: Daily, 24 hours. (315) 732–6204.

☆
Garfield Park Conservatory
300 North Central Park Boulevard

This 4-acre conservatory is one of the finest in the world, with extensive collections and seasonal displays—notably azaleas and rhododendron in February. Garfield Park also contains outdoor formal gardens, pool gardens, and a Braille-labeled Garden for the Blind.
Open: Park and gardens, daily, except winter, daylight hours; conservatory, daily 9:00 a.m.–5:00 p.m., during flower shows until 9:00 p.m. (312) 533–1281.

Graceland Cemetery
1300 block of West Clark Street and 4000 block of North Irving Park Road

Dating from the 1860s, Graceland Cemetery is regarded as the masterwork of landscape architect-engineer Ossian C. Simonds, the only Chi-

cagoan to become a charter member of the American Society of Landscape Architects when it was founded in 1899. The cemetery continues to be a pleasant park for the living as well as the final resting place for many well-known residents of the city.
Open: Daily until 5:00 p.m. (312) 525–1105.

Grant Park
Lakefront between Randolph Street and 14th Boulevard

This large central-city park features Buckingham Fountain—a lakefront landmark since 1927, a fine rose garden, and other formal gardens. In the Court of the Presidents, at Congress Parkway, stands Saint-Gaudens's statue of Abraham Lincoln. Grant Park is the core of Chicago's famous lakefront: nearby are the Art Institute, the Field Museum of Natural History, Shedd Aquarium, and the Adler Planetarium.
Open: Park, daily, sunrise–sunset. (312) 294–2493 or 294–2420.

Humboldt Park
Division Street and Humboldt Drive

Humboldt Park was designed in 1892 by landscape architect Jens Jensen, who served as its superintendent until 1900. Unfortunately, Jensen's work here, as in Columbus Park (1918), has been neglected to the point where his subtle portrayal of nature is hardly discernible. The garden now features annuals and perennials in organized flower beds.
Open: Daily, sunrise–sunset. (312) 276–0107.

Jackson Park
59th Street and Stony Island Avenue

Jackson Park was the site of the 1893 Columbian Exposition. The design and planning effort for the exposition was led by Daniel Burnham; Frederick Law Olmsted was responsible for site design. The former Palace of Fine Arts building still stands, housing the Museum of Science and Industry. Nearby along the Midway, which stretches west toward Washington Park, are the Victorian Gothic buildings of the University of Chicago. A circular perennial dry-wall garden borders a large sunken lawn area in Jackson Park. There are also annual beds, bulbs, and an Oriental Garden.
Open: Daily, sunrise–sunset. (312) 643–6363.

☆
Lincoln Park
2400 North Stockton Drive

This park is spread out along the Lake Michigan shore on Chicago's Near North side. Within the park are 6 acres of outdoor gardens, including the main garden of formal flower beds, with a fountain by Saint-Gaudens; a rock garden; and a "Grandmother's Garden" of old-time flowering plants. The Lincoln Park Conservatory offers 5 glass buildings of palms, ferns, tropical plants, and seasonal shows, coinciding with those at Garfield Park. Chicago's Lincoln Park Zoo is located here.
Open: Outdoor gardens, daily, daylight hours; conservatory, daily 9:00 a.m.–

5:00 p.m., during flower shows until 9:00 p.m. (312) 294–4770.

Marquette Park
6700 South Kedzie Avenue

Marquette Park's Rose Garden, located in the southwestern corner, is notable for its large collection, as well as for its unusual naturalized border of shrub roses and old-fashioned varieties. To the west of the Rose Garden are trial gardens, where new varieties, annuals, and perennials are displayed in formal beds, as well as a rock garden and gardens of cactus and succulent plants, herbs, and topiary.
Open: Daily, sunrise–sunset. (312) 776–9879.

Richard J. Daley Center and Plaza
Randolph and Clark Streets

The high-rise building and plaza, formally called the Civic Center, were designed in 1964 by Jacques Brownson of C. F. Murphy Associates, with Skidmore, Owings and Merrill, and Loebl, Schlossman and Bennett Associates. The granite-paved plaza, covering an entire city block, is the site of official Chicago speeches and ceremonies. It is most famous, however, as the location of Pablo Picasso's huge birdlike steel sculpture, his gift to Chicago.
Open: Daily, 24 hours. (312) 294–4790.

Washington Park
Cottage Grove Avenue at 55th Street

Originally an Olmsted design, the park has undergone many changes.

Today it contains one of the city's largest flower displays, a formal arrangement of popular bedding plants.
Open: Daily, sunrise–sunset. (312) 294–2200.

5. Danville

Dr. Fifthian Herb Garden
Vermillion County Museum, 115 North Gilbert Street

This herb garden was planted in 1967 using a modified Williamsburg design to represent the original Fifthian Garden. The first medicinal garden and adjacent residence, now the County Museum, were constructed by Dr. William Fifthian, a Danville pioneer.
Open: Tuesday–Sunday 9:00 a.m.– 5:00 p.m.
Closed: Major holidays. (217) 442– 2922.

6. Decatur

Scoville Gardens Park
Country Club Road, south of U.S. 36

There is an Oriental garden in this park.
Open: June–August, Tuesday–Sunday. (217) 422–5911.

7. East St. Louis

Cahokia Mounds State Park
U.S. 40 (Business), 5 miles east

The site of this 740-acre park and archaeological preserve was once the regional center of Mississippian culture (a.d. 850–1500). Archaeological evidence has revealed the ceremonies and everyday activities of the most highly developed prehistoric Indian civilization north of Mexico. Designated a World Heritage Site by UNESCO.
Open: Daily 9:00 a.m.–5:00 p.m.
Closed: Holidays. (618) 344–5268.

8. Elgin

Elgin Botanical Garden,
Trout Park
Trout Park Boulevard

The 18-acre botanical garden is a unique, undisturbed native plant community adapted to alkaline conditions. Self-guided trails lead the visitor through this "living museum."
Open: Daily, sunrise–sunset. (312) 741–5660.

9. Elmhurst

Elmhurst Public Library, Wilder Park
Cottage Hill and Church Streets

The library occupies a former residence built in 1868. The original greenhouse and a newly planted sunken garden are on the grounds, which in the past displayed rare trees and rose and herb gardens.
Open: Daily 9:00 a.m.–5:00 p.m. (312) 279–8696.

10. Evanston

Dawes Garden
225 Greenwood Street, off Sheridan Road

The original nineteenth-century terraces, gardens, and lawns of the chateau-style home of former Vice-President Charles Dawes (1925–29) have been restored. The residence is now the Evanston Historical Society Museum.
Open: Daily except Wednesday and Sunday, 1:00–5:00 p.m. (312) 475–3410.

Ladd Arboretum
McCormick Boulevard between Emerson and Green Bay Roads

This 25-acre strip of land along the Skokie Canal has been planted with hardy shrubs and many spring-flowering trees. In addition to the naturalized area of prairie grasses and the bird sanctuary, there is an Ecology Center and the Rotary International Club's Friendship Garden.
Open: Monday–Friday 8:30 a.m.–5:00 p.m. (312) 264–5181.

Lighthouse Landing Park
2535 Sheridan Road

The park features a small garden, lakeshore nature trails, and a nature interpretive center and art gallery. This is also the site of Historic Grosse Point Lighthouse (1870), a fine swimming beach, and a lakefront mansion with grounds designed by Jens Jensen (1928).
Open: Garden, daily; best in summer. (312) 864–5181.

Merrick Park Rose Garden
Oak Street and Lake Avenue

This garden, containing 65 varieties of roses, was honored by the American Rose Society as the finest public rose garden in the five-state area. The historic Centennial Fountain is located here.
Open: Daily, sunrise–sunset. (312) 328–1500.

Shakespeare Garden
Northwestern University, Sheridan Road

Plants named in Shakespeare's works are displayed. The design is attributed to Jens Jensen.
Open: Daily, sunrise–sunset. (312) 492–7271.

11. Freeport

Bohemiana, Stephenson County Historical Museum
1440 South Carroll Avenue

The mansion was built in 1857. Many of the large old trees in the 4-acre arboretum were part of the original estate. Also on the grounds are a farm museum and an industrial museum.
Open: Friday–Sunday 1:30–5:00 p.m. Donation. (815) 232–8419.

12. Geneva

Japanese Garden
Fabyan's Forest Preserve, South Batavia Avenue

This garden was once a part of Colonel Fabyan's estate. Through his contacts with the Japanese government, a royal gardener was sent to design the Buddhist garden, which features an authentic teahouse, pools, and a curved bridge. First built in 1914, the garden has been restored.
Open: Daily 8:00 a.m.–9:00 p.m. (312) 232–6060.

13. Glencoe

☆
Chicago Botanic Garden
Take Eden's Expressway (I-94 North) from Chicago; exit Lake Cooke Road East, on Glencoe Road

This 300-acre complex for horticultural study is being developed on reclaimed marshlands—an excellent example of land reclamation. The landscape design was by John Simonds, the Education Center by architect Edward Larrabee Barnes. The gardens are new and very modern. Educational exhibits include demonstration gardens, nature trails, and a prairie restoration area. Also featured are a Japanese Garden, Sensory Garden, Rose Garden, Aquatic Garden, and Illinois Native Plant Garden. Tram ride tours.
Open: Daily 10:00 a.m.–sunset. Closed: Christmas. Parking fee. (312) 835–5440.

14. Lake Forest

Market Square
Downtown Lake Forest

The redevelopment of an early town business center uses European design elements to achieve a well-scaled center for this north suburban village. It was designed in 1916 by architect Howard Shaw (1869–1926) and planner Edward H. Bennett (1874–1954).
Open: Daily, 24 hours. (312) 234–4282.

15. Libertyville

Cook Memorial Park Rose Garden
North Milwaukee Avenue, downtown

A lovely rose garden is adjacent to the Cook Mansion.
Open: During the growing season; 24-hour lighting allows night viewing.
(312) 680–0750.

16. Lisle

☆
Morton Arboretum
Ill. 53 and East-West Tollway

This arboretum, covering 1,500 acres, was established in 1922. One of its purposes has been to collect woody plants from around the world and evaluate their suitability for landscape use in the Midwest. Thirty miles of trails loop through plant collections and naturalized areas. Features of special interest are flowering crab apples, lilacs (April–mid-May), an old-fashioned rose garden, a prairie restoration project, and a fragrance garden.
Open: Grounds, February–March, September–October 9:00 a.m.– 5:00 p.m.; April–August 9:00 a.m.– 6:00 p.m.; November–January 9:00 a.m.–4:00 p.m. Fee. (312) 968–0074.

17. Lombard

Lilac Park
120 West Maple Street

The park's exceptional lilac collection was bequeathed to the city in 1927 by the lilac connoisseur, Colonel William Plum. Today the park comprises 7.5 acres: 275 varieties of lilacs are represented. The city holds an annual lilac festival, usually during the first two weeks of May.
Open: Daily 9:00 a.m.–9:00 p.m. Fee during lilac time. (312) 627–1281.

18. Mahomet

Early American Museum and Botanical Garden
Lake of the Woods Forest Preserve

The 8-acre botanical garden surrounds lakes and waterfalls carved from native rock. Horticultural displays include a rose garden and arbor; there is also an area of virgin forest. Lake of the Woods is a Champaign County forest preserve of 500 acres, offering outdoor recreation, picnic areas, natural areas, and several garden displays.
Garden open: Daily 7:00 a.m.–sunset. (217) 586–3360. Museum hours vary, closed in winter. (217) 586–2612.

19. Moline

**Deere and Company
Administrative Center**
John Deere Road

This is one of the finest examples of the suburban campus office setting that has become commonplace since the early 1950s. The slender, delicately framed 8-story building (designed by Eero Saarinen and Associates in 1962) bridges a naturalized ravine overlooking two lakes.
Open: Office hours. No children under 12. (309) 752–8000.

20. Monticello

Robert Allerton Park
Ill. 47, 4 miles southwest
of Monticello

The former private estate, which was given to the University of Illinois in 1946, contains 1,500 acres of formal and natural grounds. The design of Allerton House and the park was influenced by late seventeenth-century English examples. Gardens near the house include walled perennial beds, a sunken garden, and a vast meadow. The Sangomon River flows through the natural forested areas. The grounds are open to the public.
Open: Daily 10:00 a.m.–sunset. (217) 762–2721.

21. Morris

Goose Lake Prairie State Park
Pine Bluff-Lorenzo Road

This state park in Grundy County contains 1,513 acres of dedicated Illinois nature preserve. It represents one of the last significant remnants of North American tall-grass prairie. The park's interpretative program emphasizes man's relation to the environment and natural resources from Indian and pioneer times to the present.
Open: Daily, sunrise–sunset. (815) 942–2899.

22. Peoria

**Glen Oak Park Conservatory
and Rose Garden**
Prospect and McClure Avenues

A formal garden with shrub borders adjoins the conservatory.
Open: Daily, sunrise–sunset; conservatory, weekdays 8:00 a.m.–4:00 p.m., weekends noon–4:00 p.m. (309) 685–4321.

**Pettengill–Morron House
Gardens**
1212 West Moss Avenue

The Second Empire house was built in 1868. The grounds have been landscaped in typical nineteenth-century American style. Special features include a fragrance garden, wildflower walk, and hosta garden.

Open: Sunday 2:00–5:00 p.m. and by appointment. Fee. (309) 674–1921.

23. Riverside

Village of Riverside
West of Ill. 43 (Harlen Avenue)
and U.S. 34 (Ogden Avenue)

This suburban village was created in 1868 according to a plan by Olmsted, Vaux and Company. Riverside, located on the Burlington Railroad, was the first planned commuter suburb; the town became a prototype of suburban town planning. The sylvan character of the original plan remains today: tree-lined parkways wind through residential areas, and park commons stretch along the banks of the Des Plaines River. Nearby is Chicago's Brookfield Zoo. This 200-acre mainstream zoological garden, established in 1934, was the first in America to use the barless system of animal enclosure throughout. The village development can be seen only from public areas; the homes are private.
Open: Zoo, daily 10:00 a.m.–5:00 p.m. Fee. (309) 485–2200.

24. Rockford

**Sunken Gardens,
Sinnissippi Park**
1300 North Second Street

The gardens feature flowering crab apples, roses, a lagoon, and a greenhouse.
*Open: Daily 9:00 a.m.–4:00 p.m.
(815) 987–8800.*

25. Rock Island

Hauberg Civic Center Grounds
1300 24th Street

These charming grounds, designed by Jens Jensen in 1909–11, exhibit wildflowers, a variety of trees, tulips, and roses.
Open: Daily, sunrise–sunset. (309) 788–6311.

26. Saint Charles

**Peterson–Durant House
Kitchen Garden**
Leroy Oakes Forest Preserve,
Dean Street

This authentic restoration of a pioneer garden features a typical kitchen garden as well as a small orchard and herb gardens.
Open: Daily. (312) 377–6161.

27. Springfield

Abraham Lincoln Memorial Garden and Nature Center
2301 East Lake Drive

The 80-acre garden includes more than 5 miles of nature trails, planted with native flowers, shrubs, and trees that Abraham Lincoln might have known as a boy growing up in the region. Designed by Jens Jensen in 1935.
Open: Daily, sunrise–sunset; Nature Center, Monday–Saturday 10:00 a.m.–4:00 p.m., Sunday 1:00–5:00 p.m. (217) 529–1111.

Abraham Lincoln Memorial Garden and Nature Center, Springfield, Ill.

Washington Park and Thomas Rees Memorial Carillon
Chatham Road and West Fayette Avenue

There are four seasonal gardens for year-round color, including a rose garden. A conservatory and greenhouse are located near the carillon, where summer concerts are given.
Open: Daily. (217) 544–1751 or 546–0684.

28. Wheaton

Illinois Prairie Path

The Prairie Path crosses DuPage County, extending from Elmhurst west to Wheaton, where it branches into two routes, joining the Fox River at Elgin and Aurora. The 40 miles of foot and bicycle paths were developed on an abandoned right-of-way of the Chicago, Aurora, and Elgin Railroad, where remnants of the tall prairie grasses still thrive year-round. Guided walks are offered. For information write Illinois Prairie Path, P.O. Box 1086, 616 Delles, Wheaton, Ill. 60197.

Robert R. McCormick Gardens
Catigny Estate, 151 Winfield Road

This 10-acre garden, part of the 500-acre estate, displays plants seldom used in the Chicago area, and includes demonstration plots. Once the property of *Chicago Tribune* publisher Colonel Robert McCormick, the residence is now a museum. In addition to other gardens, the grounds contain World War I memorial exhibits. *Open: Sunrise–sunset; house, from noon. (312) 668–5161.*

29. Wilmette

Baha'i Temple and Gardens
112 Linden Avenue

A 9-part formal garden surrounds the 9-sided house of worship, located on the shore of Lake Michigan. The gardens, bordered by evergreen hedges, feature seasonal displays of flowering trees, annuals, and perennials. The temple building itself is a magnificent structure, with intricately decorated surfaces and a circular dome spanning 90 feet. French-Canadian architect Louis J. Bourgeois (1856–1930) used many forms and styles to achieve a Near Eastern character.
Gardens open: Daily 10:00 a.m.–5:00 p.m. (312) 492–7271 or 256–4400.

30. Winnetka

Hadley School for the Blind Discovery Garden
700 Elm Street

The Discovery Garden was designed for all to enjoy, but special emphasis was placed on features appealing to the blind. There are handrails for guidance; a center island with raised beds for easy, tactile plant discoveries; and plants with unusual shapes, textures, and fragrances. A sculptured copper fountain attracts birds and creates sound.
Open by appointment through the Hadley School. (312) 446–8111.

Other Places of Interest

ArchiCenter, Chicago
Bishop Hill Swedish Colony State
 Historic Site, Bishop Hill
Carl Sandburg Birthplace, Galesburg
Cave-in Rock State Park
Chicago Portage National Historic
 Site, River Forest
Dickson Mounds State Museum
 (Indian Burial Grounds),
 Lewistown
Fort de Chartres State Historic Site,
 Prairie Du Rocher
Frank Lloyd Wright House and
 Studio, Oak Park
Illinois Beach State Park, Waukegan
Lincoln Home National Historic Site,
 Springfield
Lincoln Log Cabin State Park,
 Charleston
Lincoln's New Salem State Historic
 Site, New Salem
Mississippi Palisades State Park,
 Savanna
Nauvoo Mormon Settlement Historic
 Site, Nauvoo
Old State Capitol, Springfield
Starved Rock State Park, Utica
Ulysses S. Grant House, Galena
Vandalia Statehouse, Vandalia
White Pines Forest State Park, Dixon
Wildlife Prairie Park, Peoria

Indiana

Area: 36,291 square miles

Population: 5,499,000

Statehood: December 11, 1816
(19th state)

Indiana extends from the Great
Lakes, in the north, to the Ohio River
Valley, which forms its southern
border. A large part of the state is
occupied by the Central Lowlands, a
flat area of rich glacial soils. A series
of sand dunes arise along the Great
Lakes; part of this area is preserved
in the Indiana Dunes National Lakeshore. The land is hilly in the south
beyond the limits of the glaciers.
Here lies an interesting topography
of scenic knobs and deep valleys. In
areas underlaid with limestone are
found sinkholes, underground rivers,
caves, and springs. Before its settlement, most of the state was covered
by northern deciduous forest.

Early settlers to Indiana came by
way of the Ohio River. This waterway, and later the railroads, tied
the state to urban markets. Indiana
was the site of several experimental
Utopian communities. Robert Owen,
a Scottish industrialist, attempted to
found at New Harmony a community
offering a new model for industrial
society. Modern Indiana is a land of
great industrial productivity and rich
farmlands.

There is one national forest and
one national lakeshore in the state. At
Vincennes is found a national historic
monument to military hero George
Rogers Clark, and in Spencer County,
near Lincoln City, is located the
Lincoln Boyhood National Memorial.
Spring Mill State Park features a
reconstructed pioneer village; it also
has many caves displaying unusual
rock formations and rare blind fish.
Turkey Run State Park near Rockville
and McCormick's Creek State Park
near Spencer have beautiful rocky
glens.

Columbus possesses a dazzling
collection of contemporary buildings
designed by the country's most dis-
tinguished architects. Information
and directions are provided at the
Visitors' Center, 506 Fifth Street,
Columbus. (812) 372–1954.

1. Columbus

Irwin House and Gardens
608 5th Street

Landscape architect Henry Ayling
Phillips modeled these gardens after
the Tivoli Gardens in Italy. The
house—a Wendell Phillips design,
completed in 1910—is covered with
tapestry brick.
*Open: Weekends only; arrangements
made through the Visitors' Center.
(812) 372–1954.*

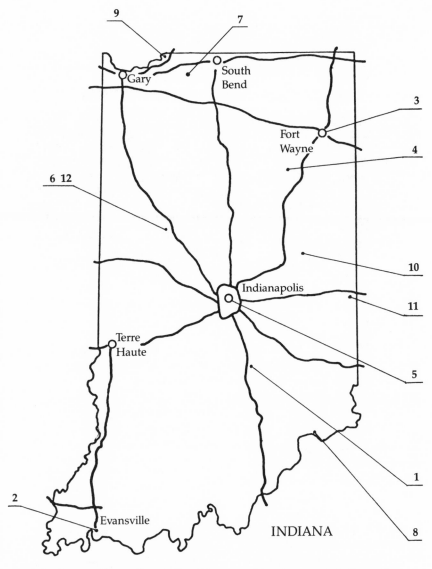

1. *Columbus*   2. *Evansville*   3. *Fort Wayne*   4. *Huntington*   5. *Indianapolis*
6. *Lafayette*   7. *La Porte*   8. *Madison*   9. *Michigan City*   10. *Muncie*
11. *Richmond*   12. *West Lafayette*

The Rappite hedge maze, New Harmony, Ind.

2. Evansville

New Harmony
Route 460 on the Wabash River,
27 miles west of Evansville

A National Historic Landmark, built
in 1814 by the Rappite Harmonists,
the site was sold in 1825 to Robert
Owen who developed it as an experiment in communal living. Ten
of the original 25 Harmonist homes
have been restored. New Harmony
contains the Paul Tillich Park and
the Roofless Church, which houses
Jacques Lipchitz's sculpture. There
is also an interesting Rappite hedge
maze (located on South Main Street).
Walking tours by appointment.
Atheneum Visitors' Center (at North
and Arthur Streets) open: May–

October 9:00 a.m.–4:30 p.m. Fee.
(812) 682–4474 or 682–4488 for winter
schedule.

Wesselman Park
551 North Boeke Road,
north of Division Street

Set aside within the city and designated a National Natural Landmark
are 200 acres of virgin hardwood forest. Some trees are 300–400 years
old. There is a nature center with
interpretive trails.
Open: Park, daily. Nature Center,
summer, Tuesday–Saturday
9:00 a.m.–5:00 p.m., Sunday noon–
4:00 p.m.; winter, Tuesday–Friday
9:00 a.m.–4:00 p.m., Saturday–
Sunday noon–4:00 p.m. (812)
479–0771.

3. Fort Wayne

Foelinger–Freimann Botanical Conservatory
1100 South Calhoun Street

Three separate display houses comprise this modern conservatory. A show house features frequent exhibitions; an arid house, desert plants of North America; and a tropical house, rare and exotic plants from around the world.
Open: Monday–Saturday 10:00 a.m.–4:30 p.m., Sunday 1:00–4:30 p.m. Closed: Major holidays. (219) 422–3696.

Foster Park
Broadway Avenue to Fairlan Street

An excellent iris collection is surrounded by peonies and lilacs.
Open: Sunrise–sunset. (219) 424–1435.

Lakeside Rose Garden
Lakeside Park, Lake Avenue

Over 5,000 rose plants are grown on 3.2 acres of formal sunken gardens. This is the largest rose garden in Indiana, and it is certified to display new rose varieties. June is the peak month for viewing the roses.
Open: Daily, sunrise–sunset. (219) 423–7346.

4. Huntington

Huntington College Botanical Garden and Arboretum
College Avenue

An educational and research center extends over 40 acres.
Open: Daily 9:00 a.m.–5:00 p.m. (219) 356–6000, ext. 142.

5. Indianapolis

Butler Botany Garden
Butler University,
4600 Sunset Avenue

Established in 1950, this 20-acre garden (also called the "Holcomb Garden") has 700 trees, many flowering shrubs, and bulbs. It is used to study the breeding and cultivation of plants.
Open: Daily 7:00 a.m.–sunset. (317) 283–8000.

Eagle Creek Park
7840 West 56th Street

This 4,000-acre education and recreation center is used extensively by the Indianapolis School System for native study.
Open: Park, daily, sunrise–sunset; Indian Heritage Museum, Monday–Friday 8:00 a.m.–5:00 p.m., Saturday–Sunday 11:00 a.m.–5:00 p.m. (317) 293–4827.

Garfield Park Conservatory and Sunken Gardens
2400 Shelby Street

Long famous for its beauty as a city park in southside Indianapolis, Garfield Park offers sunken gardens and well-tended floral arrangements in the greenhouses. Entertainment areas include fountains, an open-air theater, and acres of shady grasslands. *Open: Tuesday–Saturday 10:00 a.m.– 5:00 p.m., Sunday noon–5:00 p.m. Closed: Holidays. (317) 784–3044.*

Hillsdale Rose Garden
7800 North Shadeland Avenue

Reputed to be the largest rose garden in the Midwest, Hillsdale contains more than 20,000 plants of some 150 varieties. A rose festival is held during the second weekend of June. *Open: Daily 8:00 a.m.–dusk. (317) 849–2810.*

Holliday Park
6349 Spring Mill Road

This park includes a sculpture garden, an allée of trees with specimens marked for identification, and extensive seasonal flower gardens. *Open: Daily 7:00 a.m.–10:00 p.m. (317) 639–4282.*

Indianapolis Museum of Art
1200 West 38th Street

The 140-acre park around this museum contains a four-seasons garden. *Open: Tuesday–Sunday 11:00 a.m.– 5:00 p.m. Closed: Holidays. (317) 923–1331.*

Lockerbie Square
Bounded by Michigan, New York, College, and East Streets

This 20-acre residential area dating from the mid-1800s includes the home of James Whitcomb Riley. There are 6 acres of landscaped gardens. *Riley House open: Tuesday–Saturday 10:00 a.m.–4:00 p.m., Sunday noon–4:00 p.m. (317) 631–5885.*

6. Lafayette

Jerry E. Clegg Botanical Gardens
North of Ind. 25 to airport; right on County Road; north to 400 East

Nature trails and gardens on this 20-acre site offer an excellent opportunity to observe the beauty and diversity of native trees and wildflowers. A lookout point provides a panorama of miles of wooded hilltops, glacier-made ridges, and ravines along Wildcat Creek. *Open: Daily 10:00 a.m.–sunset. (317) 742–0325.*

7. La Porte

Hesston Monastic Gardens
10254 North 215 East

Father Joseph Sokolowski labored for 50 years to create this garden, which is most beautiful in May and June. Sunday Mass is held at 10:00 a.m. in

a tiny Greek Orthodox Chapel in the woods.
Open: May–October, sunrise–sunset. (219) 778–2421.

8. Madison

Broadway Fountain Park
Between Main and Third Streets

The very elaborate, 50-by-550-foot cast-iron fountain was manufactured by the James and Kirkland Company, which was in business around 1870. While on display at the Philadelphia Centennial in 1876, it was purchased, brought to Madison, and erected in this park.
Open: Sunrise–sunset. (812) 265–2956.

Dr. William Hutching's Medicinal Herb Garden
120 West Third Street

This medicinal herb garden, established in 1845, is a rare occurrence in the Midwest.
Open: May 1–November 1, Monday–Saturday 10:00 a.m.–4:30 p.m., Sunday 1:00–4:30 p.m. (812) 265–2967.

James F. Lanier House and Garden
511 West First Street

The grounds around the house, which cover two city blocks, were designed by Francis Costigan in 1840. They show a marked Italian influence. The garden is one of the only mid-

nineteenth-century gardens to use heated greenhouses for raising flowers and citrus fruits.
Open: Sunday–Tuesday 1:00–5:00 p.m., Wednesday–Saturday 9:00 a.m.–5:00 p.m. (812) 265–3526.

Shrewsbury House Garden
301 West First Street

Here is a fine example of the residential landscaping of the wealthy, mid-nineteenth-century homeowner. It displays original cast-iron fences and gates, a brick patio and walks, and is laid out into garden rooms. The garden contains a great wealth of plant materials.
Open: April–December, daily 10:00 a.m.–4:30 p.m.; January–March, by appointment. (812) 265–4481.

Sullivan House Garden
304 West Second Street

The Jeremiah Sullivan House and Gardens were constructed in 1818 and reflect the Federal style. The garden was one of the first domestic gardens established for a large house on the Ohio River. This was a period of rapid expansion and opulence generated by the steamboats just coming into large-scale use.
Open: May 1–November 1, Monday–Saturday 10:00 a.m.–4:30 p.m., Sunday 1:00–4:30 p.m. (812) 265–2967.

Talbott–Hyatt Pioneer Garden
First Street and Poplar Lane

This is one of the few pioneer gardens to be developed in the Midwest. It was constructed in 1820 and shows many of the plants that were popular in the early nineteenth century and some of the ways they were used.
Open: Daily, sunrise–sunset. (812) 265–2967.

9. Michigan City

International Friendship Garden
Pott Park, 1.5 miles east on U.S. 12 (turn right at Liberty Trail)

Dedicated to world peace and harmony, this garden is among Indiana's most beautiful attractions. Sixty-five distinct gardens blend into a natural setting of pines, wood, and marsh. Many of the floral specimens were donated by foreign countries and then planted to represent their individual garden styles.
Open: May 1–November 1, daily 9:00 a.m.–sunset. (219) 874–3664.

10. Muncie

☆
Ball State University Greenhouse
University Campus

This greenhouse contains the W. O. Wheeler Orchid Collection, the largest such floral exhibit on any campus.

Open: Monday–Friday 7:30 a.m.– 5:00 p.m., Saturday 9:00 a.m.– 3:00 p.m., Sunday 1:30–4:00 p.m. (317) 285–5341.

Christy Woods Arboretum
Riverside and Tillotson

Utilized by zoology and botany students as an outdoor laboratory, Christy Woods is also a pleasant place for a quiet walk. Along a self-guided trail through the woods, markers indicate the various species of trees.
Open: Monday–Friday 7:30 a.m.– 5:00 p.m. (317) 285–5341.

11. Richmond

Hayes Regional Arboretum
801 Elk Road

Over 140 woody plant species and native ferns are collected in this arboretum. Markers are conveniently placed along the path to identify the species. Colorful flora are displayed in the Nature Center.
*Open: Tuesday–Sunday 1:00– 5:00 p.m.
Closed: September 1–15. (317) 962–3745.*

12. West Lafayette

Horticultural Park,
West Woods Trail
Purdue University,
McCormick Road near State Street

The Horticultural Park exhibits a vast collection of ornamental plants, shrubs, and annuals, as well as a rose garden.
Open: Daily, sunrise–sunset. (317) 494–6191.

Other Places of Interest

Amish Acres, Nappanee
Brown County State Park, Nashville
Columbus (contemporary
   architectural town)
Conner Prairie Pioneer Settlement,
   Noblesville
Dunes National Lakeshore, Porter
   County
Fort Ouiatenon Historical Park, West
   Lafayette
Grassyforks Fisheries, Martinsville
Honeywell Gardens, Wabash
Indiana Dunes State Park, Chesterton
Limestone Quarries, Bedford
Mounds State Park, Anderson
Notre Dame University, South Bend
Tippecanoe Battlefield, Battle Ground
Victory Noll, Huntington
Whitewater State Park, Brookville
Wyandotte Caves, Corydon

Iowa

Area: 56,290 square miles

Population: 2,884,000

Statehood: December 28, 1846
(29th state)

Iowa is located in the Great Plains.
Over a million years ago much of
the land was leveled by glaciers,
which pulverized the existing rock
and deposited rich layers of soil.
The land's primary features are the
various glacial deposits and the cuts
of rivers through the thick layers
of subsoil. The last glacial period
bypassed the northeastern portion of
the state, leaving this area rugged and
hilly with quite a different landscape
character. The climate is continental:
very cold in winter, very warm in
summer. Rainfall averages 32 inches
per year. Over 90 percent of the
land's surface is in cultivation.

Before the state was settled by
Europeans, the major part consisted
of tall prairie grasses and marsh.
Trees grew only in the wet spots.
Iowa was acquired by the United
States through the Louisiana Purchase. Early settlers lived near
streams where they could obtain water and wood for fuel and shelter.
Only in the western part of the state
was the prairie sod used for housing. On the prairie, with its grasses
and marshes, lived the bison, around
which the Plains Indians built their
culture. First the Mississippi River
and its tributaries, then the railroads tied the rich agricultural land to
urban markets. Today Iowa remains
one of the nation's most productive
agricultural states.

Iowa's landscape is primarily an
agricultural one. It has evolved as
the form and methods of agriculture
have evolved, from small family
farms to larger commercial units.
There are eighty state parks and one
national historic monument, Effigy
Mounds. Here prehistoric Indians
built huge earth sculptures in the
shape of snakes, birds, bears, and
wolves.

1. Amana

Old-World Gardens

Although the town is primarily
known for its many artisans and
craftsmen, it is one of the few places
left in the United States where old-
world gardens are clustered around
quaint brick cottages.
*Open: Daily; some facilities only
April–November. (319) 622–3828.*

2. Ames

Iowa State University
Central Campus Farmhouse
Lincoln Way

Designed by landscape architect John
Olmsted, the campus features Lake
Laverne and many old trees dating

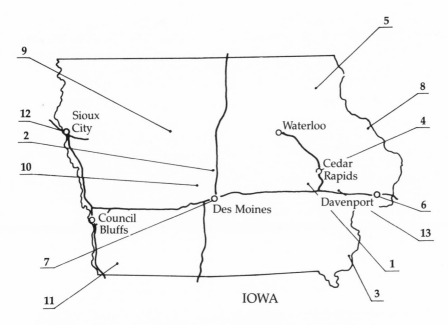

1. *Amana* 2. *Ames* 3. *Burlington* 4. *Cedar Rapids* 5. *Clermont*
6. *Davenport* 7. *Des Moines* 8. *Dubuque* 9. *Manson* 10. *Perry*
11. *Shenandoah* 12. *Sioux City* 13. *West Branch*

from the 1800s. The farmhouse, home of the university president, is a National Historic Landmark. There is a 2-acre horticulture garden. *Open: Daily, sunrise–sunset. (515) 294–2436.*

3. Burlington

Crapo Park
Great River Road,
southeastern end of Burlington

Established 70 years ago, the 172-acre park includes formal gardens and an arboretum of native trees. *Open: Daily, sunrise–sunset. (319) 753–8101 or 752–6942.*

4. Cedar Rapids

Hanging Bog Nature Conservancy
Northwest of Cedar Rapids
on a country road off Iowa 94

Red oak and basswood dominate this 16-acre natural area. Many cold springs are found on the site. A bog environment is formed on north-facing terraced slopes that remain waterlogged throughout the year. Because of the cold springs and bogs, this area is many degrees cooler than the surrounding uplands in the hot Iowa summer. This allows skunk cabbage, marsh marigold, and less common Iowa wildflowers to grow here. Jewelweed is found in the

area, and, after the frost kills many other forms of plant life, mosses and liverworts cover the ground.
Open: Sunrise–sunset. (515) 244–5044.

Shakespeare Garden
Ellis Park

This 1.4-acre site, developed in 1927 to honor William Shakespeare, features flowers and shrubs that are named in his plays. There is a bust of Shakespeare sculpted by the French artist Roubilac.
Open: Daily 8:00 a.m.–5:00 p.m.
(319) 364–2591.

5. Clermont

Montauk
U.S. 18, 0.5 miles north of Clermont

The two-story brick and limestone home of Iowa Governor Larabee (1886–90) is located on high bluffs overlooking the Turkey River. It is surrounded by 100,000 pines which the governor had planted over the 80-acre area. The original furnishings and art objects from around the world are on display. The grounds feature large statues of Civil War heroes.
Open: Daily 10:00 a.m.–5:00 p.m.
(319) 423–7173.

6. Davenport

Vander Veer Park
Lombard and Main Streets

Four major flower shows are held each year at the conservatory. The park offers a year-round display of tropical and subtropical plants and cacti. There are also very fine rose gardens containing 2,500 plants.
Open: Daily, sunrise–sunset;
conservatory, daily 9:00 a.m.–
5:00 p.m. (319) 326–7812.

7. Des Moines

☆
Arie den Boer Arboretum
1003 Locust Street
(Fleur Drive entrance)

Located in a city park of 150 acres, the 20-acre arboretum exhibits over 300 varieties of flowering crab apples collected by Mr. A. F. den Boer.
Open: Dawn–dusk. (515) 283–8791.

☆
Des Moines Botanical Center
909 East River Drive, off I-235

A 150-foot geodesic dome displays 15,000 tropical plants. There are bonsai trees and an herb garden outside.
Open: Daily 10:00 a.m.–6:00 p.m.,
Friday until 9:00 p.m.
Closed: Thanksgiving, Christmas, New Year's Day. Fee. (515) 283–4148.

Des Moines Center of Science and Industry

Greenwood Park, 4500 Grand Avenue

The grounds are the work of the eminent modern landscape architect Thomas Church. The Art Collection Building is by architect Eero Saarinen.

Open: Daily, grounds, sunrise–sunset; building, 10:00 a.m.–5:00 p.m. (515) 274–4138.

Ewing Park Lilac Arboretum

5100 Southeast Indianola Drive

This arboretum is particularly noted for its collection of some 200 varieties of French lilacs. A children's forest contains 4,000 trees native to Iowa. And an 11-acre area is devoted to wildflower trails, with a large weeping willow tree planted in tribute to Mrs. Yamamota, a famous floral designer.

Open: Daily 8:00 a.m.–sunset. (515) 283–4227.

Formal Rose Garden, Greenwood Park

48th and Grand Avenue

Designed in 1931, the garden displays over 3,100 varieties of roses and is one of the 24 trial gardens recognized by the National Rose Society.

Open: Daily, sunrise–sunset. (515) 286–4971.

Terrace Hill

2300 Grand Avenue

Built in 1869, this great mansion is considered one of America's finest remaining examples of Victorian architecture. The restored grounds include a native forest, flower gardens, pools, and fountains.

Open: Grounds, all times; house, Monday–Thursday. House closed: January–February, holidays. (515) 281–3604.

Union Park

East Ninth Street and Saylor Road

Union Park is noted for its annuals. During the late spring and early summer, marigolds, petunias, snapdragons, and other annuals flourish in the formal gardens. The park is situated on a high promontory overlooking the Des Moines River.

Open: Daily, sunrise–sunset. (515) 283–4111.

8. Dubuque

Madison Street Steps

These remarkable steps were built in the early 1900s to serve as a pedestrian link between the downtown and the residential areas on the bluffs above. They demonstrate that movement in the vertical dimension can be a joyful experience. Their restoration won a special award for excellence from the American Society of Landscape Architects.

Open: All times. (319) 557–9200.

9. Manson

Kaslow Prairie
1 mile west and 4.5 miles
north of Manson

This 160-acre area has a varied
topography and is an example of
native prairie that has been set aside
for its botanical interest. A total of
230 species of plant life have been
identified. A particularly large selection of native wildflowers adds color
to the prairie scene.
Open: Sunrise–sunset. (712) 469–3880.

10. Perry

Victor Fagan Wildflower Preserve
Iowa 141

The preserve contains 2 acres of
wildflowers and trails.
*Open: Daily, spring only. (515)
465–4601.*

11. Shenandoah

Earl May Trial Gardens
North Elm Street

These gardens, which form part of
a commercial nursery, display more
than 200 different types of flowers
and plants in season.
*Open: Weekdays 9:00 a.m.–5:00 p.m.
Tours by appointment. (712) 246–
1020.*

12. Sioux City

Grandview Park
24th and Douglas Streets

The park features rose gardens with
3,000 plants of 300 varieties. Concerts and civic gatherings are held
here.
*Open: Daily, sunrise–sunset. (712)
255–7903.*

13. West Branch

Herbert Hoover National Historic Site
Parkside Drive off I-80

Located within a 33-acre park are the
Herbert Hoover Presidential Library
and Museum, and the Hoover Birthplace, which was restored in 1938 to
its original appearance. These and
other points of interest are maintained by the National Park Service.
*Open: Daily 9:00 a.m.–6:00 p.m.
Closed: Major holidays. (319) 643–
2541.*

Other Places of Interest

De Soto National Wildlife Refuge,
   Missouri Valley
Eagle Point Park, Dubuque
Effigy Mounds National Monument,
   Marquette
Heritage Village, Des Moines
Living History Farm, Des Moines
Maquoketa Caves, Maquoketa
Nelson Pioneer Farm, Oskaloosa
Pella Historical Village, Pella

Kansas

Area: 82,264 square miles

Population: 2,450,000

Statehood: January 29, 1861
(34th state)

Kansas is located on the Great Plains at the very center of the nation. Its highest elevation is 4,000 feet above sea level in the northwestern corner. The land slopes gradually down to the south and east. Rainfall diminishes from the eastern part of the state, where it averages 40 inches per year, to the west, where the average is 15 inches. The inland continental climate is severe, and the constant wind causes a soil conservation problem. In the eastern part of the state, bluestem prairie grass is the natural vegetation. Trees are found along water courses. In the drier west, short stem grasses dominate. Bison grazing on the prairie grasses were once very numerous. The Indians used the bison for food, clothing, tools, and lodging. In the late nineteenth century, settlers nearly exterminated the species. Some hunters would kill as many as 1,000 a day.

The opening of Kansas for settlement in 1854 caused a national conflict over the issue of slavery. Violent clashes occurred between free-state and slave-state factions. The early settlers came to the state by overland trails; the Santa Fe and Oregon trails both passed through Kansas. At this time, the shipment of freight by wagon was very expensive. With the railroad's arrival in the 1870s, bulky agricultural produce could be shipped to urban markets at a much lower cost. To encourage their efforts, the federal government granted the railroad companies large tracts of land. In addition, Kansas was divided into square sections and sold to settlers. Roads followed these section lines and created a grid pattern on the land that persists to this day.

Kansas is one of the nation's great wheat-producing states. An important influence on the modern landscape has been an effective program of water control to prevent runoff and flooding and save water for irrigation. A number of large lakes of recreational value have been created by these projects.

The Museum of Kansas State History in Topeka features relics of Indian culture and frontier life. Numerous state parks recall the historic days of the Old West.

1. Abilene

Eisenhower Museum Home
201 Southeast 4th Street

This site is noted for its tulip beds. There are 75,000 plants and 1,000 rose bushes.
Open: Daily 9:00 a.m.–5:00 p.m. Closed: Major holidays. Fee. (913) 263–4751.

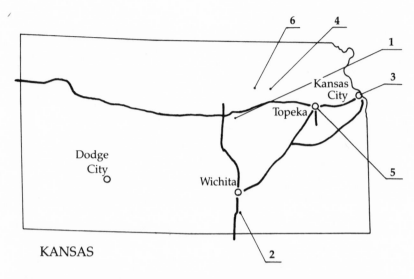

KANSAS

1. *Abilene* 2. *Belle Plaine* 3. *Kansas City* 4. *Manhattan* 5. *Topeka*
6. *Wakefield*

2. Belle Plaine

☆
Bartlett Arboretum
Kans. 55 and Line Street,
2.5 miles east of U.S. 81

Founded in 1910, this is the "only
mature arboretum between the Mississippi River and the Rocky Mountains." The 20-acre site is well maintained with many flowering bulbs
and annuals, especially tulips, and
includes virtually every variety of
tree and shrub that grows in Kansas.
*Open: April 1–November 30, daily
9:00 a.m.–6:00 p.m. Fee. (916)
488–3451.*

3. Kansas City

Municipal Rose Garden
Huron Park, adjacent to library between 6th and 7th on Ann Avenue

The garden was planted in 1936 by
the Works Progress Administration
to improve the downtown district.
The well-planned project includes
2,500 roses and a test garden.
*Open: Daily, sunrise–sunset. (913)
321–5800.*

Konza Prairie Research Center, I-70, between Exits 307 and 313, Kans.

4. Manhattan

Konza Prairie Research Center
I-70 east toward Topeka
between exits 307 and 313

Located here are 8,616 acres of tall grass prairie. This section of the true grass prairie, maintained by Kansas State University, is becoming more rare each year.
Open: Tours by appointment. (913) 532–6415.

University Gardens
Kansas State University, 17th and Anderson Streets

Each of five gardens is designed to display plants suitable to the Kansas climate.
Open: May–October, daily, sunrise–sunset. (913) 532–6415.

5. Topeka

Gage Park Tropical Rain Forest and Conservatory
Gage Park, 4320 West 10th Street (enter at 6th and Gage)

The rain forest is maintained at a constant temperature and features appropriate plantings. Winter is a good time to see the tropical jungle collections, because the conservatory is crowded with the 4,000 annuals that are started here for later spring planting in the city parks.
Open: Daily 10:00 a.m.–4:30 p.m. Fee. (913) 272–5821.

Indian Hill Arboretum
Menninger Foundation,
6500 West 6th Street

This arboretum features a group of woody trees and shrubs, oaks, pines, junipers, and lilacs that are used for therapeutic purposes.
Open: By invitation only to qualified

Reinisch Rose Garden, Gage Park, Topeka, Kans.

persons; write: P.O. Box 829, Topeka,
Kans. 66601. (913) 273–7500.

**Meade Park Gardens
and Arboretum**
124 North Filmore Gardens

The peak display is in early April and
May, when the lesser known woody
plants (500 kinds) bloom. Near the
arboretum are formal gardens and
fountains—a part of the landscaping
for Meade Mansion, which serves as
the garden center.
*Open: Garden center, Monday–Friday
10:00 a.m.–4:00 p.m; arboretum and
garden, daily 8:00 a.m.–11:00 p.m.,
Saturday–Sunday 1:00–4:00 p.m.
(913) 235–0806.*

Reinisch Rose Garden
Gage Park

Planted in 1930, the 3-acre rose garden contains 7,000 plants of 400
varieties, including a rose test garden.
Adjacent to the rose garden on the
west is the Doran Park Garden, which
displays 3,000 plants and shrubs
suited to the local environment.
*Open: Daily, sunrise–sunset. (913)
272–6171.*

6. Wakefield

Kansas Landscape Arboretum
Dogwood Street

The arboretum was established in 1972 on a plot of 193 acres. Besides the 140 varieties of trees and shrubs native to Kansas, this facility displays many exotics.
Open: March 1–November 1, 8:00 a.m.–dusk. Tours by appointment. (913) 263–2540.

Other Places of Interest

Fort Larned National Historic Site, Larned
Frontier Historical Park, Hays
Gypsum Hills, Medicine Lodge
Pawnee Indian Village Museum, Republic
Quivira National Wildlife Refuge, Great Bend
Scott County State Park, Scott City
Sedgewick County Zoo, Wichita
Tulip Festival, Pella (early May)

Kentucky

Area: 40,395 square miles

Population: 3,726,000

Statehood: June 1, 1792 (15th state)

Kentucky is called the "Bluegrass State." The Bluegrass is a region of fertile soils overlying disintegrated limestone bedrock. These soils owe their fertility to the high amounts of nitrogen and phosphorus they contain. The Bluegrass is known for its racehorses, tobacco, and bourbon.

The eastern part of Kentucky is occupied by the Cumberland Plateau. The highest peak in the state is Big Black Mountain in Harlan County, standing 4,150 feet above sea level. Long isolated by the mountains, the people of eastern Kentucky, a coal-mining region, have developed their own culture. Cultural institutions of interest here include Berea College and Pine Mountain Settlement School.

The Pennyroyal Plateau of central Kentucky is an unusual geologic area. It sits atop limestone bedrock. The rock is so porous that rainwater infiltrates the ground very rapidly, and rivers flow underground. Mammoth Cave National Park is located in this region. The name "Pennyroyal" comes from a small aromatic plant indigenous to the plateau.

Daniel Boone was an early visitor to "Kaintucke." He came first as a hunter, later as the leader of a party of settlers. These early adventurers from Virginia and North Carolina crossed the Appalachians at the Cumberland Gap. Sons of Virginia planters established estates in the fertile Bluegrass. Hemp, tobacco, whiskey, and flour were early cash products. Before the railroad arrived in 1830, produce from this area had to be shipped downriver to New Orleans in order to reach urban markets. Today tobacco is the state's leading crop.

There are two National Historic Sites in Kentucky: Cumberland Gap and Abraham Lincoln's Birthplace. Daniel Boone National Forest features beautiful natural scenery. An American Land Trust Project, "Pilot Knob," is located several miles from Natural Bridge State Park. Daniel Boone had his first overlook of Kentucky from this vantage point. There are many other historic points of interest and lovely old homes to be discovered in Kentucky.

1. Bardstown

My Old Kentucky Home State Park
U.S. 150 (Springfield Road)

This is the home that Stephen Foster memorialized in song. The gardens are quite extensive and filled with old-fashioned flowers. Iris and tulips bloom in April and May, roses in June and throughout the summer. *Open: Daily, June–August 9:00 a.m.– 6:00 p.m., September–May*

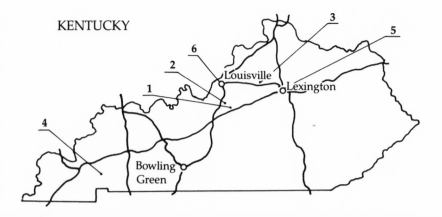

KENTUCKY

1. *Bardstown*   2. *Clermont*   3. *Frankfort*   4. *Golden Pond*   5. *Lexington*
6. *Louisville*

*9:00 a.m.–5:00 p.m. Fee. (502)
348-3502.*

2. Clermont

☆
Bernheim Forest Arboretum
Ky. 245, 14 miles west of Bardstown

This 10,000-acre forest preserve
of indigenous plant materials has a
nature center and museum. The arboretum comprises 250 acres of plants
labeled for identification. There are
also collections of heathers, shrubs,
flowering trees, and hollies, as well as
several small garden research projects
developed in cooperation with the
University of Kentucky.
*Open: March 15–November 15, daily
9:00 a.m.–1 hour before sunset. (502)
543-2451.*

3. Frankfort

Liberty Hall
West Main and Wilkinson Streets

The eighteenth-century garden is
noted for its fine boxwoods and collection of old roses. Restoration was
done by the Garden Club of Kentucky
in the 1930s.
*Open: March–December, Tuesday–
Saturday 10:00 a.m.–4:00 p.m.,
Sunday 2:00–4:00 p.m. Fee. (502)
227-2560.*

4. Golden Pond

**Tennessee Valley Environmental
Education Center**
Land Between the Lakes, U.S. 68
between Hopkinsville and Paducah

The center consists of 5,000 acres of
woodlands and native plants main-

tained by the Tennessee Valley Authority. It features primarily educational projects, with programs for youth and for the handicapped. There are also reforestation projects and nature trails.
Open: March–November, daily 9:00 a.m.–5:00 p.m.; some facilities close December–February. (502) 924–5602, ext. 238.

5. Lexington

Ashland
Richmond Road at Sycamore Road

Ashland was the estate of Henry Clay. Designed by Benjamin Latrobe and Pierre L'Enfant in 1805, it was reconstructed in 1856 using the original floor plans. The house is bordered by a formal garden which was restored by the Garden Club of Lexington.
Open: May–October, Monday–Saturday 9:30 a.m.–4:30 p.m., Sunday 1:00–4:30 p.m.; November–April, Monday–Saturday 10:00 a.m.–4:00 p.m., Sunday 1:00–4:00 p.m. Fee. (606) 266–8581.

Hunt–Morgan House
201 North Mill Street

This Georgian house has a small city garden of historical interest.
Open: February–December, Tuesday–Saturday 10:00 a.m.–4:00 p.m., Sunday 2:00–5:00 p.m. Fee. (606) 253–0362.

☆
Lexington Cemetery
833 West Main Street

This is reputed to be one of the most attractive cemeteries in the United States because of its parklike appearance. Established in 1849, it features a wide variety of unusual plant materials as well as rose, dahlia, and chrysanthemum gardens.
Open: Daily 8:00 a.m.–5:00 p.m. (606) 255–5522.

6. Louisville

Cave Hill Cemetery
East end of Broadway Street

The cemetery is used as an arboretum for the Louisville area. Specimen plants include American basswood, pink horse chestnuts, and golden chain trees.
Open: Daily 8:00 a.m.–4:45 p.m. (502) 452–1121.

Farmington
3033 Bardstown Road

Built in 1810 by John Speed to a design by Thomas Jefferson, the house and 14 acres of grounds have been restored. One of the gardens features plant materials used before 1820.
Open: Monday–Saturday 10:00 a.m.–4:30 p.m., Sunday 1:30–4:30 p.m. Closed: Some holidays. Fee. (502) 452–9920.

Locust Grove

561 Blankenbaker Lane

The 1790 structure is regarded as one of the finest Georgian houses in Kentucky. Restored gardens on the 55-acre estate are appropriate to the period.
Open: Daily 10:00 a.m.–4:30 p.m., Sunday 1:30–4:30 p.m.
Closed: Major holidays. Fee. (502) 897–9845.

Other Places of Interest

Abraham Lincoln Birthplace National Historic Site, Hodgenville
Hobson Mansion, Bowling Green
Homeplace 1850, Golden Pond
Mammoth Cave National Park, Mammoth Cave
Natural Bridge State Resort Park, Slade
Shaker Village, Pleasant Hill (Lexington)

Louisiana

Area: 44,521 square miles

Population: 4,481,000

Statehood: April 30, 1812 (18th state)

Louisiana occupies both sides of the lower Mississippi to the mouth. Its principal city, New Orleans, is the nation's second port in international trade. The farmlands of Louisiana benefit from rich alluvial soils deposited by the Mississippi and other rivers. The northern part of the state is occupied by low, pine-covered hills. Here, the land rises to its highest elevation, 535 feet above sea level. Coastal marshes extend south from New Orleans to the Gulf of Mexico. New Orleans itself lies below the mean river level. When it rains, storm drainage must be pumped up from the city's sewers into Lake Pontchartrain. Flood control is a serious problem along the Mississippi. The vast flood control system consists of sluices and spillways.

Louisiana's climate is mild in winter, hot and stormy in summer. In the fall, hurricanes are a major threat. Southern floodplain forests originally covered the rich alluvial soils along the river. Today, rice, soybeans, and sugar are important crops. In the low marshlands are prairies displaying many beautiful and unusual plants, including iris, lilies, and hibiscus.

La Salle planted the French flag at the mouth of the Mississippi in 1682.

With this act, he claimed the entire midsection of the continent that was drained by its waters. Later, the colony passed to Spanish hands. At the time of the American Revolution, New Orleans was a flourishing city with a population of 3,000. Its Latin culture has given New Orleans a unique style of architecture and gardening, cuisine, and language, and, of course, Mardi Gras. The Louisiana Territory was purchased by the United States in 1803. Industry and mining are fast-growing sectors of the state's present economy, with rich oil and gas reserves along the Gulf Coast. The expanding economy has brought new wealth, but threatens many cultural traditions.

New Orleans is a fascinating and cosmopolitan city. Not to be missed are the Vieux Carré (French Quarter) where the French and Spanish styles of urban gardening are most apparent. A good way to see the Garden District, an area settled by the Anglo-Americans, is to take a ride on the St. Charles Avenue streetcar.

New Orleans was the birthplace of jazz. At Preservation Hall, one can hear many great old jazzmen in an informal setting. St. Louis Cathedral, built in 1794, and St. Louis Cemetery are unique in this country. The Piazza d'Italia is a stylish modern urban square designed by the eminent architect Charles Moore. Throughout Louisiana are old plantations of interest. At Oakley, in Audubon Memorial State Park, the naturalist John James Audubon worked as a tutor and painted many of his wonderful representations of birds.

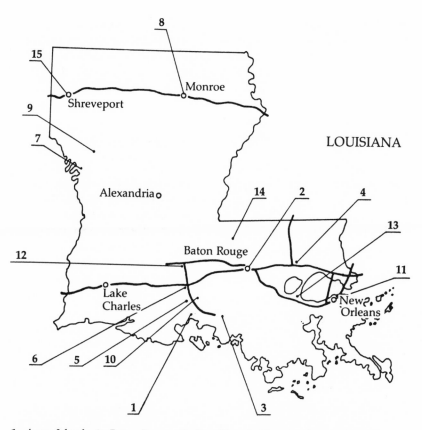

1. *Avery Island*   2. *Baton Rouge*   3. *Franklin*   4. *Hammond*   5. *Jefferson Island*   6. *Lafayette*   7. *Many*   8. *Monroe*   9. *Natchitoches*   10. *New Iberia* 11. *New Orleans*   12. *Opelousas*   13. *Reserve*   14. *Saint Francisville* 15. *Shreveport*

Louisiana is a low, flat land. Flood control problems have had a significant impact on the forms of settlement and land use. The visitor should be sensitive to water as an essential element in this landscape.

1. Avery Island

☆

Jungle Gardens
La. 329, 8 miles southwest
of New Iberia

Located on a salt dome, the gardens of the McIlhenny estate feature extremely rich collections of azaleas

and camellias. There are many rare and exotic specimens from around the world. The iris are spectacular from March to the end of April. Also of great interest is the bird sanctuary established in 1892 to protect the egret. In spring, the lookout platform affords—at dusk—a wonderful view of the egrets returning to nest.
Open: Daily 9:00 a.m.–5:00 p.m. (318) 365–8173.

2. Baton Rouge

Burden Research Plantation
Intersection of Essen Lane and I-10

This area is dedicated to horticultural, agronomic, wildlife, and landscape design research. In spring, during the height of their blooms, two ornamental gardens are open to the public: the Rose Test Garden and the Louisiana State University Annuals Garden. Also of interest is the Rural Life Museum.
Open: Monday–Friday 8:30 a.m.– 4:00 p.m. Fee. (504) 766–8241.

Cohn Memorial Arboretum
12056 Foster Road,
just off Comite Drive

Wide, paved walkways meander through this 16-acre tract of rolling terrain which is covered by more than 200 varieties of trees and shrubs, each labeled for identification. There is a greenhouse for propagation and exhibits of rare and exotic species.
Open: Monday–Friday 8:00 a.m.–

5:00 p.m., Saturday–Sunday 9:00 a.m.–5:00 p.m. (504) 775–1006.

3. Franklin

Arlington Plantation
56 East Main Street

On the banks of Bayou Teche, this stately Greek Revival mansion (ca. 1840) is surrounded by moss-covered live oaks. There are both formal and informal garden areas.
Open: Tuesday–Saturday 10:00 a.m.– 4:00 p.m. Fee. (318) 828–2644.

Oak Lawn Manor
10 miles west on U.S. 90, to Irish Bond Road; then 4 miles

This antebellum home, built in 1837, is surrounded by a large grove of live oaks and lovely gardens.
Open: Tuesday–Sunday 10:00 a.m.– 4:00 p.m.
Closed: Thanksgiving, Christmas, New Year's Day. Fee. (318) 828–0434.

4. Hammond

Zemmurray Gardens
La. 40, northeast of Hammond

A rich variety of foliage plants and perennials give this 150-acre garden year-round interest. The most exciting seasons are late winter and early spring when the camellias and azaleas blossom.

Open: March–July, 10:00 a.m.–
6:00 p.m. Fee. (504) 878–6731.

5. Jefferson Island

Live Oak Garden
Jefferson Island on La. 675,
7 miles southwest of New Iberia

Situated in the heart of Acadia is
a beautifully landscaped botanical
garden in a subtropical setting. It is
carved out of a moss-draped woodland on the rolling hillsides bordering
Lake Peigneur. Leading up to the historical home of George Jefferson is
a 2-mile allée of live oaks. The gardens around the home were designed
in the English tradition. A series
of colorful small gardens are joined
together by winding paths through
tropical vegetation.
Open: Daily 9:00 a.m.–6:00 p.m.
Closed: Holidays. Fee. (318) 367–3485.

6. Lafayette

University of Southwestern
Louisiana Horticulture Center
2206 Johnston Street

At this site is an outstanding horticultural library with many first
editions. The center contains tropical
botanical gardens, an orchid collection, and an experimental garden

of unusual flowers. A collection of
Louisiana flora is on file.
Open: Monday–Friday 8:00 a.m.–
5:00 p.m. (318) 231–6064.

7. Many

Hodges Gardens
U.S. 171, 12 miles south of Many

This 4,700-acre garden was constructed in an abandoned rock quarry
as a reforestation project by A. J.
Hodges. In addition to the thousands
of acres of pines that were planted
to establish a forest, 500 acres were
cultivated with flowers and shrubs,
creating a "garden in the forest."
This lovely garden is especially noteworthy for its design, which uses
existing natural features to aesthetic
advantage.
Open: Daily 8:00 a.m.–sunset. Fee.
(318) 586–3523.

8. Monroe

ELsong Garden
2006 Riverside Drive

Part of the Emmy-Lou Biedenharn
Foundation complex contains formal
English gardens, an Italian Garden,
and a Water Garden, created in 1947.
A Walled Garden was designed espe-
cially for small musical events.
Open: Tuesday–Friday 10:00 a.m.–

4:00 p.m., Saturday–Sunday
2:00–5:00 p.m.
Closed: Holidays. (318) 387–5281.

**Louisiana Purchase
Gardens and Zoo**
Standifer and Wilson Streets

Located in the Mississippi Delta,
where the soil is rich and deep, the
grounds surrounding the zoo are
lush and abundant with plant life.
Encompassing 100 acres, the park
is a picturesque setting for formal
gardens, huge oak trees covered with
Spanish moss, natural scenic areas,
and winding waterways. Also of
interest are the many rare animals
present.
Open: Daily 10:00 a.m.–5:00 p.m.
(318) 329–2400.

9. Natchitoches

Beau Fort Plantation
10 miles south via La. 1 and 119
(Bermuda)

This Creole-style cottage (ca. 1790) is
at the head of an avenue of live oaks.
The house was restored in 1948 and
the plantation-style gardens are now
in beautiful condition.
Open: Daily 1:00–4:00 p.m.
Closed: Holidays. Fee. (318) 352–2106.

Lemee House
310 Jefferson Street

This colonial house, built in 1840,
has a fine restored garden.
Open: By appointment. (318) 352–
8072.

10. New Iberia

Justine
Highway 86, 2 miles east
of New Iberia

Furnished in early Victorian style,
Justine was built in 1822, then added
to in 1848 and again in the 1890s.
Purchased by Aleen Veutter in 1965,
it was floated 54 miles up Bayou
Teche on two barges and completely
restored.
Open: By appointment only for tour of
house and garden. (318) 364–0973.

Shadows-on-the-Teche
117 East Main Street

The Shadows calls to mind plantation days before the Civil War. The
grounds reflect the Weeks family's
fascination with gardening. Mrs.
Weeks collected and exchanged cut-
tings with people as far away as
Philadelphia and Charleston in order
to create a lush setting for her home.
Later, Weeks Hall made changes
that significantly reduced the maintenance required; his landscape is
the one visitors see today. Owned
by the National Trust for Historic
Preservation.
Open: Daily 9:30 a.m.–4:30 p.m.
Closed: Thanksgiving, Christmas, New
Year's Day. Fee. (318) 369–6446.

11. New Orleans

Beauregard–Keyes House
1113 Chartres Street

This 1826 home features a French parterre and herb garden reconstructed from the 1830s. *Open: Monday–Saturday 10:00 a.m.–3:00 p.m. Donation. (504) 523–7257.*

☆
City Park
Lelong and City Park Avenues

In 1850 the land for this park was left to the city of New Orleans by John McDonough, who asked in return only that "the little children shall sometimes come and plant a few flowers about my grave." The 1,500-acre park has been beautifully developed with a huge floral clock, rose gardens, camellia garden, an azalea garden, boating lagoons, a casino, and an 1890 carousel. City Park is also the home of the New Orleans Botanical Garden and the New Orleans Museum of Art. *Open: Park, daily, sunrise–sunset (504) 482–4888; Botanical Garden, daily 9:00 a.m.–5:00 p.m., fee (504) 488–6439.*

Hermann–Grima House and Courtyard
820 Saint Louis Street

This reconstruction of an early nineteenth-century courtyard parterre is located in the Vieux Carré district. *Open: Monday–Saturday 10:00 a.m.–3:30 p.m., Sunday 1:00–5:00 p.m. Closed: Wednesday. Fee. (504) 525–5661.*

Historic New Orleans Collection—Museum/Research Center
533 Royal Street

One of the most impressive and impeccably restored gardens in the Vieux Carré displays lush evergreen courtyards that are colored and perfumed by typical southern Louisiana seasonal plants. The first of three courtyards is included in the tour; the remaining courtyards are available for public viewing on request. *Open: Tuesday–Saturday 10:00 a.m.–3:15 p.m. Closed: Major holidays. (504) 523–4662.*

Leon Heymann Conservatory
Audubon Park,
6500 St. Charles Avenue

In this conservatory are exhibited many kinds of exotic plants, including some 20 types of orchids. The surrounding gardens are planted with a variety of indigenous Louisiana flora. *Open: Daily 10:00 a.m.–4:00 p.m. (504) 891–2419.*

Longue Vue Gardens
7 Bamboo Road

Begun in 1942 and now one of America's outstanding city estates, Longue Vue Gardens provides 8 acres of stylistic diversity. In addition to a formal English Garden, wildflowers, and a pastoral wooded area,

Longue Vue Gardens, New Orleans, La.

smaller gardens—organized by color scheme—are featured. A major attraction is the Spanish Court, inspired by the Generalife Gardens of Spain.
Open: Tuesday–Friday 10:00 a.m.–4:30 p.m., Saturday–Sunday 1:00–5:00 p.m. Fee. (504) 488–5488.

Pitot House
1440 Moss Street

This West Indies type of plantation house facing Bayou St. John has a French parterre and secondary gardens.
Open: Wednesday–Saturday 10:00 a.m.–3:00 p.m. Fee. (504) 482–0312.

12. Opelousas

Louisiana State Arboretum
Chicot State Park
36 miles northwest
via U.S. 167 and La. 3042

The 301-acre preserve forms part of the 6,000-acre state park. A system of nature trails reveals over 150 species of plant life native to Louisiana.
Open: Daily, sunrise–sunset. (318) 363–6287.

13. Reserve

San Francisco Plantation
River Road (off U.S. 61 and La. 637),
60 miles west of New Orleans

The 1853 unique plantation-style home has been restored. The gardens have been partially restored. *Open: Daily 10:00 a.m.–4:00 p.m. Fee. (504) 535–2341.*

14. Saint Francisville

Afton Villa Garden
U.S. 61, 3.6 miles north of La. 10

An avenue of oaks provides a half-mile winding approach to the home of a mid-nineteenth century U.S. senator. The formal gardens surrounding the site of the former Gothic chateau are terraced. A boxwood maze and sunken gardens are part of the terraced plan. One of Louisiana's outstanding visual floral attractions, this garden is also characterized by a profusion of floral scents. *Open: March, daily 9:00 a.m.–5:00 p.m. Fee. (504) 635–4196.*

Myrtles Plantation
West Feliciana Parish, U.S. 61

The 1795 plantation house is set among live oak trees festooned with Spanish moss. The informal gardens are not large, but maintain a peaceful atmosphere. *Open: Daily 9:00 a.m.–5:00 p.m. (504) 635–6277.*

Rosedown Plantation and Gardens
Great River Road (La. 10)

Nowhere is the opulence of plantation culture more apparent than at Rosedown Plantation. The mansion and garden were built in 1835 by Daniel Turnbull, a wealthy cotton planter, and his wife Martha. The riverboats that took cotton to New Orleans returned with wall coverings, chandeliers from Paris, silver, and marble statuary from Italy. There are numerous landscape features, including formal gardens, and water features. *Open: Daily 9:00 a.m.–5:00 p.m. Fee. (504) 635–3332.*

15. Shreveport

American Rose Center
Exit 5 off I-20, then follow signs to Jefferson-Paige Road
(16 miles from Shreveport)

The 118-acre American Rose Center and Cascade Gardens are particularly beautiful when the roses or camellias are in bloom, from April through December. Over 20,000 rose bushes and 500 camellias. *Open: Monday–Friday 9:00 a.m.–6:00 p.m., Saturday–Sunday 10:00 a.m.–6:00 p.m. (318) 938–5402.*

Barnwell Memorial Garden and Art Center

501 Clyde E. Faust Memorial Parkway

A combination art and horticulture facility features changing exhibits. Indoor facilities include tropical plants; outdoors there are ornamental trees and shrubs.
Open: Monday–Friday 9:00 a.m.– 4:30 p.m., Saturday–Sunday 1:00–5:00 p.m. (318) 226–6495.

Other Places of Interest

Audubon Memorial State Park, Saint Francisville

French Quarter Vieux Carré Gardens (seen in various restaurants that are in old houses), New Orleans
Garden District of New Orleans
Jean Lafitte National Historic Park, New Orleans
Marksville Prehistoric Indian Park, Marshville
Old Chautauqua Grounds, Reston
Stuart Forest Nursery, Alexandria

Towns of special interest include Baton Rouge, Grand Isle, Houma, Lafayette, Natchitoches, New Iberia, and Saint Martinville.

Maine

Area: 33,215 square miles

Population: 1,164,000

Statehood: March 15, 1820
(23rd state)

Maine, "The Pine Tree State," occupies the extreme northeastern corner of the nation. Its topography was much altered by the epoch of glaciation one million years ago. Retreating glaciers left long narrow ridges of soil and rock called horsebacks. Glacial till blocked many river valleys, forming the state's innumerable lakes. The seashore was left rugged and highly indented. Cadillac Mountain on Mount Desert Island rises 1,350 feet above the sea. In central and western Maine are the Longfellow Mountains. Maine's highest peak is Mount Katahdin, which stands 5,268 feet above sea level. The state is rich in forests; white pine, maple, beech, birch, spruce, fir, and hemlock are important tree species. The state's relatively cool summers make it a popular vacation spot. Even in July, the temperature of ocean waters does not exceed 60° F.

The coast of Maine was first settled by traders and fishermen. Lumbering, fishing, and shipbuilding are traditional industries. Before the days of refrigeration, the exporting of ice was also an important industry. The poet Henry Wadsworth

Longfellow was a native of Portland; his family home stands at 487 Congress Street. Longfellow and novelist Nathaniel Hawthorne both graduated from Bowdoin College in Brunswick, Maine, in 1825. Harriet Beecher Stowe wrote *Uncle Tom's Cabin* while residing in Brunswick. The summer home of President Franklin D. Roosevelt was located at Campobello, on the Canadian border. Today its lands form the Campobello International Park.

Maine's places of interest include many old and historic homes, fine beaches, lakes, and forests. Acadia National Park, located on Mount Desert Island, features a rugged and beautiful landscape. The Allagash Wilderness Waterway in northern Maine is a National Wild and Scenic River. Remote coastal towns offer a particular attraction. They blend the elegant simplicity of traditional New England settlements with a natural landscape of particular beauty.

1. Augusta

Governor's Mansion
Corner of State and Capitol Streets

The mansion (1830) is sometimes known as "the Blaine House." It was presented to the state of Maine in 1919 by Harriet Blaine Beale for use as the governor's residence. The well-maintained grounds were designed by Olmsted Brothers in 1921.
Open: Garden, daily 10:00 a.m.–4:00 p.m. (207) 289–2121.

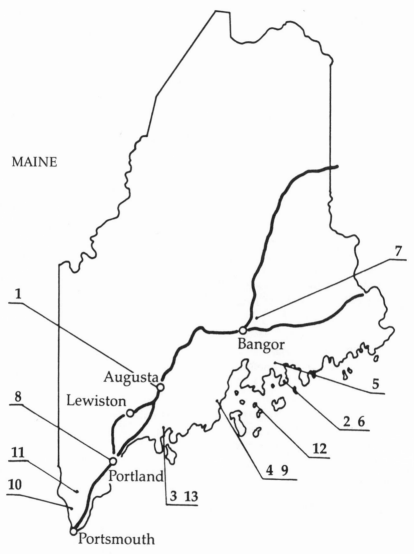

MAINE

Bangor

7

1

Augusta

8

Lewiston

11

10

Portland

3 13

4 9

12

2 6

5

Portsmouth

1. *Augusta* 2. *Bar Harbor* 3. *Bath* 4. *Camden* 5. *Ellsworth* 6. *Northeast Harbor* 7. *Orono* 8. *Portland* 9. *Rockport* 10. *South Berwick* 11. *Springvale* 12. *Stonington* 13. *Woolwich*

2. Bar Harbor

College of the Atlantic
Bar Harbor Road (Maine 3)

The vegetable gardens of this college (established in 1972) are of interest to environmentalists. Only organic methods of gardening are used, and many ecological experiments are under way.
Open: Daily 9:00 a.m.–5:00 p.m. (207) 288–5015.

Wild Gardens of Acadia
Sieur De Monts Spring,
Acadia National Park

The land in this area is filled with oddities of interest to ecologists, botanists, students, and laymen. The gardens contain plants native to Mount Desert Island, displayed in their specific habitats. The site is the northernmost limit of many southern species and the southernmost limit of a number of Arctic varieties.
Open: May–October, daily, sunrise–sunset. (207) 228–3338.

3. Bath

Bath Marine Museum and Garden
963 Washington Street

Adjacent to the Marine Museum Mansion, the Bath Garden Club has constructed a garden in the style of the 1850s.
Open: May–October, daily. (207) 443–1316.

4. Camden

Bok Amphitheater
Atlantic Avenue

Designed after the style of ancient Greece, this large amphitheater hosts many outdoor events. The grounds are well landscaped.
Open: Daily, sunrise–sunset. (207) 236–4404.

Merry Spring Park
Conway Road and U.S. 1

A memorial arboretum and garden are features of this 66–acre nature reserve. Nature trails have been developed in the naturalized areas, which display indigenous plants.
Open: Daily, sunrise–sunset. (207) 236–4885.

Old Conway House Complex
Conway Road and U.S. 1,
1 mile south of Camden

The authentically restored eighteenth-century farmstead includes a small kitchen herb garden.
Open: July–August, Tuesday–Sunday 1:00–5:00 p.m. and by appointment. Fee. (207) 236–2257 or 236–2720.

5. Ellsworth

Stanwood Museum
Bar Harbor Road (Route 3)

This wildlife sanctuary was developed around the property of ornithologist and writer Cordelia J. Stanwood (1865–1958). Native plants and wildlife habitats can be seen at the site, which has been listed in the National Register of Historic Places. *Open: House, June–October, Tuesday–Sunday 10:00 a.m.–4:00 p.m.; grounds, daily, sunrise–sunset. Donation. (207) 667–8460.*

7. Orono

Fay Hyland Botanical Plantation
University of Maine Campus

This botanical plantation, established on nearly 10 acres of land, consists largely of the native plants of Maine. There are 200 species and varieties. The site is named in honor of Dr. Hyland, a famous botanist of the Northeast who has done much to popularize the plants indigenous to the area. *Open: Daily, sunrise–sunset. (207) 581–7461.*

6. Northeast Harbor

Asticou Gardens
Asticou Way (Routes 3 and 198)

These gardens, which have been patterned after the Zen temple at Kyoto, enjoy a view of mountains and ocean. The subtlety of a Japanese garden is achieved with plant materials native to Maine. *Open: April–Labor Day, sunrise–sunset. (207) 276–5456.*

Thuya Lodge Gardens
Seal Harbor Road (Route 3)

Terraced gardens feature native plants at the former summer home of landscape architect Joseph Henry Curtis. *Open: Mid-June–mid-October, daily 9:00 a.m.–6:00 p.m. Donation. (207) 276–5130.*

8. Portland

Deering Oaks Park
Deering and Forest Avenues

The park, which dates back to the 1880s, includes an All-American Rose selection garden established in 1974. *Open: Daily, sunrise–sunset. (207) 772–2811.*

Eastern Cemetery
Congress Street and Washington Avenue

This cemetery is a National Historic Site. The grounds contain a mini-arboretum of 3 acres in Payson Park. *Open: Daily, sunrise–sunset. (207) 772–2811.*

Henry Wadsworth Longfellow House and Garden
487 Congress Street

The restored eighteenth-century garden provides a beautiful green oasis in downtown Portland. Lilacs and elms, hosta, geraniums, old roses, and strawberry shrubs highlight the carefully researched and reconstructed garden.
Open: May 31–September 30, Monday–Saturday 9:30 a.m.– 4:30 p.m. Fee. (207) 772–1807.

9. Rockport

Gardens of Vesper Hill Children's Chapel
Calderwood Lane

The chapel, open on all sides and built on a rock foundation overlooking the Atlantic Ocean, is a favorite setting for weddings. The garden leading to the chapel is composed of lawn, beds of flowers, rock gardens, and a biblical herb garden.
Open: Daily, garden, sunrise–sunset; chapel, 10:00 a.m.–4:00 p.m. (207) 236–4404.

10. South Berwick

Hamilton House and Gardens
Vaughan's Lane, Maine 236 and 91

The house and gardens, which date from 1785, are located in Vaughan

Woods State Park. There is an elaborate formal garden, flowering trees and shrubs, and a charming "doll house."
Open: May 30–October 15, daily. (207) 384–5269.

11. Springvale

Harvey Butler Rhododendron Sanctuary
Route 11-A

A 5-acre stand of rhododendrons blooms in early July, and a fine display of painted trillium in May. Also featured are an outstanding stand of black birch and a spice bush stand along the trail. The sanctuary is operated by the New England Wildflower Preservation Society.
Open: Daily, sunrise–sunset. (207) 324–4280.

12. Stonington

Ames Pond
Indian Point Road, off Maine 15

Ames Pond may not be classified as a "garden," but it is certainly of interest to the plant enthusiast. In 1932, 24 pink water lily roots were tied to rocks and thrown into the pond. They have multiplied into the thousands that now cover the pond completely from early July through early September. The blooms close each day at about 3 p.m. *Open: Daily, sunrise–sunset. (207) 348–6124.*

13. Woolwich

Robert P. Tristram Coffin Wild Flower Reservation

This 185-acre tract operated by the New England Wildflower Preservation Society displays a rich variety of ferns. Members of the Conservation Committee of the Bath Garden Club provide guided field trips in early June.
Open: Daily, sunrise–sunset. (207) 443–9751.

Other Places of Interest

Acadia National Park, Bar Harbor

Towns of special interest include Bath, Boothbay Harbor, Brunswick, Camden, Portland, and Wiscasset.

Maryland

Area: 10,577 square miles

Population: 4,392,000

Statehood: April 28, 1788 (7th state)

The state of Maryland falls midway between North and South; the Mason-Dixon line forms its border with Pennsylvania. The bountiful Chesapeake Bay divides the Eastern Shore from the major part of the state. Baltimore, located 200 miles up from the bay's mouth, is an important industrial city and seaport. The Eastern Shore is a low, flat agricultural area of sandy soils. Many broad lazy rivers cross it. The estuaries currently threatened by pollution are very productive of seafood. Along the shore are forests of water oak, cypress, sweetgum, and pine.

Most of the state's population is located in central Maryland. An almost continuous line of suburbs joins Baltimore to Washington, D.C., 40 miles to the south. The new town of Columbia is in this region. West of Frederick, Maryland, is a remote area of scenic beauty and coal mines. Many fine state parks are located there.

The first permanent settlement in Maryland was established in 1634 at Saint Mary's. The colony's major source of wealth was tobacco. The colonial capital at Annapolis was laid out in 1696 by Governor Francis Nicholson.

Owing to its excellent harbor, situated to the west of other Atlantic ports, Baltimore grew early to commercial prominence. During the War of 1812, the city was attacked by British forces. While observing the naval bombardment of Fort McHenry, Francis Scott Key wrote the National Anthem. Fort McHenry stands today as a National Historic Landmark at the Baltimore harbor. A walk through Federal Hill Park provides an excellent view of the city's modern downtown. On reclaimed land along the Inner Harbor are a modern promenade and public park. This development has opened the city to the pleasures of its waterfront.

In its small area, the state of Maryland contains a rich cross section of the nation's history. The city of Baltimore is exceptional in the beginnings it has made, despite serious economic problems, in developing a vital civic environment for the last part of the twentieth century.

1. Annapolis

Hammond–Harwood House and Garden
19 Maryland Avenue

The house is a fine example of Georgian architecture dating back to 1774. The surrounding grounds were redesigned in 1947 by landscape architect Alden Hopkins.
Open: April–October, Tuesday–Saturday 10:00 a.m.–5:00 p.m., Sunday noon–4:00 p.m.; November–

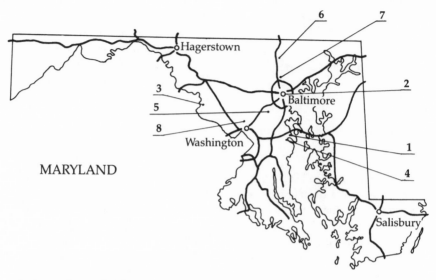

MARYLAND

1. *Annapolis* 2. *Baltimore* 3. *Dickerson* 4. *Edgewater* 5. *Laurel*
6. *Monkton* 7. *Towson* 8. *Wheaton*

March, Tuesday–Saturday
10:00 a.m.–4:00 p.m., Sunday
1:00–4:00 p.m. Fee. (301) 269–1714.

Helen Annalyne Tawes Garden
Tawes Office Building,
580 Rowe Boulevard

This modern garden is located on the
axis leading to the historic Maryland
State House. It endeavors to represent the various plant communities
of the state in a concentrated area;
its design permits special attention to
the needs of handicapped persons. In
1982 the garden received the American Society of Landscape Architects
award of excellence for design.
Open: Daily, sunrise–sunset. (301)
269–3717.

☆
William Paca House and Garden
186 Prince George Street

The garden designed by a Maryland
signer of the Declaration of Independence and governor, William Paca,
was described in 1769 as "the most
elegant in Annapolis." In later days,
the land was used for buildings and
a parking lot. Through careful research, the garden has been restored
to its original condition and today
provides an outstanding example of
Middle-Colony gardening.
Open: Garden, Monday–Saturday
10:00 a.m.–4:00 p.m., Sunday 1:00–
5:00 p.m. House closed: Monday. Fee.
(301) 263–5553.

2. Baltimore

Baltimore Museum of Art
Wyman Park, Art Museum Drive
and Charles Street

The small enclosed courtyard garden
is particularly delightful. The classic revival museum was the work of
architect John Russell Pope. It houses
an internationally renowned collection of twentieth-century French
painting and sculpture.
*Open: Tuesday–Friday 10:00 a.m.–
4:00 p.m., Saturday–Sunday
11:00 a.m.–6:00 p.m. (301) 396–6300.*

Carroll Mansion and Garden
800 East Lombard Street

Built in 1812, the Carroll Mansion
is Baltimore's finest surviving townhouse of the period. The courtyard
garden has been redesigned. Plantings in the garden are of the kind
supplied by local vendors or found in
catalogs in 1840.
*Open: Tuesday–Saturday 10:00 a.m.–
5:00 p.m., Sunday noon–5:00 p.m.
(301) 396–4980.*

Cylburn Arboretum
4915 Greenspring Avenue

The site includes an herb garden, a
garden for the blind, formal gardens,
flower gardens, an arboretum, and
nature trails through the wildflower
preserves and wooded areas.
*Open: Daily 6:00 a.m.–sunset. (301)
396–0180.*

Evergreen House and Garden
4545 North Charles Street

The house is a 42-room mansion currently owned by the Johns Hopkins
University. Dating from 1876, the
gardens are mostly formal in design
with fountains and statuary.
*Open: 2nd Tuesday of each month.
Guided tours of the house: 10:00–
11:00 a.m., 2:00–3:00 p.m. (301)
435–3376.*

Mount Vernon Place
Charles and Monument Streets

Situated on a dramatic site overlooking the Baltimore harbor, this formal
urban square contains the first monument erected to honor George Washington. The cruciform park is a fine
example of early nineteenth-century
urban design. Around it are many
historic townhouses, the Peabody
Conservatory, Mount Vernon Place
Methodist Church, and a historical
information center. (301) 396–7761.

Sherwood Gardens
Greenway and Highfield Roads

This is one of the most famous tulip
gardens in the world; over 70,000
tulips are planted annually. The garden also features azaleas and specimen trees.
Open: Sunrise–sunset. (301) 366–2572.

3. Dickerson

Sugar Loaf Mountain
Route 85

The mountain has been registered as a National Natural Landmark because of its geological interest and striking beauty. It is owned by Stronghold, Inc., a charitable corporation whose basic purpose is to bring back the native chestnut by developing a species resistant to the blight that has destroyed so many chestnut trees and forests. Currently, the site offers a walking trail, wildflower garden, forest demonstration area, and nature center.
Open: Daily 11:00 a.m.–sunset. (301) 874–2024.

4. Edgewater

Londontowne Publik House and Gardens
839 London Town Road

Located next to a historic brick house built in 1758, the modern naturalistic gardens feature a wide variety of plant types, many of which are labeled. Educational programs are offered here.
Open: Tuesday–Saturday 10:00 a.m.–4:00 p.m., Sunday noon–4:00 p.m. (301) 956–4900. Fee.

5. Laurel

Montpelier Mansion
Md. 197, 3 miles southeast of Laurel

Built in 1780, this Georgian mansion of the Snowdon family included George Washington among its early visitors. The grounds feature boxwood gardens and a shrubbery maze.
Open: March–December, Sunday 1:00–5:00 p.m. (301) 779–2011.

6. Monkton

Breezewood
7322 Hess Road

The grounds include a very fine Oriental garden. A museum displays sculpture from India and Southeast Asia.
Open: May–October, 1st Sunday of the month, 2:00–5:30 p.m. Fee. (301) 472–9438.

☆☆
Ladew Topiary Gardens
3535 Jarretsville Pike

This garden, famous for its extraordinary topiary, covers 22 acres and ranges in design from formal to absolute whimsy. A dozen different small garden rooms are arranged around a central lawn and pool. Topiary hedges depict exotic animals, simple geometric shapes, and other interesting figures.
Open: April–October, Tuesday–Friday 10:00 a.m.–4:00 p.m., Saturday–

Ladew Topiary Gardens, Monkton, Md.

Sunday, 10:00 a.m.–5:00 p.m.
Separate fees for house and gardens.
(301) 557–9466.

7. Towson

Hampton National Historic Site
535 Hampton Lane

The gardens around this Georgian colonial mansion date from the late eighteenth century and have evolved in form over the years. Italian, French, and English styles have influenced the design of the landscaped gardens. Six parterres on three levels of descending terraces can be viewed from the broad lawn separating the gardens and the mansion. Restored (ca. 1825) classic revival orangerie. *Open: Monday–Saturday 11:00 a.m.–*

4:30 p.m., Sunday 1:00–4:30 p.m. (301) 823–7054.

8. Wheaton

Brookside Botanical Gardens
1500 Glenallen Avenue

The 25-acre site includes formal gardens, an azalea collection, and a garden for the blind. Three greenhouses contain excellent seasonal displays. *Open: Tuesday–Saturday 9:00 a.m.–5:00 p.m., Sunday 1:00–6:00 p.m. Closed: Christmas. Partial handicapped access, wheelchair available. (301) 949–8231.*

Other Places of Interest

Assateague Island, Ocean City
Fort McHenry National Monument,
 Baltimore
Hampton National Historic Site,
 Baltimore
Haven Meeting House, Easton
Historic St. Mary's City, St. Mary's
 (Route 5)

Lily Pons Water Garden, Lily Pons
National Aquarium, Baltimore
Sub-Artic Swamp, Oakland

Towns of special interest include
Annapolis, Baltimore, Cambridge,
and Columbia.

Massachusetts

Area: 8,257 square miles

Population: 5,822,000

Statehood: February 6, 1788
(6th state)

Glaciers of one million years ago
reshaped the topography of Massachusetts. They stripped away much of
the topsoil and left boulders strewn
over New England. Thousands of
lakes were created by this change in
the drainage pattern.

The state has a varied and irregular coastline. Cape Cod is a sandy
spit stretching out into the Atlantic Ocean. The North Shore above
Boston has a rocky coast. Along the
North Shore on Nantucket Island
and in the town of Edgartown on
Martha's Vineyard can be found
many historic homes of the Federal
period. In Salem are the customhouse
where author Nathaniel Hawthorne
worked and the House of the Seven
Gables, immortalized by his novel of
the same name. Plymouth Rock is
located on the South Shore.

The majority of the state's in-
habitants live in the busy industrial
eastern section between Boston and
Worcester. Boston was developed as
a great port from colonial times. In
the nineteenth century, the towns
of eastern Massachusetts became
manufacturing centers. The Merri-
mac River powered the state's textile
mills. The town of Lowell developed
a beautiful riverfront, earning it the
title of "Venice of North America."
Lowell has been restored to become
the first National Urban Park.

The Boston National Historic Park
preserves many sites of significance
in the nation's early history. They
include Fanueil Hall, the Paul Re-
vere House, Old North Church, the
Old State House, and the berth of
the USS *Constitution*. The Isabella
Stewart Gardner Museum, built in
the style of a Venetian palace, houses
the works of many great artists.
The Boston Public Library (designed
by Charles F. McKim), at Copley
Square, is an excellent example of the
Romanesque Revival style of architecture. Louisburg Square on Beacon
Hill exemplifies nineteenth-century
urban housing. The city was a leader
in developing a public park system;
an ambitious design was proposed
by landscape architect Frederick Law
Olmsted.

Slightly west of Boston are Lexington and Concord. A National Historic
Park commemorates the momentous
events of April 1775 that occurred in
these quiet towns. Concord was the
birthplace of Henry David Thoreau.
Walden Pond, where Thoreau lived
as a hermit, gave its name to his little
book which proposes a guiding ethic
for man's relationship to the land.
Another great New England Tran-
scendentalist, Ralph Waldo Emerson,
also lived in this tiny town.

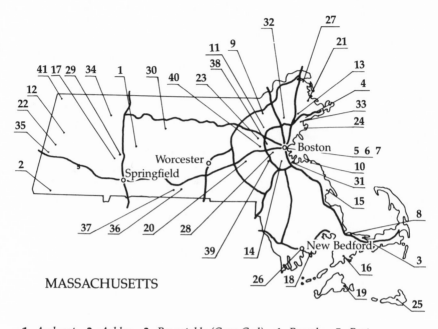

MASSACHUSETTS

1. *Amherst*   2. *Ashley*   3. *Barnstable (Cape Cod)*   4. *Beverly*   5. *Boston*
6. *Brookline*   7. *Cambridge*   8. *Cape Cod*   9. *Chelmsford*   10. *Cohasset*
11. *Concord*   12. *Dalton*   13. *Danvers*   14. *Dedham*   15. *Duxbury*
16. *East Falmouth*   17. *East Hampton*   18. *East Marion*   19. *Edgartown*
20. *Framingham*   21. *Ipswich*   22. *Lenox*   23. *Lincoln*   24. *Marblehead*
25. *Nantucket*   26. *New Bedford*   27. *Newburyport*   28. *Newton*
29. *Northhampton*   30. *Petersham*   31. *Quincy*   32. *Reading*   33. *Salem*
34. *Shelburne Falls*   35. *Stockbridge*   36. *Sturbridge*   37. *Wales*
38. *Waltham*   39. *Wellesley*   40. *Weston*   41. *Williamstown*

1. Amherst

Rhododendron Gardens, Amherst College
Route 116

Established in 1912, these gardens serve educational purposes and are used for special events. Azaleas, mountain laurel, and rhododendron bloom from May to mid-June.
Open: Daily during school term. (413) 542-2320.

2. Ashley

Bartholomew's Cobble
Rannapo Road, 1 mile west of Ashley Falls

Typical of the "Berkshires," this 235-acre cobble contains many trails and diverse natural areas, along with the restored eighteenth-century house of Colonel John Ashley, one of the original frontier settlers. A National Natural Landmark.

The Fenway, Boston, Mass.

Open: April 15–October 15,
Wednesday–Sunday 9:00 a.m.–
5:00 p.m. (413) 229–8600.

3. Barnstable (Cape Cod)

St. Mary's Church Garden
Main Street

A small garden of great charm and significance has its peak in the spring. *Open: Daily, sunrise–sunset. (617) 362–3977.*

4. Beverly

☆
Sedgewick Gardens at Long Hill
572 Essex Street

The Charleston-style house, built in 1918, is now headquarters of the Massachusetts Trustees of Reservations. Extensive gardens, both formal and informal, surround the house. Among the over 400 varieties of plant species are azaleas, rhododendron, Japanese flowering cherry, roses, and a large collection of bulbs.
Open: Daily 8:00 a.m.–sunset. Fee. (617) 922–1536.

5. Boston

☆☆
Arnold Arboretum
of Harvard University
Arborway, Jamaica Plains

Founded in 1872 and designed by
Frederick Law Olmsted, this 265-acre
arboretum is one of the oldest and
most important centers of worldwide
horticultural research. It contains
an extensive library and large herbarium. The collection of plants
includes many rare exotics, specimen
trees, and flowering shrubs carefully
landscaped for the public's enjoyment.
*Open: Daily, sunrise–sunset; library,
9:00 a.m.–5:00 p.m. (617) 524–1717
(recording) or 524–1718 (information).*

Boston Public Garden
Arlington and Beacon Streets

The first public botanical garden in
the United States was begun here
in 1838. Plant materials have been
chosen for ornamental excellence as
well as botanical diversity. Situated
across the street from the Boston
Common, the garden provides a
green and flowering oasis—including
swan boats in the lagoon—in the
heart of a great metropolis.
*Open: Daily, sunrise–sunset. (617)
323–2700.*

Fenway Park Garden
Park Drive

Established in 1893, this public garden features tulips in spring and
other seasonal displays; it also contains formal gardens and some rare
trees.
*Open: Daily, sunrise–sunset. (617)
725–4006.*

Isabella Stewart Gardner
Museum
280 Fenway and Worthington Street

A wealth of art is housed in this
Venetian palace. The superb inner
court garden features some rare
plants. Outside are seasonal gardens,
rock gardens, and flowering trees.
*Open: May–October, Tuesday–
Thursday, Saturday 10:00 a.m.–
4:00 p.m., Sunday 2:00–5:00 p.m.
(617) 566–1411.*

6. Brookline

Frederick Law Olmsted
National Historic Site
99 Warren Street

This was the home and office of
the "Father of American Landscape
Architecture." Drawings for many of
the parks, campuses, and great private
estates designed by Olmsted and his
sons are stored here.
*Open: Friday–Sunday 10:00 a.m.–
4:00 p.m. (617) 566–1689.*

7. Cambridge

☆
**Harvard University
Botanical Museum**
24 Oxford Street

Although not a garden, this is a
unique exhibit of extraordinary life-
like flowers made of glass. There
are over 800 species of flowers in
the collection, all made with perfect
anatomical detail by Leopold and
Rudolph Blaschka.
*Open: Daily 9:00 a.m.–4:30 p.m.,
Sunday 1:00–4:30 p.m. (617)
868–7600.*

Longfellow House
105 Brattle Street

The 1759 house contains Longfellow's
books, manuscripts, and furniture.
The garden has been restored by the
Cambridge Plant and Garden Club
according to Longfellow's design.
*Open: Daily 10:00 a.m.–4:30 p.m.
(617) 876–4491.*

☆
Mount Auburn Cemetery
580 Mount Auburn Street

The oldest garden cemetery in the
United States features an arboretum
of 100-year-old trees, including
many rare specimen trees that are
labeled. The Asa Gray Memorial
Garden appropriately honors this
famous botanist.
*Open: Daily, May–October 8:00 a.m.–
7:00 p.m.; November–April, until
5:00 p.m. (617) 547–7105.*

8. Cape Cod

Heritage Plantation of Sandwich
Grove and Pine Streets

This 76-acre estate features 35,000
Dexter hybrid rhododendrons. There
is also a collection of plants native to
the Cape Cod area.
*Open: May–October, Daily
10:00 a.m.–5:00 p.m. (617) 888–3300.*

9. Chelmsford

Bartlett Park
Acton Road (Route 27)

An arboretum in the park is maintained by the Conservation Commission. Specimen plants are established
in their natural habitat and labeled.
*Open: Daily, sunrise–sunset. (617)
256–0028.*

10. Cohasset

**Cohasset Historic House
and Maritime Museum**
Cohasset Village Center, Elm Street

The house dates back to 1800. The
garden, built and maintained by
the Cohasset Garden Club, features
plants of the period.
*Open: June–September, Tuesday–
Sunday 1:30–4:30 p.m. Fee. (617)
383–6930.*

11. Concord

Walden Pond State Reservation
915 Walden Street
(south of town on Mass. 126)

The reservation is 300 acres. A cairn marks the site of Thoreau's cabin, made famous by *Walden, or Life in the Woods*, the naturalist author's account of his two years (1845–47) spent living by the pond. Walden Pond is now used for recreational activities such as swimming, boating, and fishing.
Open: Daily, sunrise–sunset. (617) 369–3254.

12. Dalton

Crane Estate
South Street off Mass. 9,
10 miles east of Pittsfield

The lovely perennial gardens surrounding the museum offer exciting vistas.
Open: June–September, weekdays 10:00 a.m.–5:00 p.m. (413) 684–2600.

13. Danvers

Glen Magna Mansion
U.S. 1 and 57 Forest Street

Gardens of the mansion were designed by Frederick Law Olmsted and Joseph Chamberlain. The Derby summerhouse was designed by Samuel McIntire in 1793. There are 140 acres of fields and woods.
Open: May 30–October 1, Tuesday and Thursday 10:00 a.m.–5:00 p.m. or by appointment. Fee. (617) 774–9165.

14. Dedham

Fairbanks House and Gardens
511 East Street

Fairbanks House is the oldest wooden frame house in America, dating back to 1636. Both the house and gardens are maintained by the Fairbanks Garden Club.
Open: May–October, Tuesday–Sunday and by appointment. (617) 326–1170.

15. Duxbury

King Caesar's Garden
King Caesar's Road

The garden was probably laid out when the house was built by Ezra Weston in 1808. Weston, one of the wealthiest shipowners in the country, was known as "King Caesar." In 1886, restoration of the gardens to their original condition was begun by Mrs. Frederick B. Knapp. In the old garden Mrs. Knapp found rare iris reticula brought from Asia Minor in King Caesar's ships. Descendants of these plants flourish to this day.
Open: Mid–June–Labor Day, Tuesday–Sunday 2:00–4:00 p.m. Fee. (617) 934–2378.

16. East Falmouth

**Ashumet Holly Reservation
and Wildlife Sanctuary**
Ashumet Road

Old favorite hollies are grown on this 45-acre wildlife preserve, as well as new varieties tested for the Holly Society. There is also an herb garden. *Open: Tuesday–Sunday, sunrise–sunset. Closed: Holidays. Fee. (617) 563–6390.*

17. East Hampton

Arcadia Wildlife Sanctuary
Fort Hill Road

The 500-acre preserve of woods, meadows, and marsh also includes the Mendenhall Wildflower Garden. *Open: Tuesday–Sunday 9:00 a.m.–5:00 p.m. Fee. (413) 584–3009.*

18. East Marion

Stone Estate
Off U.S. 6 (reached by I-95)
on Delano Road

This is the site of Great Hill Farm, home of the famous "Stone Acacias." There are also plantings of rhododendrons and laurels. *Open: June–September, weekdays 10:00 a.m.–5:00 p.m. (617) 748–1052.*

19. Edgartown

Mytoi Japanese Garden
Chappaquidick Island
(Ferry ride from Edgartown)

This lovely 3-acre garden is part of an 11-acre reservation owned by the Massachusetts Trustees of Reservations. It was originally planned by the late Hugh Jones, an architect who once resided in Japan. The garden is simple, covered mainly with native pitch pine similar to that of Japan. Japanese iris and primroses border a reflection pond. *Open: Daily, 8:00 a.m.–sunset. (617) 627–8644.*

20. Framingham

☆
Garden in the Woods
Hemenway Road

The headquarters of the New England Wildflower Preservation Society features a 42-acre botanical garden. There is an outstanding collection of the native plants of North America. *Open: April–November, Monday–Saturday 8:30 a.m.–5:00 p.m. (617) 237–4924.*

21. Ipswich

**Arthur Shurcliff Memorial
Gardens, Whipple House**
U.S. 1-A, 0.25 miles south
of Ipswich Center

A pleasantly restored seventeenth-
century garden has clamshell walks
and formal flower beds. Plantings
replicate those originally used in the
garden. Some old roses are descendants of the original plants.
*Open: April 1–November 1, Tuesday–
Friday 10:00 a.m.–5:00 p.m., Sunday
1:00–5:00 p.m. (617) 356–4070.*

22. Lenox

**Pleasant Valley
Wildlife Sanctuary**
472 West Mountain Road

This site includes an Audubon Nature
Center with several wooded trails.
*Open: May–October, Tuesday–Sunday
10:00 a.m.–5:00 p.m. (413) 637–0320.*

Tanglewood
West Street (Mass. 183)

This 210-acre summer residence of
Nathaniel Hawthorne is now the
summer home of the Boston Symphony Orchestra and the Boston
Pops. The estate is characterized by
broad sweeping lawns and separate
formal garden areas.
*Open: Summer. There is no fee to view
the grounds except when concerts and
other special events are held. (413)
637–1940.*

23. Lincoln

Codman House Garden
Codman Road

The house and garden are owned
by the New England Society for the
Preservation of Antiquities. Restoration of the Italian Garden, originally
constructed in 1899, was begun in
1975.
*Open: June 1–September 30, Tuesday,
Thursday, Sunday 1:00–5:00 p.m.
Fee. (617) 259–8843.*

24. Marblehead

Lee Mansion Garden
161 Washington Street

This is a fine example of a restored
eighteenth-century garden. It is
owned and maintained by the Marblehead Historical Society.
*Open: May 15–October 15,
10:00 a.m.–4:00 p.m. Fee. (617)
631–2608.*

25. Nantucket

Jethro Coffin House
Sunset Hill Road

Surrounding a house that dates back
to 1686, the gardens are maintained
as a project of the Nantucket Garden
Club.
*Open: June–September, daily
9:00 a.m.–5:00 p.m. Fee. (617)
228–1894.*

26. New Bedford

Rotch–Jones–Duff House and Garden
396 County Street

This 1834 Greek Revival mansion includes a restored formal garden. *Open: June–August, Wednesday–Friday 9:00 a.m.–5:00 p.m.; rest of year, Sunday 1:00–5:00 p.m. Fee. (617) 997–1401.*

27. Newburyport

Cushing House Museum
98 High Street

This 21-room Federalist mansion (ca. 1808) features a French-style garden. *Open: May–November, Tuesday–Sunday 10:00 a.m.–5:00 p.m. Closed: Holidays. Fee. (617) 462–2681.*

28. Newton

Jackson Homestead Garden
527 Washington Street

The garden surrounds the Newton Historical Museum. It was planted by the Garden Club of Newton in keeping with the period of the homestead. *Open: July–August, Tuesday–Friday 10:00 a.m.–4:00 p.m.; rest of year, Monday–Friday. Fee. (617) 552–7238.*

29. Northhampton

Smith College Botanical Garden and Lyman Plant House
College Lane, Smith College Campus

The entire 300-acre campus is an educational garden. Plants of over 3,500 species are arranged according to taxonomic relationships. An outstanding rock garden, a collection of herbaceous plants, water and bog plantings, a cactus area, and an area of shade-loving plants are found here. There are also conservatories of tropical plants and a greenhouse. *Open: Daily, conservatories 8:00 a.m.–5:00 p.m. (413) 584–2700, ext. 373.*

30. Petersham

Fisher Museum of Forestry
Mass. 32

A tract of forest and woodlands belonging to Harvard University provides a demonstration of the management of forestland lots. The main building features an interesting exhibit showing changes in the New England countryside. *Open: Weekdays 10:00 a.m.–5:00 p.m. (617) 724–3285.*

31. Quincy

Adams Mansion and Gardens
135 Adams Street

Built in 1731 with additions in 1800 and 1869, this mansion housed four generations of the Adams family including two U.S. presidents. The grounds were designed by John Adams's wife, Abigail. Today, the property is maintained by the National Park Service.
Open: April 19–November 12, daily 9:00 a.m.–5:00 p.m. (617) 773–1177.

The Quincy Homestead
34 Butler Street

This restored eighteenth-century Georgian mansion was once the home of Dorothy Quincy. There is a small colonial herb garden.
Open: June–October, Tuesday–Saturday 9:00 a.m.–4:00 p.m., Sunday 1:00–4:00 p.m. (617) 472–5117.

32. Reading

Parker Tavern Dooryard Garden
Washington Street

The Parker Tavern and garden were built in 1694. The garden includes herbs, flowers, trees, and shrubs.
Open: May–October, Sunday 1:00–5:00 p.m. or by appointment. Fee. Call Mrs. Trites at (617) 944–7449.

33. Salem

Essex Institute Gardens
132 Essex State

Featured are a China Trade Garden, an herb garden, and a flower garden.
Open: May–November, Tuesday–Saturday 9:00 a.m.–5:00 p.m. (617) 744–3390.

First Church of Salem
316 Essex Street

The 300-year-old colonial garden may be the oldest garden in constant use in the United States.
Open: Daily, sunrise–sunset. (617) 744–4323.

Greenlawn Cemetery
57 Orne Street

This old New England cemetery is extensively planted with trees and shrubbery. It also includes a chapel, a greenhouse, several pools, and a summer planting of flowering plants in formal beds.
Open: Daily, sunrise–sunset. (617) 744–4323.

House of Seven Gables
54 Turner Street

The 1668 house is said to be the setting for Hawthorne's novel of the same name. On the restored grounds are period knot gardens and some fine trees, as well as Hathaway House (1740), the birthplace of Nathaniel Hawthorne.
Open: July–September 1, daily 9:30 a.m.–6:30 p.m.; rest of year,

10:30 a.m.–4:30 p.m.
Closed: Major holidays. Fee. (617)
744–0991.

Japanese Garden at Peabody Museum of Salem
161 Essex Street

Designed in 1960, this garden is considered a "viewing garden" because it can be seen from the sidewalk.
Open: Monday–Saturday 8:00 a.m.–5:00 p.m., Sunday 1:00–5:00 p.m. Fee. (617) 745–1876.

Ropes Garden
318 Essex Street

The grounds of the Ropes Mansion feature a formal garden and a small pool.
Open: June 1–October 15, Tuesday–Saturday 10:00 a.m.–4:30 p.m., Sunday 1:00–4:30 p.m.; rest of year, Tuesday–Saturday 2:00–4:30 p.m. Fee. (617) 744–3390.

34. Shelburne Falls

The Bridge of Flowers
South of Mass. 2

A spectacular and unique garden is located on a bridge over the Deerfield River. Once a trolley span, the bridge now has a complete watering system, is planted with flowers, and is lighted at night from spring to fall. There is an excellent view from the bridge.
Open: April–November, daily, sunrise–10:30 p.m. Donation. (413) 773–5463.

35. Stockbridge

Berkshire Garden Center
Larryway Street (Mass. 102 and 183)

Situated on well-landscaped grounds, the 15-acre garden center offers a year-round assortment of activities including lectures, horticultural displays, workshops, and nature walks.
Open: Daily 10:00 a.m.–5:00 p.m. during the growing season; greenhouses, year-round. (413) 298–3926.

Chesterwood
2 miles west of Stockbridge (take Mass. 102 to Mass. 183 South and follow the signs)

Daniel Chester French (1850–1931), the eminent sculptor, made Chesterwood his summer home. The gardens were developed by French between 1898 and 1931 to reflect his philosophy that a garden should be a "continuation of the house, a room of living green, with plenty of shade to sit in and seats in the right places." The Chesterwood gardens contain many sculptures and have been maintained much as French knew them, with the help of his extensive garden records which note plant names and sources of supply, planting locations and dates, flowering dates, and seasonal interest. The property is administered by the National Trust for Historic Preservation.
Open: May–September 31, daily 10:00 a.m.–5:00 p.m.; October, weekdays. Fee. (413) 298–3579.

Naumkeag Gardens
The Choate Estate,
Prospect Hill Road

Dating back to 1885, the large, formal gardens of this Stanford White-designed grand summer estate have a Victorian air. They are tucked into a hillside with a view westward to the Berkshires.
Open: Memorial Day–Columbus Day, Tuesday–Saturday, 10:00 a.m.–5:00 p.m., Sunday 11 a.m.–4:00 p.m. (413) 298–3239.

36. Sturbridge

Old Sturbridge Village
U.S. 20, I-84, or the Massachusetts Turnpike (I-90), Exit 9

This historic village, which depicts the period 1790–1830, was entirely re-created beginning in 1930; it was first opened for public exhibition in 1946. The large herb garden and the several flower gardens adjacent to houses within the village contain only those plants known to have been used during the period.
Open: April 1–October 31, daily 9:00 a.m.–5:00 p.m; rest of year, Tuesday–Sunday 10:00 a.m.–4:00 p.m. Fee. (617) 347–3362.

37. Wales

Norcross Wildlife and Wildflower Sanctuary
Monson-Wales Road

This magnificent wildflower sanctuary contains over 3,000 acres of rare wildflowers. There are two museums and self-guiding trails. Most interesting during the spring.
Open: Daily 9:00 a.m.–4:00 p.m. Closed: Major holidays. (413) 267–9654.

38. Waltham

Gore Place
U.S. 20 between Watertown Square and Waltham Center

Christopher Gore, later governor of Massachusetts, purchased this farm in 1786 and subsequently redesigned it in the manner of Sir Humphrey Repton with herb garden, ha-ha fence, native American trees, and shrubs planted in a "naturalistic" design.
Open: April 15 –November 15, Tuesday-Saturday except holidays, 10:00 a.m.–5:00 p.m., Sunday 2:00–5:00 p.m. Fee. (617) 894–2798.

Lyman Estate and Greenhouses
185 Lyman Road

Regarded as one of New England's finest examples of a Federal period country estate, "The Vale" was

owned by the Lyman family for over 150 years. The 30 acres of gardens were styled in the English manner of Sir Humphrey Repton. An important feature of the estate is its five greenhouses; the earliest, dating back to 1800, is no longer in use but is thought to be the oldest standing greenhouse in America. The other greenhouses feature grapes, camellias, tropicals, and plant propagation and sales. The property is now owned by the Society for the Preservation of New England Antiquities.
Open: House, only by appointment for groups—(617) 893–7431; grounds and greenhouses, year-round, Thursday–Sunday 10:00 a.m.–4:00 p.m. Fee. (617) 891–7095.

39. Wellesley

Walter Hunnewell Pinetum
845 Washington Street

Situated on the edge of Lake Waban, the pinetum adjoins the campus of Wellesley College. On the hillside above the lake, the clipped trees, reputed to be the "oldest topiary in America," are patterned after the trees in Italian gardens of the mid-1800s. In this pinetum, the spruces, hemlocks, yews, cedars, firs, elms, and junipers cover the hillsides and surround the broad lawns. The rhododendrons represent one of the finest collections in New England.
Open: By appointment only. (617) 235–0422.

40. Weston

Case Estate
135 Wellesley Street

Experimental gardens of the Arnold Arboretum are located on 112 acres.
Open: Daily 9:00 a.m.–6:00 p.m. (617) 524–1718.

Hubbard Trail
Ridgeway Road and Orchard Avenue

A 22-acre suburban tract is owned by the Weston Trail and Forest Association, and operated by the New England Wildflower Preservation Society as a natural garden. April and May are the best months.
Open: Sunrise–sunset. (617) 893–7320.

41. Williamstown

Buston Garden
Northwest Hill Road

Located in the Hopkins Memorial Forest of Williams College, this garden contains grapes, perennials, and shrubbery planted at the turn of the century.
Open: Daily, sunrise–sunset. (413) 597–3131.

Other Places of Interest

Boston Common
Cape Cod National Seashore
Copley Square, Boston
Fenway, Boston
Fogg Museum, Harvard University

Freedom Trail, Boston
Government Center, Boston
Martha's Vineyard
Mohawk Trail, Pittsfield
Nantucket Island
Old Deerfield, Deerfield
Pilgrim Trail, Plymouth
Pilgrim Village, Plymouth
Pioneer Village, Salem
Plymouth Plantation, Plymouth
Storrowton, West Springfield

The Massachusetts Trustees of Reservations is a unique organization founded in 1891 for the preservation and acquisition of public open space of historic and environmental significance. Currently it lists 70 properties throughout the state, several of which are included in this guide. For further information, write Trustees of Reservations, 572 Essex Street, Beverly, Mass. 01915. (617) 921–1944.

Michigan

Area: 58,216 square miles

Population: 9,088,000

Statehood: January 26, 1837
(26th state)

Michigan is an industrialized and highly productive state rich in natural resources. The Great Lakes and the Saint Lawrence Seaway tie Michigan's products to the ports of the world. The southern part of the state is heavily settled; it is rich in agriculture and industry. Northern Michigan is a resort area of rivers, lakes, and forests.

Most of Michigan lies in the Central Lowlands. Its land was reshaped by the glaciers of the Ice Age, when many lakes were created and the Great Lakes were given their current form. The glaciers deposited rich clay in the soils in southern Michigan; receding, they deposited poorer sandy soils farther north. The western part of Michigan's Upper Peninsula lies in the Superior Upland, a region of rugged, highly eroded landforms. Michigan's highest elevation is found in this region at Huron Mountain, which stands 1,980 feet above sea level.

Michigan's mid-continental climate is tempered by the proximity of the Great Lakes. The growing season ranges from about 80 to 190 days. Rainfall over most of the state exceeds 30 inches per year. Vast hardwood forests originally covered the rich clay soils of southern Michigan. On the poorer sandy soils of the north, pine forests are prevalent.

Michigan's first industries were fur trading and lumbering. By the 1850s, a prosperous agricultural economy had developed. The state's major industry today is automobile manufacturing. Iron is mined in the Upper Peninsula. Grand Rapids is famous for its fine furniture, which is displayed twice yearly at its furniture mart. Holland, Michigan, is the nation's tulip bulb producer; it holds a tulip festival each May.

The state offers great variety in its cultural and natural attractions. The Detroit Institute of Art has an internationally known collection of paintings. Cranbrook Institute, in Bloomfield Hills, combines a leading art school and science research institute; its beautiful campus features buildings designed by Eliel Saarinen, and statuary and fountains by sculptor Carl Milles. Mackinac Island, once a great fur trading post, is now a peaceful resort community. Isle Royale National Park in Lake Superior is a magnificent wilderness area. The Pictured Rocks National Lakeshore features colorful sandstone cliffs, dunes, and beaches. The sand dunes of Sleeping Bear Dunes National Lakeshore are particularly impressive. The Soo Locks, which serve shipping between Lake Huron and Lake Superior, are a formidable work of man's technology.

MICHIGAN

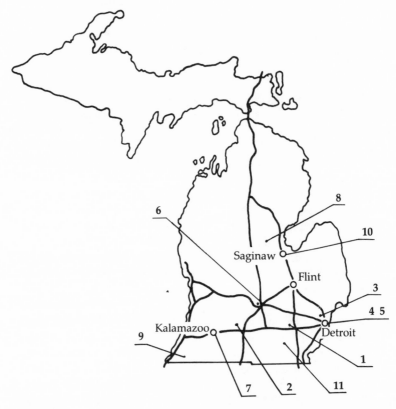

1. *Ann Arbor*   **2.** *Battle Creek*   **3.** *Bloomfield Hills*   **4.** *Dearborn*   **5.** *Detroit*
6. *East Lansing*   **7.** *Kalamazoo*   **8.** *Midland*   **9.** *Niles*   **10.** *Saginaw*   **11.** *Tipton*

1. Ann Arbor

☆

Matthaei Botanical Gardens
University of Michigan,
1800 Dixboro Road

The major part of the 250-acre site is
maintained as a natural area, which
encompasses a diversity of habitats.
Over 700 native plant species are

grown in the gardens. The habitats
serve a variety of biological research
projects, particularly those of an
ecological nature. The gardens' special features include a conservatory,
medicinal plant garden, rose garden,
wildflower garden, and prairie.
*Open: Grounds, sunrise–sunset;
greenhouses, daily 10:00 a.m.–
4:30 p.m. (313) 764–1168.*

Cranbrook Art Museum, Bloomfield Hills, Mich.

Nichols Arboretum
Geddes Road

This 125-acre tract has an assemblage of interesting trees and shrubs, many unique to the area. There is also a lilac and peony collection.
Open: Daily, sunrise–sunset. (313) 763-4636.

Open: Grounds, all times; museum, year-round, Tuesday–Saturday 9:00 a.m.–5:00 p.m., Sunday 1:00– 5:00 p.m.; summer–Labor Day, open also on Monday 9:00 a.m.–5:00 p.m. (616) 965-5117.

3. Bloomfield Hills

2. Battle Creek

Leila Arboretum
West Michigan Avenue at 20th Street

The arboretum is situated on 72 acres of rolling hills and contains specimens of nearly every species of tree found in the United States. The Kingman Museum of National History is located on the grounds.

☆
Cranbrook House and Gardens
Cranbrook Educational Community, 380 Lone Pine Road

The community, consisting of the Cranbrook Institute of Science, the Art Museum, the Kingswood School, and the Booth House, lies on 320 acres of beautifully landscaped grounds. It contains, among other attractions, the Circular Orpheus

Fountain created by Swedish sculptor Carl Milles. The Booth House is surrounded by 40 acres of gardens.
Open: June–August, daily 10:00 a.m.–5:00 p.m., Sunday 1:00–5:00 p.m.; May and September, daily 1:00–5:00 p.m.; October, weekends only, 1:00–5:00 p.m. Fee. (313) 645–3149.

4. Dearborn

Fair Lane
4901 Evergreen Road

The 70-acre estate was the home of Henry Ford. The mansion, built in 1915, is surrounded by an English flower garden. Now owned by the University of Michigan.
*Open: Grounds, daily 9:00 a.m.–5:00 p.m.; house, Sunday 1:00–4:30 p.m.
Note: May be closed for special events. (313) 593–5590.*

Ford Motor Company World Headquarters Arboretum
American Road,
Michigan and Southfield Roads

This 30-acre arboretum contains native Michigan trees.
Open: Sunrise–sunset. (313) 322–3000.

5. Detroit

☆
Belle Island Conservatory and Park
Detroit River (MacArthur Bridge)

Belle Island Park, designed by the Olmsted, Olmsted and Eliot firm of landscape architects, is located on the Detroit River, a short distance upstream from the center of Detroit. The wooded areas remain essentially the same as they were in 1882, with deer and other animals roaming free. The park contains the Whitcomb Horticultural Conservatory and an extensive canal system which facilitates canoeing. The majority of the structures were erected between 1890 and 1915, giving the entire park a turn-of-the-century atmosphere. The park also features the Henry A. Johnson Memorial Gardens.
Open: Daily 9:00 a.m.–6:00 p.m. (313) 224–1097.

Detroit Zoological Park
Woodward Avenue and
Ten-Mile Road

The park includes 122 acres of the finest botanical specimens in Detroit. Hundreds of varieties of trees and shrubs are used to create a natural atmosphere on the 40-acre zoo site. The Holden Museum of Living Reptiles is also located here.
Open: April 15–September 14, Monday–Saturday 10:00 a.m.–5:00 p.m., Sunday 9:00 a.m.–6:00 p.m.; rest of year, Wednesday–

Sunday 10:00 a.m.–4:00 p.m. Fee.
(313) 398–0900.

Elmwood Cemetery
1200 Elmwood Avenue

A fine example of nineteenth-century landscape architecture, the 46-acre cemetery was designed by Frederick Law Olmsted after the Mount Auburn Cemetery of Cambridge, Massachusetts. The Gothic Revival chapel is made of limestone.
Open: Daily, sunrise–sunset. (313) 567–3453.

Grosse Pointe
War Memorial Garden
Grosse Point Farms,
32 Lakeshore Drive

Formal "trial gardens" have been established on the grounds of an old estate on Lake St. Clair.
Open: Monday–Saturday 9:00 a.m.–9:00 p.m. (313) 885–6600.

Meadow Brook Hall and Gardens
Adams Road (Rochester)
I-75, 25 miles north of Detroit

The house, built in 1926, is a copy of Compton Wynyates, an English Tudor mansion (ca. 1520). The grounds include rose, topiary, and rock gardens. Formerly the Wilson home, it is now owned by Oakland University.
Open: Gardens only, year-round, Monday–Friday 10:00 a.m.–5:00 p.m.
(313) 370–3140.

Moross House
1460 East Jefferson Avenue

Typical mid-nineteenth century gardens surround the historic 1840 house, currently the headquarters of the Detroit Garden Center.
Open: 2nd Tuesday and 4th Thursday of the month, 8:00 a.m.–5:00 p.m.
(313) 259–6363.

6. East Lansing

☆
W. J. Beal–Garfield
Botanical Gardens
Michigan State University
West Drive, off Michigan Drive
(Mich. 43)

Begun in 1873 and reputed to be the oldest, continuously operated botanical garden in the United States, the gardens have more than 5,500 plant species and varieties. The campus horticultural gardens are the only trial gardens that display the plants in a landscape setting. They operate as a teaching and research facility as well as for public education.
Open: Daily 8:00 a.m.–5:00 p.m.
(517) 355–9582.

7. Kalamazoo

Memorial Arboretum
7000 North Westedge Avenue

The 25-acre arboretum is part of 500 acres that make up the Kalamazoo Nature Center.
Open: Monday–Friday 9:30 a.m.–5:00 p.m., Sunday 1:00–5:00 p.m. Fee. (616) 381–1574.

8. Midland

Dow Gardens
1018 West Main Street

The gardens were begun in 1899 by Dr. Herbert H. Dow, founder of Dow Chemical Company. One of the finest collections of crab apples grows in these gardens. May is the peak month for floral displays. The Dow Foundation sponsors many displays and educational programs on gardening techniques.
Open: Daily 10:00 a.m.–5:00 p.m. Closed: Thanksgiving, Christmas, New Year's Day. (517) 631–2677.

9. Niles

Fernwood, Inc.
1720 Range Line Road, 3 miles north of Niles

Formerly a private home, the garden now serves as a nature center. In the 100-acre arboretum is found an interesting variety of native trees, tall grass prairie, ferns, wildflowers, and bog plants.
Open: April 1–November 30, Monday–Friday 9:00 a.m.–5:00 p.m., Saturday 10:00 a.m.–5:00 p.m., Sunday noon–5:00 p.m. Fee. (616) 695–6491.

10. Saginaw

Tokushima Saginaw Friendship Garden
Ezra Rust Drive at Washington Avenue

The 1-acre Japanese garden was designed by Yotaro Suzue, a well-known landscape architect of Tokushima, Japan. The garden was completed in 1960.
Open: Daily, sunrise–sunset. (517) 776–1480.

11. Tipton

Hidden Lake Gardens
Mich. 50, 4 miles west of Tipton

Started in 1926 by Harry A. Fee, the gardens were given to Michigan State University in 1946. A wide variety of trees, shrubs, and flowers can be seen on the 670-acre site. In both natural and man-made environments, some 150 genera and 1,800 species are represented. There is also an extensive collection of dwarf and rare conifers. The conservatory complex has separate domes in which tropical, arid, and temperate plants are exhibited. *Open: April 1–November 1, weekdays 8:00 a.m.–sunset, Saturday–Sunday 9:00 a.m.–sunset; rest of year, 9:00 a.m.–4:30 p.m. (517) 431–2060.*

Other Places of Interest

Gaslight Village, Grand Rapids
Greenfield Village, Dearborn

Hartwick Pines State Park, Grayling
Isle Royale National Park
Little Netherlands, Holland
Mackinac Island, Lake Huron
Porcupine Mountains State Park, Ontonagon
Sleeping Bear Dunes National Lakeshore, Glen Haven

Minnesota

Area: 84,068 square miles

Population: 4,193,000

Statehood: May 11, 1858 (32nd state)

Minnesota is a land of varied and interesting topography. Situated in the exact center of North America, it lies at the confluence of three great continental drainage systems. In the Arrowhead region of northeastern Minnesota, the pre-Cambrian volcanic rocks of the Laurentian shield—the continent's ancient center—are exposed. Sharp ridges and deep valleys makes this region America's major source of iron ore. The surface of Minnesota was reshaped in the last Ice Age. Soils deposited in bands by the receding glaciers underlie the several distinctive landscape types. Water is an important element in Minnesota's landscape, which is known for its thousands of lakes.

Owing to the state's mid-continent location, the climate is extreme. Temperatures have been known to range from 35° below to 108° above zero. The growing season varies from 160 days in the south to less than 100 days in the extreme north. Rainfall ranges from 20 to 30 inches over most of the state. Due to its long summer days and rich soils, Minnesota is well suited to agriculture.

The first Europeans to visit Minnesota were trappers and fur traders. At the time of their arrival, huge coniferous forests covered northern Minnesota. South of these stretched "the Great Woods," a band of maple-basswood forests. Soon, the ancient trees were floating down Minnesota's waterways to the sawmill. The grasses of the Great Plains start in southern Minnesota.

Modern Minnesota has a diversified economy. The countryside owes its beauty to thousands of well-kept family farms. The nation's center of iron production is located in the Arrowhead region. The twin cities of Minneapolis–St. Paul occupy a dramatic site astride the Mississippi River. Minneapolis was a national leader in developing a public park system. A comprehensive plan for the city's system was prepared in 1883 by landscape architect H. W. S. Cleveland. In recent years, downtown Minneapolis has undergone extensive redevelopment. Projects include an innovative "skywalk" system of pedestrian bridges and the world-famous Nicollet Mall.

The people of Minnesota have long been concerned with preserving their state's natural beauty. The state park system was initiated in 1889 and today covers over 150,000 acres. Lake Itasca State Park celebrates the source of the Mississippi River. In the Arrowhead region are Voyageurs National Park and Superior National Forest.

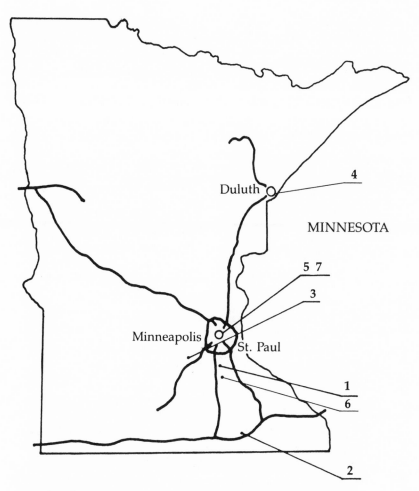

1. *Apple Valley*   2. *Austin*   3. *Chaska*   4. *Duluth*   5. *Minneapolis*
6. *Northfield*   7. *St. Paul*

1. Apple Valley

☆
Minnesota Zoological Gardens
12101 Johnny Cake Ridge Road
(20 miles south via I-35 West,
exit at Route 13 North)

On 467 acres, these gardens have established a kaleidoscope of northern hemispheric plant/animal life. Rockwork, bodies of water, and planting zones have been carefully designed to replicate the natural environments of the animals displayed. The five-story Tropic Building houses specimens primarily from southeastern Asia. Six major tropical ecosystems are exhibited with over 40,000 plantings (1,500 of which are orchids). The Minnesota Wildlife portrays scenes from the deciduous forests, coniferous forests, and vast tall and short grass prairies of the state. Along a 2.5-mile walkway, the Northern Trek expansively displays animals and plants from the steppes of Asia to the boggy marshes of North America.
Open: Daily, summer, 9:30 a.m.–5:00 p.m.; winter, until 4:30 p.m.
(612) 432–9000.

2. Austin

**Hormel Foundation
Nature Center**
21st Street, Northeast

Once the private estate of J. C. Hormel, the 240-acre site features established evergreens and woody shrubs. Interpretative paths wind through woods and meadows and cross streams in this delightful natural area.
Open: Daily, sunrise–sunset. (507) 437–7519.

3. Chaska

University of Minnesota Landscape Arboretum
3675 Arboretum Drive (entrance on Minn. 5, 0.5 miles west of intersection with Minn. 41)

The arboretum features labeled plants, wildflowers, and trees. Picnic grounds.
Open: Daily 8:00 a.m.–sunset. Fee. (612) 443–2460.

4. Duluth

Glensheen
3300 London Road

The 7.6 acres of this former estate (ca. 1905) are now owned by the University of Minnesota. Formal and informal grounds surround the house.
Open: June–September, Thursday–Tuesday 10:00 a.m.–4:00 p.m.; October–May, limited hours. (218) 724–8863.

Leif Erikson Park
11th Avenue East and London Road

There is a statue of the explorer and a half-scale replica of the boat he sailed to North America in a.d. 997. There is also a municipal rose garden.
Open: Daily, sunrise–sunset. (218) 724–8863.

5. Minneapolis

Eloise Butler
Wild Flower Preserve
Glenwood Avenue and North Abbot

Paths wind through 13 acres of woodland gardens and 7 acres of upland gardens blooming with flowers and plants native to Minnesota.
Open: April 1–November 1, daily 10:00 a.m.–6:00 p.m. (612) 374–4305.

Greenhouse of the
College of Pharmacy
University of Minnesota Campus

Medicinal plants are grown, observed, and studied here.
Open: Daily during school hours. (612) 373–2126.

Lake Minnetonka Gardens
Lyndale Park, West 42nd Street

A rose garden, rock garden, and bog garden are featured. The rose garden has more than 5,000 plants and a wide variety of hybrids.
Open: Daily, sunrise–sunset. (612) 348–2142.

Nicollet Mall
Downtown

This semi-pedestrian mall area (buses and taxis are allowed) was designed by landscape architect Lawrence Halprin. It features attractive landscaping, seating, fountains, and sculpture.
Open: All times. (612) 348–4313.

Summit Avenue

This notable area offers many magnificent nineteenth-century styles of architecture and garden art, as well as the former residences of such celebrities as F. Scott Fitzgerald and Frank B. Kellogg. The Burbank–Livingston–Griggs House and the governor's mansion are also located here.
Open: All times. Houses open to the public, generally daily 10:00 a.m.–4:00 p.m. (612) 348–3413.

6. Northfield

Carleton College Arboretum
Minn. 19, northwestern edge of town

The 455-acre arboretum of this liberal arts college, founded in 1866, also features a 35-acre tall grass prairie.
Open: By appointment. (612) 633–4309.

7. St. Paul

Como Park Conservatory
North Lexington and Como Avenues

This Victorian structure houses a wide variety of plants as well as many temporary exhibits. It is famous nationwide for its colorful, varied, and well-arranged floral displays. In addition to the conservatory, Como Park has many other attractions including formal gardens, waterfalls, an amusement park, a zoo, and rental boats.
Open: Winter, daily 10:00 a.m.– 4:00 p.m.; summer, until 6:00 p.m. (612) 489–1740.

Town Square Park
445 Minnesota Street

Reputed to be one of the largest indoor parks (28,000 sq. ft.), this unique facility features waterfalls, streams, pools, and an abundance of tropical vegetation.
Open: Monday–Friday 9:00 a.m.– 9:00 p.m., Saturday 9:00 a.m.– 6:00 p.m., Sunday noon–6:00 p.m. (612) 227–3307.

Other Places of Interest

Forest History Center, Grand Rapids
Freeboron County Historical Village, Athert Lee
Iron Range Interpretative Center, Hibbing
Lake Harriet Garden Center, Minneapolis
Lake of the Woods, Burdette
Mayowood, Rochester
Pioneer Village, Workington
Pipestone National Monument, Pipestone
Rice Lake National Wildlife Refuge, Aitkin
Village of Yesteryear, Owatonna
Voyageurs National Park, International Falls

Mississippi

Area: 47,716 square miles

Population: 2,613,000

Statehood: December 10, 1817
(20th state)

The "Magnolia State" is located entirely in the low Gulf Coastal Plain. Its highest elevation is 806 feet above sea level at Woodall Mountain in the extreme northwestern part of the state. Rainfall is plentiful everywhere. Summers are very hot and winters mild. The state's various soils are reflected in a variety of vegetation and landforms. In the extreme west lie the rich alluvial soils of the Mississippi and Yazoo rivers; in the south, sandy hills are dominated by pine trees. An area of rich clay loam known as "The Black Belt" occurs in the northwest. Heavy summer rains cause serious soil erosion throughout the state.

Britain, Spain, and France competed in colonial times for control of the area, then known as West Florida. The decline of farmlands along the seaboard where the cotton plantation system was practiced pressured planters to seek new land in the west. By the close of the War of 1812, the Mississippi Territory was firmly controlled by the United States. Cotton long dominated Mississippi's agriculture.

Before the advent of the railroad, produce from states west of the Appa-lachians had to be shipped to market via the Mississippi River. Farmers from Kentucky and Ohio would load their produce on flatboats and float it downstream to the great riverport of Natchez. Unable to return upriver against the Mississippi's strong current, they would sell their boats for lumber and return home overland by a trail called the Natchez Trace. After the 1830s the steamboat, which could navigate upriver, gave them an easier way home. The 450-mile Natchez Trace National Historic Parkway follows the old overland route.

Mississippi has many interesting homes of the pre-Civil War era. The town of Natchez is particularly rich in these. Every year, in mid-March, the Natchez Pilgrimage offers the public an opportunity to visit a number of these historic homes. For information, write P.O. Box 347, Natchez, Miss. 39120. (601) 442–5849.

1. Belzoni

Wister Gardens
Highway 49, 0.5 miles north of Belzoni

This 14-acre floral garden is located in the heart of the Mississippi Delta. It is noted for its many varieties of azaleas and camellias. On the grounds are a lake, fountains, an astrolab, and gazebos.
Open: Daily 8:00 a.m.–5:00 p.m. (601) 247–3025.

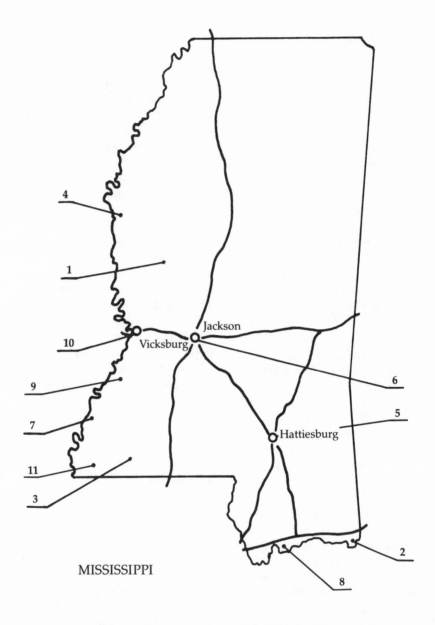

MISSISSIPPI

1. *Belzoni* **2.** *Biloxi* **3.** *Gloster* **4.** *Greenville* **5.** *Hattiesburg* **6.** *Jackson*
7. *Natchez* **8.** *Pass Christian* **9.** *Port Gibson* **10.** *Vicksburg* **11.** *Woodville*

2. Biloxi

Beauvoir Gardens
West Beach Boulevard,
5 miles west on U.S. 90

This was the last home of Jefferson Davis, president of the Confederate States of America, and the plantings are kept just as they were by President and Mrs. Davis and their daughter, Winnie. The gigantic trees, which were spared by the killer hurricane "Camille," continue to flourish on the grounds.
Open: Daily 9:00 a.m.–5:00 p.m. Closed: Christmas. Fee. (601) 388–1313.

3. Gloster

Gloster Arboretum
Arboretum Road (take Railroad Avenue past the Georgia Pacific Building)

The 327-acre arboretum was established by Mr. and Mrs. Frank Gladney in 1956. Thousands of unusual native plants abound on the bluffs and in spring-fed ravines.
Open: Monday–Friday 9:00 a.m.–5:00 p.m., weekends by appointment. (601) 225–4743 or (Mrs. Stephens) 225–7579.

4. Greenville

Wetherbee House
509 Washington Avenue

A typical small-town home of the 1870s with a cottage garden is located on the main street. Shaded by five giant water oaks, it features a simple parterre of old-fashioned fragrant flowers, a cistern, and a carriage house.
Open: By appointment, P.O. Box 595.

Winterville Indian Mounds State Park
Miss. 1, 3 miles north of Greenville

The site contains fourteen Indian mounds. The Greenville Garden Club donated the 43 acres as a park to protect the mounds from erosion and bulldozers. There is a museum.
Open: Tuesday–Saturday 9:00 a.m.–6:00 p.m., Sunday 1:00–6:00 p.m. Fee. (601) 334–4684.

5. Hattiesburg

University of Southern Mississippi
Hardy Street

The 840-acre campus includes an American Rose Society test garden. Best seen between spring and December.
Open: Daily, sunrise–sunset. (601) 266–4491.

6. Jackson

7. Natchez

Governor's Mansion
300 East Capitol Street

This 1838 Greek Revival mansion was extensively restored in 1972. The grounds have been designed to complement the restoration and feature a gazebo, formal perennial beds, roses, and a fountain. *Open: Grounds, daily 9:00 a.m.– 6:00 p.m.; different hours for house. (601) 359–3818 or 948–7575.*

Mynelle Gardens
4738 Clinton Boulevard

Today the 6-acre gardens are rich in lush plant materials. They feature statuary, a rustic Garden and Summer House, Wedding Lawn, English Bog Garden, and Japanese Garden Island. The gardens are very colorful in all seasons. *Open: Daily, dawn–dusk. Fee. (601) 960–1894.*

The Oaks
823 North Jefferson Street

This Greek Revival cottage (1846) was occupied by General William T. Sherman during the siege of 1863. The grounds include a restored garden. *Open: Daily 10:00 a.m.–5:00 p.m. Fee. (601) 948–7575.*

Conelly's Tavern
Jefferson and Canal Streets

Built in 1797, the house and grounds have been restored by the Natchez Garden Club. *Open: Daily 9:00 a.m.–5:00 p.m. Closed: Christmas, New Year's Day. Fee. (601) 442–2011.*

Longwood Grounds
140 Lower Woodville Road

Longwood was designed by Samuel Sloan for Dr. Haller Nutt. Construction began in 1858 but was stopped when workmen left for the Civil War. Today the house remains as the workmen left it. With its octagonal plan, the structure is an outstanding example of the Oriental style that was briefly popular in the mid-nineteenth century. An artificial lake was formed from a bayou and magnolias were planted along the drive; several orchards and 10 acres of roses were also planted. The dam broke, destroying the lake, and much of the grounds have been allowed to return to their natural state. Maintained by the Pilgrimage Garden Club. *Open: Daily 9:30 a.m.–5:00 p.m. Fee. (601) 442–5849.*

Rosalie Plantation
100 Orleans Avenue

Built in 1820, this plantation is the state headquarters of the Daughters of the American Revolution. Its

gardens feature azaleas and native plants.
Open: Daily 9:00 a.m.–5:00 p.m. Closed: Holidays. Fee. (601) 445–4555.

Stanton Hall Gardens
401 High Street

Frederick Stanton purchased one city block in 1850 to build the magnificent Stanton Hall; seventeen live oaks were planted. In 1938, the Pilgrimage Garden Club bought the home. The original trees still remain. Azaleas, camellias, and other flowering plants have been added.
Open: Daily 9:00 a.m.–5:00 p.m. Closed: Christmas, New Year's Day. (601) 446–6631.

8. Pass Christian

Wildflower Gardens
Menge Avenue

Many of Mississippi's native trees and shrubs can be seen in this 11-acre woodland.
Open: Daily, sunrise–sunset. (601) 452–2252.

9. Port Gibson

Oak Square
U.S. 61, 1 mile off
Natchez Trace Parkway

This 1850 mansion has been beautifully restored. There are extensive grounds, a courtyard garden, and a gazebo.
Open: Daily 9:00 a.m.–5:00 p.m. Fee. (601) 437–4350.

10. Vicksburg

Cedar Grove
2200 Oak Street

An antebellum mansion with gardens that extend down to the river.
Open: Monday–Saturday 9:00 a.m.– 5:00 p.m., Sunday 1:00–5:00 p.m. Fee. (601) 636–1605.

McRaven
1445 Harrison Street

The lovely gardens surrounding McRaven have century-old oaks, boxwoods, magnolias, camellias, and other Deep South traditional plants from before the Civil War.
Open: Mid-February–mid-November, Monday–Saturday 9:00 a.m.– 5:00 p.m., Sunday 1:00–5:00 p.m. (601) 636–1663.

Planters Hall
822 Main Street

This is the site of Vicksburg's first bank. The garden, contained within a brick wall, has a central fountain and is planted with species indigenous to the area.
Open: By appointment. (601) 636– 9421.

11. Woodville

Rosemont Plantation

East of town on Miss. 24
(Main Street)

This 1810 mansion was the family home of Jefferson Davis. The 300-acre plantation has been restored to its early nineteenth-century character.

Open: March–December, Monday–
Friday 9:00 a.m.–5:00 p.m. Fee. (601)
888–6809.

Other Places of Interest

Battlefield Park, Jackson
Navish Waiya Mound, Noxapater
Vicksburg National Military Park

Towns of special interest that have spring garden tours include Columbus, Laurel, Natchez, Oxford, Port Gibson, and Vicksburg.

Missouri

Area: 69,686 square miles

Population: 5,029,000

Statehood: August 10, 1821 (24th state)

Located along the western bank of the Mississippi River, America's "Gateway to the West" enjoys an exciting diversity of landforms. The Ozark Plateau, a scenic green and hilly region, covers most of the southern part of the state. In the extreme southeastern corner is a low area of the Mississippi alluvial plain with distinctive southern vegetation. The Great Plains begin in northwestern Missouri. The average yearly rainfall diminishes from about 50 inches in the southeast to about 30 in the northwest. Early settlers found oak-hickory covering large areas of Missouri.

Missouri's first permanent settlement was founded at Saint Genevieve in 1732 by French settlers who came to mine rich lead ores. This small town has several early homes. Mining continues to be an important industry in this part of the state. Numerous parks in southeastern Missouri display the caves and unusual rock formations carved by water in the calcareous bedrock. The Mark Twain National Forest and many state parks are located in this region. Elephant Rocks, Johnson's Shut-Ins, and Millstream Gardens State Forest all feature interesting rock formations.

Saint Louis was founded as a trading post near the junction of the Missouri and Mississippi rivers. At this historic site many settlers began their migration to the West. Furs and other valuable products of the frontier were brought here for processing and market. Today, the 82-acre Jefferson National Expansion Memorial and the Gateway Arch decorate the waterfront. Nearby is the "Old Courthouse," a fine example of Greek Revival architecture. Forest Park, site of the 1904 World's Fair, is not to be missed. Aloe Plaza near Union Station features a fountain by eminent sculptor Carl Milles.

Northeastern Missouri is a fertile farming region. Hannibal, situated on bluffs overlooking the Mississippi River, was Mark Twain's boyhood home. The house where he lived—owned by the city—is open to the public. The Oregon and Santa Fe trails started in western Missouri. Kansas City is a modern, growing city. The many fountains gracing its public spaces recall the bubbling springs of the Ozarks.

Missouri offers a delightful mixture of landscapes and cultures.

1. Centralia

Chance Gardens
319 Sneed Street

Mr. A. B. Chance started these very colorful gardens in 1935. They are

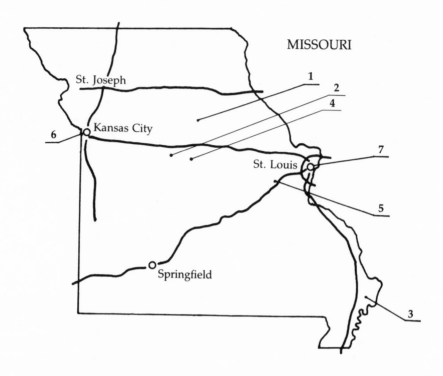

1. *Centralia* 2. *Columbia* 3. *East Prairie* 4. *Fulton* 5. *Gray Summit*
6. *Kansas City* 7. *Saint Louis*

now maintained by the Chance Foundation, which continues the tradition of sharing a garden's beauty with visitors.
Open: Daily 9:00 a.m.–8:00 p.m.
(314) 682–5521

eties of trees. There is a restored one-room schoolhouse. Garden concerts are provided Sunday evenings during June and July.
Open: Daily 8:00 a.m.–dusk. (314)
445–8441.

2. Columbia

Shelter Insurance Gardens
1817 West Broadway

The focus of several of the city's cultural events, the gardens feature waterfalls, pools, and over 200 vari-

3. East Prairie

Big Oak Tree State Park
10 miles south of East Prairie
(take Mo. 80 to Mo. 102)

This 1,004-acre virgin forest contains a number of the largest specimen

Gateway Arch National Monument, Saint Louis, Mo.

trees in North America, including green ash, swamp privet, and water locust.
Open: Daily, sunrise–sunset. (314) 649–3149.

4. Fulton

Winston Churchill Memorial English Garden
Westminster Avenue and West 7th Street

A beautiful garden adjoins the St. Mary Aldermanbury Church building and the Westminster College campus. The building was originally in London where it was the site of Churchill's "Iron Curtain" speech.
Open: All times. (314) 642–3361 or 642–6648.

5. Gray Summit

Shaw Arboretum
Junction of Route 144 and Mo. 100

This 2,400-acre facility of the Missouri Botanical Gardens includes a 200-acre landscaped pinetum and a number of native Ozark plant communities. The arboretum is maintained for research and public education.
Open: Daily 8:00 a.m.–5:00 p.m. Fee. (314) 742–3512.

6. Kansas City

Loose Park Garden Center
51st and Wornall Streets

The 75-acre park features a famous rose garden. There is also a horticultural reference library.
Open: Daily 8:00 a.m.–4:00 p.m. (816) 561–9710

Missouri Town
East side of Lake Jacomo

This reconstructed Missouri town of the mid-nineteenth century features vegetable gardens, orchards, and ornamental plantings typical of the period.
Open: Daily 9:00 a.m.–5:00 p.m. Fee. (816) 474–9600.

☆
The Plaza
47th Street and
J. C. Nichols Parkway

Started in 1922, this 55-acre complex of city shops, restaurants, and painstakingly cared for landscaping was the vision of department store owner J. C. Nichols. Strict architectural standards and a commitment to provide outdoor enrichment through sculpture, fountains, and richly planted areas suggest an approach to downtown urban development from which others can still learn.
Open: All times. (816) 753–0100.

Unity Village
Colburn Road and Mo. 350, southeast off I-470

Founded in 1889 by the Unity School of Christianity, the 1,400-acre Mediterranean-style village provides a tranquil atmosphere which is enhanced by the attractively developed landscaping. Formal areas include the Lowell Filmore Memorial Garden and the Unity Rose Garden.
Open: Daily, sunrise–sunset. Tours available Monday–Saturday. (816) 524–3550.

William Rockhill Nelson Gallery of Art
4524 Oak Street

There are extensive gardens including the Pierson Sculpture Garden.
Open: Tuesday–Saturday 10:00 a.m.–5:00 p.m., Sunday 2:00–6:00 p.m. Fee (except Sunday). (816) 561–4000.

7. Saint Louis

Forest Park
Between Kings Highway, Lindell Boulevard, and Oakland Avenue

The site of the 1904 World's Fair, this is one of the finest large urban parks in the country. The "Jewel Box" is a spectacular conservatory; when built in 1936, it was considered an architectural curiosity. An electric chime carillon provides a musical background for visitors. The zoo, where many animals are in their natural habitats, and a modern planetarium are also of exceptional interest.
Open: Daily 9:00 a.m.–5:00 p.m. (314) 535–5050.

Laumeier Sculpture Park
12580 Rott Road

This 96-acre park is devoted mainly to the outdoor display of contemporary sculpture. There is also an art gallery.
Open: Daily, sunrise–sunset. (314) 821–1209.

☆☆
Missouri Botanical Gardens
4344 Shaw Boulevard

The Missouri Botanical Gardens, Arboretum, and Nature Preserve is undoubtedly one of the most complete nature centers in the United States; there are 79 acres in the Botanical Gardens and 2,400 acres in the separate arboretum at Grey Summit. The Botanical Gardens were founded in 1859 by Henry Shaw.

Missouri Botanical Gardens, Saint Louis, Mo.

Located here is the Climatron, an internationally famous geodesic dome that contains over 1,200 exotic plants representing the tropical regions of the world. Built in 1969, it is believed to be the largest indoor garden of this type in the United States. There are also a desert house, floral display house, camellia house, scented garden, and much more. *Open: May–October, 9:00 a.m.– 8:00 p.m.; November–April, until 5:00 p.m. Fee. (314) 577–5100 or 577–5125.*

Adjoining the Botanical Gardens is the headquarters of the National Council of State Garden Clubs, Inc. (4401 Magnolia Avenue), surrounded by a beautifully landscaped green area—(314) 776–7574. Tower Grove House, the restored country residence of Henry Shaw, is also open to the public on a more restricted schedule—(314) 577–5150.

☆
Seiwa-En, The Japanese Garden
Missouri Botanical Gardens

Constructed in 1977, this traditional Japanese garden encompasses 14 acres, making it the largest such garden in North America. It features many water elements, three styles of Japanese bridges, and an extensive variety of Japanese plant species. *Open: May 1–October 15, 9:00 a.m.–*

7:30 p.m.; October 16–April 30, until
4:30 p.m.
Closed: Christmas. Included in
admission fee for Missouri Botanical
Gardens. (314) 535–0400.

Tower Grove Park

4255 Arsenal Avenue

Tower Grove Park rambles over 279
acres. It has been called one of the
finest remaining examples of a Victorian park in the United States and is
likely one of the finest in the world.
Its gazebos, statuary, sailboat pond,
stately entrances, and tree-lined
walks convey Henry Shaw's vision
of a strolling park in the English
tradition.
Open: Daily 7:00 a.m.–11:00 p.m.
(314) 771–2679.

Other Places of Interest

Arrow Rock State Historic Site,
    Arrow Rock

Gateway Arch, Jefferson National
    Expansion Memorial, Saint Louis
Grants Farm, Saint Louis
Harry S. Truman Library,
    Independence
Highway 94 from Saint Charles to
    Jefferson City (scenic drive)
Highway 21 from Saint Louis to
    Ironton (scenic drive)
Lakes of the Ozarks, Central
    Missouri
Mark Twain Museum, Hannibal
Missouri Wine Country, Highway 94
Ozark National Scenic Riverways,
    Van Buren
Shark Brothers Nursery, Louisiana
Test Rose Garden, Cape Girardeau
Watkins Woolen Mill State Historic
    Site, Lawson

Montana

Area: 147,138 square miles

Population: 826,000

Statehood: November 8, 1889
(41st state)

Montana is known as the "Treasure
State." The Great Plains occupy
its eastern portion. These vast and
empty grasslands are divided into
huge ranches and worked by giant
agricultural machines. In the western
part of the state rise the northern
Rocky Mountains. Snow-capped
peaks, alpine meadows, coniferous
forests, lakes, and waterfalls make
this a spectacular landscape.

Montana has a climate of hot and
cold extremes. Rainfall averages less
than 20 inches per year in the Plains
area. Droughts caused the ranches
of many early homesteaders to fail.
Despite the fact that the lack of water
limits productivity, Montana is the
nation's third largest wheat producer.
Cattle raising and sheep raising are
significant uses of land too poor for
crop production. Coniferous forests
cover the mountain areas. There are
eleven national forests in Montana
as well as many commercial forests.
Lumbering is an important industry.

The settlement of Montana was
limited to a few fur trading posts
until gold was discovered. The ghost
town of Bannack marks the site where
the first great strike occurred in 1862.

Copper mining and coal mining are
important industries today. The city
of Butte sits on the edge of the now
closed Anaconda copper mine, an
open pit one mile across and hundreds of feet deep. Regulation of the
coal strip mining planned for the
eastern prairies is a current concern
of residents.

A large part of the state consists
of publicly owned lands. Glacier
National Park and part of Yellowstone National Park are located in
Montana's mountains. Custer Battlefield and Big Hole Battlefield national
monuments mark the sites of historic Indian battles. Medicine Rocks
State Park, featuring unusual rock
formations of an intense white color,
includes land sacred to the Indians
and once was the site of their medicine dances. Montana has seven
Indian reservations; periodically,
colorful Indian ceremonies are held.
At Browning is located a museum of
the Plains Indians. Montana's favorite artist is Charles M. Russell, who
came to Montana as a young man and
spent his life vividly recording scenes
of the western frontier. Many of his
works are on display at the Russell
Gallery in Great Falls.

The visitor will find the beautiful
Rocky Mountains to be Montana's
most magnificent garden.

1. *Deer Lodge* 2. *Missoula* 3. *Moccasin*

1. Deer Lodge

Grant–Kohrs Ranch National Historic Site
Northern edge of town

Once the headquarters for over one million acres of ranchland, this fine old ranch house and its surrounding buildings and grounds have been preserved in their original pioneer condition.
Open: Daily 9:00 a.m.–5:00 p.m. Closed: Major holidays. (406) 846–2070.

2. Missoula

Memorial Rose Park
U.S. 93 South (Brooks Street)

About 2,000 roses are grown in a memorial rose garden and rose testing field. Flowering continues from June through most of October.
Open: Sunrise–sunset. (406) 543–6623.

3. Moccasin

Moccasin Experiment Station
Montana State University, Mont. 200

The plants maintained in the experimental plots are grown primarily to

determine the hardiness of various ornamentals in relation to the rigorous climate. There are some plantings and a flower garden.
Open: Sunrise–sunset. (406) 994–3681.

Other Places of Interest

Big Hole Battlefield National
 Monument, Mont. 43
Bighorn Canyon National Recreation
 Area, Hardin
Custer National Forest, Hardin

Flathead National Forest, Kalispell,
 U.S. 2
Gallatin National Forest, Bozeman
Glacier National Park, Columbia
 Falls, Mont. 40, U.S. 2
Medicine Rocks State Park, Enkalaka,
 Mont. 7
National Fish Hatchery, Ennis
Pictograph Cave State Monument,
 Billings
Russell Studio Museum, Great Falls

Nebraska

Area: 77,227 square miles

Population: 1,606,000

Statehood: March 1, 1867
(37th state)

Nebraska's land is flat, rising gradually from the Missouri River on its
eastern border to the Rocky Mountains in the west. Its continental
climate is harsh, with severe blizzards
in the winter. In the western part of
the state, rainfall averages only about
17 inches a year; the dominant vegetation is grama and buffalo grass. In
the east, rainfall will average up to
30 inches per year; bluestem prairies
occur in these more humid regions.
In the west, where rainfall is less
frequent, wind plays a more important role in shaping the land. The
Sandhills form a significant geologic
area. They are composed of loess
transported from the western deserts
by the prevailing winds. Grasses
rooting in these soils hold the sand
in place. Lakes and marshes in low
areas account for its scenic beauty. In
the western Platte Valley, a favorite
landmark for pioneers traveling the
Oregon Trail was Chimney Rock, a
wind-sculpted formation. Nebraska's
rivers cut wide valleys in its thick
soils. In the spring they carry melting snow from the mountains; at
other times they become only narrow
rivulets.

The tree is a precious item in Nebraska. Early settlers missed the
forests they were accustomed to see-
ing in the eastern states or in Europe.
It was a Nebraska settler, J. Sterling
Morton, while serving as secretary
of agriculture in President Grover
Cleveland's administration, who
initiated Arbor Day. The Nebraska
National Forest, established in 1902
in the Sandhill country, is the largest
section of national forest planted by
man. Forest fires are a great danger in
this dry country. Modern westerners
recognize the prairies as a natural
form with their own unique beauty.
In 1960, the Ogallala National Grassland was established in Dowes and
Sioux counties.

Nebraska has many historic re-
minders of the Old West. There are
several Indian museums, and the
state capitol building at Lincoln displays works of Indian art. The Joslyn
Art Museum in Omaha exhibits
paintings of the frontier as well as the
works of European masters. Agate
Fossil Beds National Monument is of
interest to paleontologists. There are
several frontier forts of note. Willa
Cather's childhood home in Red
Cloud is a state park, as is Buffalo
Bill's ranch near North Platte.

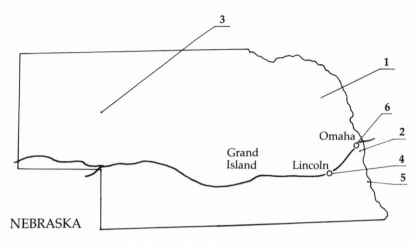

NEBRASKA

1. *Bancroft*   2. *Bellevue*   3. *Elsworth*   4. *Lincoln*   5. *Nebraska City*   6. *Omaha*

1. Bancroft

Sioux Prayer Garden
Corner of Elm and
Washington Streets, off I-29

This small garden is at the former
home of Dr. John G. Neihardt, poet
laureate of Nebraska until his death
in 1973. It is a unique, living symbol
of the Sioux "Hoop of the World."
Open: April 1–November 15,
Monday–Saturday, 8:00 a.m.–
5:00 p.m., Sunday 1:00–5:00 p.m.
(402) 648–3388.

2. Bellevue

Fontenelle Forest
and Nature Center
1111 Bellevue Boulevard, North

Begun in 1912, this wilderness area
offers 17 miles of hiking trails and
features many kinds of birds and
animals. There are public workshops
and guided tours.
Open: 362 days/year, 8:00 a.m.–
5:00 p.m. (402) 371–3140.

3. Elsworth

Sandoz Fruit Farm
6 miles north of Elsworth
on Nebr. 27

Jules Sandoz, immortalized by his daughter Mari in the biography *Old Jules*, was a pioneer horticulturist in the Nebraska Sandhills. His "experimental farm" boasted one of the best collections of fruit trees suited to the North-Central Plains.
Open: Daily 9:00 a.m.–5:00 p.m. (308) 282–1546.

4. Lincoln

Chet Ager Nature Center
Pioneers Park, Van Dorn and Southwest 40th Streets

The center is dedicated to making the public aware of the beauty of nature, with nature trails, recycling displays, and many other ecologically oriented exhibits. Guided tours.
Open: Daily 9:00 a.m.–5:00 p.m. (402) 471–7895.

Pioneers Park
0.25 miles south of Coddington and Van Dorn Streets

This park was designed by Ernest Herminghaus in 1933 to reflect a beaux-arts combination of the English and French landscape styles. Thousands of Austrian pines are used to create a contrast to the prairie.
Open: Sunrise–sunset. (402) 476–7511.

Wilderness Park
South 1st Street and
Pioneers Boulevard

Established in an urban setting, this 1,455-acre park aims to provide a refuge where visitors can enjoy nature. Land for the park was purchased with funds from the Federal Open Space Act. It includes a hiking trail and bridle path.
Open: Daily, sunrise–sunset. (402) 476–7511.

5. Nebraska City

Arbor Lodge State Historical Park
Second Avenue
(U.S. 75, 1 mile north)

When J. Sterling Morton came to the Nebraska frontier from New York State, he brought many trees from the East to plant on the grounds of this 65-acre treeless prairie lot. Later, as secretary of agriculture under Grover Cleveland, he founded Arbor Day. Begun in 1855, the grounds and the lodge have undergone many renovations. The Italian formal garden was established in 1923.
Open: Park, daily, sunrise–sunset; mansion, April 15–October 31, daily 1:00–5:00 p.m. (402) 873–3221.

6. Omaha

☆
General Crook House
30th and Fort Streets

This Italianate house (1878) was originally the quarters of the commanding officer of Fort Omaha. A Victorian flower garden is maintained during the summer.
Open: Daily 9:00 a.m.–5:00 p.m. Tours by appointment. Closed: Major holidays. Fee. (402) 455–9990.

Mount Vernon
Municipal Gardens
5833 South 13th Street

At this site is a reproduction of the George Washington Gardens at Mount Vernon, Virginia. (402) 444–4660.

Other Places of Interest

Agate Fossil Beds National
  Monument, Scottsbluff
Boys Town, Omaha (U.S. 6)
Buffalo Bill State Historical Park,
  North Platte
Chimney Rock National Historic
  Site, Bridgeport (U.S. 26)
Harold Warp Pioneer Village,
  Minden
Historic Bellevue, Omaha (Nebr. 73
  and 75)
Homestead National Monument,
  Beatrice
Railroad Town, Grand Island
Scottsbluff National Monument,
  Gering (Nebr. 92)

Nevada

Area: 110,540 square miles

Population: 936,000

Statehood: October 31, 1864
(36th state)

Most of Nevada lies within the Great Basin formed by the Rocky Mountains to the east and the Sierra Nevada Mountains to the west. Eroded mountain ranges divide the land into long valleys trending north and south. Boundary Peak, at 13,143 feet above sea level, is Nevada's highest point.

Because of the barrier formed by the encircling mountains, the average annual rainfall never exceeds 20 inches anywhere in the state. The average rainfall at Las Vegas, the state's largest city, is only 5 inches per year. Water is a precious resource and determines the land's potential use. Extensive water conservation projects have been undertaken to conserve this resource and to use it wisely to support agriculture and human settlements. Hoover Dam, built in the 1930s to catch the waters of the Colorado River, created Lake Mead which is an important recreational area.

Because of the state's basin topography, most rivers have no outlet to the sea. They either flow into lakes or are absorbed into huge mud flats. Lake Tahoe, lying 6,225 feet above sea level and surrounded by snow-clad mountains, is of great scenic beauty. The remarkable clarity of its waters is threatened, however, by the heavy resort development it has attracted.

Much of northern Nevada is grazing land. Remote cattle ranches feed their herds on the sagebrush steppe. At higher elevations coniferous forests are found. There are four national forests in Nevada.

The first impetus to settle this arid land came in 1859 when the Comstock Silver Lode was discovered. Virginia City at that time became a boisterous boomtown of 30,000 residents. Today, its population is close to 700. Souvenir shops and abandoned mansions recall its days of glamour. In 1931 Nevada, seeking to attract the tourist dollar, legalized gambling, an Old West tradition. The economic base and the water supply furnished by Lake Mead allowed Las Vegas, originally a tiny Mormon trading post, to grow into a glittering, air-conditioned resort city with a population of over 100,000.

1. Carson City

Sandy Bowers Mansion
Old U.S. 395, 10 miles north of Carson City

The mansion on this 1.5-acre site was built in 1864. The entire structure and grounds were restored in 1968. A large circular driveway with fountains and pathways now surrounds the mansion. Some of the grounds are

NEVADA

1. *Carson City*

lushly planted; much has been left in
its natural state.
Open: Mid-May–October, 9:00 a.m.–
4:30 p.m. Fee. (702) 849–0201.

State Capitol Grounds
101 North Carson Street

The grounds surrounding the capitol
buildings encompass 3.67 acres. The
original design was installed in 1870,
much of which was supervised by

Sagebrush desert in Nevada.

the architect of the buildings, Joseph Gosling. In 1974, a restoration of the grounds was completed under the direction of Allen Scott, landscape architect for the State Parks Department.
Open: Daily, sunrise–sunset. (702) 882–1565.

Other Places of Interest

Cathedral Gorge
Elko-Center (for visits to ghost towns)

Humboldt National Forest, northern Nevada
Ichthyosaur Paleontologic State Monument, central Nevada
Lake Mead National Recreation Area, southern Nevada
Lake Tahoe
Lehman Caves National Monument, northern Nevada
Valley of Fire State Park, southern Nevada

New Hampshire

Area: 9,304 square miles

Population: 998,000

Statehood: June 21, 1788 (9th state)

The "Granite State" is remarkable for the scenic beauty of its mountains. Its Presidential Range contains the highest peaks in New England. The tallest of these, Mount Washington, stands 6,288 feet above sea level. Snowstorms occur on its summit in August. From the summit, on a clear day, the Atlantic Ocean can be seen. In this state, the naturalist will find large areas of alpine vegetation and some of the last remaining primeval forests in the East. Extensive hiking trails and cabins are operated by the Appalachian Mountain Club. At Franconia Notch, towering above Profile Lake, is a cliff carved by nature to look like a human profile; Nathaniel Hawthorne called this formation "The Old Man of the Mountain." Water descending from the mountains has carved many scenic ravines; one of the most spectacular of these is the Lost River Gorge.

East of the White Mountains lie the New England Uplands. The average elevation in this area is 1,000 feet above sea level. "Monadnocks," granite domes that have eroded more slowly than the surrounding rock, are striking landscape features. Soils here are poor and boulder-strewn due to glaciation. The Merrimack River cuts through this area in south-central New Hampshire. Once Indian fishing villages lined the river where great salmon and shad runs occurred. In the nineteenth century, the waters of the Merrimack powered New England's textile industry, and mill towns and company-built tenements replaced fishing villages. The Amoskoeg Manufacturing Company of Manchester was once the largest textile operation in the world. Finding new uses for these fine old buildings presents a significant challenge to contemporary New Englanders. Many beautiful old homes still remain in this area. In Franklin is the boyhood home of statesman Daniel Webster. Concord, the state capital, was once famous for the beautiful coaches that it produced.

A narrow section in the southeastern portion of the state falls into the low, flat Atlantic Coastal Plain. New Hampshire has 18 miles of ocean beach. At Portsmouth is Strawberry Banke, a lovely area of restored colonial homes.

New Hampshire, a state of poor, thin soils, has derived its wealth from other natural resources: abundant water, rich forests, and the scenic beauty of its mountains. Each year there is growing pressure to protect these valuable resources through appropriate conservation programs.

NEW HAMPSHIRE

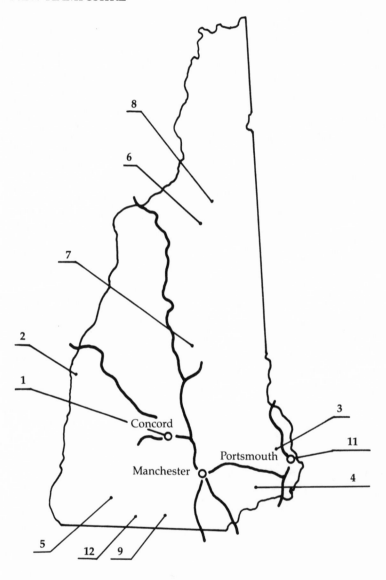

1. *Concord* 2. *Cornish* 3. *Durham* 4. *Exeter* 5. *Fitzwilliam* 6. *Kinsman's Notch* 7. *Meredith* 8. *Mount Washington* 9. *New Ipswich* 10. *North Hampton* 11. *Portsmouth* 12. *Rindge*

1. Concord

Pierce Manse
14 Penacook Street

Built in 1838, this was the home of Franklin Pierce, fourteenth president of the United States. The gardens re-create the style of the period with lilacs, flowering trees, shrubs, and an herb garden.
Open: Summer, Monday–Friday 11:00 a.m.–3:00 p.m. Fee. (603) 224–9620 or 225–2068.

2. Cornish

Saint-Gaudens
National Historic Site
Off N.H. 12A

The site features the studio, home, and restored garden of the sculptor Augustus Saint-Gaudens.
Open: Mid-May–October 31, daily 8:30 a.m.–4:30 p.m. Fee. (603) 675–2175.

3. Durham

Lilac Arboretum
University of New Hampshire Campus

A fine collection of varieties of common lilacs can be found on the campus as well as in the lilac arboretum, which is operated by the Department of Horticulture.
Open: Daily 8:00 a.m.–5:00 p.m. (603) 862–2190.

4. Exeter

Gilman Garrison House
12 Water Street

A seventeenth-century log house with eighteenth-century additions, this was one of the original garrisons in New Hampshire. Restoration included the grounds, which feature an eighteenth-century herb garden with raised beds and a dooryard garden.
Open: June 1–September 30, Tuesday, Thursday, Saturday–Sunday noon– 5:00 p.m. Fee. (603) 778–7183.

5. Fitzwilliam

Rhododendron State Park
Troy Road, 2.3 miles west of Fitzwilliam

This 16-acre National Natural Landmark contains the largest stand of *Rhododendron maximum* north of the Allegheny Mountains, which is best seen in early July. A wildflower trail is maintained by the local garden club.
Open: Daily, sunrise–sunset. (603) 271–2155.

6. Kinsman's Notch

Lost River Reservation
Route 112

This area features a natural garden containing about 100 varieties of wildflowers plus various trees and shrubs, ferns, and club mosses. All are labeled for identification.
Open: May 15–October 15, Monday–Friday 9:00 a.m.–5:30 p.m. Guided tours. Fee. (603) 745–8031.

7. Meredith

Huntress Farm Gardens
U.S. 3, 4 miles north of Meredith

These gardens are noted for choice bearded iris, which are at their best in mid-June. There are also Oriental poppies and daylilies.
Open: June–October, daylight hours. (603) 569–5437.

8. Mount Washington

Mount Washington Arctic Gardens
Via toll road or cog railroad

Alpine flowers grow above the timberline. June is the best month for blossoms.
Open: Memorial Day–Columbus Day 9:00 a.m.–6:00 p.m. (603) 466–3388.

9. New Ipswich

Barrett House
Main Street

Built by Charles Barrett for his son, "Forest Hall" remained in the Barrett family until 1948. The grounds include a Gothic summer house, vegetable garden, and annual garden.
Open: June 1–September 30, Tuesday, Thursday, Saturday–Sunday noon–5:00 p.m. Fee. (603) 227–3956.

10. North Hampton

Fuller Gardens
10 Willow Avenue, off Route 1A

These colonial revival gardens were designed in the 1920s by landscape architect Arthur Shurcliff. An ocean view combining roses, a conservatory, and hedge topiary are featured, as well as a Japanese garden and wildflower walk.
Open: Mid-May–October, daily 10:00 a.m.–6:00 p.m. Fee. (603) 964–8414.

11. Portsmouth

Garden of the Moffatt–Ladd House
154 Market Street

The colonial mansion was built in 1763 for Samuel Moffatt by his father John; it was later the home of Gen-

eral William Whipple, a signer of the Declaration of Independence. The garden is densely planted with flowering trees, shrubs, and a variety of annuals and perennials. Both are maintained by the National Society of Colonial Dames in New Hampshire.
Open: June 15–October 15, Monday–Saturday 10:00 a.m.–4:00 p.m., Sunday 2:00–5:00 p.m. Fee. (603) 436–8221.

Governor John Langdon Mansion
143 Pleasant Street

The house, built in 1784 by the Revolutionary leader John Langdon, is surrounded by extensive gardens, wildflowers, and formal areas. Maintained by the Society for the Preservation of New England Antiquities.
Open: June 1–October 15, Tuesday–Sunday noon–5:00 p.m. Fee. (603) 431–1800.

Strawberry Banke Museum
Marcy Street

Chartered by the state of New Hampshire as a nonprofit educational institution, Strawberry Banke is a unique achievement in historic preservation. This was one of the earliest settlements in North America. Some of the houses were owned and occupied by captains of sailing ships and by government dignitaries. Almost all of the 35 houses have gardens typical of the seventeenth century.

Open: April 15–November 15, daily 9:30 a.m.–5:00 p.m. Fee. (603) 436–8010.

Wentworth–Coolidge Mansion
Little Harbor Road

The garden features plantings of lilacs dating from the 1700s.
Open: June–September, 10:00 a.m.–5:00 p.m. (603) 436–6607.

12. Rindge

Garden of Remembrance, Cathedral of the Pines
Cathedral Road

A memorial to those lost in the wars, this site has been proclaimed a national shrine. The gardens circling the cathedral knoll are informally planted with rhododendrons, azaleas, lilacs, flowering quince, and beds of annuals and perennials.
Open: May–October, daily 9:00 a.m.–6:00 p.m. Guided tours and organ recitals. (603) 899–3300.

Other Places of Interest

Canterbury Shaker Village, Concord
Crawford Notch, Bartlett
Dartmouth College, Hanover
Franconia Notch
Lost River Reservation, North Woodstock
Shelburne Birches, Gorham

New Jersey

Area: 7,836 square miles

Population: 7,562,000

Statehood: December 18, 1787
(3rd state)

New Jersey's low coastal plain has several distinct landscapes. Around New York the saltwater-inundated meadows were once at the bottom of a glacial lake. The sandy New Jersey shore extending south as far as Cape May, a popular vacation resort area, is threatened by pollution of the ocean waters. A little inland from the coast are the Pine Barrens. The nearby ocean moderates the winters. Species of plants that grow in the Pine Barrens are generally found much farther south. In southern New Jersey are fertile farmlands. Many historic brick farmhouses built by the Quaker settlers still remain.

New Jersey's major cities are located in the Piedmont. In 1791, Alexander Hamilton planned the location of the city of Paterson to take advantage of the water power of the Passaic River at the fall line. It was the nation's first planned industrial city. Newark is a center for the production of fine gold jewelry. Thomas Edison established research laboratories at Menlo Park. His home in West Orange is a national historic park; visitors can see his laboratory much as he left it. Princeton is a major research center today.

The northern part of the state was settled by Puritans from New England, and its early villages resembled those of New England. The Palisades, great rock cliffs cut by the Hudson River, are an interesting landform.

Across western New Jersey runs the ridge and valley province of the Appalachians. New Jersey's highest elevation is 1,803 feet above sea level in the Kittatinny Mountains near the state's northwestern corner. The Delaware Water Gap, a narrow valley cut by the Delaware River as it flows south through the mountains, is an area of great scenic beauty.

In early colonial days the British, Swedes, Dutch, and Germans made New Jersey their home. The state benefits from a population of great ethnic diversity.

The state offers many attractions, including historic homes, battle sites of the Revolutionary War, industrial sites, and old mines. Driving along the New Jersey Turnpike, one is struck by the colossal scale of the twentieth-century industrial landscape.

1. Barnegat

Edith Duff Gwinn Garden
Barnegat Light Museum

A seashore garden at the Barnegat Light Museum is maintained by the Historical Society and Garden Club of Long Beach Island.
Garden open: Daily, sunrise–sunset.
(609) 494–9196.

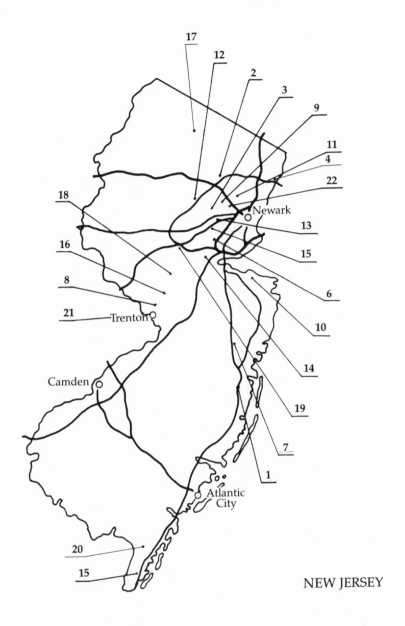

NEW JERSEY

1. *Barnegat* **2.** *Boonton* **3.** *Chatham* **4.** *Englewood Cliffs* **5.** *Fishing Creek*
6. *Iselin* **7.** *Lakewood* **8.** *Lawrenceville* **9.** *Livingston* **10.** *Middletown*
11. *Montclair* **12.** *Morristown* **13.** *Mountainside* **14.** *New Brunswick*
15. *Plainfield* **16.** *Princeton* **17.** *Ringwood* **18.** *Rocky Hill* **19.** *Somerville*
20. *Swainton* **21.** *Trenton* **22.** *West Orange*

2. Boonton

Toure Park
Powerville Road

The historic 225-acre park, which dates back to the early 1700s, is now a bird sanctuary. It offers a variety of nature trails and is particularly noted for its wildflowers.
Open: Daily, sunrise–sunset. (201) 334–0598.

3. Chatham

Outdoor Environmental Education Center
Southern Boulevard

This 40-acre sanctuary adjoins the 6,000-acre Great Swamp National Wildlife Refuge. It is a haven for naturalists and horticulturalists alike. A boardwalk extending into the swamp affords a view seldom seen of the terrain. Approximately 180 species of birds and over 500 species of swamp plants have been identified. Naturalists provide tours of the center.
Open: Daily 9:00 a.m.–5:00 p.m. (201) 635–6629.

Access to the National Wildlife Refuge is from Pleasant Plains Road, Basking Ridge.
Open: Daily 9:00 a.m.–5:00 p.m. (201) 647–1222.

4. Englewood Cliffs

Prentice-Hall Publishing Co.
Sylvan Avenue

The campuslike setting of this publishing house is enhanced by a Japanese garden built in 1960 to honor the one-hundredth anniversary of Japanese-American cultural relations. A copy of the Imperial Palace "Benkei-Bashi" bridge spans a small stream.
Open: Office hours. (201) 592–2000.

5. Fishing Creek

The Hedge Garden
Tabernacle Road, 6 miles from Wildwood

Since 1927, Gus Yearick has been shaping over 175 different hedge plants into a variety of figures. Many outstanding examples of topiary art have received worldwide recognition.
Open: Daily 9:00 a.m.–5:00 p.m. Donation. (609) 886–5148.

6. Iselin

Garden for the Blind and Handicapped
1081 Green Street

Called the "Circle of Senses," the circular planter—3 feet high and 18

feet in diameter—is the focal point of a botanic garden for the blind.
Open: May–October, daily, sunrise–sunset. (201) 283–1200.

7. Lakewood

Japanese Garden at Georgian Court College

This 1-acre garden was laid out in the early 1900s by Japanese landscape architect Takeo Shiota. Mr. Shiota, who came to the United States in 1907, is credited with designing the greatest number of Japanese gardens on the Atlantic seaboard.
Open: Year-round, weekdays 10:00 a.m.–5:00 p.m. (201) 364–2200.

8. Lawrenceville

Lawrenceville School Garden
U.S. 206

The campus was designed in 1880 by Frederick Law Olmsted. Many of the original trees and shrubs that were imported from around the world still survive.
Open: Daily, sunrise–sunset. (609) 896–0400.

9. Livingston

Force House Herb Garden
South Livingston Avenue

A small, interesting Early American herb garden featuring a sundial and four beds is divided into scented herbs, culinary herbs, and medicinal herbs.
Open: Daily. (201) 992–2343.

10. Middletown

Eighteenth-Century Herb Garden
Marlpit Hall, Kings Highway

The oblong garden features herbs of the period used for fragrance, seasoning, and medicines. It has a diamond-shaped center with sundial and oyster path, and is bordered with English boxwood. Designed, planted, and maintained by the Village Garden Club of Middleton.
Open: April–December, Tuesday and Sunday 1:00–4:00 p.m., Saturday 10:00 a.m.–4:00 p.m. Fee. (201) 462–1466.

11. Montclair

Israel Crane House Gardens
110 Orange Road

The Kitchen, Herb, and Pleasure gardens feature indigenous plantings

that are typical of the late 1700s.
*Open: Sunday 2:00–5:00 p.m.
School programs, Monday–Tuesday.
Adult groups and individuals by
appointment. (201) 744–1796.*

Presby Memorial Iris Garden
Mountainside Park

This National Historic Landmark
contains over 75,000 irises, representing most of the more than 200
species and 5,000 varieties from
around the world. The garden preserves historic iris rootstock from as
early as the 1500s. The historic beds
are arranged chronologically.
*Open: Daily, sunrise–sunset. (201)
744–7660.*

12. Morristown

Acorn Hall Victorian Garden
68 Morris Avenue

The restored authentic Victorian garden was designed by Alice Dustan
Kollar; it was planted and is maintained by the Home Garden Club of
Morristown.
*Open: Thursday 11:00 a.m.–
3:00 p.m., Sunday 1:00–3:30 p.m.
Closed: January–February. Fee. (201)
267–3465.*

Frelinghuysen Arboretum
53 East Hanover Avenue

Many of the ornamental trees in
this 127-acre arboretum date back

to the nineteenth century when the
collection was started. Formal and
informal flower gardens have been
developed, and there are orchards and
a pinetum.
*Open: Monday–Friday 9:00 a.m.–
5:00 p.m., Saturday–Sunday until
6:00 p.m. (201) 285–6166.*

MacCulloch Hall
45 MacCulloch Avenue

The gardens of this imposing brick
home, built in 1806, were restored
by the Garden Club of Morristown.
Some of the original plantings still
survive.
*Open: April–November, house by
appointment; garden, daily 9:00 a.m.–
5:00 p.m. (201) 538–2404.*

Schuyler–Hamilton House
5 Olyphant Place

The grounds around the house,
built in 1774, feature gardens of the
period. This site is now the headquarters of the state chapter of the
Daughters of the American Revolution.
*Open: Tuesday and Sunday
2:00–5:00 p.m., other times by
appointment. (201) 267–4039.*

Tempe Wick House
Jockey Hollow
Morristown National Historic Park,
Tempe Wick Road

The 1748 farmhouse of "Temper-
ance" Henry Wick has a restored
colonial garden. Plants are those
needed for daily living, including

medicinal herbs, flax for linen, and soapwort for soap.
Open: Daily 9:00 a.m.–5:00 p.m. (201) 539–2016.

13. Mountainside

Union County Rhododendron Display Garden
Near Surprise Lake

This garden was designed in 1958 by John Jennings. More than 5,000 plants have been identified.
Open: Daily, sunrise–sunset. (201) 232–5930.

14. New Brunswick

Rutgers Display Gardens
U.S. 1 and Ryder Lane

Operated by the Cook College of Rutgers University, this 41-acre site is known for its collections of American and Japanese hollies as well as abundant native flora.
Open: 8:30 a.m.–sunset. (201) 932–9639.

15. Plainfield

Cedar Brook Park
Park Avenue

The park contains three unique gardens: the Iris Garden, the Cornus

Collection, and the Shakespeare Garden. They were designed in part by Olmsted Brothers.
Open: Daily, sunrise–sunset. (201) 754–7250.

16. Princeton

Kuser Farm Mansion and Park
10 miles southeast of Princeton via U.S. 206

This 1890 summer mansion of impressario Fred Kuser was built by German craftsmen. The 22 acres of grounds include formal gardens, a bowling green, nature trails, and an English park.
Open: April–November, Thursday–Sunday, grounds 9:00 a.m.–6:00 p.m., house 11:00 a.m.–3:00 p.m. (609) 890–3782.

☆
Princeton University Campus

Founded in 1719, this 215-acre campus of one of the great Ivy League schools is a delightful arrangement of harmoniously designed buildings and landscaped spaces. The Putnam Sculpture Collection of contemporary outdoor sculpture is one of the best. Guided tours require 10 days' notice.
Open: All times. (609) 452–3603.

17. Ringwood

Ringwood State Park Complex
North of town

The park has two historic areas and a recreation complex. Around Ringwood Manor are located a series of formal gardens which were started in 1880. Adjacent to Skyland Manor are several informal English gardens, an arboretum, and specialized gardens including a wildflower garden, a bog garden, and a rhododendron garden. *Open: Daily, sunrise–sunset; different hours for the mansions. Parking fee. (201) 962–7031 or 962–6377.*

18. Rocky Hill

Rockingham
County Route 518, near U.S. 206

George Washington's military headquarters for a time, the estate features eighteenth-century herb and rose gardens. *Open: Tuesday–Saturday 10:00 a.m.– 5:00 p.m., Sunday 2:00–5:00 p.m. (609) 921–8835.*

19. Somerville

☆
Duke Gardens Foundation, Inc.
U.S. 206, 1.25 miles south of the Somerset Shopping Center

A re-creation of the world's horticulture is presented in a series of exquisite gardens, all contained under an acre of glass. This display embodies the precision of a sculptured French parterre garden, the lushness of a tropical jungle, the arid beauty of an American desert, and the stylized naturalism of Japan. *Open: Daily 8:30 a.m.–10:30 p.m. Closed: Major holidays. Tours by reservation. Fee. (201) 722–3700.*

20. Swainton

Leaming's Run Botanical Gardens
N.J. 9, Avalon exit
off Garden State Parkway

Almost a mile in length but only 20 acres in area, the gardens follow the stream known as Leaming's Run. There are 27 separate gardens, each with a different theme or plant collection. Included are colonial, fern, herb, bog, evening, blue, orange, and English cottage gardens. Thomas Leaming's house, built in 1706, is the only remaining whaler's house in New Jersey. *Open: July 1–October 31, 9:30 a.m.– 5:00 p.m. Fee. (609) 465–5871.*

21. Trenton

William Trent House Gardens
15 Market Street

Miss Isabella Pendleton redesigned the grounds in 1938 based on a description of the property in the "Pennsylvania Journal" of 1759. Her interpretation has been continued by the Garden Club of Trenton.
Open: Weekdays 10:00 a.m.–5:00 p.m. Fee. (609) 695–9621.

toric Site. The landscaped grounds, designed by Olmsted and Vaux, feature fine old beech trees, a flower garden, and a conservatory.
Open: Monday–Saturday 10:00 a.m.–4:00 p.m.
Closed: Holidays. (201) 736–0550.

Other Places of Interest

Long Beach Island
Menlo Park, Somerville
Morristown National Historic Park

22. West Orange

Glenmont
Llewellyn Park

The home of inventor Thomas Edison has been preserved as a National His-

New Mexico

Area: 121,666 square miles

Population: 1,450,000

Statehood: January 6, 1912
(47th state)

New Mexico, called the "Land of Enchantment," is an arid state of great scenic beauty. The form of the land sculpted by the wind is visible under a light vegetative cover.

The Great Plains and the Rocky Mountains meet in New Mexico. The entire state is over 2,800 feet above sea level. Its highest point, Wheeler Peak, rises to 13,161 feet. Only at higher elevations does rainfall exceed 20 inches per year. At lower altitudes there is a sparse desert vegetation; at higher elevations are found a variety of needle-leaf trees. The desert climate is hot and dry during the day but temperatures cool rapidly at night. Heavy snows cover the mountains in winter. There are seven national forests in the state; about one-fourth of the land is forested. A large part of New Mexico was once open range land. Stock raising is an important industry.

The state is rich in natural wonders. They include the majestic Carlsbad Caverns; White Sands National Monument, a spectacular basin filled with white gypsum and deposits; and Capulin Mountain National Monument, a landscape formed by recent volcanic activity.

New Mexico's contemporary culture is influenced by its Spanish and Indian populations. The periods of Spanish and Mexican domination left behind an interesting architectural heritage. The ancient "Palace of the Governors" in Santa Fe was built in 1610. The mission at Ranchos de Taos dates from the eighteenth century. There are numerous Indian pueblos of interest; some are still occupied. The Museum of International Folk Art includes a fine collection of Spanish colonial folk art.

The scarcity of water, the importance of shade, and the unusual vegetation demand a particular gardening style in this desert land. Paving materials, water features, and man-made structures become especially important landscape elements.

1. Alamogordo

Garden Center
10th and Orange Streets

The center contains an experimental garden of plants that will survive in this area of New Mexico, including trees, shrubs, and flowers. There is also a Memorial Rose Garden.
Open: Daily, sunrise–sunset. (505) 437–6120.

NEW MEXICO

1. *Alamogordo*   2. *Albuquerque*   3. *Carlsbad*   4. *Deming*   5. *Las Cruces*

2. Albuquerque

Sandia Peak Botanical Gardens
At the foot of the aerial tramway

These gardens feature over 900 species and varieties of native shrubs and trees, cacti, and wildflowers found in the zone between 5,000 and 7,000 feet.
Open: Daily, sunrise–sunset. (505) 298–8518.

University of New Mexico
Central Avenue and Yale Boulevard

This is an excellent example of modern campus design. An interesting array of native desert and semitropical plant materials has been used to harmonize with the surrounding environment. An arboretum, a rose garden, and a garden of indigenous plants are also featured.
Open: Daily, sunrise–sunset. (505) 277–2421.

Sandia Peak Botanical Gardens, Albuquerque, N.Mex.

3. Carlsbad

Living Desert State Park
Off U.S. 285 North

This park combines zoological and horticultural aspects. The animal exhibits are arranged along trails that wind through a series of cactus gardens. Over 1,000 varieties of cacti grow here. Native and exotic succulents are displayed.
Open: May 15–September 15, daily 8:00 a.m.–8:00 p.m.; September 16–May 14, daily 9:00 a.m.–5:00 p.m. Fee. (505) 887–5516.

4. Deming

Pancho Villa State Park
N.Mex. 11, 27 miles south of Deming

Located in Luna County near the Mexican border, this park is the site of Pancho Villa's raid into the United States territory on March 9, 1916. The remains of Camp Furlong, headquarters of John J. Pershing's expedition, and a botanical garden of desert vegetation are the major features. Picnicking facilities are provided.
Open: Daily. Fee. (505) 546–2674.

5. Las Cruces

Leding Cactus Gardens

University Park,
New Mexico State University

Most of the cacti, agaves, and shrubs are natives of this area. May is the best season for blossoms.
Open: Daily 8:00 a.m.–5:00 p.m.
(505) 646–3221.

Other Places of Interest

Abo Site National Monument, Mountainair
Acoma Rock Pueblo, Casa Blanca (I-40)
Aztec Ruins National Monument, Aztec
Capulin Mountains National Monument, Folsom
Carlsbad Caverns National Park, Carlsbad
Chaco Culture National Historical Park
Gila Cliff Dwellings National Monument, Silver City
Los Alamos Energy Research Center, Los Alamos
Navaho Indian Reservation, Gallup
Old Town, Albuquerque
Palace of the Governors, Santa Fe
Taos Pueblo, Taos
White Sands National Monument, Alamogordo

New York

Area: 49,576 square miles

Population: 17,783,000

Statehood: July 26, 1788 (11th state)

The spine of the "Empire State" consists of a series of deeply eroded uplands—the Taconic, Adirondack, and Catskill mountains—that are dissected by broad fertile river valleys. The Palisades, a particularly striking feature, are formed where the Hudson River cuts through the Taconics and Catskills just above New York City. In western New York, the land drops off to the Great Lakes Plain. Glacial deposits in this area created the eleven Finger Lakes, an interesting irregular landscape. The Atlantic Coastal Plain stretches east from New York City across Long Island.

The state of New York has a typical four-season climate. Rainfall is plentiful, although severe summer droughts sometimes occur in the western plains. The growing season varies from 200 days on Long Island, where ocean waters moderate temperatures, to less than 100 days at mountain elevations. The eastern deciduous forest originally covered most of New York State except for higher elevations where coniferous forests were prevalent. Under the state constitution, millions of acres of forestland are now "Forever Wild"; the 2.75-million-acre Adirondack

Forest Preserve and the 272,000-acre Catskill Forest Preserve are the two areas so designated.

The state benefits from a diversity of peoples. The Dutch were the first Europeans to settle New York. The colony passed to English hands as a result of the fierce Indian Wars. The state grew rapidly during the early nineteenth century. Many new residents came from exhausted farms in New England to settle throughout the state; a large number of them flocked to New York City.

The great city stands at a dramatic site where the uplands drop down to the sea. Manhattan Island is located on the ancient rocks of the upland. The city's location, which provided a deep harbor on the extensive river system of the Hudson and the Mohawk, destined it for greatness. In 1825, the Erie Canal was completed, tying New York City via the Hudson and Mohawk rivers to the Great Lakes at Buffalo. This event assured New York's prominence as America's outstanding commercial node.

New York City played a leadership role in the development of public parks in the nineteenth century. During the 1850s, social reformers concerned with the blighted condition of the city's environment urged the development of open spaces. Central Park, designed in 1857 by Frederick Law Olmsted and Calvert Vaux, was a landmark in America's development of quality urban environments. This preserve, intended for the common man, set a standard of excellence in public park design that remains to

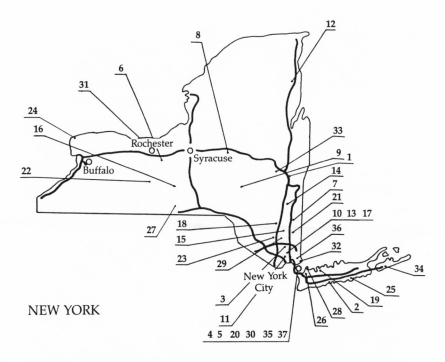

NEW YORK

1. *Albany*   2. *Bay Shore*   3. *Beacon*   4. *Bronx (New York City)*   5. *Brooklyn (New York City)*   6. *Canandaigua*   7. *Clermont*   8. *Clinton*   9. *Cooperstown* 10. *Cross River*   11. *Croton-on-Hudson*   12. *Elizabethtown*   13. *Garrison-on-Hudson*   14. *Hudson*   15. *Hyde Park*   16. *Ithaca*   17. *Katonah*   18. *Kingston* 19. *Locust Valley*   20. *Manhattan (New York City)*   21. *Millbrook*   22. *Naples* 23. *New Paltz*   24. *Niagara Falls*   25. *Oakdale*   26. *Old Westbury*   27. *Owego* 28. *Oyster Bay*   29. *Poughkeepsie*   30. *Queens (New York City)*   31. *Rochester* 32. *Rye*   33. *Schenectady*   34. *Southampton*   35. *Staten Island (New York City)*   36. *Tarrytown*   37. *Yonkers*

this day. Brooklyn's Prospect Park, by the same designers, is another great work. Rockefeller Plaza in midtown Manhattan was an innovative downtown space of the 1930s. More recently, Paley Park in the East Fifties of Manhattan has demonstrated the innovative use of very small spaces to improve the quality of urban living.

1. Albany

Saint Michael's Episcopal Church Garden
49 Kilean Park

Three acres of intensively developed gardens adjoin the church, including an herb garden, an extensive fern collection, and many varieties of suc-

Paley Vest Pocket Park, Manhattan, N.Y.

culents. There is also a greenhouse with over 2,000 species of plants.
Open: 9:00 a.m.–5:00 p.m. (518) 869–6417.

Ten Broeck Mansion
Arbor Hill

Extensive lawns and an herb garden are features of this 1798 restoration.
Open: Tuesday–Sunday 9:00 a.m.–5:00 p.m.
Closed: Holidays. Fee. (518) 436–9826.

2. Bay Shore

Sagtikos Manor
3 miles west on Montauk Highway (N.Y. 27A)

The house, which dates from 1692, features a colonial herb and cutting garden.
Open: Memorial Day, June, September, Sunday 1:00–4:00 p.m.; July–August, Wednesday, Thursday, Sunday 1:00–4:00 p.m. (516) 661–8348 or 665–0093.

3. Beacon

Madame Brett Homestead and Brinkerhoff Foster Memorial Garden
50 Van Nydeck Avenue

The formal garden behind the historic house (ca. 1709) is in the style of colonial times.
Open: May–October, Friday–Sunday 1:00–4:00 p.m. (914) 831–6533.

4. Bronx (New York City)

☆☆
New York Botanical Garden
Bronx Park, 1 East 200th Street

This botanical garden is not to be missed. On the beautiful 230-acre site are grown shrubs, trees, and flowers from every part of the world. Special features include a 3.5-acre rock garden, rose gardens, aquatic gardens, an extensive herb garden, and a hemlock forest. The conservatory provides displays throughout the winter.
Open: Daily 9:00 a.m.–sunset; conservatory, Tuesday–Sunday 10:00 a.m.–4:00 p.m. Fee. (212) 220–8728.

Wave Hill Center for Environmental Studies
675 West 252nd Street

The center offers 28 acres of wild-flowers; rose, herb, and aquatic gardens; and nature trails.
Open: Daily 10:00 a.m.–4:30 p.m. (212) 549–2055.

5. Brooklyn (New York City)

☆☆
Brooklyn Botanic Garden
1000 Washington Avenue

This 50-acre oasis in the heart of Brooklyn features a Cherry Esplanade, Rose Garden, Fragrance Garden for the Blind, Rock Garden, Iris Garden, Magnolia Garden, Herb Garden, and Bonsai Garden Collection; three Japanese gardens; a conservatory; and more.
Open: Tuesday–Friday 8:00 a.m.–4:30 p.m., Saturday–Sunday 10:00 a.m.–4:30 p.m.; summer hours to 6:00 p.m.; conservatory, weekdays 10:00 a.m.–4:00 p.m., weekends and holidays 11:00 a.m.–4:00 p.m. Japanese gardens closed in winter. Grounds are free. Fee for conservatory and Japanese gardens. (212) 622–4433.

Prospect Park
8th Avenue, Parkside Avenue, Flatbush Avenue, and Prospect Park West

Designed in 1866–68 by Frederick Law Olmsted and Calvert Vaux, Prospect Park is considered by some critics to have the best design of any

in which Olmsted was involved. As in the case of Central Park, this park was intended to provide rural scenery within the urban environment, as well as recreational areas for people of all backgrounds and classes. The spatial organization of the Long Meadow is particularly skillful. The 526-acre park is currently in need of restoration.
Open: All hours. (212) 788–0055.

6. Canandaigua

☆
Sonnenberg Gardens
151 Charlotte Street (Route 21)

This turn-of-the-century estate has a variety of elegant gardens. Of particular interest are the Rose Garden, Italian Garden, Japanese Garden, Rock Garden, and Blue and White Garden. Other features include the mansion, conservatory, and reflecting pool.
Open: June–August, daily 9:30 a.m.–5:30 p.m.; May, September–October, Monday–Friday 9:30 a.m.–5:00 p.m. Fee. (716) 924–5420 or 394–4922.

7. Clermont

Clermont State Park
Route 9G, 5 miles west of Clermont (U.S. 9)

Clermont was an early seat of the Livingston family. The grounds were first developed by Robert Living-ston during the late 1700s and have been embellished over time. Early landscape architects such as A. J. Downing (1815–52) and Charles Eliot (1859–97) wrote of their beauty. The site is famous for its ancient Black Locust allée.
Open: Daily 8:00 a.m.–sunset. (518) 537–4240.

8. Clinton

Root Glen Foundation
107 College Hill Road

This pleasant site, owned by Hamilton College (founded in 1812), features fine specimen trees dating from 1850.
Open: Daily, sunrise–sunset. (315) 859–7680.

9. Cooperstown

Fenimore House
N.Y. 80, 1 mile north of Cooperstown

There is an extensive medicinal herb garden here. Also of interest is the fine collection of American folk art and sculpture.
Open: July–August, 9:00 a.m.–9:00 p.m.; other months, until 5:00 p.m. Fee. (607) 547–2533.

10. Cross River

Meyer Arboretum
Ward Pound Ridge Reservation
Route 121 south of Route 35

The 175-acre arboretum features primarily native plants. Educational programs for children and adults are offered.
Open: Tuesday–Sunday, 9:00 a.m.–sunset.
Closed: Winter. (914) 763-3493.

11. Croton-on-Hudson

Van Cortlandt Manor
9 miles north of Tappan Zee Bridge (Exit 9 on I-90)

For nearly 300 years this manor house has stood on a rise overlooking the Hudson River. Eighteenth-century gardens and apple, peach, and pear trees flank the famous "Long Walk." The restoration is noted for its authenticity.
Open: Daily 10:00 a.m.–5:00 p.m.
Closed: Holidays. Fee. (914) 631-8200.

12. Elizabethtown

Colonial Garden of the Adirondack Center Museum
Court Street

The garden is an authentic reproduction of a formal colonial garden. There is also a wildflower walk. The Indian and pioneer exhibits in the museum are of interest.
Open: June 15–September 15, daily 9:00 a.m.–5:00 p.m. Fee. (518) 873-6466.

13. Garrison-on-Hudson

Boscobel
4 miles north on N.Y. 9D

The 36-acre site overlooking the Hudson River was originally developed in 1805 as a formal garden, with hedges, large trees, a rose garden, and perennial beds. It was restored in 1960 with as much authenticity as possible.
Open: April–October, Wednesday–Monday 9:30 a.m.–5:00 p.m.; March, November–December, until 4:00 p.m. Closed: January–February. Fee. (914) 265-3638.

14. Hudson

Olana State Historic Site
Take I-87 to N.Y. 23, to N.Y. 9G; 1 mile south of Rip Van Winkle Bridge

Olana was the home of Frederick Church, noted landscape artist. His "castle" was begun in 1870; its landscaping is considered one of the primary artistic expressions of late nineteenth-century America. Tours.
Open: Memorial Day–last weekend in October, Wednesday–Sunday 9:00 a.m.–4:30 p.m.; grounds, daily, sunrise–sunset. Fee. (518) 828-0135.

15. Hyde Park

**Vanderbilt Mansion
National Historic Site**
U.S. 9 North

The 50-room mansion was designed by Stanford White in 1896. A Belgian landscape gardener planted the 700-acre estate to frame the magnificent view of the Hudson River and the Catskills. Many original trees survive. There is also a handsome Italian garden.
Open: Tuesday–Sunday, 9:00 a.m.–5:00 p.m. Fee. (914) 229–8114.

16. Ithaca

Cornell Plantations
Cornell University,
100 Judd Falls Road

The 1,500-acre site features azalea, synoptic shrub, and wildflower gardens; plant collections; marked nature trails; and the Mary Rockwell Azalea Garden. Guided tours.
Open: Sunrise–sunset. (607) 256–3020.

17. Katonah

John Jay Homestead
Jay Street
(Exit 6 off I-684 on N.Y. 22)

This house was built in 1787 by John Jay, first chief justice of the United States. The grounds include herb, formal, and twentieth-century gardens.
Open: Wednesday–Saturday 9:00 a.m.–5:00 p.m. (914) 232–5651.

18. Kingston

The Senate House
312 Fair Street

Great care has been taken to make a small dooryard garden appear as it might have in the late eighteenth century. The historic house is also of interest.
Open: April 1–December 31, Wednesday–Saturday 10:00 a.m.–5:00 p.m., Sunday 1:00–5:00 p.m.; rest of year, Saturday–Sunday only. (914) 338–2786.

19. Locust Valley

Bailey Arboretum
194 Bayville Road

The 42-acre estate features over 600 kinds of trees and shrubs, many labeled. There are nature trails and greenhouses.
Open: March–November 15, daily 9:00 a.m.–4:00 p.m. Fee. (516) 676–4497.

20. Manhattan (New York City)

Cathedral Church of St. John the Divine Biblical Gardens
Amsterdam Avenue at 112th Street

The garden displays plants mentioned in the Bible.
Open: 9:00 a.m.–5:00 p.m. (212) 316–7540.

Central Park
57th–110th Streets, Central Park West–Fifth Avenue

This 88-acre urban park, which lies in the heart of Manhattan, was the "grandfather" of the parks built in the United States during the nineteenth-century Urban Park movement. Its design was the winning entry submitted by Frederick Law Olmsted and Calvert Vaux, under the name "Greensward," in a design contest for the park in 1857. Olmsted and Vaux envisioned the park as a rural retreat within the hustle of city life, which would boost the morale of the socially disadvantaged and oppressed as well as the well-to-do. A National Historic Landmark, the site is currently being restored. Many urban wildlife species and Victorian architectural gems can be found in this venerable park. A visitors' center is located at "The Dairy." *Park open: Daily, all hours. (212) 397–3156.*

The Cloisters–Metropolitan Museum of Art
Fort Tryon Park, North Avenue and Cabrini Circle

The gardens of the Metropolitan Museum contain only plants that were known to Europeans during the Middle Ages.
Open: Tuesday–Saturday, 10:00 a.m.–5:00 p.m., Sunday 1:00–5:00 p.m. Fee. (212) 923–3700.

Ford Foundation
320 East 43rd Street

The 11-story building surrounds a unique contemporary indoor courtyard garden designed by landscape architect Dan Kiley.
Open: Monday–Friday 9:00 a.m.–5:00 p.m. (212) 573–5000.

Garden of the Museum of Modern Art
11 West 53rd Street

The Museum of Modern Art was the first museum in America to create a garden for the exhibition of modern sculpture. The sunken garden, designed by Phillip Johnson and opened in 1953, is simple, elegant, and rich in detail. Two reflecting pools and a grove of Japanese cedars divide the garden into areas for the exhibition of the permanent collection of sculpture by Matisse, Rodin, Maillol, Lachaise, Moore, and Lipchitz.
Open: Monday–Tuesday, Friday–Sunday 11:00 a.m.–5:45 p.m., Thursday until 9:00 p.m. Fee for entry to museum and garden. (212) 708–9500.

21. Millbrook

Innisfree Gardens
Tyrrell Road, 3 miles southwest of
Millbrook

The 1,000-acre estate features walks,
waterfalls, lakes, specimen trees,
native plantings, and terraced gardens
near the house. The plantings follow
Eastern design principles.
*Open: May–October, Wednesday–
Friday 10:00 a.m.–4:00 p.m.,
Saturday–Sunday 11:00 a.m.–
5:00 p.m. (914) 677–8000.*

22. Naples

Cummings Nature Center
Gulick Road, 30 miles south
of Rochester

The preserve of the Rochester Museum and Science Foundation covers
800 acres of woodlands and meadows, including trails. There is an
educational center.
*Open: Daily, sunrise–sunset. Fee.
271–1880 or 271–4320.*

23. New Paltz

Mohonk Gardens
Mohonk Mountain House, on Mohonk Lake

Established in 1869, the landscaped
gardens cover 15 acres of a 7,500-acre
preserve. There is a Victorian flower

garden and an annual show garden.
*Open: Daily, sunrise–sunset; peak
season in summer. Fee. (914) 255–
1000.*

24. Niagara Falls

Winter Gardens
Rainbow Boulevard

One end of an indoor shopping mall
has been developed as a 7-story glass-
enclosed tropical garden. Designed
by landscape architect Paul Friedberg,
the gardens feature over 7,000 tropical and semitropical plants, pools,
waterfalls, and a multilevel skywalk.
*Open: Daily; mall hours, usually
10:00 a.m.–10:00 p.m. (716) 278–
8196.*

25. Oakdale

Bayard–Cutting Arboretum
Village of Green River

The 690-acre site was designed by
Frederick Law Olmsted in 1886.
Outstanding among its many fine
collections is the pinetum. From its
trails, waterfowl can be observed in
the Connetquot River.
*Open: Wednesday-Sunday
10:00 a.m.–5:00 p.m.; winter and
spring, until 4:00 p.m. Fee. (516)
581–1002.*

26. Old Westbury

☆☆
Old Westbury Gardens
Old Westbury Road

The Georgian mansion is representative of the large estate on Long Island during the pre-World War II era. It is furnished with the same furniture, paintings, and art objects as when it was occupied. Outside are five beautiful gardens, a magnificent view down avenues of linden and beech trees, and sparkling pools and lakes. The site is listed in *Great Gardens of the Western World*.
Open: May–October, Wednesday–Sunday 10:00 a.m.–5:00 p.m. Fee. (516) 333–0048.

27. Owego

Tioga Gardens
Route 17C

The solar-domed conservatory features exotic plants. There is also a 2-acre water garden and an herb garden.
Open: May 31–September 6, Monday–Saturday 9:00 a.m.–7:30 p.m., Sunday 1:00–7:30 p.m.; September 7–May 29, Monday–Saturday 9:00 a.m.–6:00 p.m., Sunday 1:00–6:00 p.m. (607) 687–5522.

28. Oyster Bay

☆
Planting Fields Arboretum
Planting Fields Road

The arboretum covers 409 acres, with 200 under cultivation and the rest in woodlands. Designed by Olmsted Brothers in 1919, it serves today as a nature sanctuary and outdoor living classroom. There are teaching facilities for children.
Open: Daily 10:00 a.m.–5:00 p.m. Fee, May 1–September 1; free rest of year. (516) 922–9200.

29. Poughkeepsie

Shakespeare Garden
Vassar College, Raymond Avenue

Created in 1916, the garden features plants mentioned in Shakespeare's plays.
Open: Daily 9:00 a.m.–4:30 p.m. (914) 542–7000.

30. Queens (New York City)

Queens Botanical Garden
42–50 Main Street, Flushing

These 26 landscaped acres include a fragrance garden, a heather garden, a rose garden, dwarf conifers, and an extraordinary collection of rhododendron.
Open: Daily 9:00 a.m.–sunset. (212) 886–3800.

31. Rochester

Gardens of the George Eastman House
900 East Avenue

The grounds of this Georgian Revival mansion (now the International Museum of Photography) feature a series of formal gardens and an arboretum. The gardens, established in 1905, have been restored to their original condition.
Open: Tuesday–Sunday, 10:00 a.m.– 4:30 p.m. Fee. (716) 271–3361.

George Ellwanger Perennial Garden
625 Mount Hope Avenue

This 1-acre garden was established in 1867 by a cofounder of the famous nineteenth-century Ellwanger and Barry, Mount Hope Nursery. The garden is especially attractive at its peak flowering period in early May. Across the street is the estate of Patrick Barry, the other founder of the nursery; the grounds contain an outstanding collection of trees and shrubs. The Barry house is owned by the University of Rochester and is not open to the public. For hours of the Ellwanger garden, call (716) 546–7029. Fee.

☆
Highland Park
Mt. Hope–Highland Historic District

Plant specimens from the greatest nurseries of Europe and America are displayed here. The park is reputed to have the world's most extensive collection of lilacs. The former director, Bernard Slavin, contributed several new hybrids to the horticultural industry. The conservatory is also of interest.
Open: Daily 7:00 a.m.–10:00 p.m. (716) 546–3070.

32. Rye

Rye Marshlands Conservancy
873 Boston Post Road

The woodland and meadow trails on this 120-acre site provide the only access to Long Island Sound wetlands between New York City and New England. There is a small museum.
Open: Daily 9:00 a.m.–5:00 p.m. (914) 835–4466.

33. Schenectady

Jackson Garden
Union College Campus, Nott Street

The 18-acre garden, established in 1834, features special collections of rare plants.
Open: Daily, sunrise–sunset. Closed: Winter. (518) 370–6000.

34. Southampton

Halsey Homestead
South Main Street

The Southampton Garden Club has restored the grounds of this historic home, which is the state's oldest saltbox house. *Open: Summer–early fall, Tuesday–Sunday 11:00 a.m.–4:30 p.m. Fee. (516) 283–3527.*

35. Staten Island (New York City)

Billiou Stillwell Perine House and Gardens
1476 Richmond Road

This garden imitates the elegant simplicity of the design of colonial times. Only plant materials available then are used. *Open: Daily 10:00 a.m.–4:00 p.m. (718) 351–1617.*

High Rock Park Conservation Center
200 Nevada Avenue, off Rockland Avenue

Trails through upland swamp and marsh cover this 72-acre site. *Open: Daily 9:00 a.m.–5:00 p.m. Closed: Christmas. (718) 987–6233.*

36. Tarrytown

Lyndhurst
635 Broadway

Designed by Alexander Jackson Davis in 1838, the picturesque parklike landscape is in the style of Andrew Jackson Downing, who collaborated with Davis on many projects. A 400-foot-long greenhouse/conservatory complex was added in 1881. At that time, it was the largest in the United States and contained one of the finest orchid collections in the world. Property of the National Trust for Historic Preservation. *Open: April 14–November 4, Wednesday–Sunday 10:00 a.m.–4:00 p.m. Fee. (914) 631–0046.*

Sunnyside
West Sunnyside Lane,
1 mile north of Tappan Zee Bridge

Washington Irving, author of *The Legend of Sleepy Hollow*, designed the grounds of this estate which was his home. The house is a peculiarly whimsical building. *Open: Daily 10:00 a.m.–5:00 p.m. Closed: Thanksgiving, Christmas, New Year's Day. Fee. (914) 631–8200.*

37. Yonkers

Open: Daily 10:00 a.m.–10:00 p.m.
(914) 965–4027.

Greystone Mansion

Untermyer Park and Gardens
North Broadway Street
and Odell Avenue

This mid-nineteenth century estate
was continually embellished by its
various owners. It is one of the few
grand beaux-arts garden designs
completed in America. Fountain
networks, marble mosaics, sculpture,
and unique landscaping are integrated
on this 24-acre site overlooking both
the Hudson River and the Palisades.

Other Places of Interest

Ausable Chasm, northeastern New
York
Boldt Castle, Heart Island
F. D. Roosevelt Mansion, Hyde Park
Fire Island National Seashore
Genesee Gorge ("Grand Canyon of
the East"), Letchworth State Park
Howe Caverns, Albany
Jones Beach State Park, Long Island
Niagara Falls
Saratoga National Historic Park
Watkins Glen State Park, Corning

North Carolina

Area: 52,586 square miles

Population: 6,255,000

Statehood: November 21, 1789
(12th state)

King Charles I generously granted
the royal Proprietor of North Carolina all the land "from sea to sea
lying between 31 degrees and 36 degrees north latitude." Frontiersmen
in Tennessee subsequently formed
their own state and put a limit to
this munificence. Modern-day North
Carolina stretches 524 miles from
the East Coast in three great geologic provinces: the Coastal Plain,
the Piedmont, and the mountains.
The Great Smoky and the Blue Ridge
mountains are in North Carolina.
Mount Mitchell, in the Blue Ridge
Mountain section, is the Appalachian's highest peak, standing 6,684
feet above sea level.

North Carolina has a mild climate.
The average yearly rainfall exceeds
30 inches per year throughout the
state; on the windward slopes of the
mountains, rainfall will average 60
inches per year. The growing season
varies from 239 days at Wilmington
to 194 at Asheville. In winter, frequent snowfalls are experienced at
the higher elevations.

Due to its diverse relief and abundant rainfall, the state has a rich
variety of vegetation. Swamps dominated by cypress, oak, and blackgum

occur along the coast. Dogwood,
sourwood, and redbud trees color the
upland forests. In the mountains are
found great stands of hemlock and
other northern species. In the Piedmont, pine trees can be seen growing
back over abandoned fields. Despite
the fact that most of the work force
is engaged in nonagricultural occu-
pations, the countryside preserves
its rural character. North Carolina's
major industries include tobacco
processing, textiles, and furniture
making.

North Carolina enjoys a rich variety of scenic and recreational areas.
On the Outer Banks, Cape Hatteras
National Seashore offers an environment of great sand dunes and
wind. Near Kitty Hawk is the Wright
Brothers National Memorial. At the
other end of the state, at Flat Rock
near the Great Smoky Mountains
National Park, one finds "Conne-
mara," the home of poet Carl Sandburg, a National Historic Memorial.

The Blue Ridge Parkway is a
masterpiece of design on a grand
scale, achieved by the National Park
Service. Following the ridgetops of
the Blue Ridge Mountains, it links
the Great Smoky Mountains to
Shenandoah National Park in Virginia. With great sensitivity, the
road follows the land's contour and
permits striking views of western
North Carolina's valleys. Turnoffs
and walking paths invite motorists
to stop and observe the landscape at
closer range. Masses of laurel and
rhododendron dot the countryside
during the spring and summer. The
fall foliage is spectacular. To experi-

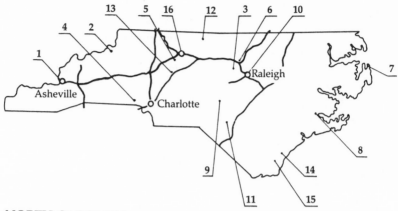

NORTH CAROLINA

1. *Asheville*   2. *Boone*   3. *Chapel Hill*   4. *Cherryville*   5. *Clemmons*
6. *Durham*   7. *Manteo*   8. *New Bern*   9. *Pinehurst*   10. *Raleigh*
11. *Red Springs*   12. *Reidsville*   13. *Salisbury*   14. *Wilmington*
15. *Winnabow (Wilmington)*   16. *Winston-Salem*

ence the parkway is to appreciate the idea of design for joyous movement.

1. Asheville

☆☆

Biltmore Estate and Gardens
On U.S. 25, 3 blocks north of its intersection with I-40 (Exits 50 or 50B), near Biltmore Forest

This 12,000-acre estate on a spectacular mountain site—unique in the United States—belonged to George Washington Vanderbilt, son of Cornelius Vanderbilt. Originally the estate covered 125,000 acres. The 250 acres around the house were intensively managed for landscape effects, whereas the bulk of the prop-erty was devoted to forestry and agricultural pursuits. The nation's first national forest was once part of the estate; though now owned by the federal government, it still serves as a buffer around the area. Frederick Law Olmsted designed the grounds, which include a large shrub garden, an Italian Garden, a Walled Garden, and the Glen. The extensive azalea collection was created by Chauncey Beadle, longtime manager of the grounds. The approach road to the mansion is noteworthy for its harmonious blending with the land and for its plantings; it was nearly a textbook example of the Picturesque ideal for estate approach roads in the nineteenth century when it was constructed. The drive evokes images of wild nature, with no distant outlooks; the visitor is surprised by the

Biltmore Estate and Gardens, Asheville, N.C.

formal contrast of the esplanade in front of the main house. The French Renaissance-style chateau, designed by Richard Morris Hunt, has a fascinating collection of Tudor furniture, Napoleon's chess set, and a variety of great works of art.
Open: Daily 9:00 a.m.–5:00 p.m. Closed: Thanksgiving, Christmas, New Year's Day. Fee, but free for children 11 and under when accompanied by an adult. (704) 274–1776.

Craggy Gardens
Blue Ridge Parkway,
17 miles north of Asheville

On this 600-acre site are featured wild rhododendron and flame azaleas; extensive nature trails provide excellent ways to enjoy the splendid mountain scenery. Best seen in May–June.
Open: Daily, sunrise–sunset. (704) 248–4612.

The Pink Beds
U.S. 276, south of Asheville,
near the "Cradle of Forestry"
in the Pisgah National Forest

A natural garden displays wild azaleas, rhododendron, and mountain laurel. The terrain is fairly level, with a 5-mile loop trail and picnic area.
Open: All times. (704) 877–3265.

University Botanical Gardens
University of North Carolina at
Asheville, W. T. Weaver Boulevard

This 10-acre garden is primarily a center for study and conservation research; it is "dedicated to the preservation and display of the native flora of North Carolina."
Open: Daily, sunrise–sunset. (704) 252–5190.

2. Boone

Daniel Boone Native Garden
Horn-in-the-West Drive

A project of the Garden Club of North Carolina, the 8-acre garden has a colorful collection of mountain plants informally displayed. *Open: May–October, daily 9:00 a.m.– 5:00 p.m. Fee. (704) 264–6390.*

3. Chapel Hill

Coker Arboretum, University of North Carolina at Chapel Hill Campus, and North Carolina Botanical Garden, Laurel Hill Road

Combined, the arboretum and botanical garden cover 329 acres where native plants and endangered species can be observed in a variety of habitats. *Open: Arboretum, all times; botanical garden, Monday–Friday 8:00 a.m.– 5:00 p.m., Saturday 10:00 a.m.– 4:00 p.m., Sunday 2:00–5:00 p.m. (919) 967–2246.*

4. Cherryville

The Iron Gate Garden
Route 274 South

The garden has 5 acres of flowering plants, including an outstanding collection of daylilies. *Open: Daily 9:00 a.m.–5:00 p.m. (704) 435–3451.*

5. Clemmons

Tanglewood State Park
U.S. 158, off I-40

Old boxwoods, oaks, a rose garden, a fragrance garden for the blind, and a botanical garden are featured on this former estate of Mr. and Mrs. William N. Reynolds. *Open: Daily 7:00 a.m.–11:00 p.m. Parking fee. (919) 766–0591.*

6. Durham

☆

Sarah P. Duke Memorial Gardens
West entrance,
Duke University Campus

The 55-acre site displays extensive plantings of annuals, perennials, and flowering shrubs, with formal landscaping. There are also naturalized areas in the pine forest. *Open: Daily 8:00 a.m.–5:00 p.m. (919) 684–3698.*

7. Manteo

Elizabethan Gardens
Roanoke Island

These gardens—adjacent to the "Lost Colony" site of 1585—are a memorial to the Elizabethan men and women who were "lost." Their formal design, by M. Umberto Innocenti and Richard Webel, is typical of the Elizabethan era. Surrounding the gardens is a park of native shrubs, wildflowers, and ferns.
Open: Daily, year-round; summer, 8:00 a.m.-8:15 p.m.; other months, 9:00 a.m.–5:00 p.m. Fee. (919) 473–3234.

8. New Bern

Tryon Palace Gardens
Tryon Palace, 1618 Pollock Street

The palace is the site of North Carolina's first colonial capital. Clipped hedges of the floral parterres of the ornate Maud Moore Latham Garden, a kitchen garden, and the Green Garden are featured on the restored grounds.
Open: Tuesday–Saturday 9:30 a.m.– 4:00 p.m., Sunday 1:00–4:00 p.m. Fee. (919) 638–5109.

9. Pinehurst

Clarendon Gardens
Linden Road

At this 20-acre site is displayed one of the largest collections of hollies in the United States. Its borders surround a 5-acre lake.
Open: Weekdays 9:00 a.m.– 5:00 p.m., Sunday 1:00–5:00 p.m. (919) 295–6651.

10. Raleigh

North Carolina State University Arboretum
Beryl Road

This 8-acre arboretum was begun in 1977. It now features over 5,000 species from all over the world. The 300-foot perennial border is magnificent in spring and fall. Nearby are test plots for bedding plants and roses.
Open: Daylight hours. (919) 737–3133.

11. Red Springs

Flora MacDonald Azalea Gardens
Vardell Hall Junior College Campus

This is a very old garden of mature native azaleas. Hybrids of these azaleas attract additional interest.
Open: Daily, sunrise–sunset. (919) 843–4995.

12. Reidsville

Chinqua-Penn Plantation
Route 3, 3 miles from Reidsville

A 1923 English-type house is surrounded by various gardens, an ornate Chinese pagoda, and a greenhouse. Property of the University of North Carolina.
Open: Wednesday–Saturday 10:00 a.m.–4:00 p.m., Sunday 1:30–4:30 p.m. Closed: December 15–March 1. Fee. (919) 349–4576 or 342–2035.

13. Salisbury

Poets' and Dreamers' Garden
Livingston College Campus

The unique theme of this garden honors famous poets and dreamers with special plantings. Included are a biblical garden, a Shakespeare Garden, and an international garden. A fountain is illuminated at night.
Open: Daily, sunrise–sunset. (704) 633–7960.

14. Wilmington

Airlie Gardens
Wrightsville Beach Highway

The 155-acre site contains a lake and landscaped formal and informal gardens. The woodland garden features stunning azaleas and camellias. Spar-kling water and swans animate the landscape. The specimen live oaks are magnificent.
Open: Only during blooming season, usually April 1–May 1, 8:00 a.m.–5:00 p.m. Fee. (919) 763–9991.

Greenfield Gardens
U.S. 421, Carolina Beach Highway

These gardens are centered around a lake bordered by huge cypress trees and masses of colorful azaleas. The area is reputed to be one of the nation's most sumptuous municipal parks. The azalea walk is magnificent in spring.
Open: Daily, sunrise–sunset. (919) 341–7855.

15. Winnabow (Wilmington)

Orton Plantation Gardens
Highway 133 off U.S. 17

The Orton House, a fine example of Greek Revival architecture, was built in 1735. It is surrounded by acres of landscaped grounds including a Stroll Garden, White Circle Garden, and Sun Garden. The entire area is lushly planted with flowering shrubs, and there is color in the garden almost year-round.
Open: Daily 8:00 a.m.–5:00 p.m. Fee. (919) 371–6851.

16. Winston-Salem

Old Salem
Old Salem Road and Academy Street

Salem was founded in 1766 as a center for Moravian commercial and religious efforts in the South. Church management of the community ceased during the 1840s, and in 1913 the town was merged with the newer industrial city of Winston. Preservation and restoration of the historic district of Salem began in the late 1940s. Today there are ten restored or recreated buildings and seven gardens. The gardens present designs and plant materials covering the period from 1759 to 1847. *Open: Monday–Saturday 9:30 a.m.–4:30 p.m., Sunday 1:30 p.m.– 4:30 p.m. Closed: Thanksgiving and Christmas. Fee. (919) 723–3688.*

Reynolda Gardens of Wake Forest University
Reynolda Road

These gardens, designed by Thomas W. Sears of Philadelphia in 1916,

cover 148 acres from the former estate of Mr. and Mrs. R. J. Reynolds. Features include a formal garden, greenhouse, pool, and teahouse. *Open: Daily 9:00 a.m.–3:00 p.m. (919) 761–5593.*

Other Places of Interest

Blue Ridge Parkway
Cape Hatteras National Seashore, Hatteras
Cherokee Indian Village of Oconaluftee, near Cherokee
Chimney Rock State Park, Asheville
Great Smoky Mountains National Park
Hayes Plantation, Edenton
Moravian Village, Winston-Salem
Nags Head Wood Preserve, Nags Head
Wright Brothers National Memorial, Kitty Hawk

North Dakota

Area: 70,665 square miles

Population: 685,000

Statehood: November 2, 1889 (39th state)

Two distinctive landscape types are found on the Dakota plains. A line of escarpments called "the Missouri coteau" marks the break between the continent's central lowlands and the Great Plains. East of the Missouri River is a flat landscape—smoothed by the glacier—with many small lakes. West of the Missouri, where the glaciers did not penetrate, the drainage pattern has eroded the soft soils to create a more distinct profile. This effect is particularly pronounced in the Badlands where little vegetative cover protected the soils.

The climate of North Dakota is continental and severe. Rainfall averages less than 20 inches per year and farmers frequently suffer severe losses due to droughts. The growing season is short, averaging only 130 days. Long summer days and very fertile prairie soils high in nitrogen compensate for the short growing season. The natural vegetation of the state is bluestem prairie grass in the east and wheat grass in the more arid west. Along water courses poplar, elm, and willow once were prevalent. Soil and water conservation projects have had a significant impact on the landscape.

The first economic ventures in North Dakota were fur-trading posts. Between the 1870s and the 1890s the Indians were pacified, and the railroads were laid. These railroads made feasible the marketing of bulky farm produce. On the fertile soils of eastern and central North Dakota, grain farming dominates. The poorer western soils are used for cattle ranching. Towering shiny metal grain elevators mark the points where agricultural production is tied to the transportation network and the market. The vertical line of the grain elevator is a dramatic expression of the state's grain economy.

Points of interest to the visitor include many sites of frontier times, old forts, and battlegrounds. At Bonanzaville is a re-created frontier town. Theodore Roosevelt and a French marquis both operated cattle ranges near the town of Medora. This town at the gateway to Theodore Roosevelt National Park has a joyful "wild west" flavor.

1. Cavalier

Gunlogson Arboretum
N.Dak. 5, 7 miles west of Cavalier

This arboretum, which consists of 200 acres and the original homestead of the Gunlogson family, is located in the 900-acre Icelandic State Park. The Gunlogson property, developed in the late 1800s, was one of the earliest homesteads in North Dakota. The arboretum provides an excellent

NORTH DAKOTA

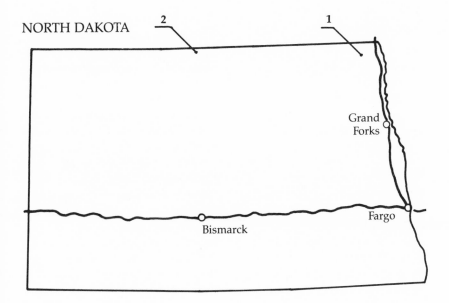

1. *Cavalier*   2. *Dunseith*

opportunity to view and study nature and has an extensive trail system along the Tongue River. Camping facilities are available.
Open: Daily, sunrise–sunset. (701) 265–4561.

2. Dunseith

International Peace Garden
Off U.S. 281

Dedicated in 1932, the International Peace Garden covers 2,300 acres along the U.S.-Canadian border. A plaque bears the inscription, "We two nations dedicate this garden and pledge ourselves that as long as men shall live we will not take up arms against one another." The formal

landscaped areas are excellent expressions of the gardening arts. The grounds include an arboretum, an international campground, and a picnic area. Also located here are a chapel, a music camp, and an athletic camp. Cultural and recreational programs are offered.
Open: April–November, daily. Fee. (701) 263–4390.

Other Places of Interest

Arrowood National Wildlife Refuge, Carrington
Bonanzaville, Fargo
Camp Hancock State Historic Site, Bismarck
Frontier Village, Jamestown
Theodore Roosevelt National Park, Medora

Ohio

Area: 41,222 square miles

Population: 10,744,000

Statehood: March 1, 1803
(17th state)

West of the peaks of the Appalachian Mountains one finds the heartland of the North American continent, a vast basin draining through the Mississippi River to the Gulf of Mexico. Ohio lies on the eastern edge of this region. Glaciation around the Great Lakes smoothed the topography of northwestern Ohio. The Appalachian Plateau in the unglaciated southeastern part of the state has a sharper topography, reflecting ages of erosion by the elements.

Weather fronts crossing the continent drop ample rain in Ohio. Before the land was cleared, deciduous forests of oak, maple, hickory, beech, and chestnut covered the state. Ohio gets its nickname, "The Buckeye State," from the horse chestnuts abundant in its forests.

The fertile soils of the central basin made Ohio the nation's breadbasket in the nineteenth century. In pioneer times produce had to be shipped down the Ohio and Mississippi rivers to market. The Erie Canal, completed in 1825, tied Ohio to the Eastern Seaboard. Many early settlers came from farms in New England and Virginia. Some old Ohio towns have a New England-like village appearance.

Ohio's central location, convenient to transportation routes and the Midwest's natural resources, helped the state to become an important steel manufacturing center and Cincinnati a center of meat processing.

Ohio is rich in cultural institutions. Among them are the fine art museums of Cleveland, Cincinnati, Columbus, Dayton, and Toledo. Cleveland, Cincinnati, and Columbus have excellent symphony orchestras. Cincinnati's May Festival and the annual Bach Festival at Berea are important musical events.

The state possesses many historic homes of interest. The nature lover may wish to visit Cedar Bog near Springfield, a rare habitat of Ice Age flora and fauna, and Glacial Groves on Kelley's Island, a unique glacier-sculptured landscape. The Ohio Historic Society in Columbus features excellent exhibits in archaeology, history, and natural history. Ohio's vanished Indian peoples left silent marks on the landscape with their giant earth-sculptured mounds; of these, Great Serpent Mound near Locust Grove is the most impressive.

Ohio was the first state to be settled under the provisions of the Northwest Ordinance, the great pattern for creating a democratic landscape of small farmers on the nation's western lands. Johnny Appleseed was an Ohioan. Intense settlement of the state began soon after the nation's war of independence. The settlers who came were no longer English colonists but Americans.

OHIO

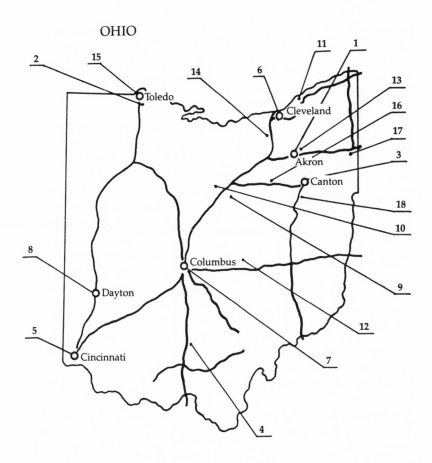

1. *Akron* 2. *Bates* 3. *Canton* 4. *Chillicothe* 5. *Cincinnati* 6. *Cleveland*
7. *Columbus* 8. *Dayton* 9. *Lucas* 10. *Mansfield* 11. *Mentor* 12. *Newark*
13. *Stow* 14. *Strongsville* 15. *Toledo* 16. *Wooster* 17. *Youngstown* 18. *Zoar*

1. Akron

Simon Perkins Mansion
550 Copley Road

Completed in 1837 by Simon Perkins, founder of Akron, the mansion sits on a hill overlooking what is now downtown Akron. Many of the trees Perkins planted are still living, and the original gardens have been re-stored. The mansion is a museum.
Open: Tuesday–Saturday 1:00–5:00 p.m.
Closed: Holidays. (216) 535–1120.

Stan Hywet Hall Gardens
714 North Portage Path

Surrounding the Tudor-style mansion are a rose garden, sunken garden, English walled garden, and Japanese garden. A rhododendron walk, a birch tree lane, terraces, pools, and statuary all add to the beauty of the grounds. Guided tours.
Open: Tuesday–Saturday 10:00 a.m.–4:00 p.m., Sunday 1:00–4:00 p.m. Closed: Holidays. (216) 836–5533.

2. Bates

Hale Homestead and Village
2686 Oak Hill Road

The gardens, reconstructed according to the original plans, have been restored by the Garden Club of Cleveland. The grounds include herb and formal gardens and a nature trail.
Open: Daily 9:00 a.m.–5:00 p.m. (216) 575–9137.

3. Canton

Canton Garden Center
Stadium Park, 1615 Stadium Parkway, Northwest

The building is "home" to 74 area garden clubs. The grounds around the center offer a dazzling display of flowers each season.
Open: Patio (flower display), 8:00 a.m.–7:00 p.m.; Cupboard Shoppe, Tuesday–Friday 10:00 a.m.–
noon, 1:00–4:00 p.m.; grounds, daily until 9:00 p.m. (216) 455–6172.

4. Chillicothe

Adena–Thomas Worthington Estate
Adena Road, Ohio 104

The mansion, built in 1807, was regarded as "one of the finest homes in the west." The formal gardens and herb garden behind the house are typical of the period.
Open: May 26–October 31, Wednesday–Saturday 9:30 a.m.–5:00 p.m., Sunday noon–5:00 p.m. Fee. (614) 466–1500.

5. Cincinnati

Cornelius J. Hauck Botanic Garden
Reading Road and William Howard Taft Avenue

Once a private garden, this 8-acre site has many and rare specimen plantings including the Manchurian sawtooth oak. A dwarf evergreen garden contains over 50 varieties of pine, spruce, fir, and other conifers.
Open: Monday–Friday 9:30 a.m.–4:00 p.m. Closed: Holidays. (513) 221–0981.

Krohn Conservatory
Eden Park off Columbia Parkway,
U.S. 50

The displays emphasizing the visual qualities of the plants are an aesthetic delight. The collections in the palm, cacti, and fern houses include many rare species from the tropics. *Open: Monday–Saturday 10:00 a.m.– 5:00 p.m., Sunday 10:00 a.m.– 6:00 p.m. Special late hours during the Christmas and Easter seasons. (513) 352–4090.*

Mount Airy Arboretum
5083 Colerain Avenue

This arboretum houses a 120-acre collection of trees and woody plants. Also featured are a Green Garden; a demonstration area for ground covers, vines, hedges, and flowers or shrubs from each of the 50 states; and an outstanding perennial garden. *Open: Daily, sunrise–sunset. (513) 352–4080.*

Spring Grove Cemetery
4521 Spring Grove Avenue

This mid-nineteenth-century cemetery is in the landscape tradition of Mount Auburn and other pastoral Victorian cemeteries. The 733-acre cemetery-arboretum, designed by Adolph Strauch in 1844, is known for its collection of magnificent trees, many over 200 years old. The "Lawn Plan" cemetery was created for the first time at Spring Grove. *Open: Monday–Friday 8:00 a.m.– 5:00 p.m., Saturday until noon. (513) 681–6680.*

6. Cleveland

Cleveland Cultural Gardens
Rockefeller Park, along Liberty and East Boulevards between Superior and St. Clair Avenues

This chain of gardens represents the native countries of most of Cleveland's ethnic groups. A National Historic Landmark, the gardens are noted for their diversity as well as their beauty. *Open: Daily, sunrise–sunset. (216) 333–1167.*

Garden of the Cleveland Museum of Art
11150 East Boulevard

Elegant gardens surround the beautiful classic revival building. The sensitively designed outdoor environment provides a superb setting for the museum's fine sculpture collection. *Open: Monday–Saturday 9:00 a.m.– 5:00 p.m. (216) 421–7340.*

Rose Garden
Wade Park, to the rear of the Museum of Art; enter from East Boulevard

The garden features a well-maintained display of thousands of rose bushes. Best seen during summer months. *Open: Daily, sunrise–sunset. (216) 421–7340.*

☆

**Western Reserve
Herb Society Garden**

11030 East Boulevard

Located on the grounds of the Garden Center of Greater Cleveland, this site is arranged in the manner of a medieval monastery garden. It is maintained by members of the Herb Society.
Open: Monday–Friday 9:00 a.m.–5:00 p.m., Sunday 2:00–5:00 p.m. (216) 721–1600.

7. Columbus

Franklin Park Conservatory

1777 East Broad Street

A landmark of Columbus since 1895, the arboretum presents a rich collection of exotic plants. There are special displays at Christmas and Easter, and a chrysanthemum show in the fall.
Open: Daily 10:00 a.m.–4:00 p.m. For guided tours, call (614) 222–7447 or 252–0145.

Park of Roses

3875 North High Street in Whetstone Park, 5.5 miles north of downtown Columbus

The park features over 36,000 roses, a natural swamp ravine and bird sanctuary, and a garden of perennials.
Open: Daily 9:00 a.m.–dusk. For guided tours, call (614) 222–7410.

8. Dayton

James F. Cox, Jr., Arboretum

6733 Springboro Pike

Established in 1967, the 164-acre arboretum is tastefully designed.
Open: Daily, sunrise–sunset. (513) 434–9005.

9. Lucas

Malabar Farm

Pleasant Valley Road

Through careful husbandry, writer Louis Bromfield was able to restore fertility to the worn-out lands of this farmstead. The attractive grounds also reflect the owner's great care for the land.
*Open: Monday–Saturday 9:00 a.m.–5:00 p.m.
Closed: December–February. Fee for farm tour.* (419) 892–2055.

10. Mansfield

☆

Kingwood Center and Gardens

900 Park Avenue West, 1.5 miles west of downtown Mansfield

On a 47-acre site, the public gardens offer sumptuous seasonal plantings including Ohio's largest tulip and daffodil displays. There are conservatories, a bird sanctuary, and wildlife exhibits. The Kingwood Center fea-

tures exhibitions and a horticultural library. The gardens host many special events.
Open: Tuesday–Saturday 8:00 a.m.–5:00 p.m., Sunday 1:30–4:30 p.m. Closed: Holidays. (419) 522–0211.

11. Mentor

☆
Holden Arboretum
9500 Sperry Road (take I-90 to State Road 306, turn south and then left at 1st intersection, Kirtland Chardon Road; follow sign to main entrance)

Founded in 1931, this 3,100-acre preserve of trees, flowers, birds, and wildlife is North America's largest arboretum.
Open: April–October, Tuesday–Sunday 10:00 a.m.–5:00 p.m. Closed: Holidays. (216) 946–4400.

12. Newark

Dawes Arboretum
State Road 13, 5 miles south of Newark

On the 1,100-acre site founded in 1929, 350 acres have been developed. The collection includes 1,500 species of trees. Of special interest are the flowering crab apples, the Japanese bonsai, and the Japanese garden. Around a 5-acre lake can be seen marsh vegetation and native wildlife.
Open: Daily, sunrise–sunset; Reception Center, Monday–Friday

8:00 a.m.–5:00 p.m., Saturday 9:00 a.m.–5:00 p.m., Sunday 1:00–5:00 p.m. Closed: Holidays. (614) 323–2355.

13. Stow

Adell Durbin Arboretum
Adell Durbin Park; on State Road 91, just south of State Road 59 intersection

The arboretum's collection includes over 250 species.
Open: Daily, sunrise–sunset. (216) 688–8238.

14. Strongsville

Gardenview Horticultural Park
U.S. 42, 1 mile south of State Road 82 at 16711 Pearl Road

The plants are arranged in complete garden settings and easily adapted to the home grounds. Exotic birds are an interesting feature. May is the peak time for blossoms.
Open: Early spring to late fall; nonmembers, Saturday–Sunday noon–6:00 p.m. Fee. (216) 238–6653.

15. Toledo

Crosby Gardens
5403 Elmer Drive

The grounds feature herb, rose, and wildflower gardens; special exhibitions; craft demonstrations on the weekends during the summer and fall months. A restored frontier cabin is also of interest.
Open: Daily, sunrise–sunset. (419) 536–8365.

Secor Park Arboretum
10001 West Central Avenue (U.S. 20, Route 120)

The 250-acre arboretum features over 500 species of trees and shrubs, as well as a wildflower collection. Tours available.
Open: Monday–Friday 9:00 a.m.– 5:00 p.m., Saturday–Sunday 11:00 a.m.–6:00 p.m. (419) 829–2761.

16. Wooster

Secrest Arboretum
Ohio Agricultural Research and Development Center, U.S. 250

Established in 1908, the arboretum is noted for its unique block plantings of forest trees and for its fine collection of yews, conifers, flowering crab apples, rhododendrons, hollies, and other ornamentals.
Open: Daily, sunrise–sunset. (216) 263–3761.

17. Youngstown

Fellows Riverside Garden, Garden Center of the Greater Youngstown Area
North end of Mill Creek Park on bluffs above Lake Glacier

The colorful formal gardens feature roses and other perennials.
Open: Daily, sunrise–sunset. (216) 744–4171.

18. Zoar

Zoar Village State Memorial
The village of Zoar was established by a German religious sect in 1817. The formal community garden, based on a biblical description of the New Jerusalem, has been carefully restored.
Open: May 24–September 1, Wednesday–Saturday 9:30 a.m.– 5:00 p.m., Sunday noon–5:00 p.m.; September–October, weekends only. (216) 874–4336.

Other Places of Interest
Blue Hole, Castalia
Cedar Bog, Urbana
Cincinnati Zoological Park
Glen Helen, Yellow Springs
Hueston Woods State Park, College Corner
Inscription Park, Sandusky
Lake Hope State Park, Athens

McKinley Memorial, Canton
Mound Builders State Memorial,
  Newark
Mound City Group National
  Monument, Chillicothe

Olentangy Caverns, Columbus
Rockefeller Park, Cleveland
Schoenbrun Village State Memorial,
  New Philadelphia
Toledo Zoo

Oklahoma

Area: 69,919 square miles

Population: 3,301,000

Statehood: November 16, 1907
(46th state)

The "Sooner State" is located in the heartland of the nation. The eroded hilly landforms of North America's Central Lowland occupy eastern Oklahoma. In the extreme east, the Ozark and Ouachita plateaus display a rugged but interesting topography. Progressing westward across the state's 400-mile length, elevations increase as the continent rises toward the Rockies. On the arid High Plains of western Oklahoma, the land is extremely flat.

The natural vegetation is oak-hickory forest. Bluestem prairie grass covers the central portion of the state, and gama-buffalo prairie grass grows in the extreme west where the least rainfall occurs.

The United States acquired Oklahoma through the Louisiana Purchase. Beginning in 1819, the five civilized Indian tribes of the Southeast—Cherokees, Choctaws, Creeks, Chickasaws, and Seminoles—were relocated in Oklahoma. These tribes, influenced by European settlers, had developed written languages and constitutions of government. They established schools and laid out towns. And, like their neighbors in Arkansas and Texas, they imported black slaves and grew cotton. After the Civil War, other nomadic Indian tribes were forced to migrate to Oklahoma. Pressures by whites for settlement of the state's rich agricultural lands and encroachments by cattle drives, and finally by the railroads, threatened the Indian communities. In 1889, the old Indian territory began to be redistributed to white settlers. The well-established tribes of eastern Oklahoma were able to maintain their landholdings, but the less cultured western tribes were displaced. One-eighth of the nation's Indians still live in Oklahoma.

Oklahoma was first settled as an agricultural state. Livestock production and wheat growing continue to be important land uses. In 1901 Oklahoma's first significant oil field was opened. Oil is still an important source of the state's wealth.

The Dust Bowl of the 1930s had a great impact on the landscape. The conservation methods resulting from the lessons learned during this period have reshaped Oklahoma's countryside. Rows of trees are planted as windbreaks at the edge of the fields. Farmers practice contour plowing, strip cropping, and crop rotation. Irrigation projects have introduced major new lakes into the state.

Many cultural and scenic points of interest can be found in Oklahoma. Tulsa has two fine art museums, the Philbrook and the Thomas Gilcrease Institute. Relics of Indian culture are preserved at the Southern Plains Museum in Anadarko and at the Five Civilized Tribes Museum in Muskogee. Scenic areas in eastern

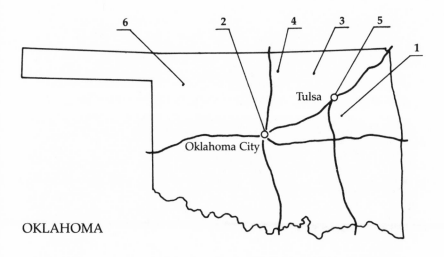

OKLAHOMA

1. *Muskogee*   2. *Oklahoma City*   3. *Pawhuska*   4. *Ponca City*   5. *Tulsa*
6. *Woodward*

Oklahoma include the Ozark and Ouachita mountains, parts of which are covered by the Ouachita National Forest.

1. Muskogee

Muskogee Azalea Gardens
Honor Heights Park

This garden is the home of some 30,000 plants of over 600 varieties of azaleas. Established in the late 1950s in the English estate style, it has won national awards. Peak blooming is during April and May when the Azalea Festival is held.
Open: Daily 8:00 a.m.–5:00 p.m.
(405) 682–6602.

2. Oklahoma City

Martin Park Nature Center
Near I-35, Arcadia/Edmond exit
on Route 3

The nature center and interpretive buildings are located within a 140-acre wildlife sanctuary. There are many wildflower displays and exhibits, as well as educational facilities, in addition to the native trails. Self-guided tours.
Open: Winter, Monday–Friday
8:00 a.m.–5:00 p.m.; summer,
Wednesday–Saturday 10:00 a.m.–
6:00 p.m., Sunday noon–8:00 p.m.
(405) 755–6676.

Oklahoma Heritage Center in Oklahoma City.

Oklahoma Heritage Center
North Robinson at 14th Street

Attractive gardens with several fountain pools can be seen on the grounds of this 1920s mansion. Inside are many interesting pieces of furniture and mementos of Oklahoma history. *Open: Daily 9:00 a.m.–5:00 p.m.; Sundays and holidays 1:00–5:00 p.m. Fee. (405) 235-4458.*

Will Rogers Park and Horticultural Center
3500 Northwest 36th Street

Included in the arboretum are lakes, rock gardens, a conservatory, botanical gardens, a greenhouse, and an exhibition building. The formal rose garden, which contains 5,000 plants

of numerous varieties, is outstanding. *Open: Daily 8:00 a.m.–sunset. (405) 943-3977.*

3. Pawhuska

Chinese Gardens
10th Street between Prudom and Leahy Avenues

The three-tiered hillside garden was begun in 1909. Plants were contributed by persons who accompanied the Osage Indians to their last reserve; friends who had traveled to the Far East donated carvings and fountains. More recent restorations of the gardens involved many members of the

community. The site is a source of pride to all members of this small Oklahoma town.
Open: Fall–winter, 9:00 a.m.– 5:00 p.m.; spring–summer, until 6:00 p.m. (918) 287–9924.

4. Ponca City

First Marland Mansion
1000 East Grand Street

The grounds of the original Marland Mansion were developed in 1914 by Henry Hatshita, a Japanese gardener. In 1967 the site was renamed the Ponca City Cultural Center; it is now operated by the city of Ponca.
Open: Monday–Saturday except Tuesday, 10:00 a.m.–5:00 p.m., Sunday 1:00–5:00 p.m. (405) 765–5268.

5. Tulsa

☆
Philbrook Art Center
Formal Gardens
2727 South Rockford Road, 3 miles southeast of downtown Tulsa (from I-44 take Peoria Street exit and follow Peoria north for approximately 2.25 miles; turn right and follow 27th Place for 1 block to Rockford Avenue)

These beautiful formal gardens on a 23-acre sloping site were designed to complement the Italian Renaissance villa that now houses the Art Center.
Open: Tuesday–Saturday 10:00 a.m.–

5:00 p.m., Sunday 1:00–5:00 p.m. Fee. (918) 749–7941.

☆
Tulsa Municipal Rose Garden
and Memorial Park
21st Street and South Peoria Avenue

This municipal rose garden, which has received numerous awards, covers 4.5 acres with 9,000 plants and 270 varieties. It is designed in the Italian Renaissance style with 6 terraces, stone steps, and rock walls. The blooms are best in mid-May and mid-September. A conservatory and a bird sanctuary are located on the grounds of the Tulsa Garden Center.
Open: Daily, sunrise–sunset. (918) 749–6401.

6. Woodward

U.S. Southern Great Plains
Field Station
2217 18th Street

The early research objectives of this station were to grow trees and shrubs in "The Great American Desert" for homestead beautification and windbreaks; at the time, the region was essentially a treeless plain with a harsh climate. By 1940, many trees, shrubs, and wildflowers had been planted. These plants—now mature—are of great interest to those concerned with horticulture on the Great Plains.
Open: Monday–Friday 8:00 a.m.– 5:00 p.m. (405) 256–7449.

Other Places of Interest

Alabaster Caverns State Park,
  Freedom
Cedarvale Gardens, Arbuckle
  Mountains

Indian City, Anadarko
Kirkpatrick Gardens, Oklahoma City
National Cowboy Hall of Fame and
  Western Heritage Center,
  Oklahoma City

Oregon

Area: 96,981 square miles

Population: 2,687,000

Statehood: February 14, 1859
(33rd state)

Oregon is a landscape of contrasts: wet and dry, rain forests and deserts, open plateaus and mountain-enclosed valleys. The Lewis and Clark expedition, and the early settlers who followed it, crossed a region they called "the Great American Desert" before arriving in the lush valleys of coastal Oregon. This great American desert—a high plateau covered by eroded ancient lava beds—extends into the eastern part of the state. Averaging less than 20 inches of rain per year, it supports a sparse prairie vegetation. Huge agricultural operations currently use the land for wheat farming and cattle grazing.

Across the rugged Cascade Mountains from this plateau lie the beautiful Willamette Valley, the Coastal Ranges, and the sea. The extensive coniferous forests on Oregon's mountains are important sources of lumber; the state produces one-sixth of the nation's supply. Douglas fir and ponderosa pine are the preferred species. The valley of the Willamette River, where the major part of Oregon's population lives, is a fertile land. The climate is wet with mild winters due to the moderating influence of the Sea of Japan current.

Portland is an important harbor, located where the Willamette meets the Columbia River. The peaks of the Cascade Ranges in the background make a dramatic setting for the city.

The Oregon coast is a splendid vacationland. Its vista is rugged and dramatic where the ancient volcano-formed Coastal Mountains are being attacked and worn away by the sea. Whales, marine creatures great and small, and sea birds animate this seascape.

The state has a wonderful variety of scenic attractions. In eastern Oregon is the Crooked Rivers National Grassland. Spectacular limestone and lava formations can be seen at Oregon Caves National Monument in the Siskiyou Mountain Range. There are 15 national forests in Oregon. Timberline Lodge in Mount Hood National Forest, a whimsical wooden structure built by the Works Progress Administration, recalls the fantastic lodges of the coastal Indian tribes. In Crater Lake National Park is found one of the world's most beautiful lakes, the 2,000-foot-deep Crater Lake, which fills the collapsed volcanic core of old Mount Mazama. Fascinating marine life is a highlight of Three Arch Rocks National Wildlife Refuge at the Oregon Dunes National Seashore. All but 23 miles of Oregon's magnificent coastline has been designated as public land to protect this great scenic resource.

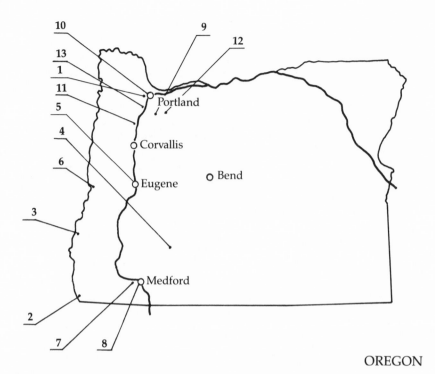

OREGON

1. *Beaverton*   2. *Brookings*   3. *Charleston*   4. *Crater Lake*   5. *Eugene*
6. *Florence*   7. *Jacksonville*   8. *Medford*   9. *Oregon City*   10. *Portland*
11. *Salem*   12. *Sandy*   13. *Wilsonville*

1. Beaverton

Jenkins Estate Gardens and Nature Trail
209 Southwest Farmington and Grabhorn Roads

The 68-acre site is noted for its formal gardens, which contain a great variety of wildflowers and of rare and exotic flowers, shrubs, and trees imported from all over the world.
Open: Monday–Friday 9:00 a.m.–5:00 p.m. (503) 642–3855.

2. Brookings

Azalea State Park
U.S. 101

Each spring this 36-acre park comes alive with many colored varieties of azaleas. The park gets its name from the many indigenous azaleas that grow here, some of them reportedly as old as 300 years. The community of Brookings sponsors an Azalea Festival each May.
Open: Daily, sunrise–sunset. (503) 469–2213.

3. Charleston

Louis J. Simpson
Estate and Gardens
Cape Arago Highway

The 600-acre site, now known as
Shore Acres State Park, is honey-
combed with trails that wander below
the Observation Building. The visitor
can hear the ocean crashing on the
rocky Oregon coastline. There are
formal gardens, display plants from
around the world, ponds, and exotic
ferns.
*Open: Sunrise–sunset. Parking fee.
(503) 888–4902.*

4. Crater Lake

Castle Crest Wildflower Garden
Crater Lake National Park

This 4-acre, naturally occurring
"garden" site is profusely watered
by dozens of springs issuing from
the Castle Crest, a long, steep rocky
ridge. The late arrival of summer
delays the blossoming period for
many flowers until about August 1.
Visitors wishing to see Castle Crest at
its best should call ahead, as the best
period for viewing is different each
year.
*Open: Summer–fall, daily. Parking fee.
(503) 594–2211.*

5. Eugene

Hendrick's Park
Rhododendron Garden
Skyline Boulevard

There are over 6,000 rhododendrons
and azaleas in this 20-acre garden.
The park contains some 300-year-old
trees. Guided tours may be arranged
by calling the Eugene Parks and
Recreation Department.
*Open: Daily, sunrise–sunset. (503)
687–5334.*

6. Florence

Darlingtonia Wayside Arboretum
U.S. 101, 5 miles north of Florence

The original 17.4-acre tract of land
was acquired principally to preserve
and show the unusual bog-loving
plants—known as Darlingtonia
plants—growing next to the highway.
The plant itself is carnivorous, often
called the Cobra or Pitcher plant because of its peculiar shape; it is native
to a limited area of southern Oregon
and northern California.
Open: Sunrise–sunset. (503) 997–3128.

7. Jacksonville

Peter Britt Gardens
First Street

This 5-acre plot, begun in 1862,
was the first "garden" in southern

Oregon. Many of the trees, shrubs, and flowers planted by members of the Britt family still flourish. It was largely through their efforts and influence that other gardens, vineyards, and orchards were begun in this area.
Open: Sunrise–sunset. (503) 899–8118.

8. Medford

Claire Hanley Arboretum
569 Hanley Road

The arboretum was established in 1961 to give residents of southern Oregon an opportunity to observe a variety of plant materials under local conditions. It contains primarily trees and rhododendrons.
Open: All times. (503) 772–5165.

9. Oregon City

John Inskeep Environmental Learning Center
19600 South Molalla

This 4-acre former industrial site has been redeveloped to demonstrate that wildlife habitats are possible in urban settings. There are also demonstration landscape developments for energy and water conservation.
Open: Weekdays 10:00 a.m.–4:00 p.m., Saturday 9:00 a.m.–5:00 p.m., Sunday noon–5:00 p.m.
(503) 657–8400.

10. Portland

Aurora Colony
Aurora Avenue

Located between Portland and Salem, the Aurora Colony was founded in 1857 by a German communal group from Pennsylvania. The colony lasted until 1883. The plants displayed in the herb and flower gardens are those grown at the time of the colony.
Open: Daily. Fee. (503) 581–1966.

Bishop's Close at Elk Rock
11800 Southwest Military Lane (Lake Oswego)
(6 miles south on Southwest Macadam to Military Road)

Scotsman Peter Kerr's ambition was to create a Scottish garden in Oregon. The 13-acre estate, designed in 1913 by J. C. Olmsted, incorporates design elements typical of Capability Brown and Charles Bridgeman. Construction took nearly 10 years to complete. Paths were left as natural as possible, wandering beneath native firs, oaks, and dogwoods. Sequoias, pines, and hemlocks were added later.
Open: Daily, summer 8:00 a.m.–7:00 p.m.; winter 9:00 a.m.–5:00 p.m. (503) 636–5613.

Bybee–Howell House and Territorial Garden
Sauvie Island, Howell Park Road

The house and grounds were planned by James and Julia Bybee in 1856. They have been restored and pre-

served as an unusual example of nineteenth-century territorial farm life. Appropriate planting, pruning, and landscaping was done to enhance the property's mid-nineteenth-century appearance; the Oregon Pioneer Orchard was planted with fruit trees found in early Oregon orchards. It is now a unique orchard museum.
Open: May–October, 10:00 a.m.–5:00 p.m. (503) 621–3344.

Crystal Springs Rhododendron Gardens
Southeast 28th Street, 1 block north of Woodstock Boulevard

These gardens are located within the boundaries of the Eastmoreland Golf Course and are surrounded by the waters of the Crystal Springs Creek. The creek is a salmon-spawning ground and a protected haven for ducks and geese.
Open: Daily, dawn–midnight. (503) 771–8386.

Hoyt Arboretum
4000 Southwest Fairview Boulevard

The 213-acre arboretum contains more than 8 miles of trails and 630 species of plant materials. It has one of the country's largest collections of different types of conifers. Self-guided tours.
Open: Daily, sunrise–sunset; Visitors' Center, 10:00 a.m.–4:00 p.m. Closed: Monday. (503) 228–8732.

☆
International Rose Test Garden
400 Southwest Kingston Avenue (Washington Park)

Covering 4 acres, this is the oldest continuously operated rose garden in the United States and one of 26 official test gardens of the All-American Rose selections. Situated on 3 terraces, the gardens overlook Portland on one side and Mount Hood on the other. They contain 8,000 roses of 400 varieties including some from Europe and the Far East. Portland merits well the title, "City of Roses."
Open: Daily, sunrise–sunset. (503) 248–4302.

☆
Ira's Fountain
Southwest 3rd Avenue and Market Street

This superb contemporary park occupies an entire city block in the redeveloped downtown area of Portland. Designed by landscape architect Lawrence Halprin, the park features a remarkable series of man-made waterfalls. The cascading waters bring the essence of the surrounding mountains to the city. The site has won many national awards for outstanding design.
Open: All times. (503) 222–2223.

Japanese Gardens
Southwest Kingston Avenue (Washington Park)

The climate of Portland helps make these among the finest examples

Ira's Fountain Square, Portland, Oreg.

of Japanese gardens in the United States. The five traditional gardens were designed in 1962, some with materials imported from Japan. There are also bonsai collections and a pavillion.
Open: May–September, daily 10:00 a.m.–6:00 p.m.; rest of year, until 4:00 p.m. Fee. (503) 223–1321.

Leach Botanical Gardens
6704 Southeast 122nd Avenue
(Foster Road exit off I-205)

Native plants of the Pacific Northwest are the focus of this 5.5-acre wooded garden. The grounds originally belonged to John and Lila Leach, who explored the region's wilderness in search of previously unknown plants. Lila, a botanist, discovered 2 genera and 11 species of plants.

Open: Grounds, daily, sunrise–sunset; home, Tuesday–Saturday 10:00 a.m.–2:00 p.m. (503) 761–9503.

Rae Selling Berry Gardens
11505 Southwest
Summerville Avenue

These gardens contain an internationally known 6-acre rhododendron collection, all grown from seed. Over 2,000 mature plants, some from the Himalayas, are exhibited. Three dozen of these species are on the threatened or endangered list of plants.
Open: Limited use by the general public; guided tours. (503) 636–4112.

11. Salem

Bush's Pasture Garden
High and Mission Streets

The garden features roses, peonies, azaleas, flowering cherry trees, flowering crab apples, and hawthorns. Many of the original fruit trees still remain.
Open: Tuesday–Sunday 9:00 a.m.–5:00 p.m. Fee. (503) 581–2228 or 363–4714.

Deepwood Gardens
1116 Mission Street

The formal gardens were originally constructed in 1894. Deepwood was the center of a principal watering, bathing, and camping place of the Calapuya Indians. Chief Quniaby, the last of the Chemeketa band, died at this camp in 1884.
Open: Monday, Wednesday–Friday, Sunday, 2nd Saturday of the month noon–5:00 p.m. Fee. (503) 363–1825.

12. Sandy

Gardens of Enchantment at the Oral Hull Park for the Blind
43233 Oral Hull Road

Sections include plants to be enjoyed through touch, taste, smell, and sound. All plants are in raised beds, and markers are in Braille.
Open: Notify caretakers; groups should make reservations. (503) 668–6195 or 668–7587.

13. Wilsonville

Grove of the States
I-5 rest area, near Wilsonville

The state tree of each of the fifty states is planted here and labeled for identification.
Open: Daily, sunrise–sunset. (503) 682–0411.

Other Places of Interest

Alton–Baker Park, Eugene
Ashland Shakespearean Festival Herb
  Garden, Ashland
Bonneville Dam,
  Oregon-Washington border
Century Drive, Bend
Columbia River Gorge
Greer Gardens, Eugene
High Desert Museum, Bend
Malheur Cave, Burns
Mount Hood National Forest
Oregon Caves National Monument,
  Grants Pass
Oregon Dunes, Florence
Silver Creek Falls State Park, Salem
Skinner Butte, Eugene

Pennsylvania

Area: 44,888 square miles

Population: 11,853,000

Statehood: December 12, 1787
(2nd state)

In 1681 King Charles II granted William Penn a charter to found a colony in the New World. Penn, son of a famous English admiral, was a Quaker, a religious sect that was persecuted in England. He aspired to develop a society where all "good" people could live together in peace. He dealt fairly with the Indian tribes of this new land and with the Swedish and German colonists who already occupied the territory.

The state of Pennsylvania stretches westward from its great port of Philadelphia, on the Delaware River, across the Piedmont and mountains to the Great Lakes in the extreme northwest. Appalachian oak forests originally covered major parts of the state. The climate is continental and humid, and the growing season varies from 160 to 200 days. Pennsylvania produces a variety of farm crops. Chester County is the nation's center of mushroom production. Members of the Amish religious sect work the land around Lancaster using eighteenth-century farm technology. Their diversified and intensive farming creates a picturesque landscape. The fertile soils and moderate temperatures of the region around Lake

Erie make this a prosperous fruit-growing region.

William Penn selected the site and laid out the initial plan for Philadelphia. He imagined a "greene country town" of ample green spaces and domestic gardens. The city has been a national leader in initiating civic improvements and welfare institutions. Fairmount Park is one of its highlights. In 1812, the city acquired a 5-acre tract on which to build a reservoir and public park. Today, the park is a unique repository of the city's great heritage, featuring two notable art museums, a zoo, numerous historic houses, and extensive recreational areas. Philadelphia's Society Hill preserves attractive townhouses dating from colonial times. In Independence National Historic Park are found many famous sites of the nation's early history, including Carpenter's Hall, where the Continental Congress met to approve the Declaration of Independence.

Pittsburgh, at the other end of the state, is located in a dramatic, hilly region. At the point of land where the Monongahela and Allegheny rivers cut through the hills and meet to form the Ohio River, a frontier military outpost once stood. In the 18-acre state park established here, a fountain of heroic proportions celebrates the place.

Pennsylvania is the site of many famous places in American history. State parks commemorate the Revolutionary War Battle of Brandywine, the desperate winter of Valley Forge, and Washington's courageous crossing of the Delaware River. Gettys-

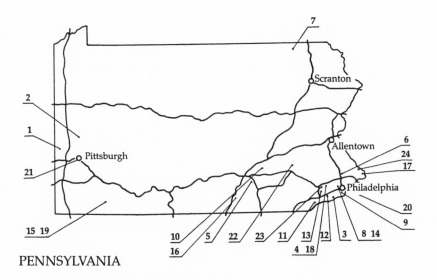

PENNSYLVANIA

1. *Ambridge* 2. *Butler* 3. *Chester* 4. *Edgemont* 5. *Elizabethtown*
6. *Fort Washington* 7. *Franklin Forks* 8. *Haverford* 9. *Havertown*
10. *Hershey* 11. *Kennett Square* 12. *Lima* 13. *Malvern* 14. *Merion Station*
15. *Mill Run* 16. *Mont Alto* 17. *Morrisville* 18. *Norristown* 19. *Ohiopyle*
20. *Philadelphia* 21. *Pittsburgh* 22. *Reading* 23. *Valley Forge*
24. *Washington Crossing*

burg National Military Park marks
the turning point of the Civil War.
Independence Hall in Philadelphia
houses the Liberty Bell.

The range of gardens to be viewed
in Pennsylvania reflects the state's
geographic diversity and rich history.

1. Ambridge

Old Economy Village
and Gardens
Pa. 65 northwest of Pittsburgh

Here are the relics of an adventure in
communal living that failed, but left
a legacy of practical gardens, flower

gardens with reflecting pools, paths,
and labyrinths. The formal gardens
have a graceful pavilion and a grotto;
the flowers are largely those of the
early nineteenth century. There is
also an excellent kitchen garden and
greenhouse.

Open: Tuesday–Saturday 8:30 a.m.–
5:00 p.m., Sunday 1:00–5:00 p.m.
Fee. (412) 266–4500.

2. Butler

Jennings Nature Preserve
Pa. 8, 12 miles north of Butler

The 400-acre site preserves the habitat of the Blazing Star. It is spectacular during the blooming season (August).
Open: Daily 10:00 a.m.–sunset. (412) 794–6011.

3. Chester

Taylor Memorial Arboretum
10 Ridley Drive

The arboretum contains 28 acres of heather, heath, azaleas, hollies, and other plant species suitable for suburban landscaping.
Open: Daily, sunrise–sunset. (215) 876–2649.

4. Edgemont

Colonial Pennsylvania Plantation
Pa. 3, 12 miles west of Philadelphia in Ridgely Creek State Park

At the plantation one can see fields, livestock, and people in a family farm setting of the 1770s and visualize how the land was used then.
Open: April–October, Friday–Sunday 10:00 a.m.–5:00 p.m.; November–March, Saturday–Sunday noon–4:00 p.m. Fee. (215) 566–1725.

5. Elizabethtown

Masonic Homes Gardens

The 5-acre site features formal gardens, rose gardens, rose arbors, and an arboretum.
Open: Daily, sunrise–sunset. (717) 367–1121.

6. Fort Washington

Hope Lodge
553 Bethlehem Pike

This eighteenth-century house is owned by the Pennsylvania Historical and Museum Commission. In its 10-acre parklike setting the gardens have been restored to portray the important historic role of gardens in the landscape. Featured are a colonial herb garden, Federal formal garden, and nineteenth-century vegetable garden.
Open: Tuesday–Saturday 9:00 a.m.–5:00 p.m., Sunday noon–5:00 p.m. (215) 646–1595.

7. Franklin Forks

Salt Springs State Park
Pa. 29, north of Montrose

The original deed of this naturalized park stipulates that the hemlock trees can never be cut; some of them

now measure more than 12 feet in circumference.
Open: Daily, sunrise–sunset. (717) 985–3239.

8. Haverford

Haverford College
College Lane

The campus arboretum features many mature specimen trees, some over 150 years old, and an outstanding collection of evergreens. The college was originally landscaped in 1834 in the style of English garden designer Humphrey Repton.
Open: Daily, sunrise–sunset. (215) 896–1101.

9. Havertown

The Grange
Myrtle and Warwick Roads

The formal gardens surrounding this eighteenth- and nineteenth-century complex of buildings were first laid out by Charles Cruikshank in 1760. The gardens consist of three terraces separated by gravel paths, and have been maintained for over 200 years. There have been minor alterations during this time, but the basic plan remains the same.
Open: April–October, Saturday–Sunday 1:00–4:00 p.m., or by appointment. (215) 446–4958.

10. Hershey

☆
Hershey Rose Gardens and Arboretum
Hotel Road

These gardens contain more than 800 varieties of roses, dwarf evergreens, annuals, perennials, and azaleas. Over 42,000 plants bloom from early June to frost time. Adjoining the rose gardens are the Tulip Gardens and the Arboretum; 25,000 tulips bloom in early May.
Open: Mid-April–December 1, daily 8:00 a.m.–7:00 p.m. Fee. (717) 534–3492.

11. Kennett Square

☆☆
Longwood Gardens
Junction of U.S. 1 and Pa. 52

One of the nation's most important horticultural showplaces, established by Pierre S. Du Pont in 1906, the Longwood Gardens are not to be missed. The water gardens, 4 acres of conservatories, arboretum, fountains, displays, and open-air theater are famous. The gardens make spectacular use of falling water. Some specimen trees date back to the early 1800s. The original site has been enlarged from 200 to 1,000 acres.
Open: Gardens, daily 9:00 a.m.–6:00 p.m.; conservatory, 10:00 a.m.–4:00 p.m. Fee. (215) 388–6741.

12. Lima

John J. Tyler Arboretum
515 Painter Road

The arboretum contains in a single tract approximately 700 acres of woods and fields, gardens, horticultural collections, and buildings. Many of the oldest trees were planted by Jacob Painter between 1830 and 1870. There are many rare specimen trees. *Open: Summer, daily 8:00 a.m.–8:00 p.m.; winter, until 5:00 p.m. Fee. (215) 566–9133.*

13. Malvern

☆
Swiss Pines Park
Charlestown Road,
3 miles north of U.S. 30

The park contains Japanese gardens, native trees, shrubs, ferns, wildflowers, and naturalized bulbs. There are also Polynesian, rhododendron, herb, and rose gardens. *Open: March 15–December 15, Monday–Friday 10:00 a.m.–4:00 p.m., Saturday 9:00 a.m.–noon. (215) 933–6916.*

14. Merion Station

Arboretum of the Barnes Foundation
300 Latches Lane

This 12-acre arboretum features magnolias, lilacs, peonies, viburnums, cotoneasters, and many conifers. *Open: By appointment only. (215) 664–8880.*

15. Mill Run

Fallingwater
Pa. 381 between Mill Run and Ohiopyle

A residence designed by Frank Lloyd Wright, this architectural masterpiece binds man's shelter superbly to the natural site—the garden. *Open: April 1–November 15, Tuesday–Sunday 10:00 a.m.–4:00 p.m., reservation required. Children under 12 not admitted. Fee. (412) 329–8501.*

16. Mont Alto

Mont Alto Arboretum
Mont Alto Campus of Pennsylvania State University

This arboretum spreads over 36 acres, with representative species from Asia, Europe, and the United States. There

are well-maintained trails with many labeled trees and shrubs.
Open: Daily, sunrise–sunset. (814) 865–7517.

17. Morrisville

☆
Pennsbury Manor
Bordentown Road and U.S. 1

This restoration of William Penn's country house (1683–84) and garden is unusual because of the time period it represents. The late seventeenth-century plan for the country manor included an "Upper Court"; this was a series of formal paths by the house, a kitchen garden, and an area for fruits and flowers.
Open: Tuesday–Saturday 9:00 a.m.– 5:00 p.m., Sunday noon–5:00 p.m. Fee. (215) 946–0400.

18. Norristown

Peter Wentz
Farmstead and Garden
Pa. 73, Skippark Pike at Shultz Road (Worcester)

The grounds surrounding this historic house are maintained by the Norristown Garden Club to interpret rural life during colonial times.
Open: Tuesday–Saturday 10:00 a.m.– 4:00 p.m., Sunday 1:00–4:00 p.m. (215) 584–5104.

19. Ohiopyle

Ferncliff Peninsula
Pa. 381

This well-known nature preserve boasts an especially outstanding variety of wildflowers.
Open: Daily, sunrise–sunset. (412) 329–8591.

20. Philadelphia

Bishop White Garden
3rd and Walnut Streets

This eighteenth-century garden expresses Philadelphia's colonial heritage.
Open: Daily 9:00 a.m. –5:00 p.m. Tours conducted by National Park Service. (215) 597–8975.

Cliveden
6401 Germantown Avenue

The historic house, held by the British during the Battle of Germantown, is surrounded by more than 6 acres of century-old trees and other plantings. Property of the National Trust for Historic Preservation.
Open: Tuesday–Saturday 10:00 a.m.– 4:00 p.m., Sunday 1:00–5:00 p.m. (215) 848–1777.

Deshler–Morris House

5442 Germantown Avenue

This lovely city garden features large specimen trees, including some tree forms of boxwood. *Open: Tuesday–Sunday 1:00 p.m.–4:00 p.m. (215) 596–1748.*

Ebenezer Maxwell Mansion and Garden

200 West Tulpehocken Street

The garden design is that of a typical suburban "pleasure ground" of the period 1850–70. The flowers in the parterre garden, ornaments, and horticultural materials, which have been carefully researched, were favorites of homeowners in mid-Victorian times. *Open: Tuesday–Saturday 11:00 a.m.–4:00 p.m., Sunday 1:00–5:00 p.m. (215) 438–1816.*

☆

Fairmount Park

East River and Aquarium Drives

Reputed to be the largest city park in the world, Fairmount contains a remarkable collection of plants. The beautifully landscaped grounds include a 4-acre azalea garden and a Japanese garden. Ten historic homes and their grounds, a zoological garden, and the Pennsylvania Museum of Art are also of great interest. *Open: Daily, park, all times; various hours for individual features. (215) 686–1776 or 879–4062.*

Independence National Historic Park

311–13 Walnut Street

In the park are eighteenth-century gardens (between 4th and 3rd on Walnut Street) and a magnolia garden (4th and Locust Streets). *Open: Daily 9:00 a.m.–5:00 p.m. (215) 597–8974.*

☆

John Bartram House and Gardens

54th Street at Lindbergh Boulevard

This is America's first botanic garden, established by naturalist John Bartram in the mid-1700s. The original house and barn still remain. The plant materials are of a kind planted by Bartram and his son William. *Open: Garden, daily, dawn–dusk; house, April–October, Tuesday–Sunday 10:00 a.m.–4:00 p.m.; November–March, Tuesday–Friday 10:00 a.m.–4:00 p.m. Fee. (215) 729–5281.*

☆

Morris Arboretum

Chestnut Hill, 9414 Meadowbrook Avenue

The arboretum contains a superb collection of native trees, shrubs, and azaleas. The fern house and laboratory are maintained by the University of Pennsylvania. *Open: April–October, daily 9:00 a.m.–5:00 p.m. (June–August, Wednesday until 8:00 p.m.); November–March, until 4:00 p.m. Fee. (215) 247–5777.*

Pennsylvania Horticultural Society

325 Walnut Street

The three colonial gardens include a formal parterre flower garden, a small orchard, and a vegetable and herb garden—all developed and maintained by members of this outstanding horticultural society.
Open: Daily 9:00 a.m.–5:00 p.m. (215) 625–8250.

Wyck

6026 Germantown Avenue

The estate contains the oldest house in Philadelphia and nearly 3 acres of developed gardens. The grounds have been cared for since 1820 by generations of Quaker families concerned about horticulture. Although no revisions have been made, severe weeding and pruning have reclaimed boxwood borders and old-fashioned roses. There is an interesting collection of shrubbery and fine old trees, as well as an active vegetable garden. Original eighteenth-century outbuildings still stand at the back of the property.
Open: Tuesday–Saturday 1:00–4:00 p.m. Fee for guided tour. (215) 848–1690.

21. Pittsburgh

Mellon Square Park

Smithfield Street and William Penn Way (downtown in the "Golden Triangle")

This well-known contemporary park, designed by landscape architect John O. Simonds, is a 2-acre oasis of trees, fountains, and waterfalls in the downtown area built atop a 6-level underground parking garage.
Open: All times; Visitor Booth, Monday –Friday 9:30 a.m.– 5:00 p.m.; Saturday during summer, until 3:00 p.m. (412) 281–9222.

☆
Phipps Conservatory

Schenley Park

The conservatory, which opened in 1893, contains tropical and subtropical plants, cacti, succulents, and orchids on 2.5 acres.
Open: Daily 9:00 a.m.–5:00 p.m. Closed: Christmas and 2 days before the opening of the annual spring flower shows. Fee. (412) 266–4500.

22. Reading

Reading Public Museum Botanical Garden

500 Museum Road

The grounds feature formal gardens, a peony garden, a special section for cacti and subtropical plants, and many spring flowering trees and lilacs. Open: Monday–Friday 9:00 a.m.– 5:00 p.m., Saturday until noon, Sunday 2:00–5:00 p.m. (215) 371–5850.

23. Valley Forge

Millgrove, Audubon Shrine and Wildlife Sanctuary
2 miles from Valley Forge

The home and farm of John J. Audubon has been preserved with nature trails and a sanctuary containing 4,000 species of trees and shrubs. Open: Tuesday–Sunday 10:00 a.m.– 5:00 p.m. (215) 666–5593.

24. Washington Crossing

Bowman Hill
State Wildflower Preserve
Washington Crossing
Historic State Park

The park contains many trails through natural areas with abundant wildflower collections typical of this area of Pennsylvania. Open: Monday–Saturday 9:00 a.m.– 5:00 p.m., Sunday noon–5:00 p.m. (215) 862–2924.

Other Places of Interest

Amish Homestead, Lancaster
Brandywine Battlefield State Park, Chester
Ephrata Cloisters, Ephrata
Gettysburg National Military Park, Gettysburg
Independence Mall, Philadelphia
Old Bethlehem, Bethlehem
Olmstead Gardens, Ludlow
Pennsburg Manor, New Hope
Pennsylvania State Park, Erie
Pocono Wild Animal Farm, Stroudsburg
Taylor Memorial Arboretum, Wallingford
Valley Forge National Historic Park, Valley Forge

Rhode Island

Area: 1,214 square miles

Population: 968,000

Statehood: May 29, 1790 (13th state)

The tiny state of Rhode Island stretches 37 miles from north to south. It is occupied by two geologic provinces, the sandy coastal plain along the shore and, farther inland, the New England uplands. The state's highest point is Jerimoth Hill, standing 812 feet above sea level in its northwestern corner. There are many glacially formed lakes; soils deposited by the glaciers are very poor, rocky, and acidic. Rhode Island's proximity to water moderates the climate. The growing season varies from 140 to 200 days per year. Oak-dominated deciduous forest was the original vegetation of the state. Currently, much of the land is being reforested, but as yet there is insufficient timber for commercial use.

The sea brought wealth to Rhode Island merchants in colonial times. A lucrative trade developed in the exchange of rum for slaves and molasses between New England, Africa, and the West Indies. Rhode Island's coastal towns have a rich legacy of stately homes from this period, and its merchants participating in the China trade introduced many Oriental plant species to this country. Fishing is another important industry. Because of poor soil, manufacturing developed early in Rhode Island. In 1790, Samuel Slater opened the first machine-powered cotton mill in the nation at Pawtucket. Modern Rhode Island is a manufacturing state; jewelry and silverware are among its many products.

The seashore is the state's major recreational area. Each year special events such as the Newport Jazz Festival and Galilee tuna-fishing tournament attract thousands of visitors. The Rhode Island coast is dotted with the opulent mansions of the Gilded Age. During the late nineteenth and early twentieth centuries, many of America's wealthiest people built glamorous summer homes here. These mansions are notable for their eclectic styles; imitating the structures of other places and other times gave expression to the whims and dreams of their owners.

1. Bristol

Blithewold Gardens and Arboretum
Ferry Road, R.I. 114

The grounds of this 33-acre property were designed in 1895. Of particular interest are the Water Garden and the largest *Sequoia gigantea* (giant redwood) in eastern North America, planted in 1911. The oldest trees on the estate are the silver maples on the front lawn and lane, said to be about 200 years old. The grounds also contain New England's largest stand of bamboo. There is a blue

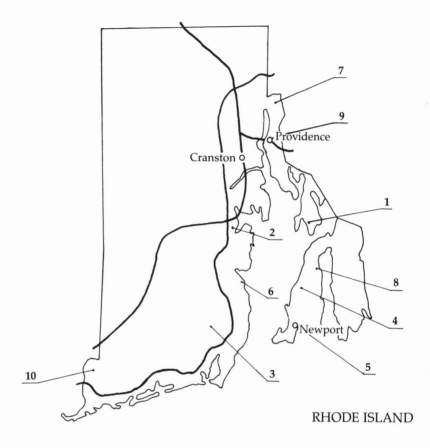

RHODE ISLAND

1. *Bristol* **2.** *East Greenwich* **3.** *Kingston* **4.** *Middletown* **5.** *Newport*
6. *North Kingston* **7.** *Pawtucket* **8.** *Portsmouth* **9.** *Providence* **10.** *Westerly*

and yellow perennial garden, a rose garden, and a bosquet.
Open: Daily 10:00 a.m.–4:00 p.m.; mansion, May–October. Fee. (401) 253–2707.

Juniper Hill Cemetery
Sherry Avenue

The 22-acre cemetery was planted in 1857 by N. B. Schubarth of Provi-

dence. Many rare trees and shrubs still survive.
Open: Daily, sunrise–sunset. (401) 253–5705.

North Farm
Hope Street

While practicing medicine in China in the 1850s, George Rogers Hall sent home to his farm many trees and shrubs, introducing them for the first time to the United States. Among the more important of these are *Zelkova serrata* (Japanese elm), *Magnolia stellata* (star magnolia), *Malus halliana* "Parkmanti" (Parkman crab), and *Taxus cuspidata* (Japanese yew). Others named after Dr. Hall are Hall's amaryllis and Hall's honeysuckle. *Open: By appointment. (401) 253–4700.*

2. East Greenwich

Varnum Gardens, General James Mitchel Varnum House
57 Pierce Street

This colorful garden features spring bulbs, annuals, and perennials that were popular in the 1700s. There is a fine copper beech on the property. *Open: June 1–September 1, Tuesday–Saturday 1:00–4:00 p.m. and by appointment. (401) 884–4622 or 884–6158.*

3. Kingston

Pettaquamscott Historical Society
2636 Kingstown Road (R.I. 128)

An informal eighteenth-century garden is featured. *Open: May–October, Tuesday, Thursday, Saturday 1:00–4:00 p.m. Closed: Holidays. (401) 783–1328.*

4. Middletown

Whitehall
Berkeley Avenue, near Green End Avenue (R.I. 114)

On the grounds of this 1729 home is a small eighteenth-century garden. *Open: July–August, daily 10:00 a.m.–5:00 p.m.; June and September, Saturday–Sunday 2:00–5:00 p.m. Fee. (401) 846–3790.*

5. Newport

The Breakers
Ochre Point Avenue

Designed by Richard M. Hunt for Cornelius Vanderbilt and built in 1895, the mansion is in the style of a sixteenth-century Italian palace. The grounds, designed by Frederick Law Olmsted, overlook the Atlantic Ocean and Cliff Walk. *Open: April–November 1, daily 10:00 a.m.–5:00 p.m.; until 7:00 p.m., Tuesday–Thursday and Sunday, July–mid-September. Fee. (401) 847–1000.*

Chateau Sur Mer
Bellevue Avenue

The mansion was built in 1852 and remodeled in 1872 by architect Richard M. Hunt. The grounds feature large and unusual trees. *Open: April–May, weekends 10:00 a.m.–5:00 p.m.; June–October,*

The Elms, Newport, R.I.

daily 10:00 a.m.–5:00 p.m. (401) 847–1000.

☆
The Elms
Bellevue Avenue

This extravagant mansion, built in 1901, is modeled after the Chateau d'Asnieres near Paris and furnished with "museum pieces." The formal French sunken gardens are particularly impressive when lighted at night. Rare trees and shrubs, fountains, and terraces are also featured. *Open: April–November 1, daily 10:00 a.m.–5:00 p.m.; until 7:00 p.m., Saturday, July–mid-September. Fee. (401) 847–1000.*

Marble House
Bellevue Avenue and Cliff Walk

Overlooking the Atlantic Ocean, the Marble House was designed in 1892 for William K. Vanderbilt by Richard M. Hunt. The lavish use of marble and gilt interior make this one of the most elaborate buildings ever constructed in America. *Open: April–November 1, daily 10:00 a.m.–5:00 p.m.; until 7:00 p.m., Friday, July–mid-September. (401) 847–1000.*

Rosecliff
Bellevue Avenue

Rosecliff, built in 1902 for Mrs. Hermann Oelrichs, was designed by Stanford White after the Grand Trianon at Versailles. The estate was

well-suited to be the scene of many large social gatherings. The restored rose garden is of interest.
Open: April–November 1, daily 10:00 a.m.–5:00 p.m.; until 7:00 p.m., Monday, July–mid-September. (401) 847–1000.

Wanton–Lyman–Hazard House
17 Broadway

Built in 1675, this is the oldest house in Newport, and one of the finest Jacobean houses in New England. The house and gardens have been carefully restored.
Open: June 15–August 31, Tuesday–Saturday 10:00 a.m.–5:00 p.m. (401) 846–0813.

6. North Kingston

Smith's Castle Garden
Richard Smith Drive, off U.S. 1

The courtyard garden is in the style of the eighteenth century.
Open: April 15–October 15, Thursday–Saturday 10:00 a.m.–5:00 p.m., Sunday 1:00–5:00 p.m. Closed: Thursday. Fee. (401) 294–3521.

7. Pawtucket

Old Slater Mill Museum, Fiber and Dye Garden
Roosevelt and Main Streets

The garden of herbs, dye plants, and fiber plants was used before the age of chemistry.
Open: Memorial Day–Labor Day, 10:00 a.m.–8:00 p.m.; rest of year, until 4:00 p.m. Fee. (401) 725–8638.

8. Portsmouth

☆
Green Animals Topiary Garden
Corey's Lane

Begun in 1880, the formal gardens are adorned with a profusion of topiary in animal and geometric forms. It has been considered an exemplary topiary garden in this country.
Open: May 1–September 30, daily 10:00 a.m.–5:00 p.m.; October, Saturday–Sunday 10:00 a.m.–5:00 p.m. Fee. (401) 847–1000.

9. Providence

Biblical Garden, Temple Beth El
Orchard Avenue

The grounds feature plants of significance in Old Testament stories.

The garden has received two national awards for excellence.
Open: Spring–fall, daily, by appointment. (401) 331–6070.

Garden for the Blind
1958 Broad Street

The plants in this garden are identifiable by scent, taste, and touch, and are labeled in Braille.
Open: Monday–Friday 8:00 a.m.– 5:00 p.m. (401) 274–1636.

John Brown House and Courtyard Garden
52 Power Street

Built in 1786 for a merchant in the China trade, the historic house and grounds overlook the harbor.
Open: Tuesday–Saturday 11:00 a.m.– 4:00 p.m., Sunday 1:00–4:00 p.m. (401) 331–8575.

Roger Williams Park
Elmwood Avenue

The park, designed by H. W. S. Cleveland, features 430 acres of beautiful landscape and lakes. The large greenhouse and exhibition halls feature numerous and diverse botanical displays, such as the tropical gardens and the cactus gardens. The park's world-famous chrysanthemum show takes place annually during the first week in November. Guided tours of the exhibition and growing areas.
Open: Daily, sunrise–sunset; greenhouses, 11:00 a.m.–4:00 p.m. (401) 785–7450 or 785–9450.

Stephen Hopkins House and Garden
Corner of Benefit and Hopkins Streets

There is a walled parterre colonial garden behind the house.
Open: Wednesday and Saturday 1:00–4:00 p.m., and by appointment. Closed: December 15–March 31. (401) 831–7440.

Truman Beckwith House and Gardens
42 College Street

The L-shaped house built on the side of a hill has a garden on three sides, including a Kitchen Garden, Tea Garden, and Terraced Garden in the back. Many of the plantings were shipped from China. The grounds have been authentically restored.
Open: By appointment. (401) 831–5337.

10. Westerly

Babcock–Smith House
124 Granite Street

Some of the boxwoods in this colonial garden are reputed to be over 150 years old. There are colorful displays of annuals and perennials.
Open: July–August, Wednesday and Sunday 2:00–5:00 p.m.; May–June, September–October, Sunday 2:00– 5:00 p.m.; also by appointment. Fee. (401) 596–4424.

Wilcox Park

High Street

Designed as a walking park by W. H. Manning, an associate of F. L. Olmsted, the 18-acre park features a dwarf conifer garden and herb and perennial gardens. There is also a fragrance garden with braille markers and a lily pond noted for its waterfowl and koi fish.
Open: Daily, sunrise–sunset. (401) 348–8362.

Other Places of Interest

Block Island State Beach
Great Swamp Wildlife Reservation, Kingston

Towns of special interest include East Greenwich, Kingston, Lincoln, Little Compton, Narragansett, Newport, and Wickford.

South Carolina

Area: 31,055 square miles

Population: 3,347,000

Statehood: May 23, 1788 (8th state)

Stretching from sandy ocean barrier islands across the Piedmont hills to the rolling Blue Ridge Mountains, the "Palmetto State" possesses landscapes of distinctive contrast.

South Carolina's coastal region is an area of low relief. Its sandy barrier islands—covered with oak, holly, and palmetto—are developing into important resort areas. Much of the low-lying land is in marshes and tidal prairies. Water is an important element in this landscape. Rice and indigo were lowland crops in colonial times, when the plantation system of the West Indies was imported to the North American continent here. Since then, Charleston has been a major commercial center for this rich agricultural land; it once served as a cultural center for the aristocratic planters' families. Lining the streets of the old city are many colorful townhouses; away from the streets on interior courts, the houses turn to catch the cooling sea breezes. Charleston's narrow streets and interior courtyards give the city a charm unique in the United States. The proud civic leaders of Charleston have been, since the 1930s, an inspiration to the nation in preserving America's architectural heritage.

In spring, from mid-March to mid-April, many of the city's splendid private homes are open to the public during the Festival of Houses and Gardens. The lowland town of Georgetown offers similar tours of the plantations surrounding it.

South Carolina's uplands were settled by small farmers descending the valley of the Blue Ridge from Virginia to Pennsylvania. The small farmers at first lived a meager frontier life, very different from that of the lowland aristocracy. In 1793 the cotton gin was invented and wealth came to the upland farmers as well. But the fertility of the upland soils was soon exhausted. After the Civil War, much of the land was share-cropped, though many agricultural workers migrated to the North to earn a living in factories. Soon after, the textile industry became established in the Piedmont region. Today, many croplands are reverting to pine forest. The nation's peach-growing capital is in the area around Spartanburg. Isolated factories surrounded by parking lots dot the landscape.

A new kind of resort community is growing up on the sunny barrier islands of the coast. Developments on Hilton Head and Kiawah Island represent superb design achievements in integrating settlement communities with the natural landscape. Here, the surroundings of the human settlement have evolved from land as a productive resource to land as a playground. Whereas the small farmer cares for the land and develops the landscape as a by-product, in these planned communities the hired care-

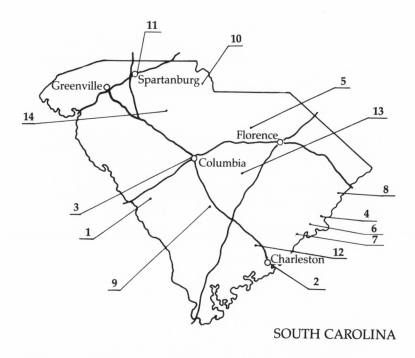

SOUTH CAROLINA

1. *Aiken*   2. *Charleston*   3. *Columbia*   4. *Georgetown*   5. *Hartsville*
6. *McClellanville*   7. *Moncks Corner*   8. *Murrells Inlet*   9. *Orangeburg*
10. *Rock Hill*   11. *Spartanburg*   12. *Summerville*   13. *Sumter*   14. *Union*

taker follows a maintenance program continually to keep nature in bounds.

the end of August, a series of city-sponsored concerts are held here. *Open: Daily, daylight hours. (803) 648–5461.*

1. Aiken

Hopeland Gardens
Whiskey Road and Dupree Place

The gardens feature tranquil terraces, reflecting pools, and a variety of flowers, shrubs, and trees imported from the world over. On Monday nights from the end of May through

2. Charleston

Boone Hall Plantation
North on U.S. 17,
7 miles from Charleston

The 2½-story mansion on this 738-acre estate is approached by a ¾-mile

picturesque avenue of moss-draped oaks.
Open: April 15–Labor Day, Monday–Saturday 8:30 a.m.–6:30 p.m., Sunday 1:00–6:30 p.m.; rest of year, Monday–Saturday 9:00 a.m.–5:00 p.m., Sunday 1:00–6:00 p.m. Closed: Thanksgiving, Christmas. Fee. (803) 556–6020.

Charlestown Landing
U.S. 7, on the Ashley River

In addition to an ancient 80-acre garden planted on the site of the first English colony in South Carolina, this 200-acre landscaped park includes an animal habitat, a pavilion, and a theater.
Open: Daily 9:00 a.m.–5:00 p.m.; June–August, until 6:00 p.m. Fee. (803) 556–4450.

Cypress Gardens
Off S.C. 52,
24 miles north of Charleston

Spectacular flowering shrubs color this cypress swamp. Boat or walking tours are available.
Open: Daily 9:00 a.m.–5:00 p.m. Fee. (803) 577–6970.

Drayton Hall
12 miles northwest via S.C. 61

One of the great plantation houses, Drayton Hall (ca. 1738), is now owned by the National Trust for Historic Preservation. The original gardens have been described as being "better laid out" than other early plantations. The site presently is used for research on crop stabilization.

Open: March 1–October 30, 10:00 a.m.–4:00 p.m.; rest of year, until 3:00 p.m. Fee. (803) 766–0188.

☆
Festival of Houses and Gardens

The Historic Charleston Foundation sponsors walking tours of downtown Charleston's many historic places from mid-March to mid-April. Information is available from the foundation's headquarters at 51 Meeting Street, Charleston, S.C. 29401. (803) 722–3405.

Hampton Park
Rutledge Avenue and Cleveland Street

In the city, adjoining The Citadel (South Carolina's military college), is lovely Hampton Park. It occupies part of the grounds that were devoted to the Interstate and West Indian Exposition of 1902. The park contains displays of azaleas and other flowers, sunken gardens, a pool, rose-bordered walks, and a zoo.
Open: Daily, sunrise–sunset. (803) 577–6970, ext. 473.

☆
Magnolia Gardens
S.C. 61, 10 miles northwest of Charleston

The grounds surrounding the historic plantation house are spectacular year-round. The winter show of camellias is not to be missed. The property has been in the Drayton family for 300 years; the gardens were begun in 1830.

Middleton Place Gardens, Charleston, S.C.

Open: Daily 8:00 a.m.–6:00 p.m.
Closed: Christmas. Fee. (803) 571–
1266.

☆
Middleton Place
S.C. 61, 12 miles
northwest of Charleston

This estate has one of the oldest gardens in America. The plantation was begun by the Middleton family in 1741 and completed a decade later. The first camellias planted in America were brought here by botanist Andre Michaux. The garden is world renowned for its uniquely designed terraces and butterfly lakes.
Open: Daily 9:00 a.m.–5:00 p.m. Fee. (803) 556–6020.

3. Columbia

Boylston Garden
829 Richland Street

The 2.5-acre park and garden, part of the governor's mansion property, are 200 years old.
Open: Monday–Friday 9:00 a.m.–5:00 p.m. Tours by appointment. (803) 737–1710.

Columbia Museum of Art Garden
1519 Senate Street

More than 50 species of flora native to South Carolina are represented in this small garden at the rear of the Science Museum. Each of South Carolina's regions (low country, midlands, and up-country) are represented.

Open: Tuesday–Friday 10:00 a.m.–
5:00 pm, Saturday–Sunday 1:00–
5:00 p.m. (803) 253–4021.

Memorial Garden, Garden Club of South Carolina
Lincoln and Calhoun Streets

Once part of the Boylston estate, this garden is around the corner from the Boylston Gardens. It is a formal garden with a water feature and statuary.
Open: Sunday 1:00–5:30 p.m., or by request. (803) 799–4413 or 737–1710.

Robert Mills Historic House and Park
1616 Blanding Street

The historic house was designed by Robert Mills, a South Carolinian who served as federal architect under seven U.S. presidents. The grounds and park were designed to highlight the house.
Open: Tuesday–Saturday 10:00 a.m.–
4:00 p.m., Sunday 2:00–5:00 p.m.
Grounds free. (803) 779–5358.

University of South Carolina Gardens
University of South Carolina Campus

There are two gardens of particular interest: the Memorial Garden behind the Caroliniana library and a small formal garden reached through a doorway in the old brick wall on Pendleton Street between Marion and Bull.
Open: Daily, sunrise–sunset. (803)
777–4061.

Woodrow Wilson Boyhood Home
1705 Hampton Street

Wilson lived as a boy in this house built by his father in 1872. The garden was originally planted by Wilson's mother, and, for a century, the tea olives, magnolias, and dogwoods have flourished.
Open: Tuesday–Saturday 10:00 a.m.–
4:00 p.m., Sunday 2:00–5:00 p.m.
Fee. (803) 779–5350.

4. Georgetown

Hopsewee Plantation
U.S. 17, 12 miles south of George-town

The large plantation is situated on a bluff overlooking the North Santee River. The house and grounds were built in 1735 and have been well maintained since then. This was the home of Thomas Lynch, a delegate to the Continental Congress, and his son, Thomas, Jr., who signed the Declaration of Independence.
Open: House, Tuesday–Friday
10:00 a.m.–5:00 p.m.; grounds, daily,
sunrise–sunset. (803) 546–7891.

Wedgefield Plantation
S.C. 701

This 618-acre estate on the Black River was established as a rice plantation in 1762. The manor house has been called the "finest example of Georgian Regency architecture in the south." The grounds are beautifully landscaped in keeping with the house. *Open: Daily 10:00 a.m.–5:00 p.m. (803) 546–8585.*

5. Hartsville

Kalmia Gardens
West Carolina Avenue

The 24-acre arboretum features over 700 varieties of trees and shrubs. The dominant species, *Kalmia latifolia*, is the source of the gardens' name. *Open: Daily, sunrise–sunset. (803) 332–1381.*

6. McClellanville

Hampton Plantation
8 miles north off U.S. 17

The ancestral home of Archibald Rutledge, once South Carolina's poet laureate, is landscaped with giant live oaks, including one that—according to legend—was saved from the ax when it caught the attention of George Washington while on a southern tour. *Open: Thursday–Monday, sunrise–sunset; house, Saturday and by appointment Thursday–Monday. (803) 546–9361.*

7. Moncks Corner

Mepkin Abbey
13 miles east off S.C. 402

Originally a 1700s rice plantation and the former summer home of Henry and Claire Booth Luce, the property is now a Roman Catholic monastery. *Gardens open: Daily 9:00 a.m.– 4:30 p.m. (803) 761–8509.*

8. Murrells Inlet

☆
Brookgreen Gardens
U.S. 17, 18 miles north of Georgetown

Beautiful live oaks, azaleas, and lily ponds provide a lovely setting for one of the largest collections of outdoor American sculpture. Special plant collections include wildflowers, best seen in April. *Open: Daily 9:00 a.m.–5:45 p.m. Closed: Christmas. Fee. (803) 237–4218.*

9. Orangeburg

Edisto Gardens
U.S. 301

These lovely gardens were created from a dismal, swampy area and river bank. Azaleas and roses provide

spectacular color from early spring through summer.
Open: Daily, sunrise–sunset. (803) 534–6376.

10. Rock Hill

Glencairn Gardens
Charlotte Avenue and Crest Street

The modern formal gardens, designed by landscape architect Robert Marvin, are outstanding in April, with terraced lawns, landscaped beds, a fountain, and a reflecting pool surrounded by tall trees and over 10,000 azaleas.
Open: Daily, sunrise–sunset. (803) 329–7000.

11. Spartanburg

Walnut Grove Plantation
Take U.S. 221 9 miles to junction of I-26; then 1.5 miles; follow signs to Walnut Grove

The plantation and gardens date from the eighteenth century.
Open: April 1–October 31, Tuesday–Saturday 11:00 a.m.–5:00 p.m.; June and August, Sunday 2:00–5:00 p.m. Fee. (803) 576–6546.

12. Summerville

Summerville Azalea Gardens
Main Street

The gardens feature a wide variety of azaleas including a favorite local variety, the pinkish "Pride of Summerville."
Open: Daily, sunrise–sunset. (803) 873–2931.

13. Sumter

Swan Lake Gardens
West Liberty Street

Swan Lake Gardens are so called because of the beautiful black Australian and white muted English swans that live on the lake. The gardens are noted for their 6 million Japanese iris, which reach full bloom in late spring. There is an Iris Festival during the last week in May.
Open: Daily 8:00 a.m.–sunset. (803) 773–9363.

14. Union

Rose Hill State Park
S.C. 16, west of U.S. 176

This 1828 house was named for its lovely rose gardens.
Open: Park, daily except Tuesday and

Wednesday; house, Saturday and by appointment, Thursday–Monday. (803) 427–5966.

Hilton Head Island
Park Seed Company, Greenwood

Other Places of Interest

Beaufort National Military Cemetery
Fort Sumter National Monument,
Charleston

South Dakota

Area: 77,047 square miles

Population: 708,000

Statehood: November 2, 1889
(40th state)

Although almost all of South Dakota is on a high plateau, the state is divided into two distinctive landscape types by the Missouri River. East of the river the land is smoothed flat by glaciation, and there are many small lakes. West of the river, the land's profile is more irregular, reflecting erosion by the drainage pattern. Upon the soft sedimentary rocks of the Badlands, where little vegetation protects the subsoil from erosion, the sculpturing done by the drainage pattern is particularly dramatic. The Black Hills, located on the Wyoming border, are an extreme eastern manifestation of the upfolded Rocky Mountains. Here stands South Dakota's highest point, Harney Peak, at 7,242 feet above sea level.

The climate of South Dakota is continental. The growing season over most of the state averages between 120 and 170 days. Rainfall averages 18 to 26 inches annually in the east and 12 to 18 inches in the west. Natural vegetation over most of the state is prairie grass. In the Black Hills are forests of Ponderosa pine. South Dakota's soils, built by generations of decaying prairie grasses, are rich in nutrients. Grain production is the major agricultural activity east of the Missouri, and cattle raising the major activity to the west. The lack of water seriously limits the land's productivity, and irrigation is an important public policy.

Several places of scenic and cultural interest are to be found in South Dakota. The Badlands National Monument features an unusually rugged and forbidding landscape. The Custer National Forest lies partly in South Dakota. The famous "Sunrise of Democracy," Mount Rushmore Monument, is located in the Black Hills. There are three National Grasslands in the state. At Deadwood, the memory of a "wild west" boomtown of gold rush days is preserved.

The Arikara Indians inhabited the Dakota Plains from pre-Columbian times. The Sioux Indians migrated from the eastern woodlands to the plains in the eighteenth century. The Sioux's economy was in harmony with the land, taking no more from it than the land could support. The Indian cultures left little mark upon the landscape. The ghosts of these tribes haunt the infamous battleground at Wounded Knee.

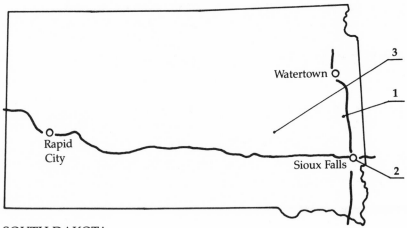

SOUTH DAKOTA

1. *Brookings*   2. *Sioux Falls*   3. *Wessington Springs*

1. Brookings

McCrory Gardens,
South Dakota State University
U.S. 14E

The 65-acre garden and arboretum on the campus grounds are used for demonstrations of home improvements, testing plants, research, and instruction. The gardens contain nearly all the ornamentals that are suitable for use in the Great Plains.
Open: Daily 8:00 a.m.–sunset. (605) 688–5136.

2. Sioux Falls

Falls Park
3rd Street and Falls Park Drive

The only surprising thing about a cactus garden so far north is that many gardeners are not aware that many varieties of the cactus family are indigenous to these areas. Part of the gardens and nearby waterfall are made of native quartzite stone.
Open: Daily, sunrise–sunset. (605) 339–7060.

McKennon Park
21st Street and 2nd Avenue

These are the oldest formal gardens in the city, covering 18 acres with nearly 11,000 plants.
Open: Daily, sunrise–sunset. (605) 339–7060.

3. Wessington Springs

Shakespeare Garden
400 College Avenue

The garden celebrates the bard's love for nature and the gardens evident in his works.
Open: Daily during growing season.
(605) 539–1691.

Other Places of Interest

Badlands National Park, Chimney Butte
Custer State Park, east of Custer
Jewel Cave National Monument, west of Custer
Mount Rushmore National Memorial, north of Keystone
Wind Cave National Park, east of Pringle

Tennessee

Area: 42,244 square miles

Population: 4,762,000

Statehood: June 1, 1796 (16th state)

Tennessee stretches west 480 miles, from the Appalachian Mountains to the Mississippi River. In mountainous eastern Tennessee are the Unaka and the Great Smoky mountains. The latter contain Clingman's Dome, the highest point in the state, with an elevation of 6,643 feet. Around Nashville is a fertile limestone basin well suited to agriculture. The low plains and fertile valleys of the Gulf Coast floodplain occupy western Tennessee. Bluffs line the banks of the Mississippi River, and in the river's floodplain are found rich alluvial soils.

Tennessee's climate is mild and humid. Rainfall averages 50 inches per year. The growing season varies from around 150 days in the mountains to up to 230 days in the Mississippi Valley. Vegetation varies greatly across the state—from spruce-pine forests in the Great Smoky Mountains National Park and Cumberland National Forest to southern floodplain forests of the Mississippi Valley where bald cypress grow. Reelfoot National Wildlife refuge in western Tennessee is an important bird sanctuary; it is centered around Reelfoot Lake, the state's largest natural lake.

Cumberland Gap National Historic Park marks the point where early settlers crossed the Appalachian Mountain chain. Tennessee was settled in the late eighteenth century by adventurous small farmers who were dissatisfied with corrupt and oppressive features of the eastern colonial governments. Andrew Jackson, who came to Tennessee as a young man, brought the state's democratic frontier spirit to the White House. In the fertile lowlands of western Tennessee, cotton was planted before the Civil War. Distinctive cultural differences exist between the people of eastern and western Tennessee.

The state has contributed greatly to America's musical heritage. Nashville is the home of the world-famous "Grand Ole Opry." W. C. Handy, often called the "Father of the Blues," began composing in Memphis. The Pi Beta Phi Settlement School at Gatlinburg and the Southern Highland Handicraft Guild help preserve traditional mountain folk crafts.

The economy of eastern Tennessee suffered greatly in the depression years. In 1933, The Tennessee Valley Authority (TVA) was established to control floods and harness the Tennessee River's waters for human use. The TVA's broad planning approach balances the growth of agriculture, industry, and recreation throughout the region. Its work has had a tremendous impact on the landscape of this great river valley. This innovative approach to comprehensive planning for a region's resources offers one possible model for national development of the land on a broad scale.

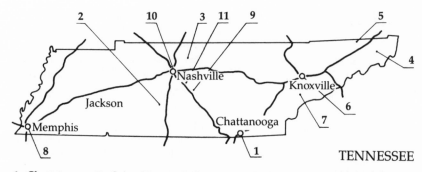

1. *Chattanooga* 2. *Columbia* 3. *Gallatin* 4. *Johnson City* 5. *Kingsport*
6. *Knoxville* 7. *Maryville* 8. *Memphis* 9. *Murfreesboro* 10. *Nashville*
11. *Smyrna*

1. Chattanooga

Cravens House and Terrace
Lookout Mountain

The well-maintained herb garden is a highlight of this completely restored house, which figured prominently in the Civil War's Battle above the Clouds.
Open: Tuesday–Sunday 1:00–5:00 p.m.
Closed: December 15–February 15.
Fee. (615) 821–6161.

Reflection Riding
Garden Road, Route 4

This wildflower preserve is located in a tranquil setting at the foot of Lookout Mountain. Most of the preserve may be viewed from an automobile.
Open: Monday–Friday 9:00 a.m.–5:00 p.m., Sunday 1:00–6:00 p.m.
Closed: Major holidays. Donation.
(615) 821–1160.

2. Columbia

Polk Garden
301 West 7th Street

The house, built in 1816, was the home of eleventh President James K. Polk during his youth. The formal garden is enclosed by a wall of hand-made brick. The garden features English boxwood, lilies of the valley, and peonies.
Open: April–October, Monday–Saturday 9:00 a.m.–5:00 p.m.; November–March, Monday–Saturday until 4:00 p.m.; year-round, Sunday 1:00–5:00 p.m.
Closed: Christmas. Fee. (615) 388–2354.

3. Gallatin

Cragfont Mansion
Tenn. 25, 5 miles east of Gallatin

The mansion and gardens were originally designed by General James Winchester in 1787; they were restored in 1973.
Open: April 15–November 1, Tuesday–Saturday 10:00 a.m.–5:00 p.m., Sunday 1:00–6:00 p.m.; November 1–April 15, by appointment. Fee. (615) 452–7070.

4. Johnson City

Tipton–Haynes Living Farm
Buffalo Road (U.S. 23)

The restored colonial farmstead (1784) of Colonel John Tipton is considered one of the "most historic sites in Tennessee." Listed on the National Register of Historic Places.
Open: Monday–Friday 10:00 a.m.–4:00 p.m., Saturday–Sunday 2:00–5:00 p.m. Closed: November 1–March 31. Fee. (615) 753–5961.

5. Kingsport

Allandale
U.S. 11-W

Attractive formal gardens surround this Greek Revival mansion (ca.

1852). Some of the trees are over 400 years old.
Open: April–December 1, Tuesday–Saturday 9:30 a.m.–4:00 p.m. Fee. (615) 246–2010.

6. Knoxville

Blount Mansion
200 West Hill Avenue

At the original home of Governor William Blount, the gardens were authentically restored by Historic Williamsburg landscape architect Donald H. Parker.
Open: March–October, Tuesday–Saturday 9:30 a.m.–5:00 p.m. (also Sunday 2:00–5:00 p.m., May–October); rest of year, until 4:00 p.m. Closed: Holidays. Fee. (615) 525–2375.

Craighead–Jackson House and Gardens
200 Hill Street

Built in 1818, the house and gardens were authentically restored in 1965 under the direction of Edith Henderson, landscape architect. They feature a formal nineteenth-century garden with circular sundial area and other plantings.
Open: Monday–Saturday 9:30 a.m.–5:00 p.m., Sunday 2:00–5:00 p.m. Fee. (615) 525–2375.

Dulin Art Gallery and Gardens
3100 Kingston Pike

Situated on bluffs overlooking the Tennessee River, the gardens include

many fine specimen trees. A gazebo, drystone retaining walls, and some trees survive from an earlier garden on the site. The elegant classic house, which today serves as an art museum, is the work of architect John Russell Pope.
Open: Monday–Friday 9:00 a.m.– 5:00 p.m. (615) 525–6101.

Ivan Racheff Park and Gardens
1945 Tennessee Avenue

Built in 1901, the park was remodeled in 1975 by the Tennessee Federation of Garden Clubs. It features flowering trees, shrubs, wildflowers, a bird sanctuary, and trout pools, and is the site of the Dogwood Arts Festival (last two weeks in April).
Open: Monday–Friday 9:00 a.m.– 4:00 p.m. Donation. (615) 637–4561 or 523–7263.

James White Garden
205 Hill Avenue

The fort and small gardens were re-constructed in 1970 by landscape architect Carl Wallis, based on research by local garden clubs.
Open: February 15–December 15, Monday–Saturday 9:30 a.m.– 5:00 p.m., Sunday 1:00–5:00 p.m.; December 16–February 15, Monday–Saturday 9:30 a.m.–5:00 p.m., Sunday 1:00–4:00 p.m. Fee. (615) 525–6514.

Ramsey House
Thorngrove Pike, 6 miles from Knoxville

The gardens of this eighteenth-century house have been restored in the "Pennsylvania Manner." There are striking boxwood gardens.
Open: April–October 31, Tuesday– Sunday 10:00 a.m.–5:00 p.m.; November 1–March 31, by appointment. Fee. (615) 546–0745.

University of Tennessee Arboretum
Oak Ridge Highway

Near the campus of the University of Tennessee is one of the South's major arboretums, covering some 250 acres. The displays include a wide range of native and exotic plants. There are foot trails and a visitors' center.
Open: Monday–Friday 9:00 a.m.– 5:00 p.m., Saturday–Sunday 1:00–5:00 p.m. (615) 483–3571.

7. Maryville

Houston Schoolhouse and Grounds
Houston Schoolhouse Road

The site was reconstructed in 1974 by Roger G. Thompson, landscape architect, in a manner consistent with Sam Houston's time. Trees and shrubs native to the area were used in the restoration.
Open: Monday–Friday 9:00 a.m.– 6:00 p.m., Saturday–Sunday 1:00–5:00 p.m. (615) 983–1550.

Dixon Gallery and Gardens, Memphis, Tenn.

8. Memphis

Dixon Gallery and Gardens
4339 Park Avenue

The gardens, begun as a private estate in 1940, resemble the great English landscape parks. Walkways and vistas are skillfully placed to take advantage of the site's magnificent trees. The art gallery is also of interest.
Open: Tuesday–Saturday 11:00 a.m.–5:00 p.m., Sunday 1:00–5:00 p.m. Fee. (901) 761–5250 or 761–2409.

Mageveny Home
198 Adams Avenue

This pioneer house, built in 1831, features herb and kitchen gardens.
Open: September 1–March 31, Monday–Saturday 1:00–4:00 p.m.; April 1–Labor Day, Monday–Saturday 10:00 a.m.–4:00 p.m. Closed: Thanksgiving, Christmas Eve and Day, July 4. Fee. (901) 526–4464.

Memphis Botanic Garden
750 Cherry Road, in the southeastern corner of Audubon Park

The 88-acre botanic garden features a variety of specialized collections in-

cluding camellias, iris, roses, dahlias, and magnolias. The magnolia collection is one of the largest in the country. The Japanese Garden features a bridge and moon-gazing pavilion. A conservatory and an orchid house are also on the grounds.
Open: Monday–Friday 9:00 a.m.–5:00 p.m., Saturday–Sunday 1:00–5:00 p.m. (901) 685–1566.

9. Murfreesboro

Oakland Gardens
North Maney Avenue

Adjacent to the historic house is a small, attractive formal garden. Plants commonly used prior to 1865 are grown.
Open: January 1–February 28, Tuesday–Saturday 11:00 a.m.–3:00 p.m., Sunday 1:00–3:00 p.m.; rest of year, Tuesday–Saturday 10:00 a.m.–4:00 p.m., Sunday 1:00–4:00 p.m. Fee. (615) 893–0022.

10. Nashville

Belle Meade Mansion
110 Leake Avenue, off U.S. 70

The mansion was originally built in 1840. A Swiss gardener is credited with placing the rare flowers, shrubs, and trees in the garden.
Open: Monday–Saturday 9:00 a.m.–5:00 p.m., Sunday 1:00–5:00 p.m. Closed: Thanksgiving, Christmas, New Year's Day. Fee. (615) 356–0501.

Belmont Mansion
Belmont Boulevard, next to Belmont College

Now owned by Belmont College, this 1850 mansion was surrounded by extensive lawns and formal Italianate gardens, statuary, and a deer park. The gardens are being restored.
Open: Grounds, year-round; mansion, Tuesday–Saturday 10:00 a.m.–4:00 p.m. Fee. (615) 269–9537 or 385–6670.

☆
Cheekwood
Tennessee Botanical Gardens and Fine Arts Center, Forrest Drive

The boxwood gardens surrounding the Georgian mansion are exceptional. Four greenhouses, which are open to the public, display a variety of orchids and camellias and a Panamanian Cloud forest. The wildflowers, towering trees, and roses are of particular interest, as are the many educational programs offered throughout the year on this 30-acre site.
Open: Tuesday–Saturday 9:00 a.m.–5:00 p.m., Sunday 1:00–5:00 p.m. Fee. (615) 352–5310.

☆
The Hermitage
12 miles east on U.S. 70 North (from I-40, Old Hickory exit)

Considered to be one of the best maintained historic mansions, the former home of President Andrew Jackson was originally constructed in 1819. The working plantation consists

of 625 acres. Fine gardens have been laid out around the mansion and the adjoining Tulip Grove house. Gardens have been restored in accordance with the extensive documentation available among the president's papers.
Open: Daily 9:00 a.m.–5:00 p.m. Closed: Major holidays. Fee. (615) 889–2941.

Travelers' Rest House and Garden
636 Ferrell Parkway

The house and original gardens were designed by Judge John Overton in 1792. The European-style gardens feature many plants indigenous to Tennessee.
Open: Saturday 9:00 a.m.–4:00 p.m., Sunday 1:00–4:00 p.m. Fee. (615) 832–2962.

11. Smyrna

Sam Davis House
Sam Davis Highway

The 1860 plantation house and garden of Sam Davis were restored in 1955. The garden is divided into four sections covering 0.5 acres. The house is listed on the National Register of Historic Places.
Open: March 1–October 31, Monday–Saturday 9:00 a.m.–5:00 p.m.; November 1–February 28, Monday–Saturday 10:00 a.m.–4:00 p.m., Sunday 1:00–4:00 p.m. Fee. (615) 459–2341.

Other Places of Interest

Chickamauga-Chattanooga National Military Park
Chucalussa Indian Village, Memphis
Cumberland Gap National Historic Park, Harrogate
Great Smoky Mountains National Park, Gatlinburg
Lookout Mountain
Norris Dam, Norris
Reelfoot Lake State Park, Tiptonville
Shiloh National Military Park, Savannah
Stones River National Battlefield and Park, Murfreesboro

Texas

Area: 275,416 square miles

Population: 16,370,000

Statehood: December 29, 1845
(28th state)

From the time of its secession from
Mexico (1836) until the date of its admission to the United States (1845),
the "Lone Star State" existed as an
independent republic.

A variety of landscape types cross
the 800-mile length of Texas. Along
the low-lying Gulf Coastal Plain,
rainfall is abundant. This warm,
humid region produces vegetables
and citrus fruit. A line of escarpments separates the plain from the
hill country to the west. The Texas
hill country is a plateau worn by
rainwater over millions of years.
This is the land of the great Texas
cattle ranches. Farther west another
line of escarpments, called the "Cap
Rock," marks the beginning of the
High Plains which stretch from Texas
north to Canada.

The Texas High Plains are one of
the flattest vast areas on earth. The
land rises gradually from 2,500 feet
above sea level in the east to 4,000
feet at its western limit. Rainfall is
meager here, and what little rain
does fall is soaked up rapidly by the
thirsty earth. During rainy times,
wet sinkholes will appear but they
rapidly dry up. Much of the land is
used for grazing. Wheat and other
crops can be grown with irrigation.
The climate is severe; at this altitude,
summer nights are cool and snowfalls
frequent in winter. Several mountain
peaks exceed 8,000 feet in elevation.
Water drains from the mountains
into the basins. When the water
evaporates, an alkaline precipitate is
left behind. This province extends to
the Rio Grande, the Mexican border.

The first Europeans to settle Texas
were Spanish missionaries. In 1821,
Texas became a state in the Mexican
Republic. Led by Stephen Austin,
many settlers from the United States
came to live here. The 1800s marked
a colorful era of Texas history, when
cattlemen drove their herds from
grazing land in Texas to railroads in
Kansas. When railroad lines were
laid to Texas in the 1870s, these cattle
drives were no longer necessary.
With the discovery of oil in 1901
at Spindle Top, the state had a new
source of wealth. The establishment
of the National Manned Space Flight
Center in Houston brought space-age
industry.

The city of San Antonio preserves
many signs of the Mexican influence on Texas life. They include the
Alamo, along with other mission sites
and an old Mexican village (La Villita). The Lyndon B. Johnson ranch
in the hill country is a National Historic Site. There are five national
grasslands in Texas and four national
forests. Big Bend National Park in
the rugged country west of the Pecos
presents a spectacular desert landscape. The 1,000-foot-deep Santa
Elena Canyon, cut by the Rio Grande,
is a magnificent feature of the park.

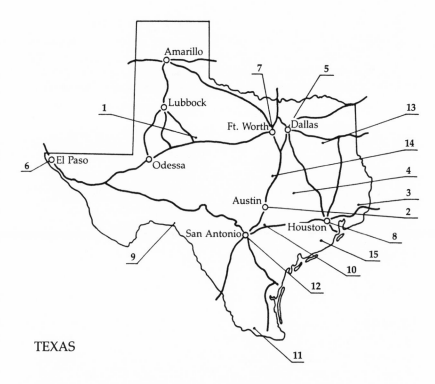

TEXAS

1. *Abilene*   2. *Austin*   3. *Beaumont*   4. *College Station*   5. *Dallas*
6. *El Paso*   7. *Fort Worth*   8. *Houston*   9. *Langtry*   10. *Luling*   11. *McAllen*
12. *San Antonio*   13. *Tyler*   14. *Waco*   15. *West Columbia*

1. Abilene

Iris Trail

Abilene is noted for its irises growing in private gardens. Each April,
tours are offered of the city's particularly fine iris gardens. For more
information, contact the Chamber of
Commerce, 325 Hickory Street. (915)
677–7241.

McMurry College Iris Garden
Sayles Boulevard and
South 16th Street

This garden is a showplace of the
American Iris Society Symposium.
Only iris considered by the symposium to be the most beautiful are
displayed, and each year 100 new
selections are added. For more information, contact the Chamber of
Commerce, 325 Hickory Street.
Open: Sunrise–sunset. (915) 692–3938.

2. Austin

Governor's Mansion and Garden
Colorado Avenue, between 11th
and 12th Streets

The mansion was built in 1854.
Through the initiative of the Texas
Garden Clubs, restoration of the
garden was begun in 1966.
Open: Mansion and garden, Monday–
Friday 10:00 a.m.–4:00 p.m. (512)
475–4101.

Japanese Oriental Garden
Zilker Park

Built in 1968–69, this Oriental garden is the creation of Isamu Taniguchi. Three acres of rugged cliffs
were transformed into a beautiful
and peaceful garden that now attracts
nearly 100,000 visitors each year.
Mr. Taniguchi said that the garden
was his gift to his adopted country
and state.
Open: Daily, sunrise–sunset. (512)
477–8672.

3. Beaumont

Beaumont Art Museum
1111 Ninth Street

Attractive gardens surround the
museum.
Open: Tuesday–Friday 10:00 a.m.–
5:00 p.m., Saturday–Sunday
2:00–5:00 p.m. (713) 832–3432.

4. College Station

Texas A&M University Arboretum and Trial Grounds
University Drive and Fine Feather
Road

There is a continual display of more
than 800 species and varieties of
plants, which the university uses
for research in its arboretum and
greenhouse.
Open: Daily, sunrise–sunset. (713)
845–2844.

5. Dallas

☆
Dallas Garden Center
Forest and 1st Street,
State Fair Grounds

A beautiful coordinating center for
garden clubs is surrounded by 7 acres
of varied and well-established small
gardens.
Open: Monday–Friday 10:00 a.m.–
5:00 p.m., Saturday–Sunday
9:00 a.m.–5:00 p.m.
Closed: Christmas. (214) 428–7476.

Old Dallas City Park
1717 Gano Street

Old City Park is a living museum de-
picting the gardens, homes, and public buildings of nineteenth-century
Dallas. Each structure has been preserved according to its period, with

authentic shrubs, trees, flowers, herbs, and vegetables.
Open: Tuesday–Friday 10:00 a.m.–4:00 p.m., Saturday–Sunday 1:30–4:30 p.m. (214) 421–5141.

Owens Fine Arts Center
Southern Methodist University Campus

A contemporary Italian sculpture garden and a courtyard garden are featured.
Open: Monday–Saturday noon–5:00 p.m., Sunday 1:00–5:00 p.m. (214) 692–2000.

6. El Paso

Chamizal National Memorial
800 San Marcial Street

A portion of the 549-acre park has been developed as a traditional Spanish colonial garden.
Open: Daily, sunrise–sunset. (915) 534–6668.

7. Fort Worth

Fort Worth Botanic Gardens
3220 Botanic Garden Drive

The formal gardens and naturalized areas of this 115-acre park display an extensive collection of plants. There are conservatories and a garden for

the blind. The 7-acre Japanese Garden is one of the largest in the South.
Open: Main garden, daily 8:00 a.m.–sunset; Japanese Garden, Tuesday–Sunday 10:00 a.m.–4:00 p.m. Fee. (817) 870–7686.

Fort Worth Water Garden
13th and Commerce Streets

This garden makes joyful use of water in the hot Texas landscape. Extensive gardens exhibit a rich variety of specimen plants.
Open: All times. (817) 870–7016.

8. Houston

Azalea Trail
River Oaks section of Houston

Local residents invite visitors to enjoy their private gardens at the height of the azalea season in March. Contact River Oaks Garden Club, (713) 523–5050 or 224–5201.

Bayou Bend
2940 Lazy Lane

Beautifully landscaped grounds surround this estate. Its fine collection of American furniture is also of interest.
Open: By appointment; contact Curator, Museum of Fine Arts, 1 Westcott Street, Houston. Fee. (713) 529–8773.

**Harris County Heritage
and Conservation Society**
Sam Houston Park, near downtown

The 21-acre park features restored
historic houses and gardens.
*Open: Monday–Friday 10:00 a.m.–
4:00 p.m., Sunday 1:00–5:00 p.m.
(713) 223–8367.*

**Houston Arboretum
and Botanical Garden**
Memorial Drive, Memorial Park

This arboretum contains 265 acres
of woodlands with gardens of fragrances, herbs, and roses.
*Open: Daily 8:30 a.m.–6:00 p.m.;
summer, until 8:00 p.m. (713)
681–8433.*

Also located here is the Aline
McAshan Botanical Hall, primarily
for children.
*Open: Monday–Saturday 8:30 a.m.–
5:30 p.m., Sunday 1:00–5:30 p.m.*

**River Oaks Garden Club
Forum of Civic Gardens**
2503 Westheimer Street

The site features a number of model
gardens with labeled plant materials.
*Open: Daily 10:00 a.m.–5:00 p.m.
(713) 523–2483.*

9. Langtry

Cactus Gardens
Judge Roy Bean Visitor's Center

Many of the Southwest's native trees
and shrubs, as well as an extensive
cactus collection, are displayed.
*Open: Daily 8:00 a.m.–5:00 p.m.
Closed: Christmas, New Year's Day.
(915) 291–3270.*

10. Luling

Palmetto State Park
U.S. 183

The 183-acre site on the banks of the
San Marcos River features many rare
plants, some found nowhere else in
the Southwest.
*Open: Daily, sunrise–sunset. (512)
672–3266.*

11. McAllen

Valley Botanical Garden
U.S. 83

Most of the work on these gardens
is done by handicapped people. The
20-acre site features herb and rose
gardens, a sunken garden, and a
collection of indigenous and exotic
plants.
*Open: Daily 8:00 a.m.–sunset. (512)
682–1517.*

Paseo del Rio (The River Walk), San Antonio, Tex.

12. San Antonio

Alamo Gardens
Alamo Plaza

Attractive gardens surround the historic Alamo shrine in downtown San Antonio.
Open: Monday–Saturday 9:00 a.m.– 5:30 p.m., Sunday 10:00 a.m.– 5:30 p.m. (512) 222–1693.

Brackenridge Park
1500 North St. Mary's Street

Expertly designed and well-maintained, this park was created from a quarry. It contains pools, a pavilion, terraced gardens, stone walkways, and spiral steps.
Open: Daily, sunrise–sunset. (512) 299–3132.

☆
Paseo del Rio (The River Walk)

A peaceful pedestrian environment in the heart of San Antonio, the sensitively landscaped walk makes superb use of the river as an urban scenic resource. Arched bridges and paved courtyards along this 21-block area give an old-world atmosphere.
Open: All times. (512) 299–8155.

San Antonio Botanical Center
555 Sunston Place

The 33-acre site was opened in 1980. It features native Texas plants and rose, herb, and old-fashioned gardens. There is a garden for the blind and a conservatory.

Open: Wednesday–Sunday 9:00 a.m.– 6:00 p.m. Fee. (513) 821–5115.

13. Tyler

Goodman–LaGrande Museum and Garden
624 North Broadway

Nine acres of attractive gardens surround the historic house.
Open: Monday–Friday 1:00– 5:00 p.m. (214) 597–5304.

Tyler Rose Garden and Park
West Front and Boone Street

Reputed to be the nation's largest municipal rose garden, these 22 acres have been developed with a magnificent collection of roses, azaleas, and other ornamental plantings. A conservatory, water features, and a sunken garden are also situated on the grounds.
Open: Daily, sunrise–sunset. (214) 593–2131.

14. Waco

Nell Pape Garden Center
1705 North 5th Street

Two acres of beautifully landscaped grounds surround the historic house.
Open: Daily. (817) 752–1960.

15. West Columbia

Varner–Hogg Plantation

Route 35, Northeast

Formal and naturalized gardens surround a Greek Revival home (ca. 1836). The plantings include many subtropical species.
Open: Tuesday–Sunday 1:00–5:00 p.m. Fee. (512) 479–4890.

Other Places of Interest

Auansas Wildlife Refuge, Corpus Christi

Big Bend National Park, southwestern border
Guadalupe Mountains National Park, northwestern border
King Ranch, Kingsville
La Villita, San Antonio
Longhorn Cavern State Park, Burnet
Padre Island National Seashore, Galveston
Palmetto State Park, Gonzales
Palo Duro Canyon State Park, Amarillo

Utah

Area: 84,916 square miles

Population: 1,645,000

Statehood: January 4, 1896
(45th state)

Utah is a landscape of dramatic line, color, and texture. Towering mountains and colorful beds of exposed sedimentary rocks lining deep water-cut canyons contrast with the pleasant farmlands of the Wasatch Basin. This basin, lying behind the steep western edge of the Wasatch Mountains, is occupied by 90 percent of Utah's population. The Wasatch and the Unita mountains are extensions of the Middle Rockies into Utah. Several peaks in these ranges exceed 13,000 feet. Stretching southeast from Salt Lake City is the Great Basin. The Great Salt Lake occupying the northeastern corner of the basin collects drainage from the surrounding mountains.

Utah has many unique landscape features. Fantastic natural rock sculptures can be found in Zion and Bryce Canyon National Park. There are numerous spectacular natural bridges. The largest of all is Rainbow Bridge National Monument. Hovenweep National Monument is the site of archaic Indian cliff dwellings. Dinosaur National Monument is known as a rich source of dinosaur fossils. The Unita National Forest preserves beautiful mountain scenery and primor-dial forests. The Wasatch Mountains, famous for their superb skiing, are an excellent recreational resource within easy access of Salt Lake City.

The Mormons were the first whites to settle Utah. Brigham Young selected the site for Salt Lake City on July 24, 1847. Mormon cities were laid out on a strict north/south axis in a gridiron pattern. The site chosen by Young for the Mormon temple was the center point for Salt Lake City's original plan. Non-Mormons, whom the established settlers referred to as Gentiles, were attracted to Utah in the late nineteenth century by the land's mineral wealth. The mining industry has had a substantial impact on the state's landscape.

The climate of Utah varies greatly due to its range of elevation and geographic latitude. The growing season in the agricultural areas ranges from 120 to 180 days. Nutrient-rich soils are present in much of the Great Basin and Colorado Plateau. Water is a limited resource for crop and livestock production. The flat low-lying areas of the state receive fewer than 16 inches of rainfall per year; mountainous areas receive up to 40 inches per year. The natural vegetation of Utah ranges from mesquite, Joshua tree, and creosote bush in the hot arid deserts, to sagebrush and grasses suitable for cattle grazing in the cooler areas, to coniferous forests on the mountainsides. Currently, about one-third of the state is forested. Utah's gardens are oases carved out of the severe natural landscape.

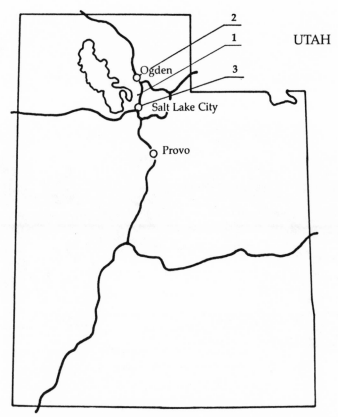

1. *Farmington*   2. *Ogden*   3. *Salt Lake City*

1. Farmington

Utah Botanical Gardens
1817 North Main Street

This 12-acre site is part of the Utah
Experimental Station, founded in
1902. The gardens exhibit a large
number of plants that have done well
in the area. There are formal planting
areas as well as test beds.
*Open: Daily, sunrise–sunset; office,
Monday–Friday 8:30 a.m.–4:30 p.m.
(801) 451–3204.*

Korean Garden in the International Peace Gardens, Salt Lake City, Utah.

2. Ogden

Municipal Grounds

Ogden, the second city of Utah, is famous for its municipal gardens and, especially, its Christmas display on the grounds. The gardens are formal in design; stepping-stone walks, dwarf shrubs, and many potted plants provide interest and color.
Open: Daily, sunrise–sunset. (801) 479–8018.

3. Salt Lake City

Garden Center, Sugarhouse Park
1602 East 21st Street, South

Colorful flower beds, rolling lawns, and groups of native trees frame a very active Garden Center. During most of the year there are exhibitions, lectures, and flower shows.
Open: Daily 9:00 a.m.–5:00 p.m.
(801) 467–0461.

Temple Gardens, Salt Lake City, Utah.

International Peace Gardens

1000 South and 900 West Streets

The idea for the International Peace Gardens originated in 1939 but World War II postponed their construction until 1947. At that time, the theme for the gardens became "Peace and Understanding between Nations." Each section was designed for a particular ethnic group, using plantings, statues, and small buildings to represent its culture. The gardens are situated on the Jordan River not far from the center of the city.
Open: Daily, sunrise–sunset. (801) 467–2467.

Perception Garden

Memory Grove Park, in the mouth of City Creek Canyon (within walking distance of downtown)

This garden features beds of fragrant and textured plants; markers are in Braille. There are broad walks, benches, and fountains. The 815 acres of Memory Grove, Salt Lake City's largest park, are dedicated to those who have lost their lives in the wars of this country.
Open: Daily, dawn–10:00 p.m. (801) 581–0755.

Rose Gardens, Sugarhouse Park

1602 East 21st Street, South

The municipal rose garden, with more than 10,000 bushes and a correspondingly large number of varieties, contains the most recent All-American selections. There are also some fine old specimens of historic roses.
Open: Daily, daylight hours. (801) 266–9095.

State Arboretum of Utah

University of Utah Campus

Since 1961, the campus of the University of Utah has served as one of the two state arboretums and as a laboratory for native and exotic trees. More than 84 varieties of trees can be found on the self-guided campus tour. Groves of trees are being used to moderate climate extremes on the campus.
Open: Daily, sunrise–sunset. (801) 581–5322.

☆
Temple Gardens

Temple Square, Church of the Latter-Day Saints

The Temple Gardens are remarkable for the quality of planting and arrangement, and have received numerous awards. They are meticulously maintained year-round.
Open: Daily. Special tours. (801) 531–2640.

Other Places of Interest

Arches National Monument, southeastern Utah

Big Rock Candy Mountain, Richfield
Bryce Canyon National Park,
southwestern Utah
Canyonland National Park,
southeastern Utah
Capitol Reef National Monument,
Torrey
Cedar Breaks National Monument,
Saint George

Dinosaur National Monument,
northeastern Utah
Great Salt Lake
Natural Bridge National Monument,
Blanding
Rainbow Bridge National Monument,
Lake Powell
Zion National Park, Saint George

Vermont

Area: 9,609 square miles

Population: 535,000

Statehood: March 4, 1791
(14th state)

The "Green Mountain State" is known for its independent ways. In the eighteenth century New Hampshire authorities granted tracts of land in Vermont to settlers. In 1764 King George recognized the New York colonies' claim to these lands, and the established settlers had to buy the lands again or be evicted. Ethan Allen and his Green Mountain Boys organized to resist enforcement of this decision. With the onset of the Revolutionary War, Vermont first declared its autonomy. From July 2, 1777 until 1791, when a compromise resolved this issue, Vermont persisted as an independent nation.

The land rises from the Connecticut River Valley in the east, crosses the spine of the Green Mountains, and descends again to Lake Champlain in the west. Vermont's highest peak is Mount Mansfield, standing 4,393 feet above sea level. The soils of Vermont are well-drained glacial deposits. Boulder-strewn fields and numerous lakes are additional effects of the glaciers' work here. Eastern deciduous forest dominated by sugar maple is the state's original vegetation. Spruce and fir are found at higher elevations. Rainfall is ample.

The growing season varies from 100 to 165 days per year.

Many early settlers of Vermont came from the worn-out farms of eastern New England. By the 1820s, the state's thin soils were depleted and Vermonters were beginning to pull up stakes and head west. Light manufacturing industries developed in the state prior to the Civil War. Today, major land uses include dairying and forestry. Vermont's mountains are an important source of building materials, such as the granite mined at Barre. The colorful marbles and slates from Vermont are popular architectural materials.

Vermont's peaceful villages and pleasant summer temperatures make it a popular resort area. Many writers and artists are attracted by its scenic beauty. Vermont's 34 state parks provide good recreational areas. The Long Trail, stretching 261 miles through the Green Mountains, is a favorite with hikers.

1. North Bennington

Park–McCullough House and Gardens
U.S. 7 via Vt. 67 and 67A

Built in 1865, the Park–McCullough House is an excellent example of Victorian domestic architecture. The grounds are in keeping with the style of the house.
Open: July 1–October 15, Monday–Friday 9:00 a.m.–4:00 p.m. Guided tours. (802) 442-5441.

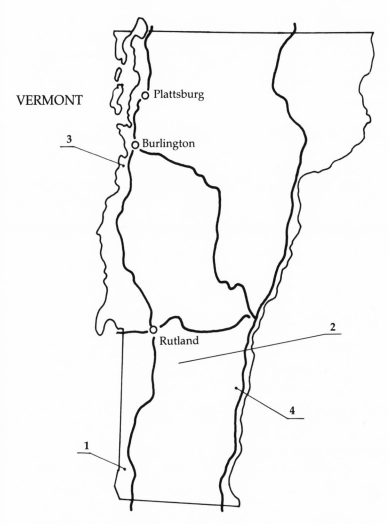

VERMONT

○ Plattsburg

3

○ Burlington

○ Rutland

2

4

1

1. *North Bennington*   2. *Plymouth Notch*   3. *Shelburne*   4. *Springfield*

2. Plymouth Notch

Coolidge Homestead
Adjoins Union Christian Church

The Presidential Garden at the Calvin Coolidge Historic Site was begun around 1895 by the president's stepmother. The 30-foot-square perennial beds were carefully restored in 1986 by the Federation of Vermont Garden Clubs. The garden can be seen from the road at all times.
House open: Mid-May–mid-October,

daily 9:30 a.m.–5:30 p.m. Fee.
(802) 672–3773.

3. Shelburne

Shelburne Museum Garden
U.S. 7

Homes, buildings, and memorabilia of New England have been assembled on 45 acres of well-landscaped grounds planted with old-fashioned roses, a fine herb garden, apple trees, and lilacs. There is also a natural rock garden. *Open: May 15–October 15, 9:00 a.m.–5:00 p.m. Fee. (802) 985–3344.*

restaurant, is surrounded by beautifully landscaped grounds. *Open: Daily, sunrise–sunset. (802) 885–2115.*

Other Places of Interest

Bellows Falls, southeastern Vermont
Green Mountain National Forest, Rutland
Quechee Gorge, Quechee
Rock of Ages Quarry, Barre
Vermont Wildflower Farm, Charlotte

Towns of special interest include Arlington, Bennington, Dorset, Grafton, Manchester, Middleburg, Weston, and Woodstock.

4. Springfield

Hartness House Inn and Gardens
30 Orchard Street

The historic house, formerly a governor's mansion and now an inn and

Virginia

Area: 40,817 square miles

Population: 5,706,000

Statehood: June 25, 1788 (10th state)

Virginia was the site of the first permanent English settlement in North America. The name "Virginia" originally applied to all land on the North American continent claimed by the Crown. The eastern portion of the state, called the Tidewater, has a low profile and is often swampy. This region is bounded on the west by the fall line that runs through Richmond and Alexandria. West of the fall line rises the Piedmont Plateau, a deeply eroded, hilly region underlaid by ancient metamorphic rocks. Farther west rise the Blue Ridge and the Allegheny mountains. In between the mountain ridges are fertile and scenic valleys.

The growing season in Virginia varies from 150 days in the mountains to 240 days at Norfolk on the coast. Rainfall is ample, averaging 40 inches per year over most of the state. Oak, hickory, and pine forests covered most of the land before it was cleared for agriculture.

The Jamestown colony was founded in 1607. Its economic viability was established when efforts to grow tobacco, first cultivated in 1612, proved successful. The plantation system of agriculture spread in colonial times from the Tidewater to the Piedmont.

Owing to poor farming practices, many soils were quickly exhausted. Before the Revolutionary War, Virginians were obliged to push westward to find more fertile lands. This westward movement provoked the French and Indian War. Today, former tobacco land is reverting to pine forests in parts of the Tidewater and Piedmont sections of the state.

Virginia is steeped in history. It was the home of great leaders such as George Washington, Thomas Jefferson, Patrick Henry, and Robert E. Lee, whose residences still stand. The Arlington National Cemetery, Jamestown National Historic Site, and Yorktown Battlefield are in Virginia. Many Civil War battlefields dot the state. Cumberland Gap National Historic Park on the Kentucky border marks the site where early settlers crossed the Appalachians. Areas of great scenic beauty in the Virginia mountains can be enjoyed from the Blue Ridge Parkway and Skyline Drive.

The colonial planters of Virginia eagerly followed garden designs imported from England. George Washington, for example, relied on Batty Langley's "New Principles of Gardening," published in London in 1728, in laying out the pleasure grounds of his Mount Vernon estate. After the Revolution, the romantic style of the English School of gardening was introduced by Thomas Jefferson at Monticello.

During the Garden Club of Virginia Annual Tour, a "must see" event, many lovely private homes are opened to interested visitors for one

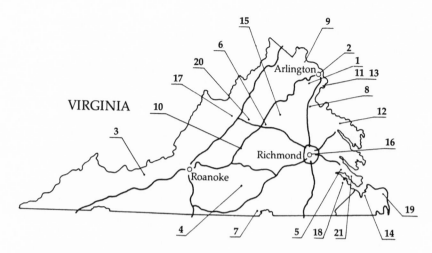

1. *Alexandria* 2. *Arlington* 3. *Blacksburg* 4. *Brookneal* 5. *Charles City County and James River Plantations* 6. *Charlottesville* 7. *Clarksville* 8. *Fredericksburg* 9. *Leesburg* 10. *Lexington* 11. *Lorton* 12. *Montross* 13. *Mount Vernon* 14. *Norfolk* 15. *Orange* 16. *Richmond* 17. *Staunton* 18. *Surry* 19. *Virginia Beach* 20. *Waynesboro* 21. *Williamsburg*

week. For the 186-page guidebook, "Historic Garden Week in Virginia," and map, write Kent–Valentine House, 12 E. Franklin St., Richmond, Va. 23219; enclose $1.00 for postage. (804) 295-3141.

1. Alexandria

Lee–Fendall Garden
429 North Washington Street

The Alexandria Council of Garden Clubs has restored carefully the grounds surrounding this historic townhouse. The gardens are in the style of the Federal period.
Open: Tuesday–Saturday 10:00 a.m.– 4:00 p.m., Sunday noon–4:00 p.m. Fee. (703) 548-1789.

Ramsay House and Gardens
221 King Street

Considered the oldest building in Alexandria, the Ramsay House is in the heart of Old Town and serves as the city's official Visitors' Center. The house was built in 1724 and restored in 1955. The colonial garden was designed by landscape architect Alden Hopkins and planted by the Hunting Creek Garden Club.
Open: Daily 10:00 a.m.–4:30 p.m. (703) 549-0205.

River Farm
7931 East Boulevard Drive

Part of the early Mount Vernon estate, the 25 acres of gardens were developed by Mr. and Mrs. Malcolm Matheson, who owned the property

from 1920 until 1974 when it was acquired by the American Horticultural Society. It is now the society's headquarters. There are period gardens and a unique ha-ha wall prefacing a graceful sweep to the Potomac River.
Open: Weekdays 8:30 a.m.–5:00 p.m. For information, write to the American Horticultural Society, Mount Vernon, Va. 22121. (703) 768–5700.

2. Arlington

Lee Mansion Garden (Arlington House or Custis–Lee House)
Arlington National Cemetery, end of Memorial Bridge

William Spencer, a gardener of Mount Vernon, designed this garden in 1802, with some assistance from Martha Washington. The garden and mansion grounds can be seen from the tourmobile that leaves frequently from the parkway area at the west end of Memorial Bridge.
Open: Daily 9:00 a.m.–5:00 p.m. (703) 521–0772.

3. Blacksburg

Smithfield Plantation
0.25 miles west, off U.S. 460 Bypass

The grounds of this prerevolutionary house (ca. 1773) have been restored by the Garden Club of Virginia.
Open: Mid-April–November 1,

Wednesday, Saturday–Sunday 1:00–5:00 p.m. Fee. (703) 951–2060.

4. Brookneal

Red Hill Shrine
Route 677, east of Brookneal

The restored site preserves the modest homestead of Patrick Henry, one of America's great patriots. Plantings on the grounds are modest and utilitarian. The huge Osage orange tree on the front lawn is reputed to be the largest of its species in the nation.
Open: Daily 1:00–5:00 p.m.; until 4:00 p.m., November 1–March 31. Closed: Christmas. Fee. (703) 376–2044.

☆
5. Charles City County and James River Plantations

Berkeley Plantation
Va. 5, between Richmond and Williamsburg

The historic plantation house is surrounded by terraced boxwood gardens. Built in 1726, it was the home of the Harrison family and the birthplace of two presidents. The working plantation was started in 1619 and has been operated continuously as a plantation.
Open: Daily 8:00 a.m.–5:00 p.m. Fee. (804) 795–2453.

Brandon Plantation

Off Va. 10, 45 miles east of Richmond, 22 miles from Hopewell

This is one of the most magnificent of the James River estates, with superb gardens that extend to the river.
Open: House, Historic Garden Week (late April); grounds, daily 9:00 a.m.–5:30 p.m. (804) 866–8486.

Sherwood Forest

John Tyler Memorial Highway (Va. 5)

This has been a working plantation for over 245 years. The Tyler home is 300 feet long and is probably the longest frame house in America. It was originally built in 1730 and was enlarged in 1844. The grounds cover 27 acres.
Open: Daily 9:00 a.m.–5:00 p.m. Fee. (804) 829–5377.

Shirley Plantation

Va. 5

This plantation overlooking the James River was established in 1613. The present historic home dates from 1723. Agricultural practices and grounds give a view of the rural lifestyle of times past.
Open: Daily 9:00 a.m.–5:00 p.m. Fee. (804) 795–2385.

Westover

Va. 5, 25 miles east of Richmond

The house, considered by some to be the finest example of Georgian architecture in America, was built in 1730 by William Byrd II. Lawns sweep down to the river's edge.

Open: Walled garden only, daily 10:00 a.m.–5:00 p.m. (804) 829–2882.

6. Charlottesville

Ash Lawn

2.5 miles past Monticello on Route 795

Ash Lawn was the home of James Monroe, fifth president of the United States. It has become known for its boxwood gardens, believed to have been designed after gardens that Monroe had seen as U.S. minister to France. The garden has a vista facing Monticello, Thomas Jefferson's estate 2.5 miles away. A focal point of the garden is the statue of Monroe. The house was designed and built by Thomas Jefferson.
Open: Daily 7:00 a.m.–7:00 p.m. Fee. (804) 293–9539.

☆☆
Monticello

Va. 53

Designed by Thomas Jefferson in 1808 to complement his primary residence, the gardens were restored in 1939–41 by the Garden Club of Virginia in accordance with Jefferson's drawings and notes. Restoration of the rest of the grounds is an ongoing process. Jefferson's design owes much to eighteenth-century English landscape gardening. It features an expanse of lawn edged with thickets and clumps of trees and shrubs. The flower borders display the same plants used by Jefferson.

Open: March 1–October 31, daily
8:00 a.m.–5:00 p.m.; November
1–February 28, daily 9:00 a.m.–
4:30 p.m.
Closed: Christmas. Fee. (804) 295–
8181.

University of Virginia Campus
U.S. 29 and U.S. 250

Thomas Jefferson developed the original site plan for the campus. The
Garden Club of Virginia has faithfully restored portions of the grounds
in accordance with Jefferson's plans as
recorded by Peter Maverick's engrav-
ings.
Open: Daily, sunrise–sunset. (804)
924–0311.

7. Clarksville

Prestwould Plantation
U.S. 15, 2 miles north of U.S. 58

The garden of Lady Jean Skipwith,
which she described in her garden
journal as "simple," has been reconstructed. The 46-acre estate includes
the 1795 house, conservatory, bee-
house, summer house, orchards, and
flower gardens.
Open: May 1–September 30, Tuesday–
Sunday 11:30 a.m.–4:30 p.m.; other
times by appointment. Fee. (804)
374–8672.

8. Fredericksburg

Kenmore
1201 Washington Avenue

George Washington's sister lived
on the original 863-acre estate. The
historic mansion was restored by the
Kenmore Association and the garden
by the Garden Club of Virginia in
keeping with the original design.
Open: Daily 9:00 a.m.–4:30 p.m.
Closed: January 1–2, December 25–26.
Fee. (703) 373–3381.

Mary Ball Washington House
1200 Charles Street

This was the home of George Washington's mother. In the garden,
re-created by the Garden Club of
Virginia in 1968, is some of the
original boxwood planted by Mary
Washington as well as her sundial.
Open: April 1–October 31, daily
9:00 a.m.–5:00 p.m.; rest of year,
until 4:00 p.m.
Closed: Christmas, New Year's Day.
Fee. (703) 373–1569.

9. Leesburg

Morven Park
2 miles north of Leesburg
on Morven Park Road

This 7,200-acre estate was established
in 1780 by a Major Swann. Enor-
mous boxwood parterre gardens, a
reflecting pool, and a boxwood-edged

nature trail leading to a wildflower
area are featured.
Open: April 1–October 31, Tuesday–
Saturday 10:00 a.m.–5:00 p.m.,
Sunday 1:00–5:00 p.m. Fee. (703)
777–2414.

Oatlands
6 miles south of Leesburg on U.S. 15

Terraced formal gardens surround
the classic revival plantation house
(ca. 1800). It is considered to have
one of the finest boxwood gardens in
America.
Open: April–October, Monday–
Saturday 10:00 a.m.–5:00 p.m.,
Sunday 1:00–5:00 p.m. Fee. (703)
777–3174.

10. Lexington

Stonewall Jackson House
8 East Washington Street

Both the house and the gardens have
been restored to their 1859 appearance.
Open: Monday–Saturday 9:00 a.m.–
4:30 p.m., Sunday 1:00–4:30 p.m.
from March to December.
Closed: Major holidays. (703) 463–
2552.

11. Lorton

☆
Gunston Hall Plantation
20 miles south of Washington, D.C.,
via I-95 or the George Washington
Parkway to U.S. 1

Authentic colonial knot gardens can
be found behind the elegant Georgian
home of George Mason, built in
1755.
Open: Daily 9:30 a.m.–5:00 p.m.
Closed: Christmas. Fee. (703) 550–
9220.

12. Montross

☆
Stratford Hall Plantation
Route 214, off Va. 3,
6 miles west of Montross

The great house, built in 1725 by
Thomas Lee, is one of the finest examples of Georgian architecture in
this country. The gardens were restored by the Garden Club of Virginia
in 1930–32. Since the property was
acquired by the Robert E. Lee Memorial Foundation over 40 years ago,
it has been restored completely and
is today maintained as an authentic
example of a colonial estate.
Open: Daily 9:00 a.m.–4:30 p.m.
Closed: Christmas. Fee. (804) 493–
8038.

Gunston Hall Plantation, Lorton, Va.

13. Mount Vernon

☆

**Mount Vernon
House and Gardens**
Mount Vernon Memorial Parkway

George Washington loved the land and had a lively interest in horticulture and farming. He felt great regret each time he was called away from his plantation by civic duty. The Mount Vernon Ladies Association has faithfully maintained this estate, which expresses one aspect of the great man's spirit. The relation of the estate to the Potomac River is significant. Washington conceived of the Potomac as a potential water connection to the interior of the continent. His original plan, which included

flower gardens, kitchen gardens, and orchards, has been preserved. *Open: March 1–October 31, daily 9:00 a.m.–5:00 p.m.; November 1–February 28/29, until 4:00 p.m. Fee. (703) 780–2000.*

Woodlawn Plantation
George Washington Memorial Parkway (U.S. 1), 3 miles from Mount Vernon

Dr. William Thornton, first architect of the U.S. Capitol, designed this elegant brick plantation house. The formal gardens bordering the mansion have been restored by the Garden Club of Virginia. Also located on the site is a demonstration Usonian House, known as the Pope–Leighey House, by Frank Lloyd Wright. The Usonian House represents Wright's

Mount Vernon House and Gardens, Mount Vernon, Va.

effort to design efficient, functional, and economic housing for the middle-class family.
Open: Daily 9:30 a.m.–4:30 p.m. Closed: Christmas. Fee. (703) 780–3118.

14. Norfolk

☆
Norfolk Botanical Gardens
8 miles east on Azalea Garden Road (adjacent to airport)

The gardens' 175 acres display constantly changing, year-round colors. An azalea festival in April celebrates a rich azalea collection. Other special gardens include colonial, Japanese, holly, and orchid gardens and a fragrance garden for the blind.
Open: Daily 8:30 a.m.–sunset. Fee. (804) 853–6972.

15. Orange

Montpelier
Va. 20, 4 miles west of Orange

Once the home of James Madison, fourth president of the United States, Montpelier was built in 1760 by President Madison's father. The large horseshoe-shaped garden features the original boxwood, topiary, terraced perennial and annual beds, and rose gardens. Pierre L'Enfant, planner of the city of Washington, D.C., also designed these gardens.
Open: Daily 10:00 a.m.–4:00 p.m. Fee. (703) 672–1162.

16. Richmond

Agecroft Hall
4305 Sulgrave Road (intersection of Malvern Avenue and Cary Street, next door to Virginia House)

Built nearly five centuries ago in pre-Elizabethan England, Agecroft Hall was transported across the Atlantic Ocean and reconstructed in Richmond. Now overlooking the James River, the estate enjoys a beautiful setting, with English gardens, tree-shaded lawns, and sunny meadows. *Open: Tuesday–Friday 10:00 a.m.– 4:00 p.m., Saturday–Sunday 2:00–5:00 p.m. Fee. (804) 353–4241.*

Capital Square
9th and Grace Streets

Designed in 1785 by Thomas Jefferson, this area represents the introduction of neoclassicism into public building in America. The square is beautifully landscaped. The governor's mansion and a walled garden are located in the northeastern corner. *Open: Square, all times; mansion, Historic Garden Week (late April). (804) 648–1234 or 644–7776.*

Edgar Allan Poe Museum
1912–1914 East Main Street

Edgar Allan Poe spent much of his boyhood in Richmond. The "Enchanted Garden" in the courtyard of the museum attempts to capture the great writer's spirit. Also on the site is the "Old Stone House," erected in 1737. *Open: Tuesday–Saturday 10:00 a.m.– 4:00 p.m., Sunday–Monday 1:30–4:00 p.m. (804) 648–5523.*

Maymont
Hampton Street and Pennsylvania Avenue

The grounds spread over 100 acres and include an Italian parterre garden, complete with a columned pergola and an elaborate cascade surrounded by a serpentine Renaissance staircase of stone. A natural waterfall parallels the staircase, then falls into the Japanese Garden below. The elaborate Victorian mansion, built in 1890, houses an interesting collection of furniture. Rare trees from the world over—such as the "Chinese Scholar" tree—are featured. *Open: March 31–October 31, daily 10:00 a.m.–7:00 p.m.; rest of year, until 5:00 p.m. (804) 358–7166.*

St. John's Mews
Carrington Square on Church Hill, near St. John's Church, 25th and East Broad Streets

A pleasantly restored and well-landscaped historic area features more than 70 houses built before 1861. *Open: Daily, all times. Note: Houses and gardens are private and open for viewing only during Historic Garden Week (late April). (804) 649–7938— church; (804) 643–7407—Historic Garden Week.*

Virginia House

4301 Sulgrave Road (0.25 miles off Va. 147 in Windsor Farms)

This Tudor house, originally built in 1125, was transplanted from England to the banks of the James River in 1925. Extensive gardens overlook the river.
Open: Tuesday–Saturday 10:00 a.m.–4:00 p.m., Sunday by appointment only after 1:00 p.m. (804) 353–4251.

White House and Museum of the Confederacy

12th and Clay Streets

The White House of the Confederacy (1861–65) is partially renovated. Next door, the Museum of the Confederacy contains interesting records and memorabilia. The large building is complemented by the formal gardens adjacent to it. Mature trees and shrubs are interspersed with curving brick pathways.
Open: Monday–Saturday 10:00 a.m.–5:00 p.m., Sunday 1:00–5:00 p.m. (804) 649–1861.

Wilton

Grove Street

A beautifully restored colonial mansion is flanked by formal gardens.
Open: Tuesday–Saturday 10:00 a.m.–4:30 p.m., Sunday 2:30–4:30 p.m. Closed: Sunday, July 1–August 31, and Saturday in August. Fee. (804) 282–5936.

17. Staunton

Woodrow Wilson Birthplace and Garden

24 North Coalter Street

A restored nineteenth-century Victorian Garden is situated below the mansion's west front. Century-old shrubs and fruit trees decorate the grounds. The historic house was built in 1846.
Open: Daily 9:00 a.m.–5:00 p.m. Closed: Holidays. (703) 885–0897.

18. Surry

Bacon's Castle

Across the James River from Jamestown Island, about 6 miles east of Surry

It is believed that the oldest English colonial garden in North America is located at this castle.
Open: Tuesday–Saturday 10:00 a.m.–4:00 p.m., Sunday noon–4:00 p.m. (804) 294–3292.

Chippokes

Across the James River from Jamestown Island, about 6 miles east of Surry

Considered to be the oldest working plantation in the United States, Chippokes contains 7 acres of formal gardens. It is owned by the Commonwealth of Virginia, Division of Parks.
Open: Daily, sunrise–sunset. (804) 294–3625.

Smith's Fort Plantation
Route 31 to Jamestown Ferry Landing

The seventeenth-century garden setting is in keeping with the house, which was built in 1652. (804) 795–2453.

19. Virginia Beach

Adam Thoroughgood House and Garden
1636 Parish Road

One of the oldest brick houses in the country was built by Adam Thoroughgood, who came to America in 1636. Behind the house is a seventeenth-century "gentlemen's pleasure garden" which has been restored by the Garden Club of Virginia.
*Open: April–November, Tuesday–Saturday 10:00 a.m.–5:00 p.m.; Sunday noon–5:00 p.m.; December–March, Tuesday–Sunday 1:00–5:00 p.m.
Closed: Major holidays. Fee. (804) 622–1211.*

20. Waynesboro

Swanannoa Marble Palace and Sculpture Garden
University of Science and Philosophy
Route 250, 4 miles from Waynesboro

The sumptuous house is flanked by terraced sculpture gardens featuring a superb mountain view and spiritually inspirational subjects. The grounds display many of the artistic works of Walter and Lao Russell.
Open: Daily, summer 8:00 a.m.–6:00 p.m.; winter 9:00 a.m.–5:00 p.m. (703) 942–5161.

21. Williamsburg

Carter's Grove Plantation
U.S. 60, 6 miles southeast of Williamsburg

The historic Georgian plantation house was built in 1760. Noted architect and author Samuel Chamberlain called it "the most beautiful house in America." Across the open greensward, the house is situated elegantly in relation to the James River.
Open: March 1–November 30 and during Christmas season, daily 9:00 a.m.–5:00 p.m. (804) 229–6883.

☆☆
Colonial Williamsburg

The landscape of the colonial capital of Virginia has been restored with careful attention to detail. The gardens of the Governor's Palace and many of the residential houses are magnificent in spring. This straightforward expression of early town planning is not to be missed. The town is also of interest as an intelligent answer to the demands of modern tourism while preserving the character of the place.
Open: Visitors' Center, daily 9:00 a.m.–5:00 p.m.; longer hours

Restored garden, Colonial Williamsburg, Va.

in spring and summer. Fee. (804)
229–1000, ext. 2751.

Williamsburg Garden Symposium

The 5-day lecture series on garden design and related subjects occurs in April. For information, write the Registrar, Box C, Williamsburg, Va. 23185.

Other Places of Interest

Arlington National Cemetery, Arlington
Blanford Cemetery, Petersburg
Blue Ridge Parkway

Breaks Interstate Park, western Virginia
Colonial National Historic Park, Jamestown
Dismal Swamp National Wildlife Refuge
Shenandoah National Park, Front Royal
Skyline Drive, Shenandoah National Park
Stratford Hall, Westmoreland County

Towns of special interest include Alexandria, Fredericksburg, Lexington, Richmond, Winchester, and Yorktown.

Washington

Area: 68,192 square miles

Population: 4,409,000

Statehood: November 11, 1889
(42nd state)

Washington is known as the "Evergreen State" for its splendid coniferous forests. These forests cover the state between the Cascade Mountains and the Pacific Ocean. The native vegetation of eastern Washington was that of the high-grass–covered plain. Washington is now a major grape-growing area.

Tall, sometimes snow-capped, mountains, alpine meadows, and lush, green bottomlands are in western Washington. Thick alluvial soils along river courses provide fertile growing areas. The Japanese current moderates the climate of western Washington. Rainfall is ample, averaging 34 inches per year in Seattle. At some places on the Olympic Peninsula, the annual rainfall has been known to exceed 100 inches.

The Cascade Mountains contain some of the nation's highest peaks. Five summits in Washington are perpetually covered with snow. Mount Rainier, standing 14,490 feet above sea level, is the state's highest point. East of the Cascades is the arid Columbia Plateau. In recent geologic times, the area was covered with lava flows. Soils derived from these basaltic rocks are rich in trace elements and fertile for agriculture when irrigated. Shrubs and grasses covered this dry area before its settlement.

The state of Washington has an abundance of water resources. The Columbia River carries drainage from vast areas of the Northwest through the state. Extensive water control projects have been undertaken by the federal government to hold these waters, and to use them for irrigation and power production. In the 1930s, the Bonneville and Grand Coulee dams were pioneering efforts to put the Columbia River to work. Irrigation projects have created a prosperous fruit-growing industry in central Washington. In eastern Washington, irrigation helps support large wheat-growing operations.

Washington also has a rich endowment of scenic and recreational resources. In Olympic National Park are magnificent coniferous rain forests and towering glacial peaks. At the park's Hurricane Ridge, nature puts on a wonderful wildflower pageant from early June to August. Unspoiled forests can be enjoyed at Mount Rainier National Park; during the short alpine, summer wildflower blossoms in the meadows are spectacular.

In 1974, Spokane was the site of an international exposition entitled "Man Living in Harmony with His Environment." A fine urban park and cultural center now mark this site. More significantly, the message of this exposition pervades the spirit of recent accomplishments throughout the state. Notable among these are

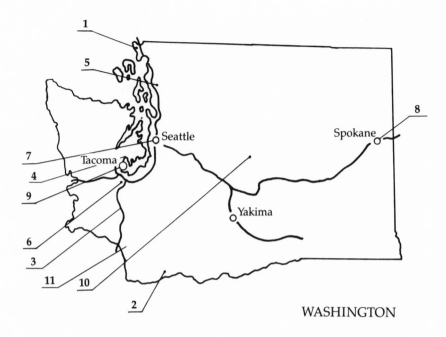

WASHINGTON

1. *Blaine*   2. *Carson*   3. *Centralia*   4. *Federal Way*   5. *Mount Vernon*
6. *Olympia*   7. *Seattle*   8. *Spokane*   9. *Tacoma*   10. *Wenatchee*   11. *Woodland*

the recycling of a derelict gas plant in Seattle, the construction of an exciting urban park over a freeway in the same city, and comprehensive planning approaches to the use of river valleys such as the Nooksack and Yakima. Washington offers a model to the nation for harmonizing the processes of industrial society with the natural environment.

1. Blaine

Peach Arch State Park
Off I-5, exit 276

The flower gardens on both sides of the border between the United States and Canada symbolize peace between the two nations.
Open: Daily, sunrise–sunset. (206) 753–2027.

2. Carson

Wind River Arboretum
Gifford Pinchot National Forest,
8 miles north of Carson

The 11-acre arboretum features a rich
collection of conifers and broad-leafed
evergreens.
*Open: Daily 8:00 a.m.–4:30 p.m.
(509) 427–5679.*

3. Centralia

Borst Blockhouse and Farmstead
1 mile west in Forst Borst Park (off
I-5, south of Harrison Street, Exit 82)

The blockhouse was built in 1852 to
defend against Indian attacks. The
farmstead (1860) is a reminder of
pioneer farm life. An arboretum
and rhododendron garden have been
developed on the site.
Open: Sunrise–sunset. (206) 736–7687.

4. Federal Way

☆
Rhododendron Species
Foundation

Over 475 species of rhododendron
and over 10,000 plants make this the
largest collection in the United States.
*Regular tours: March 1–May 30,
Wednesday 10:00 a.m.–3:00 p.m.,
Sunday 1:00–5:00 p.m.*

*Fall foliage: 3 Sundays in October,
noon–4:00 p.m.
Self-guided tours by appointment:
Year-round, Monday–Friday
10:00 a.m.–3:00 p.m. Parking at
Weyerhauser Corporation. Fee. (206)
927–6960.*

5. Mount Vernon

Fragrance Garden for the Blind
1 block south of West Division
on Ball Street

This 0.75-acre garden for the blind
features herbs and fragrant plantings
in raised beds and the cooling sound
of a central fountain.
*Open: Daily, sunrise–sunset. (206)
336–9555.*

6. Olympia

State Capitol Grounds
Capitol Way

Forty acres of flowers adorn the
grounds. A "pioneer" herb garden
and a formal rose garden are also
featured.
*Open: Dawn–dusk; herb garden,
Tuesday–Friday 10:00 a.m.–
4:30 p.m., Saturday–Sunday
noon–4:30 p.m.
Closed: Mondays and major state
holidays. (206) 753–5689.*

7. Seattle

Drug Plant Gardens
University of Washington College of Pharmacy, 17th Avenue North

Located here is one of the largest formal gardens of medicinal and culinary plants. *Open: Daily 8:00 a.m.–5:00 p.m. (206) 543–1942.*

☆
Gas Works Park
Northlake Way

A derelict gas plant with "all the nostalgia of a rested junk heap" presented the occasion for the development of a park to celebrate ground objects, a legacy of industrial society. The park is dedicated to fun, and it works. The aesthetic concept is interesting and controversial. An award-winning design by landscape architect Richard Haag. *Open: Daily, sunrise–sunset. (206) 625–4671.*

Seattle Conservatory
15th Avenue East and
East Galer Street

Located in Volunteer Park, this Victorian structure resembles Paxton's famous Crystal Palace (1851, London). Many tropical species are on display, and there is a special collection of orchids. *Open: Daily 9:00 a.m.–5:00 p.m. (206) 625–4043.*

☆
Seattle Freeway Park
Between Seneca and University Streets, over the Seattle Freeway

Essentially a 'lid' over the downtown freeway, this park is an innovative solution to a difficult urban aesthetic problem. The idea was conceived by landscape architects Angela Danadjieva and Lawrence Halprin. The sculptural quality of the park, with its waterfalls and plant materials, makes elegant reference to the nearby Cascade Mountains. *Open: All times. Fountains operate from 9:00 a.m. to 10:00 p.m. (206) 625–4043 or 447–4200.*

Seattle University
Broadway and Madison

Founded in 1891, this urban campus is noted for its fine landscaping. There are over 1,000 varieties of exotic trees and shrubs. *Open: All times. Tours of campus can be arranged. (206) 626–5656.*

☆
University of Washington Arboretum
Madison and 31st Avenue, East

The 250-acre arboretum features rare trees and plants and an Azalea Way sponsored by the Seattle Garden Center. A unique 3-acre Japanese Tea Garden is situated around a pond. *Open: Daily, sunrise–sunset; Tea Garden, 10:00 a.m.–6:00 p.m. Fee for Tea Garden. (206) 625–2635 or 543–8800.*

Seattle Freeway Park, Seattle, Wash.

Woodland Park
Freemont Avenue and
North 50th Street

The park was established by an
Englishman in the late nineteenth
century as a private garden and deer
park. In the 1880s it was opened
to the general public, and in 1900
it was purchased by the city. Now
an International Rose Test Garden
and a Zoological Garden are on the
grounds.
*Open: Daily 8:00 a.m.–sunset. Fee.
(206) 782–1265.*

8. Spokane

Duncan Gardens
and Manito Conservatory
Manito Park at 21st and Bernard

The gardens are most noted for their
flowering crab apples and tulips in
the spring. Tropicals and ferns are
displayed all year in the conservatory. Also of interest are the topiary,
flower beds, and Japanese garden.
*Open: Daily, dawn–dusk. (509)
456–4331.*

John A. Finch Arboretum
West 3404 Woodland Boulevard

Over 2,000 labeled trees and shrubs
are displayed in the 65-acre, parklike

arboretum. Also includes the Corey
Glen Rhododendron Gardens.
*Open: Daily, sunrise–sunset. (509)
456–4331.*

9. Tacoma

Point Defiance Park
North 564th and Pearl Streets

This 640-acre park contains an outstanding rose garden, as well as
rhododendron and Japanese and
native gardens. It also features an
aviary, an aquarium, and wild animals.
*Open: 8:00 a.m.–dusk; zoo,
10:00 a.m.–dusk. (206) 759–0118.*

Wright Park and Seymour Conservatory
South Third and G Streets

Established in 1908, the Seymour
Conservatory of tropical and exotic
plants is the sixth largest structure
of its kind in the United States. It
contains several hundred varieties of
plants and many temporary exhibitions. Tours are available.
*Open: Daily 8:00 a.m.–4:30 p.m.
(206) 272–5543 or 591–5300.*

10. Wenatchee

Ohme Gardens
3327 Ohme Road, 3 miles north of
Wenatchee near junction of U.S. 2
and U.S. 97

Patient efforts by the Ohme family
have transformed this barren hillside
into a delightful garden. Evergreen
trees, ground cover, the careful placing of native stone, and sensitive
exploitation of the site's superb vistas
have produced a subdued and elegant
design.
*Open: April–October 9:00 a.m.–dusk;
after hours, calls preferred. Fee. (509)
662–5785.*

11. Woodland

Hulda Klager Lilac Gardens

These 4.5 acres of gardens, a memorial to the dedicated efforts of Mrs.
Klager who emigrated from Germany
in 1865, contain not only a huge and
rare collection of lilacs but also many
exotic trees and shrubs.
*Open: Daily 9:00 a.m.–5:00 p.m.
Donation. (206) 225–8996.*

Other Places of Interest

Fort Casey Historic Park, Everett
Grand Coulee Dam National
  Recreation Area
Mount Baker National Forest,
  northwestern Washington

Mount Rainier National Park,
Longmire
Mount Saint Helens, Longview
North Cascades National Park,
northern Washington

Olympic National Park, northwestern
Washington
Pioneer Square, Seattle
Snoqualmie National Forest, west
central Washington

West Virginia

Area: 24,181 square miles

Population: 1,936,000

Statehood: June 20, 1863 (35th state)

West Virginia owes its political existence as a separate state from Virginia to its mountains. Scotch-Irish pioneers from Pennsylvania founded settlements in western Virginia prior to the Revolutionary War. Isolated by the mountains from Tidewater and Piedmont Virginia, their subsistence farming economy gave them a lifestyle and outlook very different from the lowland planters. When Virginia seceded from the Union in 1861, the West Virginians refused to join them.

The boundary between West Virginia and Virginia to the east lies in the Great Appalachian Valley. An escarpment separates the valley from the Appalachian Plateau to the west. The ancient plateau, which has been given a rugged profile from ages of erosion by rains, stretches west to the Ohio River Valley. Gorges, waterfalls, and river rapids are important landscape features. Transportation routes and settlement in this region extend linearly along the stream valleys or "hollows." West Virginia's major centers of population and industrial production are along the Ohio and Kanawha rivers.

Rainfall is abundant, averaging over 40 inches per year. The growing season ranges from 120 to 190 days.

Snow is frequent at higher mountain elevations. Deciduous forests cover most of the state. Commercial lumbering of valuable hardwoods is an important industry. Forests of beech and hemlock normally found at more northern latitudes appear here at higher mountain elevations.

West Virginia's mineral resources have played an important role in the state's history. By 1817, salt was being mined along the Kanawha River. Since 1936, West Virginia has been the nation's leading producer of bituminous coal. It has been estimated that mineable coal deposits underlie 55 percent of the state. Pure glass sands and fine pottery clays are the basis of the state's glass and ceramics industries. Valuable reserves of natural gas can also be found.

Despite the coal extracted from the soil, little wealth has accrued to West Virginians. That is because outside investors purchased mineral rights from the mountain people at low prices. Coal mining has also greatly marred the natural landscape. Slag heaps from underground mines and streams polluted by acid runoff from tailings scar the mountains. The effects of strip mining are a persistent threat to the health and beauty of the mountain environment.

West Virginia's great scenic and recreational resource is its mountains. Skiing and camping are popular in the hills. A folk music festival is held each summer at the Appalachian South Folk Center at Pipestem State Park near Hinton. Harpers Ferry, occupying a dramatic site at the confluence of the Potomac and Shenan-

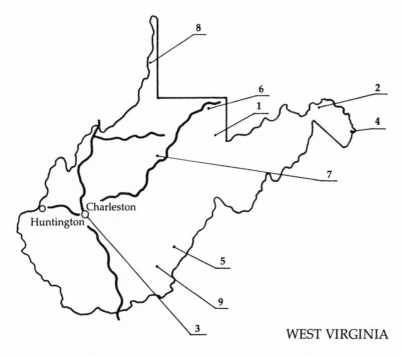

WEST VIRGINIA

1. *Aurora*   2. *Berkeley Springs*   3. *Charleston*   4. *Harpers Ferry*
5. *Mill Point*   6. *Morgantown*   7. *Weston*   8. *Wheeling*   9. *White Sulphur*
Springs

doah rivers, is a national historic park. With modern highways, the mountains, which traditionally isolated West Virginia from the rest of the Eastern Seaboard, are no longer barriers. The mountains now serve as the gateway into the predominantly rural but growing state.

1. Aurora

Cathedral State Park
U.S. 50

Located here is an outstanding collection of some of the oldest and largest trees in the eastern United States. Excellent nature trails reward visitors.
Open: Daily, sunrise–sunset. (304) 735–3771.

2. Berkeley Springs

Cacapon State Park
U.S. 522

These extensive woodlands are well known for their spring flowering shrubs.
Open: Daily, sunrise–sunset. (304) 258–1022.

342 : WEST VIRGINIA

3. Charleston

Municipal Rose Garden
Danes Park

A splendid collection of 500 roses can be seen in this well-landscaped garden.
Open: Daily, sunrise–sunset. (304) 344–5075.

Sunrise
746 Myrtle Road

Overlooking the Kanawha River and downtown Charleston, Sunrise is a center of cultural development for south-central West Virginia. The exploration of nature and the development of the arts are pursued in the two restored mansions on the 16-acre estate. The gardens contain hundreds of varieties of trees, shrubs, and flowers.
Open: Tuesday–Saturday 10:00 a.m.– 5:00 p.m., Sunday 2:00–5:00 p.m. Closed: Monday, December 24–25 and 31, January 1, Easter, Memorial Day, July 4, Thanksgiving. (304) 344–8035.

4. Harpers Ferry

Harpers Ferry Garden
Harper House, High Street

These gardens, which now form part of the Harpers Ferry National Historical Park, display the vegetable-growing methods of the nineteenth century.

Open: Daily 8:00 a.m.–5:00 p.m. (304) 535–6371.

5. Mill Point

Cranberry Glades Botanical Area, Monongahela National Forest
Forest Route 102, off W. Va. 55 west from Mill Point

Snakemouth orchids and pitcher plants are among the hundreds of unusual plants that flower between April and August in this boglike environment. A special boardwalk gives access to many areas that are otherwise difficult to reach.
Open: May 30–Labor Day, daily 9:00 a.m.–6:00 p.m.; May, September, October, Saturday–Sunday 9:00 a.m.–6:00 p.m. (304) 653–4826.

Watoga State Park Arboretum
Southeast off U.S. 219 from Mill Point

The botanical area of the 400-acre arboretum features some interesting varieties of plants. There is a wildflower pilgrimage in mid-May.
Open: Daily, sunrise–sunset. (304) 799–4087.

6. Morgantown

Core Arboretum at West Virginia University
Boulevard in front of the
Creative Arts Center

The 75-acre arboretum serves as a
testing ground for the suitability of
plants to West Virginia conditions.
Guided tours are offered.
*Open: Daily, dawn–dusk. (304)
293–3489.*

7. Weston

Jackson's Mill Museum and Garden
4 miles north off U.S. 19
(in Jackson's Mill 4-H Camp)

The exhibition illustrates pioneer
life of 100 years ago; there is also a
formal garden.
*Open: Daily 8:00 a.m.–9:00 p.m.
Museum has different hours. (304)
269–5100.*

8. Wheeling

Wheeling Garden Center
Oglebay Park

Formally known as Waddington
Farms, Oglebay Park became a city
property in 1928; it has developed
into a model urban park of 800 acres.
The garden center promotes interest
in horticulture and provides advice for gardeners. A greenhouse is
maintained for exotics and there is a
special display of chrysanthemums
in early November. There are trial
gardens for peonies, iris, and annuals,
as well as an arboretum.
*Open: Daily, sunrise–sunset;
greenhouse, 9:00 a.m.–4:00 p.m.
(302) 242–3000.*

9. White Sulphur Springs

Greenbrier Hotel
On the land around West Virginia's
oldest and most fashionable hotel and
spa are found many unique native
plants. The unusual box honeysuckle
was rediscovered here. The landscaped grounds feature attractive
flower gardens.
*Open: Daily 8:00 a.m.–sunset. (304)
536–1110.*

Other Places of Interest
Blennerhassett Historical Park
Harpers Ferry National Historical
  Park

Towns of special interest include
Berkeley Springs, Charleston, and
White Sulphur Springs.

Wisconsin

Area: 56,154 square miles

Population: 4,775,000

Statehood: May 29, 1848 (30th state)

Wisconsin is known as America's dairyland. This important land use gives much of the state a pleasant, pastoral vista.

The major structural features underlying the state's landforms are the Pre-Cambrian upfolded rocks of the Superior Upland in the north and the continent's downfolded Central Basin in the south. The glaciers of the most recent Ice Age smoothed over the eastern part of the state, creating a landscape of low relief. In the west, where the glaciers did not penetrate, relief is more pronounced. Wisconsin's many lakes are another legacy of the Ice Age.

Wisconsin has a severe continental climate. The growing season is about 180 days in the extreme north. Rainfall is adequate. Coniferous forests are the natural vegetation of the north. Maple basswood forests and some prairies originally occurred in central and southern Wisconsin. Almost half of the state is currently forested.

Settlers were first attracted to the state by lead mining in the southeast. Wisconsin's abundant forests and fertile soils drew many new residents after the Indians were pacified. Land was surveyed and subdivided according to the provisions of the Northwest Ordinance; the layout of roads, towns, and properties still reflects this influence. By the time of the Civil War, Wisconsin was an important wheat producer. The contemporary economy of the state comprises a healthy mix of farming and industry.

Wisconsin's landscape has many scenic features. The glaciated gorges of the Wisconsin River at Wisconsin Dells are spectacular. Apostle Island National Park preserves a picturesque area of the Superior lakeshore. Along the Wolf and Saint Croix rivers are national scenic waterways. The Ice Age National Science Reserve, which preserves many landforms of glacier origin, is of great interest to geologists. Frank Lloyd Wright founded a design school, Taliesin, near Spring Green. The works of this great prairie architect display remarkable sensitivity in adapting natural environments to man's habitation.

The state of Wisconsin has played a leadership role in appreciating the value of open space and in protecting it from careless development. In 1964, a comprehensive study of the state's scenic resources was undertaken, and plans were developed for their preservation and to promote public access to them. The people of the state have benefited from this farsighted approach to the economic value of tourism and, more importantly, from the access they enjoy to peaceful and restorative open spaces and natural beauty.

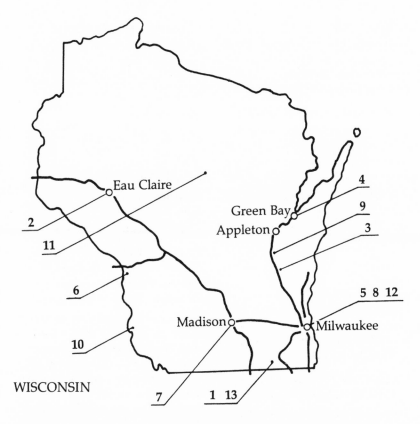

1. *Eagle* 2. *Eau Claire* 3. *Fond du Lac* 4. *Green Bay* 5. *Hales Corners*
(*Milwaukee*) 6. *La Crosse* 7. *Madison* 8. *Milwaukee* 9. *Oshkosh*
10. *Prairie du Chien* 11. *Wausau* 12. *Wauwatosa* 13. *Williams Bay*

1. Eagle

Old World Wisconsin
1 mile south on Wis. 59, 67

The state moved over 50 historic
buildings from all over Wisconsin
(Finnish, French, and German farm
buildings; houses; churches; schools;
and so forth) to create an ethnic village landscape on this 576-acre site.

Huge wagons pulled by Percherons
take the visitor from farm to farm.
Many herb gardens and cutting gardens have been created by the State
Garden Club.
*Open: May–October, daily 9:00 a.m.–
6:00 p.m. Fee. (414) 594–2116.*

2. Eau Claire

Putnam Park Arboretum
Park and Garfield Avenues

A 230-acre arboretum is part of the Eau Claire campus of the University of Wisconsin. Founded in 1916, the arboretum has maintained a tract of forest in its natural state. There are over 400 species of indigenous plants. *Open: Sunrise–sunset; greenhouses, by appointment. (715) 836–2637 or 836–4166.*

3. Fond du Lac

Saint Paul's Cathedral Cloister
51 West Division

The Gothic cathedral contains rare ecclesiastical artifacts. The small cloister garden is reminiscent of the period style of the building. *Open: Daily. Tours by appointment. (414) 921–3363.*

4. Green Bay

Hazelwood Garden
1008 South Monroe Street

The Victorian garden of this historic house (1837) reflects the taste of the mid-nineteenth century. *Open: May–October, Wednesday–Sunday 10:00 a.m.–5:00 p.m.; rest of year, Tuesday–Saturday.*

Closed: Major holidays. Fee. (414) 497–3768.

5. Hales Corners (Milwaukee)

☆
Alfred E. Boerner Botanical Gardens
Whitnall Park,
5879 South 92nd Street

Set on the crest of a hill in Whitnall Park, the gardens are dedicated to the growing of every native flower, tree, and shrub. The 450-acre park was constructed in 1932 by the Civilian Conservation Corps and the Works Progress Administration, and opened to the public in 1939. It now maintains a library, an information center, and flower shops; there are classes in horticulture, lectures, and art exhibits. *Open: Summer, daily 8:00 a.m.–sunset; winter, Monday–Friday until 4:00 p.m. (414) 425–1132.*

6. La Crosse

Gideon C. Hixon House and Garden
429 North 7th Street

The area surrounding the Hixon House encompasses half a city block. It was originally developed in 1859. Many of the older trees date from

that era, and the design of the formal rose gardens remains essentially unchanged.
Open: June 1–Labor Day, daily 1:00–5:00 p.m. Tours only. Fee. (608) 782–1980.

7. Madison

Olbrich Botanical Garden
3330 Atwood Avenue

This 51-acre garden contains over 11 acres of display gardens. The garden building includes display galleries and an atrium. Site of the National Dahlia Trial Gardens.
Open: Daily 9:00 a.m.–sunset. (608) 266–4148.

University of Wisconsin Arboretum
1207 Seminole Highway

The 1,240-acre arboretum has a wide variety of interesting plant materials arranged in ecological groupings of forest, wet and dry prairies.
Open: Daily 7:00 a.m.–10:00 p.m.; Visitors' Center, 12:30–4:00 p.m. (608) 262–2746.

8. Milwaukee

☆
Mitchell Park Horticultural Conservatory
524 South Layton Boulevard

In one of the world's most unique conservatories, samples of international horticulture and floriculture are displayed under three huge glass domes: the Flower Show House, the Desert House, and the Tropical House. Many special temporary exhibitions are offered. Outside there is a sunken garden with over 125,000 plants, best seen in August.
Open: Monday 9:00 a.m.–5:00 p.m., Tuesday–Sunday until 9:00 p.m. Fee after 10:30 a.m. (414) 649–9800.

9. Oshkosh

Paine Art Center and Arboretum
1410 Algoma Boulevard

Twenty-five acres of formal English gardens surround a Tudor-style manor house.
Open: Grounds only, Tuesday–Sunday 9:00 a.m.–5:00 p.m. House has different hours and fee. (414) 235–4530.

10. Prairie du Chien

Villa Louis
521 North Villa Louis Road

A mansion restored to its nineteenth-century splendor is surrounded by extensive grounds.
Open: May–October, daily 9:00 a.m.–5:00 p.m. (608) 326–2721.

11. Wausau

Marathon County Historical Museum and Grounds
403 McIndoe Avenue

This small garden was designed about 1900 by Van Ryn and De Gelleke. It includes a wildflower area and sunken garden, and is surrounded by old-fashioned perennials, an arbor, and other garden features.
Open: Tuesday–Sunday, 10:00 a.m.–5:00 p.m.
Closed: Holidays. (715) 848–6143.

12. Wauwatosa

Lowell Damon House and Garden
2107 North Wauwatosa Avenue

This small garden dates back to 1846; it was redesigned by Gordon Rayner

in 1972 to highlight the house, which was listed on the National Register of Historic Buildings at that time.
Open: May–October, daily 1:00–5:00 p.m. (414) 453–2330.

13. Williams Bay

Yerkes Observatory

The observatory was landscaped in the early 1900s by Frederick Law Olmsted, Jr.
Open: Grounds, daily; observatory, Saturday noon–3:00 p.m. (414) 236–5468.

Other Places of Interest

Conservation Education Center, Paynette
Heritage Hill State Park, Green Bay
Madeline Island, northern Wisconsin
Taliesin, Spring Green
The Clearing, Ellison Bay
Trees for Tomorrow, Eagle River
Whitnall Park, Milwaukee
Wisconsin Dells, Baraboo

Wyoming

Area: 97,914 square miles

Population: 509,000

Statehood: July 10, 1890 (44th state)

The Rocky Mountains give Wyoming a spectacular natural beauty. The Middle Rockies occupy the northwestern part of the state. Two sections of the Great Plains occur in eastern Wyoming: the Missouri Plateau and the High Plains. The Missouri Plateau displays a gently rolling surface interrupted by numerous escarpments. The High Plains in the southeast are extremely flat. The famous Black Hills in northeastern Wyoming and northwestern South Dakota are an extreme expression of the Rockies.

The entire state of Wyoming stands at elevations above 5,000 feet. Seven peaks are over 13,000 feet; the highest, Gannet Peak, is 13,804 feet above sea level. Rainfall exceeds 30 inches per year at higher mountain elevations, but averages less than 16 inches in the cultivable tablelands of basins and plains. Humidity is very low during the summer. Due to the low humidity and high altitude, summer nights are cool. At lower elevations, summer temperatures often exceed 100° F. Winters are severe.

Coniferous forests populate the mountains, whereas the dry basins are covered by sparse sagebrush steppes. Short tough grasses grow on the plains. Wyoming's basins and plains have nutrient-rich soils, but their productivity is limited by the lack of water. Thus water conservation is an important public policy. Cattle ranching and sheep ranching are the state's major land uses. Lumbering occurs in the northwestern mountains. The mining of coal, petroleum, natural gas, and uranium also contributes to the economy.

On Register Cliff near Guernsey can be found inscriptions made by settlers bound west from Fort Laramie to the Oregon Trail. The wheels of covered wagons have left ruts almost 3 feet deep in the soft sandstones along the trail. Fort Laramie itself is preserved as a National Historic Site.

Wyoming's wonderful scenic and recreational resources are the basis of its important tourist industry. Yellowstone Park is famous for its geysers, waterfalls, canyons, and abundant wildlife. Grand Teton National Park features mountains remarkable for their dramatic perpendicular rise above Jackson Hole, a famous winter resort. Devil's Tower in northeastern Wyoming is a striking formation of igneous rock, towering 1,200 feet above the Belle Fourche River. The majestic landscape of Wyoming is the patient work of geologic forces over time.

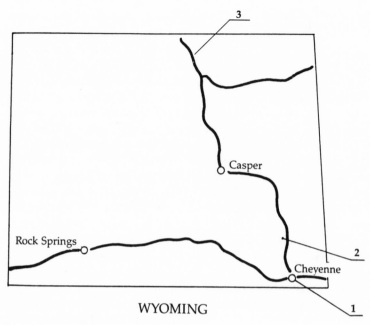

WYOMING

1. *Cheyenne*   2. *Chugwater*   3. *Sheridan*

1. Cheyenne

Cheyenne Horticultural Field Station
Plant Science Research Division

Studies on how to make things grow in the High Plains region of Wyoming are conducted at this field station.
Open: Daily 9:00 a.m.–5:00 p.m.
(307) 777–7321.

2. Chugwater

Storm Garden Center
From I-25, 9 miles east on Wyo. 313, then 1 mile north

The garden center evolved from the stubborn efforts of Lowell and Eva Storm to get the trees and shrubs to which they were accustomed to grow in the harsh Wyoming climate. There are research and display plantings of interest. A "Tulip Time in the Rockies" pageant is celebrated annually.
Open: Daily 9:00 a.m.–5:00 p.m.
(307) 422–3442.

The high desert prairie in Wyoming.

3. Sheridan

Trail End Historic Home
400 Clarendon Avenue

This Flemish revival house was owned by John Kendrick, a former governor (1915–17) and senator (1917–33). The landscaped grounds include many interesting botanical specimens.
Open: June–August, daily 9:00 a.m.– 5:00 p.m.; rest of year, Wednesday– Sunday. (307) 674-4589.

Other Places of Interest

Bighorn National Forest, northern Wyoming near Sheridan
Devil's Kitchen, Casper
Devil's Tower National Monument, northeastern Wyoming near Sundance
Fort Laramie National Historic Site, southeastern Wyoming
Grand Teton National Park, Jackson Lake
Hot Springs State Park, Thermopolis
Yellowstone National Park, western Wyoming

Index

Constitution Gardens, 68
Constitution Plaza, 52, 53
Cook Memorial Park Rose Garden, 115
Coolidge Homestead, 319
Cooperstown, N.Y., 232
Coral Gables, Fla., 72
Corbit–Sharp House, 60
Core Arboretum at West Virginia
University, 343
Corkscrew Swamp Sanctuary, 75
Cornelius J. Hauck Botanic Garden, 252
Cornell Plantations, 234
Cornish, N.H., 213
Corona Del Mar, Calif., 25
Courtview, 4
Cragfont Mansion, 299
Craggy Gardens, 243
Craighead–Jackson House and Gardens,
299
Cranberry Glades Botanical Area,
Monongahela National Forest, 342
Cranbrook House and Gardens, 179
Crane Estate, 168
Crapo Park, 129
Crater Lake, Oreg., 265
Cravens House and Terrace, 298
Creek Street Restoration, 12
Crosby Gardens, 256
Cross River, N.Y., 233
Croton-on-Hudson, N.Y., 233
Crown Zellerbach Plaza, 35
Crystal Springs Rhododendron Gar-
dens, 267
Culver City (Los Angeles), Calif., 25
Cummer Art Gallery and Memorial
Gardens, 75
Cummings Nature Center, 236
Cushing House Museum, 171
Cylburn Arboretum, 159
Cypress Gardens, 288

Dalidet Adobe, 37
Dallas, Tex., 306
Dallas Garden Center, 306
Dalton, Mass., 168
Danbury, Conn., 50
Daniel Boone Native Garden, 244

Danvers, Mass., 168
Danville, Ill., 112
Darien, Conn., 50
Darlingtonia Wayside Arboretum, 265
Davenport, Iowa, 130
Davis (Sacramento), Calif., 25
Dawes Arboretum, 255
Dawes Garden, 113
Dayton, Ohio, 254
Daytona Beach, Fla., 72
Dearborn, Mich., 180
Decatur, Ill., 112
Decatur House and Garden, 64
Dedham, Mass., 168
Deepwood Gardens, 269
Deere and Company Administrative
Center, 116
Deering Oaks Park, 154
Deer Lodge, Mont., 202
De Leon Springs, Fla., 73
De Leon Springs State Recreational
Area, 73
Delray Beach, Fla., 73
Deming, N.M., 226
Demopolis, Ala., 3
Denali National Park, Alaska, 11
Denver, Colo., 45
Denver Botanic Gardens, 45
Descanso Gardens, 27
Desert Botanical Garden, 14
Deshler–Morris House, 276
Des Moines, Iowa, 130
Des Moines Botanical Center, 130
Des Moines Center of Science and
Industry, 131
De Soto State Park, 4
Detroit, Mich., 180
Detroit Zoological Park, 180
Dickerson, Md., 160
Dickson, David, gardens designed by,
49
The Dismals, 6
Dixon Gallery and Gardens, 301
Dr. Fifthian Herb Garden, 112
Dr. William Hutching's Medicinal Herb
Garden, 125
Douglas Park, 109